THE
ABC-CLIO
COMPANION TO

The Civil Rights Movement

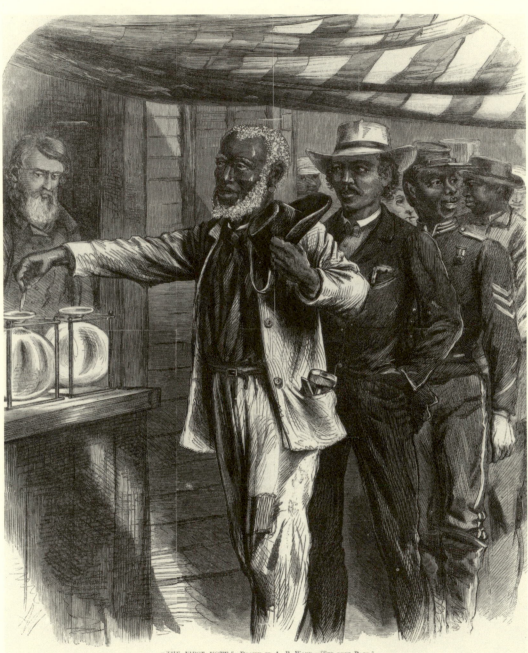

"THE FIRST VOTE."—Drawn by A. R. Waud.—[See next Page.]

The Civil Rights Act of 1866 guaranteed freedmen full rights of citizenship. A. R. Waud's drawing was published in the 16 November 1867 Harper's Weekly

THE
ABC-CLIO
COMPANION TO

The
Civil Rights
Movement

Mark
Grossman

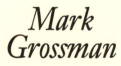

ABC-CLIO

Library of Congress Cataloging-in-Publication Data

Grossman, Mark.
    The ABC–CLIO companion to the Civil Rights Movement / Mark Grossman.
        p.   cm. — (ABC–CLIO companions to key issues in American history and life)
    Includes bibliographical references and index.
    1. Afro-Americans—Civil rights—Encyclopedias.   2. Civil rights movements—United States—History—Encyclopedias.   3. Afro-Americans—History—1877–1964—Encyclopedias.   I. ABC-Clio Information Services.   II. Title.   III. Series.
E185.61.G895   1993   305.896'073—dc20   93-38425

ISBN 0-87436-696-8 (alk. paper)

00 99 98 97 96 95 94 93   10 9 8 7 6 5 4 3 2 1 (hc)

ABC-CLIO, Inc.
130 Cremona Drive, P.O. Box 1911
Santa Barbara, California 93116-1911

This book is printed on acid-free paper ⊗.
Manufactured in the United States of America

To my parents, whose unflagging support during this project has been a source of strength; and to my grandmother, Dorothy Davidson Sapirman, whose spirit is with me in all that I do.

ABC-CLIO Companions to Key Issues in American History and Life

The ABC-CLIO Companion to the American Labor Movement
Paul F. Taylor

The ABC-CLIO Companion to the Civil Rights Movement
Mark Grossman

The ABC-CLIO Companion to Women in the Workplace
Dorothy Schneider and Carl J. Schneider

Forthcoming

The ABC-CLIO Companion to the American Peace Movement
Christine Anne Lunardini

The ABC-CLIO Companion to the Environmental Movement
Mark Grossman

The ABC-CLIO Companion to Women's Progress in America
Elizabeth Frost-Knappman

Contents

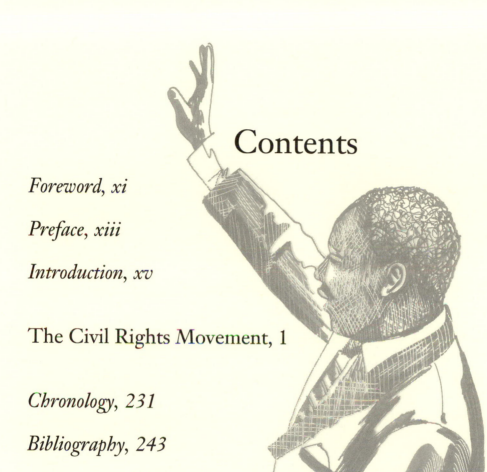

Foreword

This work provides much-needed information about the civil rights movement in capsuled and readable doses. The author has done commendable research and students of the movement, as well as just plain folks, will find this work rewarding.

The civil rights movement is still at work in a society that wants to call itself "post civil rights." One implication is that African Americans have gained their "rights" and therefore have no need for a movement.

The only thing "post" about civil rights is that some media and some folks have placed issues relating to fair and full employment, the administration of justice, voting rights, and other matters on the back burner.

But the truth will not be denied and while we have all won the right to check in at the Hilton, too few of us have the means of checking out. African Americans are still the last hired, first fired, lowest paid, most unemployed, and most underemployed. Our deprivation has been compounded by our self-deprecation and we must fight battles without and within.

We need to turn *to* each other and not *on* each other. And we need to lead the nation into a new birth of spirituality!

Dr. Joseph E. Lowery
President, Southern Christian
Leadership Conference

Preface

The *ABC-CLIO Companion to the Civil Rights Movement* is a guide to the civil rights struggle of African Americans from the end of the great Civil War, which finally brought about the destruction of slavery, to the present day. It assembles in one volume information on civil rights leaders, landmark court decisions, legislation, institutions and organizations, key concepts, watershed events, and the movement's heroes, heroines, and martyrs, as well as information on the segregationist opposition.

The ABC-CLIO Companions series is designed to provide the nonspecialist with concise, encyclopedic guides to key movements, major issues, and revolutions in American history. The encyclopedia entries are arranged in alphabetical order. Cross-references connect related terms and entries. A chronology of key events provides a handy overview, and a bibliography is provided to facilitate further research.

I would like to thank the following persons for their help in researching and writing this book: the interlibrary loan staff of the Broward County Main Library in Fort Lauderdale, Florida; the staff of the Interlibrary Loan Section, the Rare Book and Manuscript Division, and the Microforms Division of the New York Public Library in New York City; Ernie Johnston, Jr., communications director of the National Urban League in New York; Mildred Bond Roxborough, director of development of the National Association for the Advancement of Colored People in New York City; Amal Morcos, manager of editorial services at the United Negro College Fund; and the Federal Bureau of Investigation, without whose help I would have been unable to obtain the file on James William Ford.

Introduction

From the end of the Civil War, the history of black Americans has in large part been the history of a struggle to realize the full rights guaranteed by the Constitution.

The Emancipation Proclamation legally freed the slaves in the Confederate states in 1863 and slavery was formally abolished in the United States by the Thirteenth Amendment in 1865. After more than two centuries of servitude in North America, the future for black Americans was suddenly filled with bright promise. There was rapid progress almost everywhere: the Civil Rights Act of 1866 granted the rights of citizenship; the Peonage Abolition Act of 1867 provided protection against the reinstitution of slavery-like labor; the Fourteenth Amendment, which became law in 1868, guaranteed full citizenship for the freedmen. Voting rights were protected by the Fifteenth Amendment in 1870, and the Civil Rights Act of 1875 prohibited discrimination in public transportation and accommodations. Such men as Jeremiah Haralson and Charles Lewis Mitchell brought black politicians into the federal government.

As Reconstruction came to an end, however, and political power was returned to the states of the former Confederacy, the newly won rights of black Americans came quickly under attack. State laws requiring the segregation of the races were put in place, voting rights were limited by such devices as poll taxes and literacy tests, and the fabric of a segregated "Jim Crow" society was increasingly held together by the terror of the lynch mob. A reactionary Supreme Court provided the legal basis for the rescission of black rights, beginning in the 1870s with a series of rulings that both served to support racial discrimination by the states and struck down much of the civil rights legislation of the Reconstruction era. The high court's legal assault on civil rights culminated in the 1896 decision in *Plessy v. Ferguson,* which established the principle of "separate but equal" facilities for black and white. For the next half-century, Southern states employed this principle to segregate the races in schools, housing, transportation, hotels and restaurants, and virtually all aspects of society.

Black Americans struggled to regain their rights against the tide of racism and a repressive state power. Two approaches emerged: the "protest collaboration" movement led by Booker T. Washington and William H. Councill, which endorsed compromise, the peaceful resolution of racial disputes, and slow but steady progress founded on economic development and education; and the more aggressive approach favored by such black leaders as W. E. B. DuBois. With the founding of the Niagara Movement in 1905 and its institutional successor, the National Association for the Advancement of Colored People, in 1909, DuBois's views prevailed, and civil rights leaders became increasingly committed to direct legal challenges to Jim Crow.

Their prodigious efforts paid off slowly. They were hindered by an unsympathetic and sometimes hostile judicial system that generally favored property rights over individual rights, and were threatened by terrorism and the second rising of the Ku Klux Klan. Nonetheless there were some legal victories. The Supreme Court found in favor of voting rights in *Guinn and Beal v. United States* and *United States v. Moseley* in 1915, in *Nixon v. Herndon* in 1927, and in *Nixon v. Condon* in 1931. The 1917 decision in *Buchanan v. Warley* struck down segregated housing zones. And in *Aldridge v. United States* in 1931, the high court found that attorneys can legitimately question prospective jurors about racial attitudes.

With the coming of the New Deal, a fundamental shift began to occur in the political forces arrayed in the civil rights movement. The federal government, slowly and fitfully at first but with increasing commitment, began to shift toward support for the basic rights of black Americans, a position it had largely abandoned after the end of Reconstruction. Executive Order 8802, signed by President Roosevelt in 1941, established the Fair Employment Practices Committee, and in 1946 President Truman's Executive Order 9808 created the President's Committee on Civil Rights. Rights related to jury service were established by the Supreme Court in the 1938 *Hale v. Commonwealth of Kentucky* decision and in the *Patton v. Mississippi* decision in 1947. In 1941, in *Mitchell v. United States et al.*, the high court upheld the right to sue for damages resulting from discrimination in interstate transportation.

In 1938, the Supreme Court in *Missouri Ex Rel. Gaines v. Canada* held that where "separate but equal" laws related to educational facilities were in force, the educational facilities had to be equal in fact or the laws were unconstitutional. Ten years later, the Court's decision in *Sipuel v. Board of Regents of the University of Oklahoma* required that states provide equal access to education for "qualified" black students. The stage was set for the Supreme Court decision that would set segregation on the defensive. In the 1954 case of *Brown v. Board of Education of Topeka, Kansas*, the Court, having heard arguments from a team of NAACP attorneys that included future justice Thurgood Marshall, held unanimously that the "separate but equal" principle established by *Plessy* was inapplicable to public education; such separate facilities were "inherently unequal."

The following year, seamstress Rosa Parks's refusal to move to the back of a Montgomery, Alabama, bus sparked the Montomery bus boycott, and the drive for civil rights in the South was in full swing. The conflicts over voting rights, public transportation and accommodations, and school desegregation pitted grassroots activists, sometimes with the support of the federal courts and occasionally federal troops, against the Klan, state and local governments, and the police. Congress, although often divided along regional lines, brought forth the Civil Rights Act of 1957, which provided protection for voting rights, and then the Civil Rights Act of 1964, which addressed voting rights, desegregation of schools and public facilities, and employment discrimination. The landmark 1964 act provides much of the legal basis for the civil rights struggle today.

A new generation of leaders organized the movement. Martin Luther King, Jr., Ralph David Abernathy, Joseph E. Lowery, James Lawson, and others provided not only tactical leadership but a strategy of nonviolent civil disobedience.

Photographs and films of police assaulting marchers and news accounts of murderous Klan attacks on people, homes, and churches helped sway public opinion across the country. Although more radical civil rights organizations, such as the Black Panther Party, grew up in the late 1960s and promoted more violent methods, and despite destructive and deadly urban rioting, the enduring images of civil rights activism of that dramatic era are of "Bull" Connor's police attacking peaceful marchers in Birmingham; Governor George Wallace blocking a doorway at the University of Alabama to deny the admission of black students; and the stunned companions of Martin Luther King, Jr., pointing to the place where moments before an assassin had fired the bullet that cut their leader down.

By the 1970s, the legal basis for civil rights was in place. It was a plainly a triumph, not only overturning a long history of state-endorsed segregation, but changing the racial attitudes of millions of Americans, white and black. But much remains to be accomplished. In many places racism has simply gone underground, making it more difficult to fight because it is harder to see. Our inner cities are still caught up in poverty and the frustration and social ills that result. We might hope that the history of the civil rights movement so far will help to guide its success in the future.

Abernathy, Ralph David (1926–1990)

An influential civil rights advocate and associate of the Reverend Dr. Martin Luther King, Jr., the Reverend Dr. Ralph David Abernathy was one of the founders, in 1957, and president, from 1968 to 1977, of the Southern Christian Leadership Conference. Abernathy was born in Linden, Alabama, on 11 March 1926. Although the grandson of a slave and one of 12 children, he saved enough money to enroll at Alabama State College and received a bachelor of science degree from that institution in 1950. He then went to Atlanta University, where he studied sociology. There he met Reverend Dr. Martin Luther King, Jr., whose father was the pastor at the Ebenezer Baptist Church in Atlanta. In 1951, Abernathy himself became the pastor of the First Baptist Church of Montgomery, Alabama. When King took control of the Dexter Avenue Baptist Church in Montgomery, he and Abernathy decided to combine their talents to work for peaceful change in the Jim Crow laws. Following the refusal of Rosa Parks to move to the back of a Montgomery, Alabama, city bus, the two men helped establish the Montgomery Improvement Association, whose main goal was to boycott the bus system. King was the president, and Abernathy his right-hand man. In 1957, Abernathy helped King, the Reverend Joseph Lowery, and the Reverend Fred Shuttlesworth to organize the Southern Christian Leadership Conference (SCLC), which was created to advance the cause of racial integration. Abernathy continued as a close friend and associate of King's, and, following King's assassination in 1968, Abernathy took over the SCLC. He thereby became the titular head of the civil rights movement, despite criticism from other rights leaders because he was not considered a man of King's stature. He made an unsuccessful run for a congressional seat in 1976 and later served as pastor of Atlanta's West Hunter Street Baptist Church. Just before his death in 1990, Abernathy's autobiography, *And the Walls Came Tumbling Down*, charged that Dr. King had had an extramarital affair the night before his assassination. The charge led many in the civil rights community to accuse Abernathy of self-interested sensationalism.

Ralph David Abernathy

Abolition Movement

The movement to end slavery in the United States during the antebellum years was known as abolitionism. The

1

movement's antecedents included Quaker antislavery activities as early as the 1680s. In 1700, activist Samuel Sewall's *The Selling of Joseph* called for an end to slavery. Some leaders of the American Revolution, including Patrick Henry and Thomas Jefferson (himself a slave owner), spoke out against the institution. In 1775, the Society for the Relief of Free Negroes Unlawfully Held in Bondage was founded in Philadelphia. *Dialogue Concerning the Slavery of the Africans*, by Dr. Samuel Hopkins, appeared in 1776.

The Constitutional Convention in Philadelphia in 1787 nearly broke up over the demand from Southern delegates that slavery be protected in the Constitution. A compromise was reached that allowed slaves to be counted as ⅗ths of a person for purposes of congressional representation.

In 1817, a group of ministers, politicians, and even Supreme Court Justice Bushrod Washington, nephew of George Washington, founded the American Colonization Society, whose aim was to return slaves to Africa. To achieve this goal, land was purchased near the area of present-day Monrovia, in Liberia.

Among the early activists of the nineteenth century were Benjamin Lundy, who was working for the abolition of slavery about 1815 and helped form the Union Humane Society in Ohio, and writer and editor Elihu Embree. Embree's journal, *The Emancipator*, was published in Tennessee in 1820 and is believed to be the first periodical publication devoted to ending slavery. Eleven years later, the first issue of William Lloyd Garrison's antislavery publication *The Liberator* appeared with an editorial that stated: "On this subject, I do not wish to think, or speak, or write with moderation I will not equivocate—I will not excuse—I will not retreat a single inch—AND I WILL BE HEARD."

Garrison (1805–1879) is perhaps the best-known abolitionist. Born in Newburyport, Massachusetts, he began his journalistic career early. In 1828 he went to work as editor of the antislavery Bennington (Vermont) *Journal of the Times;* two years later he went to Baltimore, Maryland, where he became the editor of the Baltimore *Genius of Universal Emancipation*, where his antislavery editorials earned him a seven-week prison sentence for libeling slavetraders. Author of *Thoughts on African Colonization* (1832), Garrison was a founder, with fellow abolitionists Lewis and Arthur Tappan, of the American Anti-Slavery Society in 1833. He was shunned by more moderate abolitionists who wanted a slow approach to ending slavery without breaking up the Union. Garrison's fiery brand of activism attracted such people as Lydia Maria Child (1802–1880), author of *An Appeal in Favor of That Class of Americans Called Africans* (1833); Henry David Thoreau (1817–1862), author of *Walden* and *Civil Disobedience;* writer John Greenleaf Whittier (1807–1892); and Amos Bronson Alcott, father of writer Louisa May Alcott. On 21 October 1835, while giving a speech in Boston, Garrison proclaimed that "all men were created equal." The speech inflamed a mob of proslavery advocates, who tried to lynch Garrison. The abolitionist darted into a small jail and spent the night there under protective custody. In 1854, Garrison, who had founded the New England Anti-Slavery Society, stood in an open air rally in Framingham, Massachusetts, and publicly burned the U.S. Constitution as an evil document.

The abolitionist movement also included such women activists as the sisters Sarah and Angela Grimké, Lucretia Coffin Mott, Lucy Stone, and Prudence Crandall. The movement also brought into its fold free blacks who fought, through speeches and publications, to free Southern slaves. Among these were Samuel Ringgold Ward, James Forten, Sojourner Truth, Frederick Douglass, Robert Purvis, Frances Ellen Watkins Harper, and Harriet Tubman.

The movement against slavery did have its price. On 7 December 1837, the

Reverend Elijah Parish Lovejoy (1802–1837) was killed by a proslavery mob in Alton, Illinois. Lovejoy, editor of the antislavery journals *St. Louis Observer* and the *Alton Observer*, had founded the Illinois Anti-Slavery Society. In November 1837, proslavery mobs had wrecked his presses in Alton, but he returned to the city and published more editorials. Only days later, his shop was set afire and he was shot to death and hauled through the streets. His brother Owen (1811–1864) was a close friend of Abraham Lincoln and urged Republicans to support Lincoln in 1860. Owen Lovejoy served in Congress from 1857 to 1864, speaking out against slavery.

With Lovejoy's martyrdom, the abolitionist movement separated into two camps, known as the "moral" and "political" abolitionists. The moralists felt that with moral persuasion, slavery would slowly be rooted out. The political wing embraced electoral success as the only way to end slavery. This latter group formed the Liberty Party in New York in 1839. Their presidential tickets were headed up in 1840 and 1844 by James G. Birney, a former slaveowner. He drew about 7,000 votes in 1840 and 62,000 votes in 1844. The party collapsed in 1848 and was replaced by the more moderate Free Soil Party, which ran tickets in 1848 and 1852, with slowly improving results. The election of 1852 was the Free Soil Party's last effort; in 1854, delegates from the Whig Party, the Democratic Party, and the Free Soil Party founded the Republican party in Ripon, Wisconsin. Although the Republicans' first presidential candidate, John Charles Frémont, came in second in a close race in 1856, the party was victorious in 1860, led by Abraham Lincoln.

After 1838, Northern anger grew over slavery. The appearance of the Underground Railroad, coupled in later years with Congressional legislation like the Missouri Compromise of 1850, the horrific Fugitive Slave Act of 1850 that was upheld and strengthened, and Supreme Court decisions in *Prigg v. Pennsylvania* (1842) and *Dred Scott v. Sandford* (1857) served to polarize opinion and bring the slavery issue to the forefront, threatening to break the Union. The match to the powderkeg was the publication in 1852 of Harriet Beecher Stowe's *Uncle Tom's Cabin*. This landmark work showed the dark side of slavery and became a best-selling work.

With Abraham Lincoln's election in 1860, slavery was at a crossroads. Southern states chose to leave the Union rather than give up their "peculiar institution"; the move precipitated the Civil War. On 1 January 1863, Lincoln signed his Emancipation Proclamation, which freed the slaves in the Southern states. It was not, however, until the passage of the Thirteenth Amendment in 1865 that all slaves were freed forever.

See also American Colonization Society; Dred Scott v. Sandford; Prigg, Plaintiff in Error, v. The Commonwealth of Pennsylvania.

Adickes v. S. H. Kress and Co. (U.S., 1970)

Adickes v. S. H. Kress and Co. was the 1970 Supreme Court case in which the high court ruled that private businesses are not liable for damages from racial discrimination, even if the discriminatory action violates state policy. The case involved plaintiff Sandra Adickes, a schoolteacher from New York, who was refused service and then arrested in the restaurant of S. H. Kress and Company, a department store in Hattiesburg, Mississippi. Adickes sued the store under the provisions of 42 U.S.C. 1983, which prohibits discrimination "under the color of the law."

The District Court in Mississippi ruled that to recover damages, Adickes had to prove that the state had acted in conjunction with Kress. The court ruled that she had failed to do this, and so dismissed her suit. She then sued to the Court of Appeals, which affirmed the judgment. Adickes sued to the U.S. Supreme Court.

The Supreme Court ruled 5–2 that since Kress was not being ordered by the state to keep its segregationist policy, Adickes could not recover damages. Justice John Marshall Harlan II wrote the opinion for the Court. Justices Brennan and Douglas dissented, and Justice Thurgood Marshall did not participate.

Affirmative Action

Broadly defined, affirmative action encompasses active efforts to improve employment or educational opportunities for minority groups and women. It has included such specific actions as the setting aside of some government contracts for minority businesses and the establishment of racial quotas for college admissions. Among the most controversial aspects of the civil rights movement today, affirmative action has been championed by its advocates as a way to remedy past discrimination against minority groups; opponents often portray it as "reverse" racial discrimination.

See also DeFunis v. Odegaard; Fullilove v. Klutznick; University of California Regents v. Bakke.

Akerman, Amos Tappan (1821–1880)

Amos Akerman was the controversial attorney general during the Grant administration who fought the power of the Ku Klux Klan. Akerman was born in Portsmouth, New Hampshire, on 23 February 1821, the son of a surveyor. He attended Phillips Exeter Academy in that state and graduated from Dartmouth in 1842. Akerman traveled to Murphreesboro, North Carolina, where for a time he supported himself as a teacher. He then went to Richmond, Virginia, and later to Peoria, Illinois, taking teaching positions.

In 1845, Akerman settled in Savannah, Georgia, where he became friends with John McPherson Berrien, a noted lawyer and the attorney general in the Polk administration. Akerman became tutor to Berrien's children. He then opened a private law practice in Clarksville, Georgia, and worked there for the next 15 years. In 1860, he supported the unsuccessful Bell–Everett Union ticket in the national election, but when the South seceded after the Republican victory he supported the Confederate cause. Akerman fought in several battles under the banner of Georgia. Toward the end of the war, however, he saw the wrong in slavery and secession and spoke out against it.

In 1868, Akerman served as a delegate to the Georgia state constitutional convention and a year later was named U.S. district attorney for the State of Georgia. In July 1870, President Ulysses S. Grant named Akerman as his attorney general. Although now a moderate on several issues dear to Republicans, Akerman was a radical when it came to fighting the power of the Ku Klux Klan, which had sprung up in the years after the Civil War. In 1871, Akerman convinced President Grant to send military troops to nine South Carolina counties, to suspend the writ of habeas corpus, and to arrest Klan members. Some 2,000 Klansmen were apprehended. Akerman's opposition to the Klan grew, and he toured the North, speaking about the Klan in several cities. Some cabinet members became disillusioned by Akerman's fanaticism. According to Secretary of State Hamilton Fish, Akerman had the Klan "on the brain. It has got to be a bore to listen twice a week to this thing." In December 1871, amid a controversy over the use of railroad grants, which Akerman opposed giving to big business, Grant asked for and received his resignation. Akerman returned home to Cartersville, Georgia, and picked up his private law practice. He died there of rheumatism on 21 December 1880.

See also Ku Klux Klan.

Alabama

Alabama, one of the 11 states of the Confederacy, was governed from the end

Alabama Governor George Wallace confronts U.S. Deputy Attorney General Nicholas Katzenbach over the enrollment of two black students at the University of Alabama at Tuscaloosa in June 1963.

of the Civil War until the 1940s by a series of leaders who stood strongly for racial segregation. In 1946, however, James Elisha Folsom (1908–1987) was elected governor and served from 1947 to 1950 and again from 1955 to 1958. Folsom found himself in the middle of the Dixiecrat split of the Democratic Party in 1948 over the proposed civil rights plank that was to be added to the party platform, but managed to support President Harry S Truman for reelection as well as to improve civil rights in his state. As governor of Alabama, Folsom appointed voting rights officials who helped blacks to register to vote, labored for reapportionment that provided blacks with fair representation, either refused to sign or vetoed almost all of the segregationist legislation passed by the state legislature in the wake of the Supreme Court's *Brown v. Board of Education* decision, and, in his second term, cheered on the Montgomery Bus Boycott. Folsom was an unusual character, and a Southern politician who was surely out of step with his times. When he campaigned, he often would finish speaking to white crowds and then proceed to the fields to talk to and shake the hands of black workers. Folsom's two terms as governor were served on either side of Seth Gordon Persons (1902–1965), an Alabama native and radio tycoon. Persons was governor when the crucial *Brown v. Board of Education* decision outlawing school segregation came down. Following James Folsom's second term, John Malcolm Patterson (1921–1975) became governor and served from 1959 until 1963.

Patterson was, with the exception of George Wallace, the most segregationist of the Alabamian chief executives. As leader of the Jim Crow forces in the state, it was Patterson who expelled several white students from Alabama State College for joining with black students in a sit-in. Patterson's segregationism, however, paled in comparison with that of George Corley Wallace (1919–), whose stark figure standing in a doorway at the University of Alabama to prevent the desegregation of the school, while Assistant Attorney General Nicholas Katzenbach asked him to step aside, remains one of the most powerful images of the 1960s. When Wallace could not lawfully succeed himself as governor, his wife Lurleen Wallace (1926–1968) ran and was elected Alabama's first woman governor. She served less than a year and a half of her term. In that time, she was ordered by a federal court to desegregate Alabama schools; angered, she asked the legislature for a withdrawal of state monies from Tuskegee University, a black institution, and an increase in state colleges, which were highly segregated. She died of cancer on 7 May 1968 and was succeeded by Lieutenant Governor Albert Preston Brewer (1928–), whose administration was marked by a failure to cooperate with the federal government and the courts to desegregate schools and other areas dominated by discriminatory practices. In 1970, running for his own elected term, Brewer was defeated by a returning George Wallace, who had run for president of the United States in 1968 on the far-right platform of the American Independent party. Wallace would eventually serve as governor of Alabama through most of the 1970s and into the 1980s, surviving an assassination attempt in 1972. He finally retired in 1987, having mellowed in his racial attitudes—and after receiving a sizeable black vote in his last election. According to the 1990 census, Alabama's population included 2,975,797 whites, 1,020,705 blacks, and 44,085 people of American Indian, Asian, and other ancestry.

See also Wallace, George Corley.

Alabama Christian Movement for Human Rights (ACMHR)

The ACMHR, an affiliate of the Southern Christian Leadership Conference, was formed in Birmingham, Alabama, in 1956 by the Reverend Fred L. Shuttlesworth and the Reverend Vernon Johns, two Baptist ministers from Birmingham and Montgomery, Alabama, respectively. Shuttlesworth was the ACMHR's first president. In the six years of its existence, ACMHR used public protests at segregated restaurants and other whites-only facilities in the fight against Jim Crow laws. In 1962, the ACMHR was absorbed into the Montgomery Improvement Association, the antecedent to the Southern Christian Leadership Conference.

See also Montgomery Improvement Association; Shuttlesworth, Fred Lee; Southern Christian Leadership Conference.

Albany Movement

The Albany Movement was formed in November 1961 following the Interstate Commerce Commission's action of 1 November 1961, which outlawed segregation in interstate transport bus terminals. That same day some blacks tried to sit in the waiting room of the Trailways terminal in Albany, Georgia, and were asked to move to a waiting room for coloreds. The movement grew out of this action, and was formed as a coalition of SNCC members, the Albany chapter of the NAACP, and a partnership of black ministers. Dr. William G. Anderson, an Albany osteopath, was named the group's first president. Organized by the Albany Movement, the black community started a boycott of Albany's private bus line, and by the end of January 1962 the line was out of business. The group then tried to work through the city government to ban racial segregation in the town's laws. When this failed, the Albany Movement's members separately turned to voter registration to advance their cause.

Aldridge v. United States (U.S., 1931)

The Supreme Court held in *Aldridge v. United States* that the attorney for a defendant can reasonably question prospective jurors regarding their attitudes on race and can ask if they hold racially discriminatory views. The petitioner, Alfred Scott Aldridge, a black man, was convicted in the District of Columbia for the murder of a white policeman and was sentenced to death. Aldridge's attorney was not allowed to ask potential jurors about their racial attitudes or whether race would play a part in their deliberations. Following his conviction, Aldridge appealed, but his conviction was upheld by the Court of Appeals. Aldridge sued to the U.S. Supreme Court. The high court found in favor of Aldridge, with Chief Justice Charles Evans Hughes writing the majority decision and Justice James Clarke McReynolds dissenting.

Alexander v. Holmes County Board of Education (U.S., 1969)

Alexander v. Holmes County Board of Education was a Supreme Court case in which the high court ruled on the requirement that school segregation take place "with all deliberate speed." *Alexander* was, with *Green v. County School Board of New Kent County*, one of the last two school desegregation cases to come before the Warren Court.

In *Alexander*, the Holmes County School Board of Mississippi had asked for and received more time to end the segregation of its school system. On 28 August 1969, the Fifth Circuit Court of Appeals ruled that the school district was complying with the Supreme Court's mandate in *Brown v. Board of Education of Topeka, Kansas* that the desegregation of the nation's schools must proceed with "all deliberate speed." The Appeals Court mandate was challenged to the Supreme Court, which struck down the appeals court's ruling on 29 October 1969. No opinion was filed; the Court instead issued five strict orders demanding that the Holmes County Board of Education end segregation immediately, and that the Court of Appeals oversee the transformation.

Alexander v. Louisiana (U.S., 1972)

Alexander v. Louisiana involved Alexander, a black man, who was indicted for the crime of rape by an all-white state grand jury. The Supreme Court ruled 7–0 that Alexander was denied the equal protection of the laws by the way the grand jury was chosen. Justice Byron White wrote the decision for the Court; Justices Powell and Rehnquist did not participate.

American Colonization Society

The American Colonization Society was organized in 1817 to support the return of free blacks to Africa. Its members included U.S. senators, whites who fought against slavery, and even a Supreme Court justice, Bushrod Washington, nephew of George Washington. The work of the society led to the creation of the African state of Liberia, to which free blacks started emigrating around 1821.

An American Dilemma
See Myrdal, Karl Gunnar.

American Teachers Association (ATA)

The ATA was the first black teacher's union. Founded in 1904, it merged with the National Education Association (NEA) in 1966. The ATA was begun by John Robert Edward Lee (1870–1944) of Alabama, a black educator and reformer;

William Taylor Burnell Williams (1869–1941) of Virginia, a black educator and journalist; and Richard Robert Wright, Sr. (1853?–1947) of Georgia, a former slave and a noted black educator.

Antilynching Laws

Congressman George H. White of North Carolina introduced the first antilynching bill in the House in 1900, but it died in committee. Republican congressman Leonidas Dyer of Missouri then emerged as the champion of legislative attempts to end lynching in the United States. Dyer's efforts were unsuccessful, but they signaled a growing opposition to Southern racial violence.

See also Dyer, Leonidas Carstarphen.

Arkansas

Arkansas was one of the 11 states of the Confederacy. In 1874, the state legislature passed Article 14 of the state constitution, which read: "Intelligence and virtue being the safeguards of liberty and the bulwark of a free and good government, the state shall ever maintain a general, suitable, and efficient system of free schools whereby all persons between the ages of 6 and 21 years may receive gratuitous education." Section 4 of Article 14 gave the power over the schools to "such officers as may be provided by the General Assembly." These officers had the duty to "establish separate schools for white and colored persons." By 1954, when the Supreme Court outlawed segregation in education, Arkansas was spending $61,158,107 on its white students, and $25,297,787 on its black students—an average of $127.72 for every white student and $102.25 for every black student. Although the modern civil rights movement started in 1954 with the noted *Brown v. Board of Education* decision, Arkansas's governors were not involved to any real extent in the segregation matter, although Governor Sidney Sanders McMath (1912–), who served from 1949 to 1953, did oversee the opening up of the state's Democratic primary to black voters. But it was Orval Eugene Faubus (1910–), who served from 1955 until 1967, who was the best-known among Southern governors for standing against integration. Believing that integration was a local question, Faubus ordered the state National Guard to enforce segregation at Little Rock High School in 1957, leading to a showdown with President Dwight Eisenhower, in which the guard was overruled by U.S. Army troops sent to Arkansas by the president. Following Faubus, two more moderate governors, Republican Winthrop Rockefeller (1912–1973) and Democrat Dale Bumpers (1925–), led the way in integrating Arkansan society. According to the 1990 census, Arkansas had 1,994,744 whites, 373,912 blacks, and 32,069 people of American Indian, Asian, and other races.

Atlanta Negro Voters League

See Calhoun, John Henry, Jr.

Avery v. Georgia (U.S., 1953)

See Williams v. Georgia.

Ayers et al. v. Fordice, Governor of Mississippi

See United States v. Fordice, Governor of Mississippi, et al.

Bailey v. Alabama (U.S., 1911)

Bailey was one of two Supreme Court cases that are together considered by scholars as the "peonage cases." The Court struck down the use of peonage, the act of holding a debtor in slavery-like bondage, as a violation of both the Peonage Abolition Act of 2 March 1867 and the Thirteenth Amendment. The case involved a black laborer named Alonzo Bailey, who contracted to work off, over the period of a year, an advance paid to him. When he left the job after a month, he was arrested. The Alabama Supreme Court upheld his conviction as a case of "fraud," not peonage. In 1908, the Supreme Court agreed and refused to take the case. Bailey's lawyers appealed to the Supreme Court two years later on the grounds that the contract under which Bailey was hired constituted peonage. The Court ruled 7–2 that the Alabama statute through which Bailey was convicted was unconstitutional, with Justice Charles Evans Hughes writing the majority opinion and Justices Horace Lurton and Oliver Wendell Holmes dissenting. The Thirteenth Amendment, Hughes wrote, "render[ed] impossible any state of bondage; to make labor free, by prohibiting that control by which the personal service of one man is deposed of or coerced for another's benefit."

See also Clyatt v. United States; Peonage Abolition Act of 2 March 1867; United States v. Reynolds.

Baker, Ella Jo (1903–1986)

Ella Jo Baker, a leading civil rights activist, was the organizer of the conference that led to the creation of the Student Nonviolent Coordinating Committee. Baker was born in Norfolk, Virginia, on 7 December 1903, although she grew up in Littleton, a small village in North Carolina. She graduated in 1927 from Shaw University, and soon moved to New York City, where she helped organize the Young Negro Cooperative League, a group for black consumers. During the Depression, she wrote and lectured on civil rights and consumer matters.

In the early 1940s, Baker became affiliated with the NAACP, first as an assistant field secretary, then as national field secretary, a post in which she toured the nation setting up NAACP branches. Her main work, however, was with the New York branch. Although she left the field secretary post in 1946 to care for her niece, Baker was a moving force behind the New York NAACP branch. In 1954, she worked to supply the Supreme Court with evidence on the toll that segregation was taking on black children.

In 1957, with the founding of the Southern Christian Leadership Conference, Baker was asked by Martin Luther King to head up the SCLC's national office and serve as the organization's first executive director. She left the SCLC in 1960, disillusioned with the group's dependence on King. Her desire for a grassroots movement of young people took Baker back to Shaw University, where on 15 April 1960 she headed up a conference of young black militants that became the Student Nonviolent Coordinating Committee (SNCC). As a member of the group, she helped organize sit-ins. In 1964, she was a key mover behind the formation of the Mississippi Freedom Democratic Party (MFDP), which challenged the regular delegates to the 1964 Democratic National Convention in Atlantic City.

Ella Baker was known as a staunch independent who felt that political power should flow from the masses up and not from the leaders down. Her life work was featured in a 1983 film, *Fundi: The Story of Ella Baker. (Fundi* is a Swahili word that refers to a person who hands down a craft from one generation to another.) Ella Jo Baker died in New York City in 1986, on her eighty-third birthday.

See also Student Nonviolent Coordinating Committee.

Baker v. Carr (U.S., 1962)

Baker v. Carr was the landmark Supreme Court case in which the Court held that courts have jurisdiction to oversee state apportionment plans. In 1901, the Tennessee General Assembly passed a law establishing the formula for reapportionment as the state's population rose. The law did not provide, however, for changing demographics. By 1960, urban voters were underrepresented in the General Assembly. Baker and others sued state officials, arguing that the apportionment plan denied them due process in violation of their Fourteenth Amendment rights. The U.S. District Court for the Middle District of Tennessee dismissed Baker's suit on the grounds that such relief would have to come from the state legislature, not the courts. Baker sued to the U.S. Supreme Court. The Court held 6–2 (Justices Felix Frankfurter and John Marshall Harlan dissenting, and Justice Charles Whittaker not participating) only that the courts did have jurisdiction over the matter. Justice William Brennan wrote for the majority, "An unbroken line of our precedents sustains the federal courts' jurisdiction of the subject matter of federal constitutional claims of this nature." The Supreme Court did not directly address the matter of apportionment until two years later in *Reynolds v. Sims.*

See also Reynolds, a Judge, et al. v. Sims et al.

Baldwin, William Henry III (1891–1980)

William Baldwin III was the president of the National Urban League from 1941 to 1946. Baldwin was born in Saginaw, Michigan, on 17 September 1891, the son of railroad magnate William Henry Baldwin, Jr., and Ruth Standish Bowles Baldwin, his domineering mother, who would later become one of the founders of the National Urban League. His grandfather, William Henry Baldwin, Sr., was one of the founders of the Young Men's Christian Union in Boston. While working on, and later operating, railroads, William Baldwin, Jr., saw inequalities among blacks in the South. He later joined Booker T. Washington's movement and was a trustee of Washington's Tuskegee University from 1897 until his death in 1905. William Baldwin III was a student at the prestigious Phillips Academy in Massachusetts, then attended Harvard University, where he eventually earned his bachelor's degree, and the University of Wisconsin. He served during the early years of the First World War as a cub reporter for the New York *Evening Post*. He also served as secretary of the National Urban League, a civil rights organization his mother had helped found. In 1916, Baldwin was integral in the founding of an Urban League chapter in Brooklyn, New York, which was later merged into a greater New York chapter. In 1917, he resigned his position on the *Post* and entered the United States Naval Reserve, rising to the rank of ensign as a cable censor in Key West, Florida, before being discharged.

During the early 1920s, Baldwin was known as a worker for black causes. In 1920, he helped raise $1 million for Fisk University in Nashville, Tennessee. Black writers, poets, and musicians received prominent recognition in the white press with his help. Further, Baldwin helped fund Sydenham Hospital in Harlem, New York, which became the first hospital to be integrated in the United States. Baldwin then turned his attention to legal reform, joining such philanthropists as John D. Rockefeller, Jr., and Charles M. Schwab to found the American Arbitration Association, which aided people of limited means in settling disputes in court cheaply. From 1926 until 1942, Baldwin ran his own public relations firm, Baldwin & Mermey.

From 1942 until 1947, Baldwin was president of the National Urban League. He saw the league through the Second World War, race riots in 1943, and the black migration following the war. Baldwin stepped down in 1947. He later served as a professor at New York University. During the 1950s, he was asked by President Dwight D. Eisenhower to head up Crusade for Freedom, a national money-raising effort to help Radio Free Europe. In his final years, he retired to Kennett Square, Pennsylvania, where he died at the age of 88 on 19 May 1980.

See also National Urban League.

Barnett, Ida Bell Wells
See Wells-Barnett, Ida Bell.

Barnett, Ross Robert (1898–1987)
Ross Barnett was the segregationist governor of Mississippi who, during the mid-1960s, was one of the leaders of the Southern revolt against civil rights. Barnett was born on 22 January 1898, in the small village of Standing Pine, near Carthage, Mississippi, the youngest of 10 children in a farming family. He worked his way through high school and Mississippi College by performing odd jobs. In 1917, he entered the United States Army and served in Europe during the First World War. When he returned, he was awarded a degree from Mississippi College in 1922. While earning a law degree at the Mississippi School of Law at Oxford, Barnett was employed as a high school coach and Sunday school teacher. After earning his law degree in 1926, he began to build an influential law practice in Jackson, the state capital. One of his first major cases was to defend John Kasper, a racist indicted and convicted of

segregationist violence. From 1943 to 1944 Barnett served as bar commissioner, vice president, and president of the Mississippi State Bar Association.

Barnett became involved in politics in 1951 when he was nominated as the Democratic candidate for governor. Although he lost that race, as well as a subsequent gubernatorial attempt in 1955, he made enough political friends to receive a third nomination in 1959. By denouncing some Democrats as moderates on the racial question and pledging to do his utmost to retain segregation in Mississippi, Barnett was elected by a wide margin. He took office on 19 January 1960. Almost immediately, he worked to carry out his promise. He helped create the Citizens' Council, a segregationist group, and served as chairman of the State Sovereignty Commission. In 1960, angered by the civil rights plank in the Democratic Party platform, he refused to support John F. Kennedy in the presidential campaign.

In 1962, Barnett clashed with the federal government. In October of that year James Meredith, a young black man, sought to enter the University of Mississippi at Oxford, but was barred by school authorities. Although Meredith obtained a court order to be admitted, Barnett refused to budge. The Fifth Circuit Court of Appeals held Barnett in contempt, and he was fined $10,000 a day and ordered to jail. He never paid the fine or served prison time, and the charges were dropped in 1965. Meredith was eventually enrolled under the protection of federal troops.

Unable to run for a second term, Barnett retired. He tried to make a comeback in 1967, but was badly beaten in the Democratic primary. Ross Barnett spent his final years in retirement. He maintained the stance for which he was popular to the end. "God was the original segregationist," he once said. "He made the white man white and the black man black, and He did not intend for them to mix." Barnett died in Jackson, Mississippi, on 6 November 1987.

See also Mississippi; Mississippi Sovereignty Commission.

Barrows v. Jackson (U.S., 1953)

As in *Shelley v. Kraemer*, the Supreme Court ruled in *Barrows* that there can be no damage to homeowners or property owners if a court enjoins them from enforcing a racially restrictive covenant. The case involved Barrows and Jackson, two property owners in Los Angeles, California, who entered into an agreement to purchase a piece of residential property. Part of the agreement was that neither party could sell or rent their part of the property to anyone not of the Caucasian race. Jackson later rented her section of the property to a black couple. Barrows sued her in court for violating their agreement and asked for damages. A lower court enjoined Barrows from suing as it found the restrictive covenant to be an unconstitutional infringement of equal protection of the law. An appeals court upheld the lower court's action, and Barrows appealed to the U.S. Supreme Court to get relief. The issues in this case were unique. As Justice Sherman Minton noted in the majority opinion, no petitioner was before the Court claiming that the restrictive covenant had precluded them from occupying the land. As Minton asked, "May the respondent [Jackson], whom the petitioners seek to coerce by an action to pay damages for her failure to honor her restrictive covenant, rely on the invasion of the rights of others in her defense to this action?" Minton, in the 6–1 opinion (Justices Stanley Reed and Robert H. Jackson did not participate, and Chief Justice Fred M. Vinson dissented), decided in the affirmative. He dismissed the plaintiff's argument that he was denied due process by the failure of the court to enforce a legally binding agreement. Wrote Minton, quoting a passage from the *Shelley v. Kraemer* decision: "The Constitution confers upon no individual the right to demand action by the State which results in the denial of equal protection of the laws to other individuals."

See also Shelley v. Kraemer.

Baton Rouge Bus Boycott

The Baton Rouge, Louisiana, boycott of 1953 was the first citywide bus boycott to protest segregation in public transportation. It began when the black community of Baton Rouge convinced the city council to pass an ordinance allowing for first-come, first-served access on city buses. Blacks would still occupy the back seats of buses, but for the first time no specific seats were reserved for whites. City bus drivers ignored the ordinance, and black riders boycotted the city buses for one day. The Louisiana state attorney general then ruled that the ordinance was unconstitutional. The strike ended. Three months later, under the guidance of the Reverend T. J. Jemison, black riders again boycotted the bus system. This boycott lasted only a week, ending when the city promised to reinstate, against the bus line's wishes, the controversial ordinance. Although the Baton Rouge boycott is little known, it served as a catalyst for a larger and better-known boycott in Montgomery, Alabama, during which Reverend Jemison and his followers' methods were put into action on a wider scale.

See also Montgomery Bus Boycott.

Batson v. Kentucky (U.S., 1986)

Batson was the Supreme Court case in which the Court found that the peremptory challenges of a prosecutor to a jury could not include those based on race. James Kirkland Batson, a black man, was charged in Jefferson County, Kentucky, with second-degree burglary and the receipt of stolen goods. When he came to trial, the prosecutor removed four potential black jurors from the jury pool by way of peremptory challenges. During the examination of prospective jurors, known as *voir dire*, both the defense counsel and the prosecutor may challenge potential jurors as to cause (such as a known bias), or with peremptory challenges, those given without any explanation. When Batson was faced with an all-white jury, his attorney asked that the jury be dismissed, as his client's equal protection rights under the Fourteenth Amendment were about to be violated. The judge refused, the trial went forward, and Batson was convicted. First a circuit court, then the Supreme Court of Kentucky, affirmed the judgment, concluding that under the voir dire system, a lawyer had no obligation to explain peremptory challenges. The Supreme Court granted *certiorari*—granting the appeal from the lower court—and on 30 April 1986, held 7–2 that peremptory challenges that removed all potential black jurors must be explained by a prosecutor as having been for reasons other than race. Chief Justice Warren Burger and Justice William Rehnquist dissented, claiming that overturning the long-held belief that peremptory challenges were allowed without showing cause was unconstitutional.

Bell, Griffin Boyette (1918–)

Griffin Bell was the federal appeals court judge who was involved in desegregation cases during the early 1960s, a critical period for the civil rights movement. Bell was born on 31 October 1918 in Americus, Sumter County, Georgia. He attended public schools and Georgia Southwestern College, a local community college. Bell also worked at his father's service station and appliance store in Americus. During World War II, he was involved in the Transportation Corps and was stationed in several states. After the war, he enrolled at the Mercer University Law School, from which he earned his law degree in 1948. Until

1961, he was involved with several private law firms in Savannah, Rome, and Atlanta.

In 1958, Bell had the unique advantage of working for the campaign of Ernest Vandiver, who was elected governor of Georgia. After inauguration, Bell served as Vandiver's chief of staff from 1959 until 1961. Vandiver was a staunch segregationist, and it was the association with Governor Vandiver that would later cloud Bell's career. In 1960, Bell served as the state co-chairman of John F. Kennedy's presidential campaign in Georgia. When Kennedy was elected, Bell was the new president's first appointee to the Fifth Circuit Court of Appeals to fill one of two newly created seats on that court. Bell, at 42, was the youngest person ever named to that court. Until 1976, when he resigned from the court, he participated in more than 3,000 cases, including 141 dealing with the matter of desegregation. Although critics called his approach "conservative," Bell was noted more as a centrist on the 15-man court because, while he agreed with many desegregation efforts, he opposed busing. In a controversial case, he sided with the majority finding that Julian Bond, a black Georgia assemblyman, had been rightly denied taking his seat in the state legislature because of his opposition to the Vietnam War. The Court's decision was eventually overturned by the Supreme Court.

In 1976, Bell resigned from the Court to rejoin his old law firm and work on Jimmy Carter's 1976 presidential campaign in Georgia. When Carter was elected, Bell was chosen as attorney general. His confirmation was held up by several organizations who called into question his commitment to civil rights, as shown by his association with Governor Vandiver and the Julian Bond decision. Bell was confirmed anyway and served as attorney general from 1977 until 1979, when he left office to return to his private law practice. Despite being a Democrat, in 1993, Bell was hired as former President George Bush's personal attorney on matters dealing with the Iran-Contra arms affair.

Berea College v. Commonwealth of Kentucky (U.S., 1908)

Berea College was the Supreme Court case in which the Court ruled that schools were "institutions," and thus were a matter for local, and not federal, control. Berea College in eastern Kentucky was a mixed-race institution in which blacks and whites received equal instruction in religion. In 1904, the Kentucky legislature passed a law prohibiting the use of such facilities for the commingling of the races; as a result, all of the blacks were tossed out. The college sued the state to overturn the law, but both the district court and the Kentucky Court of Appeals upheld the constitutionality of the statute on the grounds that it preserved the "purity of racial blood." The Supreme Court also upheld the Kentucky statute, but on narrow grounds. Justice David Josiah Brewer wrote the 8–1 decision. Not only was the matter subject to local control, Brewer wrote, but the state had the right to impose the will of "free association" on the college. Justice John Marshall Harlan, in his last great dissent before his death in 1911, derided the majority for the decision. On the matter of religious instruction, Harlan was livid. "The capacity to impart instruction to others is given by the Almighty for beneficent purposes, and its use may not be forbidden or interfered with by Government."

See also Harlan, John Marshall.

Bethune, Mary McLeod (1875–1955)

Mary McLeod Bethune, a black woman, strove to improve the lot of her fellow citizens through education. Born in rural South Carolina on 10 July 1875, she attended Scotia Seminary in Concord, North Carolina, and the Moody Bible Institute in Chicago, Illinois. From 1899 to 1903, she was a teacher at the Palatka (Presbyterian) Mission School in Palatka, Florida. In 1904, she started a rural school for black women in nearby Daytona Beach with $1.50 in cash and five students. It was called the Daytona Normal and Industrial Institute for Negro Girls of Daytona Beach. Nineteen years later, the small school merged with another Florida institution and became Bethune-Cookman College. Bethune served as president of the college until 1947. In her other work in the field of civil rights, she served as the head or member of various civil rights groups, including the National Urban League and the National Council of Negro Women, which she helped to found in 1935. Bethune died on 18 May 1955.

Bevel, James Luther (1936–)

The Reverend James Bevel is the civil rights activist known chiefly for his work as the organizer of the Southern Christian Leadership Conference's Birmingham, Alabama, chapter. Bevel was born in Ittabena, Mississippi, on 19 October 1936, and was educated in local schools. Between 1954 and 1955, he served in the United States Naval Reserve. In 1961 he earned a bachelor's degree from the American Baptist Theology Seminary, having been ordained as a Baptist minister in 1959.

An intimate of John Lewis, one-time chairman of the SNCC, Bevel was active in the SNCC until 1961, when he came under the influence of the Reverend Dr. Martin Luther King, Jr., and moved to the more moderate Southern Christian Leadership Conference, being named as a youth training specialist. One source notes that it was most likely Bevel, a Gandhian pacifist, who persuaded King to oppose the Vietnam War. In 1963, King asked Bevel to go to Birmingham, Alabama, to start up an SCLC branch there. His efforts in registering blacks to vote helped lead to the movement that culminated in the Voting Rights Act of 1965. In 1966, Bevel moved to Chicago to head up King's housing program, which ultimately failed. Bevel was with King when the civil rights leader was assassinated in Memphis on 5 April 1968 and took King's place as the leader of the sanitation strike march.

Since King's assassination, Bevel has retreated into the shadows. In the 1980s, he served as pastor of the South Shore Community Church in Chicago, advocating his program of education for black youth, Students for Education and Development.

Bilbo, Theodore Gilmore (1877–1947)

Theodore Bilbo, a staunch segregationist, served as governor of Mississippi from 1916 to 1920, and again from 1928 to 1932. Bilbo was born in Juniper Grove, near Poplarville, Mississippi, on 13 October 1877. His father, James Oliver Bilbo, was a cattleman. When he was 15, Theodore Bilbo became a church worker, and at age 19 was licensed as a Baptist lay preacher. He attended the University of Nashville from 1897 to 1900, and later earned a law degree at Vanderbilt University in 1907. He entered politics in 1903 when he ran for a circuit judgeship, and, although defeated in this first race, he was elected in 1908 to the Mississippi State Senate. During the next four years, he was caught up in a bribery scandal. In 1912, he ran for lieutenant governor dogged by the allegations, but was elected anyway. In 1916, he was elected governor. His first term was marked by compassion for the sick and handicapped; shades of his support for segregation were not in evidence. Under his leadership, Mississippi became the first state to ratify the Eighteenth Amendment, prohibiting the sale of alcoholic beverages. He was defeated for reelection as governor, and then made an unsuccessful run for Congress. He tried to make a comeback as governor in 1924, but lost to a Republican whose support for women's suffrage gained him that section of the electorate. In 1928, Bilbo again ran for governor. The Republican incumbent, Henry Lewis Whitfield, had called out federal troops during the lynching of a black man. Bilbo used this matter in his campaign and received the support of the Ku Klux Klan. Elected to a second term as governor, he worked for the improvement of public roads. In 1933, he left the governorship and worked in Washington for a year until he ran for the U.S. Senate and defeated a 22-year veteran. In the Senate, Bilbo railed against a proposed antilynching bill and called for the exportation back to Africa of all blacks in the United States. He spoke constantly on the Senate floor of white supremacy and opposed the Fair Employment Practices Act. In his second campaign for reelection, in 1946, he called for the disenfranchisement of all black voters. "I'm calling on every red-blooded American who believes in the superiority and integrity of the white race to get and see that no nigger votes. And the best time to do it is the night before." Although he was easily reelected, the Senate set up a committee in 1947 to investigate whether Bilbo should be seated. During the committee hearings, Bilbo was hospitalized with cancer of the jaw. It was at the time of the investigation that Bilbo's book, *Take Your Choice—Segregation or Mongrelization*, appeared in Mississippi. The Senate committee, however, took no action on Bilbo's conduct because he was too ill to take his seat. On 22 August 1947, Bilbo succumbed to cancer. He was 69 years old.

Birth of a Nation

Birth of a Nation is the historic 1914 film directed by David Wark (D. W.) Griffith, one of early Hollywood's greatest filmmakers. It was based on the book *The Clansmen* by Thomas Dixon, and it led to the reemergence of the Ku Klux Klan into the modern era. Commented President Woodrow Wilson after seeing it, "It is like history written with lightning." Griffith, the son of a Confederate officer, adapted Dixon's controversial novel to the screen because he felt it best reflected what happened to the South during and after the Civil War. It portrayed blacks who took positions of power in Reconstructionist governments as buffoons, former slave-owners as victims of the evil North, and the Ku Klux Klan as a heroic organization that came to the defense of white womanhood threatened by vicious negroes. Although the film was a sensation, it barely earned back the $110,000 of Griffith's fortune that he had poured into it. Incensed and embarrassed by the reaction to the film's stereotypical portrayal of blacks, he made his next picture, *Intolerance* (1916), as a statement against racism. Nonetheless, the depiction of the Klan in *Birth of a Nation* had already infused new life into the Klan, and the effects are still visible today.

See also Ku Klux Klan.

Black Athletes

Once banned from the major leagues of all professional sports, black Americans today are well represented in virtually every major sport save professional hockey.

In baseball, professional black teams were organized in the Negro Leagues. Such players as "Sweet Judy" Johnson, James "Cool Papa" Bell, Josh Gibson, and "Buck" Leonard would have been stars in the majors had they not been banned because of their race. The first black athlete drafted into major-league baseball was Jack Roosevelt Robinson. "Jackie" Robinson was first signed from the Montreal Monarchs in 1946 to play for the Brooklyn Dodgers. Later, Larry Doby was signed by the Cleveland Indians in 1947, and he became the first black to play in the American League. Doby hit .318 in the 1948 World Series against the Boston Braves. Doby went on to coach the Indians in 1974 and to manage the Chicago White Sox in 1978. A former Negro Leagues star, Satchel Paige, finished his career pitching in the major leagues for various teams.

Tennis player Arthur Ashe

The second professional sport to open to blacks was football. Marion Motley signed as a fullback with the Cleveland Browns in 1946 and played until 1953.

Following the opening up of baseball and football, blacks were more widely accepted into white-dominated sports. The first black basketball player was Chuck Cooper, who signed with the Boston Celtics in 1951. Coaching spots in basketball didn't open up for blacks until the Celtics hired Bill Russell in 1966.

Tennis, once considered a whites-only sport, opened up to women like Althea Gibson, who won the U.S. Open in 1957 and Wimbledon in 1958. Arthur Ashe became the first black to compete on the U.S. Davis Cup team in 1963. In 1968 he won the U.S. Open and, in 1975, became the first black man to win Wimbledon.

Black Magazines

Magazines by and for African Americans have existed since before the Civil War.

The African Methodist Episcopal *Review*, which began publication in 1841, is often considered to be the first black magazine. However, William Whipper, head of the American Moral Reform Society of Philadelphia, published *The National Reformer*, an abolitionist journal, as early as 1839. Another early journal aimed at ending slavery was the *Demosthenian Shield*, edited by Benjamin Stanley and issued in Philadelphia. David Ruggles's *The Mirror of Liberty*, started in 1837, was aimed primarily at free blacks in the North.

Following the Civil War, many black magazines sprang up across the nation. *Howard's Negro American* was published in Harrisburg, Pennsylvania, and *The Colored American* began publication in Boston, Massachusetts, in 1900. Some of these pioneering magazines survived more than a few issues, but most have been virtually forgotten.

Following a hiatus of some 40 years, *The Voice of the Negro* appeared again in the first years of the twentieth century. It was among the finest of black magazines to come out of the South. Booker T. Washington and W. E. B. DuBois, among others, were contributors to this publication. The *Voice* was, however, the forerunner of a greater literary and reformist work.

In 1910, *The Crisis* appeared. The official publication of the recently founded National Association for the Advancement of Colored People (NAACP), *The Crisis* was fundamentally different from its predecessors: instead of bright stories, poetry, or antislavery editorials, it contained piercing articles on problems in black life in America under segregation and Jim Crow. With W. E. B. DuBois as the journal's editor, such writers as Oswald Villard and Arthur Schomburg were free to discuss controversial issues.

After the founding of the *The Crisis*, few new black magazines appeared until such slick publications as *Jet* and *Ebony*, designed to appeal to a broader audience of black Americans, showed up on news-stands for wide consumption. They often dealt with movie stars and entertainers, cooking tips and other ways to improve the household, and other articles of varied interest. To this day, these two publications rank high in the list of all magazines sold nationally.

See also The Crisis.

Black Newspapers

The black press began with attempts at communicating abolitionist sentiment to free blacks in the North. The first paper written by blacks for blacks was *Freedom's Journal*, edited by John B. Russworm and Samuel E. Cornish, which was published in New York from 1827 to 1830. Before 1860, the best-known black newspaper was Frederick Douglass's *North Star*. From 1827 until 1865, some 40 black newspapers flourished in the United States, all in the North. From 1865 until 1900, almost 1,200 new black papers were added to this list. These later papers concentrated as much on the uplifting of the freed slaves to economic betterment as they did on matters of the family and church.

The New York *Age* was the premier black newspaper of the last two decades of the nineteenth century. The forerunner of the *Age* in New York was the *Rumor*, founded by black publisher George Parker in March 1880. The *Rumor*, however, used expensive artistry to decorate its pages of black news, and soon went out of business. Late in 1880, printer Timothy Thomas Fortune and W. Walter Sampson invested in the remains of the *Rumor* and with Parker published the New York *Globe*. Four years later, Fortune struck out on his own, founding the New York *Freeman*, which in 1887 became the New York *Age* after Fortune left the paper to campaign for Grover Cleveland in Ohio. The *Age* became the leading black paper over the next several years as a voice for Republican policies. In 1888, Fortune returned to New York, took over the *Age*, and ran it until 1907, when he sold it to

Fred Moore, owner of *Colored American Magazine*. Fortune was the leading black journalist in the last years of the 19th century, and he turned the *Age* into the first daily black newspaper in America. After the sale of the *Age* to Moore, Fortune went to work for Marcus Garvey as the editor of Garvey's magazine, *Negro World*.

The oldest continuing black newspaper in the United States is the *Philadelphia Tribune*, a semiweekly paper founded in 1884 by Chris J. Perry, Sr., and carried on by his widow and two daughters after his death in 1921. Other newspapers founded at this time include the *Baltimore Afro-American*, founded in 1892 by John H. Murphy, Sr.; the *Boston Guardian*, founded by William Monroe Trotter in 1901; the *Chicago Defender*, established by Robert S. Abbott in 1905; the *New York Amsterdam News*, founded by James H. Anderson in 1909; and Robert L. Vann's *Pittsburgh Courier* and Plummer Bernard Young's *Norfolk Journal and Guide*, both founded in 1910.

With the coming of the modern civil rights movement in the 1940s, black newspapers were the key news source for the black community. Gunnar Myrdal, the Swedish writer, lauded the black press for its important influence on "a large proportion of the Negro population." The growth of new black newspapers, such as *Muhammad Speaks*, the official organ of the Nation of Islam, and the *Black Panther*, the paper of the Black Panther Party, made the black press more competitive. By the 1970s, the white press in America began to improve its coverage of the black community, undermining to some degree the black press' original purpose. Nonetheless, papers such as the *Atlanta World*, *Chicago Defender*, and *Amsterdam News* continue today to supply important coverage of the black community, and their survival seems assured.

See also Fortune, Timothy Thomas; Young, Plummer Bernard, Sr.

Black Panther Party

A radical group in the movement for black equality and civil rights, the Black Panther Party was founded by Bobby Seale and Huey Newton in Oakland, California, in 1966. The key aim of the Black Panthers was to take to the streets, employing violent tactics to force political and social change, although the organization was also involved in a variety of nonviolent social programs for the black community. The Panthers included among their membership a number of influential black radicals, including Eldridge Cleaver, author of *Soul on Ice*, who served as the group's minister of information, and Kwame Toure (Stokely Carmichael), who was the party's prime minister.

The police systematically cracked down on the Panthers, killing or sending to prison many of its leaders. Bobby Hutton was among those killed in police shoot-outs. On 4 December 1969, Fred Hampton, head of the Chicago arm of the Black Panthers, was killed in his bed after an informant working for the FBI's COINTELPRO program fingered him. COINTELPRO, short for Counter Intelligence Program, was started by FBI director J. Edgar Hoover in August 1967 to destroy black militant groups, particularly the Black Panthers.

After the turbulent 1960s, the Panthers lost much of their popular support and their power waned. Some members turned to more conventional methods of political action, while others longed for the combative days. In 1990, Huey Newton was killed in Oakland while buying crack cocaine; in 1992, former Panther Bobby Rush won a seat in the U.S. House of Representatives, representing the First Illinois Congressional District.

Black Panther leader Eldridge Cleaver

Blyew v. United States (U.S., 1872)

Blyew was the first Supreme Court case to challenge successfully the constitutionality of the Civil Rights Act of 1866. It involved John Blyew and George Kennard, two white men who murdered three blacks. Under the 1866 act, crimes committed against blacks in states where blacks could not get justice in state courts came under federal jurisdiction. Blyew and Kennard were brought before a circuit court and found guilty of the murders. They took the case to the Supreme Court to get relief. Justice William Strong spoke for the 7–2 majority in striking down Blyew and Kennard's convictions. Strong's reasoning was that Section 3 of the act mentioned crimes "affecting persons"; since the victims were dead, they were no longer considered persons within the meaning of the law. Blyew and Kennard had been, Strong opined, convicted in the wrong court. Justices Joseph P. Bradley and Noah Swayne dissented, calling the opinion "too narrow" and unacceptable to the literal meaning Congress gave to the 1866 act.

Bob Jones University v. United States (U.S., 1983)

Bob Jones University was the first Supreme Court case that challenged the right of the federal government to refuse to grant tax-exempt status to a religious school solely because it practices racial discrimination. The case involved the racially discriminatory policies of Bob Jones University in Greenville, South Carolina, and Goldsboro Christian School in Goldsboro, North Carolina, both of which at one time refused admission to black students (in 1975, Bob Jones began admitting blacks). Both institutions also precluded whites from dating blacks. In 1981, the Fourth Circuit Court of Appeals affirmed the Internal Revenue Service's right to cancel the universities' tax-exempt status under section 501 (c)(3) of the tax code. The two schools appealed to the Supreme Court. In 1983, the high court upheld the circuit court's ruling denying tax-exempt status. Writing for the court, Chief Justice Warren Burger wrote, "There can no longer be any doubt that racial discrimination in education violates deeply and widely accepted views of elementary justice."

Bob-Lo Excursion Company v. Michigan (U.S., 1948)

It was not until 1948 that the Supreme Court finally held that discrimination in foreign commerce was a violation of Article 1, section 8 of the Constitution. The Bob-Lo Excursion Company ran a pleasure ferry from Detroit, Michigan, to Bois Blanc Island, Canada, known to locals as Bob-Lo Island. In June 1945, one Sarah Elizabeth Ray, a black woman, purchased a ticket on the ferry with a group of white girls. When she boarded, she was first asked and then ordered to leave the ferry. She complied, but later filed a grievance with the state of Michigan. The ferry company was found guilty of violating the state's antidiscrimination statute and fined. The state supreme court upheld the judgment, and the ferry company appealed to the U.S. Supreme Court. On 2 February 1948, the U.S. Supreme Court held that discrimination in "foreign commerce," as the ferry company's business was labeled, was a violation of Article 1, section 8 of the Constitution, which reads, "The Congress shall have the power to regulate Commerce with foreign Nations." Justice Wiley Rutledge wrote the Court's opinion, from which Chief Justice Frederick M. Vinson and Justice Robert H. Jackson dissented.

Bolling v. Sharpe (U.S., 1954)

Bolling was a companion case to the historic *Brown v. Board of Education*, but has been overshadowed by the famous decision in *Brown*. The case concerned Spottswood Bolling, Jr., a 12-year-old black student, who, with his attorney, James M. Nabrit, Jr., challenged the validity of segregation in the public schools of the District of Columbia by suing the president of the District of Columbia Board of Education, C. Melvin Sharpe, to obtain relief. On 17 May 1954, Chief Justice Earl Warren delivered the opinion of a unanimous Court in this, his first major opinion since being named to the Court by President Dwight Eisenhower. The decision was an encompassing one, as *Bolling* had been consolidated with *Brown* and other cases. The Court held that the Equal Protection clause of the Fourteenth Amendment to the Constitution prohibited the states, as well as the District of Columbia, which was a federal enclave, from maintaining racially segregated schools. In Bolling's case, it ordered that day that segregation must be eliminated.

See also Briggs v. Elliott; Brown v. Board of Education I; Nabrit, James Madison, Jr.

Bond, Julian (1940–)

A longtime civil rights activist, Julian Bond remains today one of the most outspoken advocates of civil rights in America. Born in Nashville, Tennessee, the son of educator Horace Mann Bond, Julian Bond received his education at Morehouse College in Atlanta, Georgia. While there, he helped found the Committee on Appeal for Human Rights. Later, he served as communications director of the Student Nonviolent Coordinating Committee (SNCC). Following a short period during which he worked at a black newspaper in Atlanta, Bond was elected in 1965 to the Georgia House of Representatives. Because of his active stand against the Vietnam War, Bond was not allowed to take his seat. Although the Fifth Circuit Court of Appeals decided against him, he appealed to the U.S. Supreme Court, which ruled unanimously in *Bond v. Floyd* (U.S., 1966) that state action in denying Bond his seat due to his political beliefs, when he was a properly elected member, was unconstitutional. In 1968, several delegates at the Democratic National Convention in Chicago entered Bond's name as a contender for vice president of the United States, but were forced to withdraw it when it was realized he was only 28 years old, seven years shy of the constitutional limit. Today, Bond still speaks out on civil rights issues and is the host of a nationally syndicated television show dealing with black issues, *America's Black Forum*.

See also Bell, Griffin Boyette; Student Nonviolent Coordinating Committee.

Boynton v. Virginia (U.S., 1960)

Boynton was the landmark Supreme Court case in which the Court ruled that blacks should have the right to sit in sections of bus terminals reserved for whites. Plaintiff Boynton, a black law student, purchased a ticket on a Trailways bus from Washington, D.C., to Montgomery, Alabama. When the bus stopped in Richmond, Boynton stepped off and attempted during the stopover to purchase a sandwich and tea in the white section of the terminal restaurant. When he was refused service and ordered to move to the colored section, Boynton refused and repeated his demand for a sandwich. When the terminal called the police, Boynton was arrested and found guilty of unlawful trespass. His defense, that as a passenger in interstate travel he had the right to sit where he wanted, was ignored by several courts before the Supreme Court granted *certiorari*. On 5 December 1960, the Supreme Court ruled 7–2 (Justices Charles E. Whittaker and Tom Clark dissenting) that under section 216(d) of the Interstate Commerce Act, Boynton had a right as an interstate passenger to sit anywhere in the restaurant he chose. The Court ruled that as an interstate passenger, he was "under the authority of [federal] law," and as such was not subject to any state laws that violated this edict.

Branton, Wiley Austin (1923–1988)

Wiley Branton was a civil rights attorney who was the chief counsel for the Little Rock Nine, the name given to the first nine black students to desegregate Central High School in Little Rock, Arkansas. Branton also served as lawyer for the Freedom Riders. Born in Pine Bluff, Arkansas, Branton helped his father run the family taxi business at an early age. He graduated from Arkansas AM & N (Agricultural, Mechanical and Normal) College and served with the U.S. Army in the Pacific during the Second World War. In 1953, he earned his law degree. For the next four years, Branton was caught up in the desegregation struggle in Little Rock, where, in 1957, he successfully argued for desegregating Little Rock's public schools. After his success in Little Rock, he was named

by the nation's civil rights leaders as director of the Southern Regional Council's Voter Education Project in Atlanta, Georgia, where he oversaw the registration of some 600,000 black voters from 1962 to 1965. Branton served as executive secretary of the Council of Economic Opportunity, a Great Society antipoverty program, during the Johnson Administration, as well as special assistant to U.S. Attorneys General Nicholas Katzenbach and Ramsey Clark from 1965 to 1967. After his government work, Branton was involved with private antipoverty groups, including the United Planning Organization from 1967 to 1969, and the Alliance for Labor Action. He eventually left to become a member of the Washington, D.C., law firm of Dolphin, Branton, and Webber, which was later dissolved. In 1977, Branton was named dean of the Howard University Law School in Washington, D.C., where he served until 1983. From 1983 until his death, he was a partner in the Washington, D.C., office of the Chicago law firm of Sibley & Austin. Branton died on 13 December 1988.

Briggs v. Elliott (U.S., 1954)

Briggs was a companion case to the more famous *Brown v. Board of Education*. *Briggs* involved black plaintiffs from elementary and secondary schools in Clarendon County, South Carolina, who sued in the Court for the Eastern District of South Carolina to stop the state from enforcing the state constitutional law that called for segregated schools. The Court denied the motion to stop the state from doing this, even though it found that the black schools were "inherently inferior" to the state's white schools, and thus broke the edict of "separate but equal." It ordered the state to remedy this situation immediately. The plaintiffs appealed to the U.S. Supreme Court for relief. Chief Justice Earl Warren delivered the opinion of a unanimous Court in ruling that

South Carolina's separate but equal rule was a violation of the equal protection clause of the Fourteenth Amendment to the U.S. Constitution. He ordered the schools to be desegregated immediately, and indicated that measures to complete such a program would be announced when a second *Brown* decision was released the following year.

See also Brown v. Board of Education I; Brown v. Board of Education II; Davis v. County School Board of Prince Edward County, Virginia.

Brooke, Edward William (1919–)

Edward William Brooke was the first black elected to the U.S. Senate after the end of Reconstruction. Born in Washington, D.C., on 26 October 1919, Brooke graduated from Washington's Howard University in 1941. After military service in World War II, during which he served with the 366th Infantry, he received both a law degree and a masters of law degree from Boston University. In 1960, he was the Republican nominee for secretary of the Commonwealth of Massachusetts but was defeated. In 1962, and again in 1964, in the midst of a Democratic landslide against Republicans, Brooke was twice elected as Massachusetts's attorney general. In 1966, he defeated former Governor Endicott Peabody and was elected to the U.S. Senate, the first black to sit in that body, as well as the first to complete a full term, since Reconstruction. Brooke was defeated in 1978 by Congressman Paul E. Tsongas, later a Democratic candidate for the presidency in 1992.

Brown et al. v. Mississippi (U.S., 1936)

Brown et al. was the Supreme Court case in which the High Court found that if the only evidence against a defendant is a coerced confession, any conviction based on that confession is invalid due to violation of the due process clause of the Fourteenth Amendment. The petitioners were two black men arrested for murder in 1934. They admitted their guilt, but later testified under oath that they had been beaten and tortured to extract their confessions. In court, their attorneys tried to suppress the confessions, but to no avail. The men were convicted and sentenced to death. When the Mississippi Supreme Court upheld the convictions, the defendants appealed to the U.S. Supreme Court. In a unanimous decision, the Court struck down the convictions, ruling that the defendants had been denied their rights under the due process clause of the Fourteenth Amendment.

Brown, H. Rap (Hubert G. Brown; 1943–)

H. Rap Brown, a militant civil rights advocate, was the radical chairman of the Student Nonviolent Coordinating Committee (SNCC). Born in Baton Rouge, Louisiana, Brown became involved in the civil rights movement at an early age. When only 24, he succeeded Kwame Toure (Stokely Carmichael) as head of the SNCC. Brown found himself increasingly in trouble with the police as his tactics became more combative, and in 1970 he was charged with running from prosecution for arson and incitement to riot. He was placed on the FBI's Ten Most Wanted List and in 1971 was wounded and captured in a gun battle with police in New York City. Convicted in 1973, he was released from prison on 21 October 1976. H. Rap Brown is the author of *Die, Nigger, Die!* (1969).

Brown, Oliver

See Brown v. Board of Education I; Brown v. Board of Education II.

Brown v. Allen (U.S., 1953)

Brown v. Allen was a key Supreme Court case dealing with the constitutional rights of black prisoners. Actually, there were three cases heard at one time: *Brown v.*

Allen, *Speller v. Allen*, and *Daniels v. Allen*. The defendants were all black inmates of the North Carolina prison system. Brown sued on the grounds that petit and grand juries were chosen in North Carolina by the tax rolls, so whites would be overrepresented relative to blacks. Speller was appealing his conviction on the grounds that not enough blacks were seated to hear his case, and that his confession was inadmissible as evidence against him because it was coerced. Daniels, appealing a death sentence, said his attorney had failed to appeal his conviction 60 days after conviction, as prescribed by state law. The Court ruled 5–3 in all three cases. It found that in Brown's case, use of the tax rolls was not unconstitutional; in Speller's case, that the racial composition of the jury was not due to racism or state action, and, further, that if other evidence was not coerced, it could be used against him in trial; and in Daniels's case, that his attorney's failure to appeal during the 60-day period was not a violation of his rights.

Brown v. Board of Education of Topeka, Kansas I (U.S., 1954)

In the first *Brown* case, the Supreme Court, in a landmark decision, found that segregation in the public schools was unconstitutional. The case originated when Linda Brown, a young black girl, was disallowed by Topeka, Kansas, law to attend a white school. Her father, Oliver Brown, sued, arguing that it was a hardship for his daughter to walk to attend a black school. On appeal to the Supreme Court, *Brown* was consolidated with several similar cases from South Carolina, Virginia, and Delaware. In all but the Delaware case, district courts had found against the plaintiffs. In Delaware, the state supreme court found that it supported the separate but equal principle of *Plessy v. Ferguson*, but that Delaware schools were unequal; the court therefore ordered that the black plaintiffs be admitted to white

schools. The Supreme Court heard arguments on the consolidated cases in 1954. Chief Justice Earl Warren read the unanimous decision of the Court on 17 May 1954: "We conclude that in the field of public education the doctrine of 'separate but equal' has no place. Separate educational facilities are inherently unequal. Therefore, we hold that the plaintiffs and others similarly situated for whom the actions have been brought are, by reason of the segregation complained of, deprived of the equal protection of the laws guaranteed by the Fourteenth Amendment. This disposition makes unnecessary any discussion whether such segregation also violates the due process clause of the Fourteenth Amendment." The decision in *Brown v. Board of Education* was monumental in its effect. In one sweeping decision, the Supreme Court overturned the legal basis for school segregation established in 1896 in *Plessy*. In 1955, the Court heard arguments in *Brown II* to determine how to go about creating desegregated schools nationwide, especially in the South.

See also Bolling v. Sharpe; Briggs v. Elliott; Brown v. Board of Education II; Davis v. School Board of Prince Edward County, Virginia.

Brown v. Board of Education of Topeka, Kansas II (U.S., 1955)

Brown II was the second in a series of cases brought by the plaintiff Oliver Brown, a Topeka, Kansas, preacher, on behalf of his daughter, Linda, who was forced to attend a segregated, all-black school. In the first case, known as *Brown I*, the Supreme Court ruled that segregation was unconstitutional, and struck down the "separate but equal" doctrine used since the case of *Plessy v. Ferguson* in 1896. In the second case, *Brown II*, the Court did not vote, but instead decided on ways to move school districts to integrate their facilities as quickly as possible. In the opinion, delivered by Chief Justice Earl Warren, the Court recognized that different school

Attorneys (left to right) George E. C. Hayes, Thurgood Marshall, and James M. Nabrit celebrate on the steps of the Supreme Court in Washington, D.C. following the court's landmark Brown *decision on 17 May 1954.*

districts called for different remedial techniques to cure segregation. Yet Warren called for these districts to desegregate "with all deliberate speed."

Brownlow, William Gannaway (1805–1877)

William Brownlow was the governor of Tennessee who, as a radical Republican during Reconstruction, created a near-dictatorial state to advance the cause of black rights and destroy the power of the Ku Klux Klan. Brownlow was born in Wythe County, Virginia, on 29 August 1805. His family moved to eastern Tennessee when he was a youngster, but he was orphaned at age 11. He was self-educated and apprenticed as a carpenter. In 1826, he became a Methodist minister. Opposed to Baptists, he wrote newspaper articles espousing Methodism and condemning Baptist thinking. In 1839, he founded the Elizabethon *Whig*, which later appeared under the banners of the Tennessee *Whig*, the *Independent Journal*, and the *Rebel Vindicator*. In 1861, at the start of the Civil War, he was imprisoned for writing Unionist articles. Eventually, he was pardoned by Governor Andrew Johnson. Although a Methodist minister, Brownlow's hatred for the Confederacy led him to say that he would arm "every wolf, panther, and bear in the mountains of America ... every rattlesnake and crocodile ... every devil in Hell, and turn them loose upon the Confederacy" to end the insurrection. In 1865, Brownlow led a state convention that seceded the state from the Confederacy, freed all of the slaves in Tennessee, and called for the election of officials in sympathy with the Union cause. Brownlow was nominated for governor by the convention, and he was elected by a largely black electorate. Immediately, he set the guidelines for voting: only those white males who expressed "Unionist sentiments" during the war would be granted suffrage. Further, Brownlow called for federal aid to freedmen to pay for the purchase of private land, and he pushed for a tough law in the legislature that cracked down on the Ku Klux Klan. Brownlow was easily reelected in 1867 despite his growing dictatorial powers. In early 1869, just before he left office, Brownlow declared a Klan emergency in nine counties, but his successor, DeWitt Clinton Senter, in order to appease disen-

franchised whites, curtailed the anti-Klan activities and did little to advance black rights. Brownlow was elected to the U.S. Senate, and served one term, 1869 to 1875. The few speeches he did deliver have been eclipsed by the long periods he was absent because of illness. Paralyzed, he retired in 1875 and went home to Knoxville and worked as a writer for the *Weekly Whig and Chronicle*. Brownlow died two years later, on 28 April 1877, at the age of 71.

Brownsville, Texas, Riot (1906)

The Brownsville Riot was one of the first examples of race riot violence in the United States in the twentieth century. The trouble began in August 1906 between black troops of the First Battalion, Twenty-fifth Infantry, at Fort Brown, near Brownsville, and a white storekeeper in Brownsville. According to eyewitness accounts, sometime around midnight, 13 August, about 20 black men rode on horses through the city of Brownsville, shooting into homes and throwing objects. In the melee, one white resident was killed and several were injured. The chief of police later lost an arm due to his injuries. The residents identified the men as black troops stationed at nearby Fort Brown, but a later grand jury found no evidence that any of the black troops at the military base were involved. President Theodore Roosevelt ordered an investigation and named Brigadier General E. A. Garlington, inspector general of the U.S. Army, to head the inquiry. In October 1906, after questioning all the involved parties, Garlington issued his report. He concluded that although there was no hard evidence that the black troops at Brown were involved in the riot, he felt that some of them did know who really had caused the trouble. The black troops held to utter silence. Garlington recommended, and Roosevelt concurred, that all of the 167 black men

HARPER'S WEEKLY

JOURNAL OF CIVILIZATION

VOL. LI.   *New York, Saturday, January 12, 1907*   NO. 2612

Copyright, 1907, by HARPER & BROTHERS. All rights reserved

DISHONORABLY DISCHARGED

Harper's Weekly of 12 January 1907 acknowledged the discharge of 167 black soldiers following riots at Brownsville, Texas in 1906.

in Companies B, C, and D of the Twenty-fifth Infantry be dishonorably discharged from the military.

Sixty-six years later, in September 1972, the army announced that, after reopening the investigation, it had cleared the military records of the 167 men and changed their discharges to honorable. A year later, a single survivor of the Twenty-fifth was found still alive, and the army awarded him $25,000.

Bruce, Blanche Kelso (1841–1898)

Blanche Kelso Bruce was the only black to serve a full term, and only the second black person overall, in the U.S. Senate between Reconstruction and the election of Edward Brooke in 1967. Born into slavery in Farmville, Virginia, on 1 March 1841, Bruce was taken by his master to Missouri, where he was taught the printer's trade. In 1861, just before the start of the Civil War, he escaped and tried to enlist in the Union Army but was refused. Instead, he went to Hannibal, Missouri, and started a school for free blacks and former slaves. After the war, Bruce became a prosperous planter in Mississippi and held a number of local offices, including sheriff and superintendent of schools.

A Republican, in 1874 Bruce was elected by the Republican-controlled Mississippi legislature to serve in the U.S. Senate from the Forty-fourth to the Forty-sixth Congresses, 1875 until 1881. Up for reelection, a now-Democratic Mississipi legislature instead elected Democrat James Z. George to the seat. After leaving office, there were calls to give Bruce a cabinet position in the new Garfield administration, but, instead, President Garfield appointed him registrar of the U.S. Treasury, in which poition he served from 1881 to 1885. From 1889 until 1893, he was the recorder of deeds for the District of Columbia, during the presidency of Benjamin Harrison. From 1895 until his death three years later, Bruce served as the treasury registrar for

Blanche Kelso Bruce

the District of Columbia. He died in Washington on 17 March 1898.

Bryant, Roy

Roy Bryant was, with his stepbrother J. W. Milan, one of the accused killers of a young black man named Emmett Till. Bryant ran a grocery and meat market in Money, Mississippi, where some people claimed that Till, a Chicago youngster visiting relatives in Mississippi, whistled at and made lewd comments to Bryant's wife. Bryant and Milan apparently kidnapped and murdered Till, dumping his body into a nearby river. After a local investigation, the two men were put on trial for the murder, but an all-white jury found them not guilty after only 75 minutes of deliberation on 23 September 1955.

See also Till, Emmett.

Bryant v. Zimmerman (U.S., 1928)

Bryant, while not a civil rights case per se, illustrates the unique standards to which the Supreme Court holds organizations with differing agendas. *Bryant* was the first case before the Court that dealt with the use of the law to force an organization to open its membership lists to public scrutiny. A New York state law demanded that that the Ku Klux Klan disclose the names of its members in the state. The Supreme Court finally ruled that the New York law was constitutional; this contradicts the later case of *NAACP v. Alabama*, in which the Court ruled that an organization did not have to disclose its membership rolls to protect free speech rights.

See also NAACP v. Alabama.

Buchanan v. Warley (U.S., 1917)

Buchanan was a Supreme Court case revolving around the constitutionality of racial zones for housing. The case involved a Louisville, Kentucky, ordinance passed in 1914 that forbade blacks from moving into a neighborhood in which there were more whites than blacks. The Louisville chapter of the NAACP decided to challenge the ordinance. It arranged for William Warley, a black man, to purchase a plot of land for a house in a white neighborhood with the help of a white real estate agent, Charles H. Buchanan, who was sympathetic to civil rights. The neighborhood in question had eight white families and two black families. As part of the plan, Warley withheld $100 of the $250 purchase price until he took possession of the property, so that Buchanan could sue for relief. The Kentucky state courts ironically ruled that because of the ordinance, Warley was within his rights to hold the rest of the money until he could be allowed to move onto the land. Buchanan took the case to the U.S. Supreme Court. The Court was short-handed at the time the case was originally argued in April 1916. Justice William Day was ill, and the death of Justice Joseph Rucker Lamar left the Court with only seven justices. Eventually, Justice Louis Brandeis, who replaced Lamar, reheard arguments in

April 1917, when Day rejoined his colleagues on the bench.

Justice Day wrote the 9–0 opinion of the court striking down the Louisville ordinance. Day argued that the ordinance was "based wholly on color; simply that, and nothing more." He derided Louisville's attempt to refuse land ownership to persons based on color. Further, the ordinance restricted landowners from selling land to whomever they chose. In closing, Day wrote that the fundamental law of the Fourteenth Amendment to the Constitution had been violated because property rights had been disregarded without due process of law.

Buchanan was a landmark decision: For the first time, the high court imposed limits on Jim Crow legislation. Ironically, Justice Oliver Wendell Holmes nearly dissented in this case. He felt that the "contrived" atmosphere of the case, and the fact that Buchanan and Warley were in cahoots to overturn the ordinance, were sufficient grounds for the court to refuse to hear the case.

Bunche, Ralph Johnson (1904–1971)

Dr. Ralph Bunche was the first black man to win the Nobel Peace Prize. Born in the Detroit ghetto in 1904, Bunche was orphaned in 1915 and raised by his grandfather, a former slave. He received an athletic scholarship to the University of California and graduated with honors in 1927. In 1928, he received his master's degree from Harvard University, and in 1934 his Ph.D. from that institution. From 1928 until 1932, he taught at Howard University, where he became chairman of the political science department.

Starting in 1941, Bunche served in the U.S. government. An original member of the Office of Strategic Services, the forerunner of the Central Intelligence Agency, as well as a member of the State Department, Bunche was an integral member of the American team that helped create

Ralph J. Bunche

the United Nations. From 1948 until 1968, he held various offices at the United Nations. In 1968, he became undersecretary general, the highest U.N. office attained by a black man up until that time. Bunche was involved in a series of important diplomatic missions in the quest for international peace. His work on the Palestinian commission that settled the 1949 Arab–Israeli War won him the 1950 Nobel Peace Prize. His work in the Congo, Kashmir, and Yemen were further highlights in an illustrious career. Bunche died on 9 December 1971 at the age of 67.

Bureau of Refugees, Freedmen, and Abandoned Lands

The so-called Freedmen's Bureau was established by the U.S. government after the Civil War to aid former slaves. With the lawful cessation of slavery in the United States, the welfare, education, and labor conditions of the freed slaves became the official responsibility of the government. Before the end of the war, some organizations had been doing this on a private charitable level. This work started in 1861, with the capture of Hilton Head Island, South Carolina, when such groups as the New England Freedman's Aid Society and the New York and Pennsylvania Freedmen's Relief Organizations intervened to help the freed slaves there. President Lincoln submitted to Congress the idea for a government agency to handle these problems. The idea was pushed in the Senate by Republican Lyman Trumbull of Illinois and in the House by George Washington Julian of Indiana, a radical Republican, who insisted that amendments be made to the Second Confiscation Act to allow for permanent seizure of former Confederate properties by the federal government. The Bureau of Refugees, Freedmen, and Abandoned Lands was established on 3 March 1865, under the stewardship of the American Freedmen's Inquiry Commission. The commission was made up of Samuel Gridley Howe (1801–1876), a social and educational reformer who was married to suffragette Julia Ward Howe; Robert Dale Owen (1801–1876), another social reformer who was the creator of the socialist community New Harmony; and James McKaye, a social reformer and author. Known historically as the Freedmen's Bureau, the agency worked toward six major goals: 1) distributing food and medicine to former slaves; 2) creating schools, building shelter, and managing other charitable organizations; 3) establishing labor regulations and contract requirements; 4) governing confiscated Confederate lands and properties; 5) forming courts to oversee the problems and concerns of freed slaves; and 6) paying salaries and bounties to black soldiers who served in the Civil War. A private bank, the Freedman's Savings and Trust, was created specifically for the banking needs of former slaves. For the first two years, the bureau had no funds, but from 1868 to

1869 it did its best work with a $7 million budget. The Freedmen's Bureau lasted until its congressional mandate was exhausted in 1872.

Burton v. Wilmington Parking Authority (U.S., 1961)

Burton was the key Supreme Court case in which the Court found that states should be held responsible in the area of civil rights for the conduct of businesses to which they rent land. Burton, a black man, was refused service at the Eagle Coffee Shoppe in Wilmington, Delaware. Burton sued not the restaurant, but the Parking Authority of Wilmington, in which the Eagle Coffee Shoppe was located. It was a narrow argument: Could a state agency be responsible for the private conduct of an employer that happened to rent space in one of its office areas? Burton's case before the Supreme Court of Delaware was thrown out on the grounds that as a separate entity, the coffee shop was acting apart from the state agency and, further, that its conduct was not state-initiated. In the conclusion of its decision, the Delaware court ruled that under section 1501 of the Delaware Code, the shop was a restaurant, not an inn, and as such was not required to serve all who entered its place of business. Burton appealed the case to the U.S. Supreme Court. Justice Tom Clark delivered the 6–3 opinion of the Court, in which Justices Felix Frankfurter, John Marshall Harlan, and Charles Whittaker dissented. The Court ruled on narrow grounds that because the land on which the coffee shop was located, as well as the Wilmington Parking Authority itself, were publicly owned, the state was duty-bound to adhere to the provisions of the Fourteenth Amendment, which negated racial discrimination in public places.

Busing

Busing, the act of moving students from one geographic area to another to achieve racial integration in schools, has been a topic of great controversy since its introduction into law by the Supreme Court in the *Swann* decision of 1971. In that judgment, the Court ordered the use of busing to move both black and white children to achieve racial integration. This busing would be mandatory but could not impose an undue burden on the transported students; in other words, the trip could not take more than 35 minutes or go more than several miles.

School boards across the country balked at the Supreme Court's busing order, while white opposition to initial busing efforts contributed to so-called "white flight" from previously integrated areas, leaving many inner cities virtually black-only enclaves.

In 1974, the Court held in *Milliken v. Bradley* that where segregation was not the result of segregationist law but was caused by other factors, there was no constitutional basis for ordering desegregation. New ideas in the area of education, such as transfer student plans and magnet schools, were ways around the *Milliken* test.

In 1992, Dr. Robert Lissitz of the University of Maryland was hired by the Eighth Circuit Court of Appeals for the Eastern Division of Missouri. He was asked to study racial patterns in segregated and nonsegregated schools in St. Louis and the effects that busing had on eliminating these patterns, regardless of the geographic location of the student. The Lissitz report found that the reading, writing, and math scores of segregated and nonsegregated students, when compared to the scores of 1) black students intermingled with whites in suburban areas, 2) all-black city schools, 3) desegregated city schools, and 4) magnet schools, showed no difference with any degree of certainty in the benefits of busing. Lissitz wrote, "Achievement gains of students are not obtainable through a transfer program approach." Although Lissitz showed that busing may not ultimately be the answer to desegregating the schools, and in fact may be harmful to students who are bused, school boards nationwide still look toward busing as one factor in their drive to make the schools integrated.

See also Milliken v. Bradley I; Milliken v. Bradley II; Swann v. Charlotte-Mecklenburg Board of Education.

Butts v. Merchants & Miners Transportation Company (U.S., 1913)

In *Butts* the Supreme Court held that the public accommodations provision of the Civil Rights Act of 1875 was invalid. Plaintiff Mary Butts purchased a first-class ticket on a ship sailing between Boston, Massachusetts, and Norfolk, Virginia. Because she was black, Butts was asked to move to the segregated section of the ship designated for blacks; further, she was forced to eat after the whites were finished, with the dirty linen on the tables. Butts sued the ship line under the public accommodations section of the Civil Rights Act of 1875, which required that all persons, regardless of race, be entitled to the full use of public transportation and accommodations. A Massachusetts state court found that the Civil Rights Act of 1875 was unconstitutional and that Butts's claim was unfounded. She sued to the U.S. Supreme Court for relief. The Court ruled that since the Civil Rights Cases of 1883 had rendered the 1875 act moot, Butts's suit was without merit. Writing for the unanimous Court (Justice Oliver Wendell Holmes did not participate), Justice Willis Van Devanter declared that because the Civil Rights Cases rendered the 1875 act "altogether invalid," there was no federal protection against racial discrimination in the area of public accommodations.

Cain, Richard Harvey (1825?–1887)

Richard Cain was the first black clergyman to serve in the U.S. House of Representatives. Cain was born a free man in Greenbrier County, Virginia, on 12 April, supposedly in the year 1825, although this date has been questioned. Cain's parents migrated to Gallipolis, Ohio, when he was a child. The family eventually settled in Cincinnati. When Cain was 16, he finished what little schooling a black child could obtain in those days and went to work on the steamboats that traveled the Ohio and Mississippi rivers. Settling in Hannibal, Missouri, the hometown of Mark Twain, Cain became a lay minister in the Methodist Episcopal Church but was not allowed to preach because he was black. He moved to the African Methodist Church some time in 1848, and subsequently became a minister for the African Methodist Episcopal congregation in Muscatine, Iowa. After attending Wilberforce University to further his education, Cain served as a pastor in Brooklyn, New York. In 1865, when Charleston, South Carolina, fell to Union forces, he was sent to the embattled city to comfort the residents.

In Charleston, Cain purchased the South Carolina *Leader*, a wholly black-owned paper, which, under the new name of *The Missionary Record*, became the black organ of the state Republican Party. The associate editor was Robert Brown Elliott, who would go on to become a black congressman from South Carolina. In 1868, Cain was a delegate to the South Carolina state Constitutional Convention. That year, he was elected to serve as a state senator for Charleston, a position he held until 1870. A local Charleston paper claimed that Cain was among the eight men who controlled the state. Two years later, he was nominated by the Republicans for the South Carolina congressman-at-large seat. Cain beat his Democratic opponent by a wide margin and took his seat in the U.S. House of Representatives on 1 December 1873. Cain served in the House in the Forty-third and Forty-fifth Congresses. He was an able debater during the floor debate over the Civil Rights Act of 1875 and stood for educational reform for all in the Reconstructed South. Cain did not win re-election in 1874, but was returned to Congress in 1876. When the Republicans replaced him with a new nominee in 1878, Cain left Congress. In 1880, the African Methodist Episcopal Church elected him the organization's fourteenth bishop and made him the head of the group's Texas–Louisiana Conference. Cain spent his final years utilizing his power to educate black children. He died of Bright's disease on 18 January 1887.

Calhoun, John Henry, Jr. (1899–1988)

John Henry Calhoun, Jr., was a long-time advocate of civil rights, president of the Atlanta chapter of the National Association for the Advancement of Colored People (NAACP), and an Atlanta City councilman. Born in Greenville, South Carolina, on 8 July 1899, Calhoun was apprenticed at the age of 12 to a blacksmith for 50 cents a week during the school year and a dollar a week during the summer. He went on to attend the Hampton Institute in Virginia and graduated when he was 23 years old. Calhoun served as a bookkeeper and secretary at the Tuskegee Institute in Alabama and later was hired as the first black administrator of the Veteran's Administration in Tuskegee.

Calhoun's first involvement with civil rights advocacy came in 1948, when he and several other black leaders in Atlanta founded the Atlanta Negro Voters League to help blacks register to vote. From 1956 to 1957, Calhoun was the head of the Atlanta NAACP chapter. In that post, he initiated a series of lawsuits designed to desegregate city parks and golf courses. In 1964, when several delegates supporting Barry Goldwater helped oust blacks from leadership roles in the party, Calhoun, a staunch Republican, loudly denounced the white delegates and their actions. In 1965, he served as the head of Economic Opportunity Atlanta (EOA), a group dedicated to providing neighborhood organizations in low-income areas. Calhoun went on to serve as EOA's Model Cities chairman from 1970 to 1972.

In his final service to the Atlanta community, Calhoun served as a city councilman for the city, having been elected to the seat in 1973 when he was 74 years old. From 1978 to 1982, he was a consultant with the Atlanta Regional Commission. John Henry Calhoun, Jr., died in his home in Atlanta on 6 May 1988, at the age of 88.

Carmichael, Stokely
See Toure, Kwame.

Carter v. Texas (U.S., 1900)
Carter was the Supreme Court case in which the Court found that the exclusion of blacks from grand juries was a violation of the Fourteenth Amendment. The case involved Seth Carter, a black man accused of killing Bertha Brantley, a black woman, in Galveston, Texas, in 1897. A Galveston grand jury returned an indictment of murder against Carter. Seeing no blacks were on the grand jury, Carter's attorney sought to have the indictment dismissed. When that was overruled, the trial went forward, and Carter was convicted. On appeal, the Texas Court of Criminal Appeals affirmed the conviction, and Carter appealed to the Supreme Court. The case was heard some three years after the crime. Justice Horace Gray wrote the unanimous opinion of the Court. Striking down Carter's conviction, the Court ruled the exclusion of blacks from the grand jury was a violation of Carter's Fourteenth Amendment rights. The Court also ruled that when a defendant makes such a plea in open court, before trial, the court must hear evidence that may cause an indictment to be dismissed before trial.

Cassell v. Texas (U.S., 1950)
In *Cassell*, the Supreme Court ruled against the systematic exclusion of black people from grand jury service. Petitioner Cassell, a black man, was indicted by a Dallas County, Texas, grand jury for murder. Grand juries in the area were composed of 16 men and were selected from among the friends of the jury commissioners. These commissioners all were white and had no black friends, so no blacks were chosen for the grand juries. Cassell, upon conviction, sought to have the indictment thrown out as a violation of his equal protection rights under the Fourteenth Amendment. The trial court dismissed his argument, and the Texas Court of Criminal Appeals upheld the lower court's judgment. Cassell appealed to the U.S. Supreme Court. On 24 April 1950, the Court ruled 8–1 (Justice Robert H. Jackson dissented) that the exclusion of blacks from the grand juries was a violation of Cassell's Fourteenth Amendment rights. Justice Stanley Reed wrote the majority opinion. Wrote Justice Tom Clark, a member of the majority, "The elimination of this group [blacks] in the community from the commissioners'

consideration deprived petitioner of constitutional safeguards as defined in the decisions of this Court."

Chambers et al. v. Florida (U.S., 1940)

In *Chambers et al.*, the Supreme Court ruled that convictions in state courts that are the result of coerced confessions violate the due process clause of the Fourteenth Amendment. The case involved plaintiffs Chambers, Davis, Williamson, and Woodward, four black men who were accused of the murder of an elderly white man in Pompano Beach, Florida, on the night of 13 May 1933. The four men were arrested but denied committing the murder. Using coersive tactics, including hours of interrogation, the denial of the right to see a lawyer or relative, as well as threats, sheriffs at the Dade County (Miami) Jail finally forced the four to confess to the crime. They were tried, convicted, and sentenced to death. The case was appealed to the Florida Supreme Court, but the Court upheld the convictions. In 1940, the U.S. Supreme Court agreed to review the case. A month later, the Court struck down all four convictions unanimously (Justice Frank Murphy did not participate, making the decision 8–0). Justice Hugo Black spoke for the Court when he branded all such confessions made in a compulsory manner to be in violation of the due process clause of the Fourteenth Amendment.

Chambliss, Robert Edward (1904–1985)

Robert Chambliss was the Ku Klux Klan member sentenced to life in prison in 1977 for the 1963 Birmingham church bombing that killed four girls. He served only eight years of his sentence, dying of a heart attack in 1985.

See also Sixteenth Street Baptist Church Bombing.

James Earl Chaney

Chaney, James Earl (1943–1964)

James Earl Chaney was the black civil rights worker who was killed in 1964 by the Ku Klux Klan in Philadelphia, Mississippi, along with white civil rights workers Andrew Goodman and Michael Schwerner. Chaney was born on 30 May 1943 in Meridian, Mississippi, the son of a farmer. After attending local schools, he enrolled at Harris Junior College. It was there that he encountered his first taste of the civil rights struggle: he was suspended from school for wearing the letters "NAACP" on a small slip of paper pinned to his shirt. After being expelled a year later, he attempted to join the army but was refused because he had asthma. Instead, he and a friend hitchhiked to Wichita Falls, Texas, where they took on odd jobs. He soon returned to Meridian and joined his father in the plastering trade.

James Chaney was not formally involved in the civil rights movement until just a year before his death. In October 1963, he was introduced in Meridian to a Hispanic worker for the Congress of Racial Equality (CORE). Chaney became committed to working for the full emancipation of his race. As a native Mississippian, Chaney was soon in the forefront of CORE's campaign to register potential black voters.

In 1964, Chaney was named a staff member of the Meridian Community Center. That same year, he was teamed with white CORE activist Michael Henry Schwerner from New York. On 20 June 1964, 21-year-old CORE worker Andrew Goodman joined them. The next day, a black church in nearby Longdale, in Neshoba County, was burned down. Goodman, Chaney, and Schwerner went to the scene to investigate. Later, when they returned to Meridian, they were picked up by the police. According to court records, the three men were released but were apprehended again by the local authorities. Nothing was heard from the three activists for the next 44 days. On 4 August, their bodies were found; all three had been murdered, Chaney having suffered three gunshot wounds.

The murders of Goodman, Chaney, and Schwerner set off a firestorm of controversy across the nation. Several policemen were later tried and convicted of the murders. In 1989, the movie *Mississippi Burning* portrayed the murders and their aftermath.

See also Goodman, Andrew; Schwerner, Michael Henry; United States v. Price et al.

Chapman, John Jay (1862–1933)

John Jay Chapman was a white writer, poet, and orator who spoke out on lynching and segregation. Chapman was born on 2 March 1862, in New York City. His paternal grandmother, Maria Weston Chapman (1806–1885), was an intimate of William Lloyd Garrison and Wendell Phillips, two of the best-known abolitionists. His mother's father, John Jay, John's father William Jay, and his great-grandfather John Jay, the first chief justice of the U.S. Supreme Court, were all antislavery advocates. So it was natural that at an early age John Jay Chapman should become involved with the fight for equal justice for blacks. He attended a religious school for boys in New Hampshire, then Harvard University, where he graduated in 1884. While in Harvard Law School, he was accidentally burned, losing his left hand as a result. He later moved back to New York City, where he participated in the Good Government movement and opposition to Tammany Hall.

On 14 August 1911, a black man named Zacharia Walker attempted to rob a steel company safe in Coatesville, Pennsylvania. Caught in the act, he refused to surrender and instead fired at the police, killing one officer. He turned the gun on himself, but the wound was not fatal, and Walker was captured and taken to a hospital. Local residents were so outraged at Walker's crime that they marched on the hospital, tied Walker to his hospital bed, and set him on fire. The New York *Tribune* noted that Walker's burnt torso was kicked by local children as a plaything in the streets for hours after his death. John Jay Chapman was consumed with outrage at Walker's death. As the first anniversary of the lynching approached, he felt he needed to do something. He went to Coatesville, rented a small hall, and conducted a prayer meeting. Only three people attended. Still, it was Chapman's shining moment. He later went on to become a noted speaker against lynching.

In the last 30 years of his life, Chapman lived at his country estate, "Sylvania," on the Hudson River in Barrytown, New York. He died there on 4 November 1933, at the age of 71.

Chase, William Calvin (1854–1921)

William C. Chase was the editor of the Washington *Bee*, one of the nation's leading black newspapers. Born to free parents on 2 February 1854, in Washington, D.C., Chase, who was known throughout his life as W. Calvin Chase, was left fatherless in 1863 when his father, William, a local blacksmith, was shot by a stranger in his offices. This left his widow, Lucinda Seaton Chase, to raise and educate six children.

At a young age, W. Calvin Chase was interested in journalism as a career. He attended a local school in the basement of a church, then enrolled at an all-white private school in Methuen, Massachusetts. When he returned to Washington, D.C., he attended a few preparatory classes at Howard University, then read law and was admitted to the District of Columbia and Virginia bars. Chase then worked for various black newspapers: the Boston *Observer*, the Boston *Co-Operator*, and the Washington *Plaindealer, Argus and Free Lance*. In 1882, Chase founded and began editing the Washington *Bee*. The *Bee* was a uniquely Republican paper; however, in 1884 and 1892, following Democratic presidential victories, it flirted with the Democratic Party. In 1904, and again in 1919, it went so far as to move to the socialist realm, but it eventually returned to the Republican fold. Chase himself was a delegate to the Republican national conventions in 1900 and 1912.

The *Bee* was a controversial organ. In 1884, following a series of brutal lynchings in Louisiana, Chase himself editorialized: "In the state of Louisiana, a few days ago, the most cowardly and bloody murders were committed. Innocent colored Republicans were shot down by Democrats like dogs. The same was a repetition of the past brutalities, when helpless colored female virgins and babes were snatched from their beds and murdered. The scene in the South has raised the indignation of over five millions of true black American citizens. It is time for every American Negro in the South to make an appeal to arms and fire [on]

every Democratic home where Negro-killers live, in retaliation for the foul and dastardly murders that were committed." Chase later utilized the *Bee* to rail against racist Democratic Senators Ben "Pitchfork" Tillman of South Carolina and James K. Vardaman of Mississippi.

Chase ruled the *Bee* for four decades, opposing the Niagara Movement, the NAACP, and Marcus Garvey's Back to Africa movement. When he died on 2 January 1921, he left the paper without a firm leader or proper monetary backing. His widow and son kept the *Bee* alive for a time, but closed it in 1922 because of financial difficulties.

Chavis, Benjamin Franklin, Jr. (1948–)

The Reverend Benjamin Chavis, Jr., became the seventh executive director of the National Association for the Advancement of Colored People in 1993, succeeding Dr. Benjamin Hooks. Born in Oxford, North Carolina, on 22 January 1948, Chavis is the great-great grandson of the Reverend John Chavis, who became in the 18th century the first African American ordained a Presbyterian minister in the colonies. Benjamin Chavis joined the NAACP at the tender age of 12. During the 1960s, he was affiliated with such organizations as the Congress of Racial Equality, the Southern Christian Leadership Conference, and the American Federation of State, County and Municipal Employees (AFSCME), working on labor issues. He received his education at the University of North Carolina, where he was awarded a bachelor of arts degree in chemistry; Duke University, where he received a master of divinity degree; and Howard University, where he received his doctor of divinity degree.

In 1971, Chavis was convicted of the firebombing of a white-owned grocery in Wilmington, North Carolina. As part of the civil rights group known as the

"Wilmington 10," he served four years in prison (1976-1980) until a federal appeals court reversed his conviction. Chavis served on Jesse Jackson's 1984 presidential campaign. The following year, he was named executive director and chief executive officer of the Commission for Racial Justice, a wing of the United Church of Christ based in Cleveland. Chavis still held that position when he was chosen to head the NAACP on 9 April 1993.

See also National Association for the Advancement of Colored People.

Cheatham, Henry Plummer (1857–1935)

A black member of Congress from 1888 to 1892, Cheatham was born a slave on 27 December 1857, near the town of Henderson in Granville (now Vance) County, North Carolina. He attended local schools and graduated with a bachelor's degree from Shaw University in Raleigh, North Carolina, in 1882. He was the principal of the Plymouth Normal school from 1883 to 1884. From 1884 until 1888, Cheatham was the registrar of deeds in Granville County while he studied law. In 1888, he was Granville County's representative to the Republican state convention held that year. At the convention, he was nominated as the Republican candidate for the Second Congressional District and was elected by about 700 votes. Cheatham was the only black in Congress until he was joined by John Mercer Langston of Virginia in 1890. He was reelected in 1890, but in 1892 was defeated by a white Populist. In his two terms in the U.S. House of Representatives, Cheatham worked to have the government compile a list of accomplishments of the black race, a bill that failed to pass the House. Further, he tried to have more blacks at the Columbian Exposition at Chicago in 1893. With the collapse of the Freedman's Bank, Cheatham sought unsuccessfully to have all the bank's depositors reimbursed. In 1894, he tried to secure the Republican nomination for Congress, but he was beaten out by the last ex-slave in Congress—his own brother-in-law, George Henry White. After he left Congress, Cheatham moved to Washington, D.C., in 1897 and served as the recorder of deeds there. In 1901 he moved back to North Carolina, where he became the president of the black orphanage at Oxford, North Carolina, which he had founded before his congressional career. Cheatham died in Oxford on 29 November 1935, at the age of 78.

Chicago Riot of 1919

The Chicago riot of 1919 was the crisis in the Windy City that precipitated a summer of racial strife in the nation. Eugene Williams was one of five black youths who went for a swim at Chicago's 26th Street Beach on 27 July 1919. Earlier, an altercation had occurred at a whites-only beach, when black bathers had tried to swim there. At the the 26th Street Beach, a white man, aware of the distant fracas, assaulted the five black youths with thrown rocks. It was all "just a game," as one of the youths later recalled. The game ended tragically, however, when one of the rocks struck Eugene Williams in the head. He sank beneath the waves and drowned. When a white policeman refused to arrest the attacker, Williams's companions ran to the black section of town and spread word of the incident. A riot ensued that lasted for five days. In that time, white mobs clubbed and shot several blacks to death, mobs roamed the city unimpeded, and police wounded seven black rioters. The toll of the disorder was at least 16 blacks and 15 whites dead, and more than 500 people of both races injured. Illinois Governor Frank O. Lowden convened a commission that later issued a report on the causes of the riot. Sociologist Charles S. Johnson served on the commission and was the main author of the final report.

See also Johnson, Charles Spungeon.

Chiles v. Chesapeake & Ohio Railway (U.S., 1910)

In *Chiles*, the Supreme Court held that if Congress failed to enact laws regarding segregation in the means of interstate travel, the railway lines themselves had the right to step in and make those rules. The case involved J. Alexander Chiles, a black attorney who purchased a ticket on the defendant's railway line to travel from Washington, D.C., to Lexington, Kentucky. Chiles, who bought a first-class ticket, was ordered by the line to move from the first-class section, which was for whites only, to a less-comfortable black section in the back of the train. Chiles protested but, under threat of arrest, acceded to the demand that he move. He later sued the line, but an all-white jury ruled that the line was within its rights to make rules related to segregation. Chiles sued to the Supreme Court to reverse the lower court's ruling. Justice Joseph McKenna wrote the 8–1 decision of the Court (Justice John Marshall Harlan dissented) in which the lower court's ruling was affirmed. The case was decided on the basis of a thin argument. McKenna said that where Congress had failed to pass laws in regard to segregation in interstate travel, the railway lines themselves were within their rights to make such laws. McKenna cited the cases of *Hall v. DeCuir* and *Plessy v. Ferguson*, in which such segregationist laws were upheld for the same reasons. *Chiles* was in effect overruled 31 years later in the case of *Mitchell v. United States*.

See also Hall v. DeCuir; Mitchell v. United States; Plessy v. Ferguson.

Chisholm, Shirley Anita St. Hill (1924–)

Shirley Chisholm was the first black woman to run for Congress and the first black to put her name in contention for the presidency of the United States. Chisholm was born in Brooklyn, New York, on 30 November 1924, although she later lived with her grandmother in Barbados. It was there that she received an education in a small school. She later returned to Brooklyn and finished her education, eventually graduating from Brooklyn College in 1946 with a bachelor's degree in sociology. In 1952, she was awarded a master's degree from Columbia University. Chisholm worked as a teacher before becoming the director of a nursery school. In 1964, she was elected to the New York State Assembly as a Democrat. She served until 1968. In that year, she was elected to the U.S. House of Representatives by defeating civil rights activist James Farmer, who was running as a Republican.

Shirley Chisholm represented the Twelfth New York District from 1969 until 1983, encompassing the Ninety-first to the Ninety-seventh Congresses. Known as a liberal, she fought for child-care funding for middle- and lower-class families. In 1972, she announced a run for the presidency, the first black to campaign for that post. She entered 12 state primaries and was awarded 152 votes on the first ballot at the Democratic Convention that year in Miami Beach.

Shirley Chisholm chose not to run for reelection in 1982 and retired to her home in Williamsville, New York. In 1993, she returned to public service as ambassador to Jamaica in the Clinton administration.

Citizens' Council

The Citizens' Council was a white, ultra-racist organization that sprang up in the South to fight desegregation. The council was formed by Robert "Tut" Patterson, a former football hero at Mississippi State University. Angered by the Supreme Court's *Brown* ruling, which desegregated Southern schools, Patterson got together several white business friends and founded the first chapter of the Citizens' Council in Sunflower County, Mississippi. The council was known by many as the "white-

U.S. House of Representatives Speaker John McCormack reenacts the swearing in of New York representative Shirley Chisholm, 3 January 1969.

collar Klan" or the "reading and writing Klan" because much of the group's membership was drawn from affluent and educated businessmen. By 1956, the group claimed 85,000 members in Mississippi and Alabama alone and many thousands more in Southern states from Virginia to Florida to Texas. Although it played a key role in the Montgomery Bus Boycott, when flyers and other paraphernalia were handed out condemning the boycott, the council soon lost its power because of the quickening civil rights movement and court orders that progressively desegregated Southern society.

City of Richmond v. United States (U.S., 1975)

The Supreme Court in *City of Richmond* dealt with the complicated matter of city annexation and adequate minority representation. The case involved the city of Richmond, Virginia, which, in 1970, was allowed by a Virginia court to annex a parcel of land in Chesterfield County. The city's black population was thereby reduced from 52 percent to 42 percent. Under a new plan, minority representation on the city council, while remaining the same, would be lessened because new seats would be added to the council. Black plaintiffs in the city, with the backing of the federal government, sued to the Supreme Court to have the annexation declared null and void because its main purpose was to dilute black representation on the city council. The Court ruled 5–3 (with Justices William Brennan, William O. Douglas, and Thurgood Marshall dissenting, and Justice Lewis Powell not participating) that merely because an annexation move may dilute a minority group's political strength, it is not unconstitutional if the group is given full political representation. Writing for the majority, Justice Byron White held that "the plan here does not undervalue the postannexation black voting strength or have the effect of denying or abridging the right to vote."

Civil Rights Act of 9 April 1866

The 1866 Civil Rights Act was passed by Congress to enforce the end of slavery and protect the rights of the freed blacks before the passage of the Fourteenth Amendment. The act had three sections. Section 1 stated that "All persons born in the United States are declared to be citizens of the United States with the equal right to contract, sue, be parties to lawsuits, give evidence in a court, and benefit equally of the laws and proceedings for security of person and property." Discussed further in this section was the equal right to inherit, purchase, hold, and convey real and personal property. Section 2 held that there was a penalty for depriving, because of race, any of the rights listed in the first section. Section 3 made clear that courts of the United States were to have jurisdiction over offenses committed under the act and of all causes, civil and criminal, affecting persons who could not enforce in state

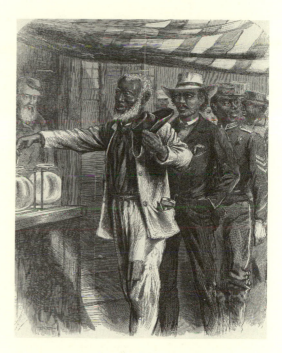

Freedmen voting in state elections, 1867

courts the rights secured under Section 1. Further, if such action were to be brought in a state court, there would be a removal of a criminal or civil suit under the act's provisions.

Upon its approval by Congress, the act was vetoed by President Johnson, but the veto was overridden. After this episode, however, some of the act's congressional supporters felt that it might be found unconstitutional—a Supreme Court packed with justices opposed to civil rights might overturn it—and thus a few weeks later, on 30 April, the Joint Committee on Reconstruction brought forth a series of proposals that when ironed out became the Fourteenth Amendment.

Civil Rights Act of 1875

The 1875 Civil Rights Act was passed by Congress to secure for blacks the rights and privileges of social contact that whites enjoyed. Basically, the act covered discrimination in public transportation, public accommodations, restaurants and other places of dining, and on grand and petit juries. Senator Charles Sumner of

Massachusetts initiated a civil rights bill in 1870, but a watered-down act was passed when he was absent due to illness. In 1873, he again introduced his bill in the Senate. The House adjourned before consideration of the bill, and it languished. In 1874, Sumner again introduced it, and this time it passed both houses. Although President Grant signed it enthusiastically, Sumner was not present for the ceremony. He had died on 11 March 1874, leaving a great void in the struggle for civil rights.

Within eight years, the law came up for examination before the Supreme Court. Five separate plaintiffs sued to have various portions of the act utilized for relief from discrimination. These are known as the "Civil Rights Cases." Instead of siding with the plaintiffs, the Supreme Court ruled that the Civil Rights Act of 1875 was unconstitutional, citing the fact that the Thirteenth Amendment, which the act was passed to strengthen, outlawed slavery and involuntary servitude, not private discrimination. The Court opined that the act, on its own, overreached the bounds of necessary law.

See also "Civil Rights Cases"; Sumner, Charles.

Civil Rights Act of 1957

The Civil Rights Act of 1957 was signed into law by President Dwight D. Eisenhower on 9 September 1957. Part I created the U.S. Civil Rights Commission, a six-member council that would investigate allegations that "certain citizens are being deprived of their right to vote." The commission was also created to collect and disseminate information on legal steps taken to enhance civil rights. Part II allowed for the creation of another assistant attorney general. Part III strengthened 28 U.S.C. 1343 in the area of civil rights and repealed section 1989 of the Revised Statutes (42 U.S.C. 1993). Part IV laid out the government's plans to protect the right to vote. Part V allowed for jury trials to punish those conspiring to infringe on the right of others to vote.

The act was passed because there was widespread harassment of blacks in the Southern states by persons who were not state officials, and thus could not be prosecuted under existing federal civil rights statutes. The act for the first time made it a federal crime for civilians to act against voting rights under the color of state action.

Civil Rights Act of 1964

The Civil Rights Act of 1964, a landmark in American legal history, provides much of the legal basis for the modern civil rights movement. The act has several sections, or titles.

Title I deals with voting rights. It bars unequal application of voting registration requirements (effectively doing away with poll taxes) and allows only those literacy tests that will later be furnished to the public. Title II concerns public accommodations. The 1964 act outlaws, in most hotels, motels, restaurants, gasoline stations, and places of entertainment and amusement, any racial discrimination that either qualifies as state action (where the state has a financial or administrative interest in the area doing the discriminating), or involves a privately owned business engaged in interstate commerce. Title III involves public facilities that bar entry to anyone on account of race. It gives the attorney general the right to sue any state that allows a public facility to remain segregated. Title IV pertains to segregation in the schools. It allows for suits to be brought by the government on behalf of those who claim discrimination; calls for financial assistance to be made available to those schools trying to end segregation; and it required the U.S. Office of Education to report to Congress in 1966 on the results of school desegregation efforts nationwide. Title VI lays out steps that allow the government to end federal assistance to any program that discriminates on the basis of race. Title VII forbids discrimination by employers or unions with more than 100 employees, with that number reduced to 25 by the end of 1969. Title VII also created the Equal Employment Opportunity Commission (EEOC), which investigates discrimination complaints across the nation. Title VIII authorizes the U.S. attorney general to involve himself or herself in cases in which the Fourteenth Amendment is involved and which the attorney general feels have "public importance." Title IX enjoins federal courts from sending civil rights cases back to state courts, where states might refuse to try them. Title X provides for a Community Relations Service to mediate disputes involving any portion of this act. Title XI, the criminal section, calls for trial by jury in all cases of criminal contempt involving any section of the act except Title I. Title XI also limits a contempt sentence to six months in prison and no more than a $1,000 fine.

Civil Rights Act of 1991

The Civil Rights Act of 1991 was an attempt to defeat the effects of the controversial *Wards Cove* Supreme Court decision, in which the high court held that the burden of proof of workplace discrimination lay with the employee, not the employer. President George Bush signed the act on 21 November 1991. Title I listed federal remedies in the areas of civil rights, including "a prohibition against all social discrimination in the making and enforcement of contracts," as well as placing the burden of proof in workplace discrimination incidents on the employer and not the employee, and allowed for damages to be awarded in cases of *intentional* discrimination in employment. Title II addresses the so-called "glass ceiling," artificial barriers in the workplace to minority and female advancement. Title III applies to government employee rights. Title IV deals with general provisions, such as the effective date of the act, and inclusion or exclusion of other "disparate impact" cases dealt with before the passage of the act.

"Civil Rights Cases" (U.S., 1883)

The "Civil Rights Cases" were the five combined litigations before the Supreme Court in 1883 that dealt with the constitutionality of the Civil Rights Act of 1875. All five—*United States v. Stanley; United States v. Ryan, United States v. Nichols; United States v. Singelton;* and *Robinson v. Memphis and Charleston Railroad Company*—were basically a test of the act's public accommodations section. In four of the cases, the federal government sued on behalf of injured parties who had suffered private discrimination that the government felt was covered by the act. In the fifth case, two blacks sued a railroad company. Twice, the cases were argued before the Court: once, on 7 November 1882, and again, on 29 March 1883. Justice Joseph P. Bradley wrote the 8–1 majority opinion of the Court. In striking down the entire Civil Rights Act of 1875, he said, "Has Congress constitutional power to pass such a law? On the whole, we are of the opinion that no countenance of authority for the passage of the law in question can be found in either the thirteenth or fourteenth amendment of the Constitution; and no other ground of authority for its passage being suggested, it must necessarily be declared void, at least so far as its operation in the several states is concerned."

Justice John Marshall Harlan, who 13 years later would be the lone dissenter in the case of *Plessy v. Ferguson*, issued in this case a strongly worded protest, while utilizing the inkwell of Chief Justice Roger B. Taney, who wrote the *Dred Scott* decision: "The opinion in these cases proceeds, as its seems to me, upon grounds entirely too narrow and artificial. ... The Thirteenth Amendment did something more than prohibit slavery as an *institution*, resting upon distinctions of race, and upheld by positive law. They [the Court majority] admit that it [the Thirteenth Amendment] established and decreed universal *civil freedom* throughout the United States. But did the freedom thus established involve nothing more than the exemption from actual slavery? Was nothing more intended than to forbid one man from owning another as property? Was it the purpose of the nation simply to destroy the institution, and then remit the race, theretofore held in bondage, to the several states for such protection, in their civil rights, necessarily growing out of freedom, as those states, in their discretion, choose to provide?"

See also Civil Rights Act of 1875; Harlan, John Marshall.

Civil Rights Commission, United States
See United States Civil Rights Commission.

Clark, Kenneth Bancroft (1914–)
Kenneth Bancroft Clark is the black sociologist whose landmark studies of the impact of segregation on black life were used by the Supreme Court in the *Brown* school desegregation case. Clark was born on 14 July 1914, in the Panama Canal Zone. When he was five, Clark was taken to the United States by his mother over the objections of his father, a worker with the United Fruit Company in Panama. Eventually the couple divorced. Clark attended local schools in New York City, then earned his bachelor's and master's degrees in psychology from Howard University. He received his doctorate in experimental psychology from Columbia University in 1940.

While at Howard, and later at Columbia, Clark and his wife, whom he met at Howard, became interested in the effects of racism on the black psyche and esteem. He worked hand in hand with Gunnar Myrdal, the famed Swedish author of *An American Dilemma*, about the Jim Crow South, on a study of black children funded by the Carnegie Corporation. The Clarks invented the "doll test," in which black children were asked to pick among black and white dolls which they felt best with. Many black children rejected the black doll as "bad," leading the Clarks to conclude that racism was indeed creating an atmosphere of self-hatred among blacks.

In 1950, Clark was asked by the White House Mid-Century Conference on Youth to write a report detailing these attitudes. His report, "Effects of Prejudice and Discrimination on Personality Development," later published as "Prejudice and Your Child" (1955), was a groundbreaking indictment of the effects of racism on current and future generations. Four years after its completion, Clark's report was utilized by the Supreme Court in the landmark *Brown v. Board of Education* decision overturning segregated schools. Reference to Clark's work can be found in footnote 11 of the *Brown* opinion.

Because of his work with children, Clark became a leading voice in the sociological area of the civil rights struggle. Author of 1966's *Dark Ghetto*, which looked at the effects of residential segregation on blacks, Clark later served as a visiting professor at Columbia and Harvard universities. He remains one of the staunchest advocates of sociological testing to study the effects of racism.

Clark, Septima Poinsette (1898–1987)
Septima Poinsette Clark was known as the "queen mother" of the civil rights movement. Born on 3 May 1898 in Charleston, South Carolina, Septima Poinsette was the daughter of Peter Poinsette, a black slave whose master, Joel Poinsette, brought a plant from Mexico to the United States that was called the poinsettia. Septima Poinsette, whose name in Haiti means "sufficient peace" (her mother grew up in Haiti), had little schooling save some time spent at a normal school run by missionaries. Desiring to become a teacher but unable to do so in the segregated South, Poinsette went to Johns Island off the coast of South

Carolina and in 1916 began to teach black children to read and write. She also joined the infant National Association for the Advancement of Colored People (NAACP).

In 1919, Poinsette returned to Charleston and, barred from teaching by state law, launched a successful crusade to have the legislature change the law. In 1920, having begun her new teaching job, she met and married Nerie Clark, a sailor. After two children (one of whom died in infancy), Septima Poinsette Clark was widowed in 1924. She never remarried.

Clark taught on Johns Island until 1927, then moved to Columbia, South Carolina. While living in Columbia, she attended several colleges, earning degrees from Benedict College in Columbia and the Hampton Institute in Virginia. In Columbia, she began to work for equal pay for black teachers. Her work earned her enmity from whites. When the civil rights movement began, the South Carolina state legislature demanded that no teacher work for the NAACP. Refusing to give up her membership in the organization, she left South Carolina for Tennessee, where she was named director of education of the Highlander Folk School, a nonsegregated educational institution.

On 31 July 1959, the Tennessee state police raided Highlander looking for evidence to close the school down. A bathtub used to offer cold drinks to visitors was used as evidence that Septima Clark, herself a teetotaler, was dealing in making illegal moonshine. In the trial, Clark was accused of being a Communist and badgered by the prosecutor. In December 1961 the school was closed.

Clark transferred her teaching seminars to the Dorchester Cooperative Community Center in McIntosh, Georgia, under the sponsorship of the Southern Christian Leadership Conference. She utilized her time there to teach people mathematics and English. She retired from the SCLC in 1970, and was awarded the Martin Luther King, Jr.,

Award. In her final years, she received back pay from the years following her firing as a teacher in South Carolina, and even served for a time on the Charleston School Board. Septima Poinsette Clark died on 15 December 1987, at the age of 89. At her funeral, she was hailed as the "queen mother of the civil rights movement" and its "mother conscience." Taylor Branch, in his *Parting the Water: America in the King Years, 1954–1963*, dedicated the book to "the memory of Septima Poinsette Clark."

Clayton, Powell (1833–1914)

Powell Clayton was the Republican governor of Arkansas noted for calling out a black militia to hunt down the Ku Klux Klan in his state during his term of office. Clayton was born in Bethel County, Pennsylvania, on 7 August 1833, the son of a surveyor. He attended the local schools, as well as a military academy, then, when he was 26, he went to Leavenworth, Kansas, where he worked as an engineer. When the Civil War began, he enlisted in the 1st Kansas Infantry, with the rank of captain. Clayton saw action at Pine Bluff, and his heroism there earned him a promotion to brigadier general. In 1865, at the end of the war, he bought a piece of property in Pine Bluff and built a small cotton farm. A supporter of black suffrage, Clayton ran unopposed for governor of Arkansas in 1868. As soon as he was inaugurated, Clayton was faced with Ku Klux Klan violence in 10 counties. He immediately placed all 10 under martial law and sent a segregated militia of blacks and Unionists under the command of former General Robert F. Catterson to guard them. More than 100 Klansmen were arrested, and three were executed. Clayton's actions earned him the enmity of the Klan and Democrats, who called into question the appropriation of some $330,000 for the Klan operation. The Democrats in the state legislature tried to impeach him on charges of election fraud and the illegal selling of railway bonds, but the majority Republican state senate acquitted him.

In 1871, the state legislature elected Clayton to the U.S. Senate, but he had to switch his cabinet around so that the state senate president, Ozra A. Hadley, could become governor. Clayton served but a single term in the U.S. Senate, and many believe that Democrats voted for his election to that body just to get him out of Arkansas. After he left the Senate in 1877, Clayton returned to Arkansas and became the director of the Missouri & North Arkansas Railroad. In 1897, President William McKinley named Clayton as U.S. ambassador to Mexico, a post the former governor held until 1905. Although he eventually retired in Arkansas, before his death he transferred to Washington, D.C. It was there that Powell Clayton died, on 25 August 1914, just 18 days after his eighty-first birthday.

Clyatt v. United States (U.S., 1905)

In *Clyatt*, the Supreme Court held that the practice of peonage, outlawed in 1867, was a legitimate method for collecting debts. The *Clyatt* decision was essentially rendered moot by *Bailey v. Alabama* (1911). Justice David Brewer wrote the Court's opinion.

See also Bailey v. Alabama; United States v. Reynolds.

Coleman, James Plemon (1914–1991)

James P. Coleman was the segregationist governor of Mississippi from 1956 to 1960. Born in Ackermann, Mississippi, Coleman attended the University of Mississippi before earning a law degree from George Washington University in 1939. He entered public life by winning a seat as local circuit judge in 1946. Four years later he was appointed to the commissioner's post on the state supreme court, but he resigned that position soon afterward to become Mississippi state attorney general. He became a member of the Democratic National Committee in

1952. From 1948 to 1955, Coleman published a weekly newspaper in Choctaw County, Mississippi. He resigned as editor in 1955 in order to run for the governorship. Although he finished second in the principal primary, in a run-off he received the Democratic nomination and, with no Republican opposition, was elected. Although considered as segregationist in his thinking as his successor, Ross Barnett, Coleman had a mixed record on civil rights. Although he set up the Mississippi Sovereignty Commission, a watchdog agency designed to intimidate and hinder civil rights workers, Coleman did resist pressure to outlaw the NAACP and even signed a bill that created an integrated hospital under the auspices of the Veterans Administration. Unable to run for reelection, Coleman ran for the state House of Representatives and served one term during 1961–1965. He tried to regain the governorship in 1963, but was defeated in the primaries. In 1965, Senator James O. Eastland of Mississippi persuaded President Lyndon B. Johnson to appoint Coleman to a vacant seat on the Fifth Circuit Court of Appeals. Coleman served on the bench from 1965 until his retirement as the circuit court's chief judge in 1981. In December 1990 Coleman suffered a severe stroke. He died on 29 September 1991.

Collins, Thomas LeRoy (1909–1991)

LeRoy Collins was the governor of Florida whose administration was marked by a strong commitment to the cause of civil rights. Collins was born in the Florida capital of Tallahassee on 10 March 1909, the great-grandson of a Confederate chaplain. He graduated from a local high school in 1927 and, four years later, earned his law degree from Cumberland University in Williamsburg, Kentucky. In 1932, he was defeated for the post of Leon County prosecutor. That same year, he married the great-granddaughter of a two-time territorial governor of Florida, Richard Keith Call.

LeRoy Collins

In 1935, Collins was elected to the first of three terms in the Florida state House of Representatives. In 1940, he ran for and was elected to a seat in the Florida state senate. He served two full terms and two years of a third in this position. During World War II, Collins was not accepted for combat duty because of his age, but instead was selected to participate in the courtmartial process. Following this service, he was reelected to another state senate term.

In 1954, he ran for governor of Florida and won. When he was inaugurated on 4 January 1955, Collins made the usual promises to preserve segregated schools in the state. In his first term, however, he refused to sign the execution warrant for a black man he felt had been convicted by mob rule, and he adjourned the state legislature when it was poised to send him a bill annulling federal law on desegregation in Florida. Collins was easily reelected in 1956. In his second inaugural address, he said, "We can find wise solu-

tions if the white citizens will face up to the fact that the Negro does not now have equal opportunities, that he is morally and legally entitled to progress more rapidly."

In his second term of office, Collins changed the direction of Southern politics. He vetoed a bill that would have allowed white schools to close if blacks were admitted. He laid the groundwork so that urban as well as suburban areas would have equal representation in the legislature. Furthermore, during sit-in protests in Jacksonville in 1960, he went on television to denounce white storeowners for refusing to offer service to black customers. Although he served as chairman of the Southern Governor's Conference from 1957 to 1960, he refused to support the conference's recommendation not to back John F. Kennedy for president in 1960. Instead, Collins served as permanent chairman of the 1960 Democratic convention in Los Angeles.

After Collins left office in 1961, he continued to serve as a conduit for racial change. In 1965, in the midst of the civil rights battles raging in the South, President Lyndon Johnson chose him as a troubleshooter to stop potential violence in the Reverend Dr. Martin Luther King, Jr.'s march in Selma, Alabama. Collins was able to work out a deal between King and the Selma sheriff that prevented bloodshed. Photos of the encounter, showing the former Florida governor speaking with King, were later used against Collins in his unsuccessful run for the U.S. Senate in 1968. After this defeat, he retired. Collins died on 12 March 1991 at the age of 82.

Columbus Board of Education v. Penick (U.S., 1979)

In *Columbus*, the Supreme Court ruled that egregious violations of a court order for a school board to desegregate were a violation of the original court order. The case involved the Columbus (Ohio) Board of Education, which had been sued in 1976 by defendant Penick and several others for "pursuing a course of conduct having the purpose and effect of causing and perpetuating racial segregation in the public schools, contrary to the Fourteenth Amendment." The district court eventually found that the Columbus Board of Education had used every method at its disposal to avoid desegregating the school system. When the case of *Dayton Board of Education v. Brinkman* was heard in 1977, the Columbus Board of Education asked that its desegregation order be modified. A court of appeals denied such relief, and the board sued to the U.S. Supreme Court. The Court ruled 7–2 (with Justices William Rehnquist and Lewis Powell dissenting) that the board must comply with the original court order to desegregate.

See also Dayton Board of Education v. Brinkman.

Committee on Fair Employment Practices

Once called the Fair Employment Practices Commission, the committee is a federal agency established under Executive Order 8802, signed by President Franklin D. Roosevelt on 25 June 1941, to initiate state and federal protections against racial discrimination in employment.

See also Executive Order 8802.

Congress of Racial Equality (CORE)

CORE is a civil rights organization founded in 1942 by members of the Gandhian pacifist Fellowship of Reconciliation (FOR), whose dictum was the nonviolent protest of segregation. The first group that made up CORE was originally called the Chicago Committee of Racial Equality (CCRE). The members of this original Chicago group, located at the University of Chicago, included both whites and blacks: James Farmer and George Houser, both pacifists in seminary studies for the ministry; Bernice Fisher and Homer Jack from Rochester, New York, who were

also at the University of Chicago studying for the ministry; and James R. Robinson, an English graduate student from upstate New York. The group was rounded out by Joe Guinn of Chicago, who in 1941 was the head of the Chicago branch of the NAACP Youth Council. In 1942, this group expanded to 50 members and renamed itself the Committee of Racial Equality, later changed to Congress of Racial Equality. The committee members utilized sit-ins and discussions to end racial segregation. Over the next several years, chapters of CORE spread across the United States, applying the same techniques to knock down discriminatory barriers. CORE remains active today under the leadership of Roy Innis.

See also Farmer, James; Innis, Roy.

Connor, Theophilus Eugene "Bull" (1898–1973)

"Bull" Connor was the commissioner of public safety in Birmingham, Alabama, from 1936 to 1952, and again from 1956 to 1963—the latter period during the height of the civil rights struggle. Films of Connor's brutal troops assaulting peaceful marchers in Birmingham with dogs and fire hoses made him infamous. Connor earned the nickname "Bull" because of the deep voice he had as a young adult. In the 1920s, he served in the Alabama legislature as a Democrat. In 1936, he was elected as police commissioner of Birmingham, a post he held for 16 years, until a sex scandal drove him from office. Four years later, however, he was reelected to the post. With the coming of the civil rights movement, Connor was unrelenting in his opposition to desegregation. As the years passed and attitudes changed, Connor saw himself become a barrier against change rather than a barrier against unwanted intrusions into Southern life. In 1960, he and commissioner L.B. Sullivan sued the *New York Times* for libeling them in an advertisement paid for by a civil rights group. Although a Birmingham jury awarded the men $500,000 and the Alabama Supreme Court upheld the damages, the U.S. Supreme Court in the landmark case of *New York Times v. Sullivan* (U.S. 1964) ruled that the advertisement was allowable under the provisions of the First Amendment to the Constitution.

By 1963, Connor was on the way out. A system that relegated the commissioner—now simply a member of the city council—to the back scenes was put in place and Connor lost much of the power he once wielded. In 1966, he suffered a stroke that left him confined to a wheelchair. In early 1973, he suffered a second stroke that led to his death on 10 March of that same year.

Cooper v. Aaron (U.S., 1958)

The Supreme Court held in *Cooper* that threats of "mob action" could not be used as excuses for schools not to desegregate. The case, known officially as *Cooper et al., Members of the Board of Directors of the Little Rock, Arkansas, Independent School District, et al., v. Aaron, et al.,* came only four years after the historic *Brown* decision. The case concerned several black students who wished to follow the order of *Brown* and enter the once all-white public schools of Little Rock, Arkansas. Due to incendiary statements by the governor and members of the state legislature, mob threats caused the students to stay away from the schools. President Dwight Eisenhower was forced to send in federal troops to quell the violence. The state sued in court to have the implementation of *Brown* put off for two and one half years so that other measures protecting the students could be worked out. Several black students sued to have the district court's order reversed. This was done by an appeals court, and the school board sued to the U.S. Supreme Court to obtain relief. In a special August session, the Court held unanimously that any delay in the implementation of *Brown* was a violation of the equal protection clause of the Fourteenth Amendment. Wrote the Court, "The constitutional rights of respondents are not to be sacrificed or yielded to the violence and disorder which have followed upon the actions of the governor and Legislature, and law and order are not here to be preserved by depriving the Negro children of their constitutional rights."

Corrigan et al. v. Buckley (U.S., 1926)

The Supreme Court's ruling in *Corrigan* sidestepped the issue of racially discriminatory covenants in housing. The suit involved Buckley and Corrigan, joint owners of a piece of property in the District of Columbia. Both persons agreed, when purchasing the property in 1921, that neither they, nor their heirs, could rent or sell the property to "persons of the negro race or blood" for a period of 21 years after the purchase. In 1922, Corrigan sold her section to Curtis, a black man. Buckley and 23 other homeowners in the area sued Corrigan for breaking their contract. A district court found for Buckley, and the District of Columbia Court of Appeals affirmed the judgment. Corrigan sued to the U.S. Supreme Court for relief. On 24 May 1926, the Court ruled that because, under the Fifth Amendment, only states were barred from "[taking] private property for public use without just compensation," the courts had no jurisdiction to stop Corrigan from selling her land. Wrote Justice Edward T. Sanford, "The prohibitions of the Fourteenth Amendment have reference to state action exclusively, and not to any action of private individuals." The high court ultimately took action against discriminatory covenants in *Shelley v. Kraemer* (1948).

See also Shelley v. Kraemer.

Council of Federated Organizations (COFO)

COFO was formed among civil rights workers stationed in Mississippi, including members of the Student Nonviolent Coordinating Committee, the Congress of Racial Equality, the Southern Christian Leadership Conference, and the National Association for the Advancement of Colored People. Founded in October 1962 to negotiate with Mississippi governor Ross Barnett over security for the Freedom Riders, its mission was extended to provide funds to all areas of civil rights work in Mississippi, including voter registration.

Councill, William Hooper (1849–1909)

William H. Councill was an intimate of Booker T. Washington who, with Washington, was one of the initiators of the Protest Collaboration Movement, established by moderate black leaders to deal rationally with white society. Councill was born a slave to slave parents on 12 July 1849, in Fayetteville, Cumberland County, North Carolina. His father, William, escaped to Canada in 1854 and, over the next several years, agitated unsuccessfully to get his family out of the country. In 1857, two of the Councill children (*Councill* was the maiden name of William Hooper's mother Mary Jane; his father's name remains unknown) were sold to another owner, and they were never heard from again. At that same slave auction, William, his mother, and a younger brother were all sold in Richmond, Virginia, taken to Alabama, and sold again to a planter. The family was moved to Tennessee. When the Union Army overran Chattanooga in 1863, William and his family were taken in by the Union troops. Soon after, however, William's brother and mother both died. Left alone, he went back to Stevenson, Alabama, and educated himself by attending a Freedmen's school. In 1866, he taught for a time at the school. At night, he educated himself by reading books on Latin, the law, and mathematics. In 1883, Councill was admitted to the Alabama bar, but he never practiced law. In 1872, and again in 1874, he served as the enrolling clerk of the Alabama legislature.

In the latter year, he was the editor of the *Negro Watchman*, as well as being an unsuccessful candidate for the state legislature.

In 1873, Councill became involved with the fight for the civil rights of freed slaves when he was a secretary at the Colored National Civil Rights Convention held in Washington. In 1875, the state legislature named him principal of the new State Normal and Industrial School in Huntsville. Councill served in this position until a sex scandal drove him from office. He was later rehired in 1888. In 1887, he was involved in a controversial Interstate Commerce Commission decision that struck down unequal and separate facilities in travel, but upheld the principle of separate but equal. It was at this time that Councill became a rival of sorts of Booker T. Washington, whose Tuskegee Institute was a model for black schools. Although both men agreed that it was in the best interest of blacks to live peacefully with Southern whites—hence the founding of the Protest Collaboration (or Accommodation) Movement—scholars consider Councill the more accommodating of the two. Several of his comments, including one stating that no one was "better suited for domestic and personal service than the Negro," angered his contemporaries. After 1895, Councill was overshadowed by Washington, as the former tried to build his school, now called the Alabama State Agricultural and Mechanical College for Negroes, into another Tuskegee. William Hooper Councill died in obscurity in Normal, Alabama, on 17 April 1909.

See also Councill v. Western & Atlantic Railroad Company; Protest Collaboration Movement; Washington, Booker Taliaferro.

Councill v. Western & Atlantic Railroad Company (1887)

Councill v. Western & Atlantic was the Interstate Commerce Commission (ICC) ruling that struck down unequal facilities as a violation of section 3 of the Interstate

Commerce Act of 1887, but held that if such facilities were equal, railroads could implement separate but equal standards. William Hooper Councill, an educator who was a close associate of Booker T. Washington, boarded a train car on the railroad at Chattanooga, Tennessee. At first, he was told by someone he connected with the train company to move to the colored car. Councill did not move. Soon, he was approached by two men, one of whom was carrying a lantern. Without provocation, Councill was seized, lifted up, and struck in the head with the lantern, breaking the glass and cutting his head. Although Councill appealed for help, his cries fell on deaf ears. He was carried to the colored car and dropped down. The car was filthy and smelled of smoke. Counsel for the railroad produced a deposition from the man with the lantern, identified as a passenger, who claimed that he tried to talk Councill into moving to the other car but was accosted. In the melee, he claimed, Councill hit his head on the lantern. Following the hearing, the ICC held that, regardless of the fight's originators, it found the conditions to which Councill was exposed in the colored car were unequal to those of the white car. However, it upheld the right of railroads to separate passengers into colored and white sections, provided that they were "equal."

See also Councill, William Hooper.

Creswill v. Grand Lodge Knights of Pythias of Georgia (U.S., 1912)

Creswill was the Supreme Court case in which the Court upheld the legality of a black organization utilizing the same name as a white organization. The Supreme Lodge of the Knights of Pythias of Georgia, a fraternal organization, had a strict policy of not allowing black members to join. The excluded blacks formed their own chapter, calling it the Grand Lodge of the Knights of Pythias. They organized in 1880 and reaffirmed their license in 1889. In 1906, when they tried to join the national organization, the original Knights cried foul, claiming that the name was theirs alone. They sued to a district court, which held that the black group could use the same name. The Supreme Court of Georgia reversed the district court decision, whereupon Charles D. Creswill, a member of the black Knights organization, appealed to the U.S. Supreme Court. The Court held that because the original Knights had not sued for a quarter of a century after the separate Knights organization was founded, they were not entitled to relief. Chief Justice Edward Douglass White, a former Confederate soldier, wrote the 7–2 decision upholding the right of the black Knights to retain their name.

The Crisis

The Crisis, the official journal of the National Association for the Advancement of Colored People (NAACP), was started

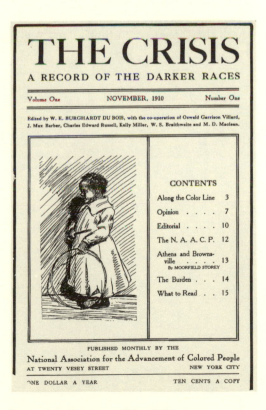

Cover of the first issue of The Crisis

in 1910 under the editorship of William Edward Burghardt DuBois and described itself as "a record of the darker races." In its November 1910 inaugural issue, the magazine's mission was spelled out: "The object of this publication is to set forth those facts and arguments which show the danger of race prejudice, particularly as manifested today toward colored people. It takes its name from the fact that the editors believe that this is a critical time in the history of the advancement of men. Catholicity and tolerance, reason and forbearance can today make the world-old dream of human brotherhood approach realization; while bigotry and prejudice, emphasized race consciousness and force can repeat the awful history of the contact of nations and groups in the past." *The Crisis* remains today the organ of the NAACP, published monthly.

Cumming v. Richmond County Board of Education (U.S., 1899)

Cumming was the Supreme Court case in which the Court ruled that a state was al-lowed to deny a high school education to black students solely on account of their race. The Board of Education of Richmond County, Virginia, closed a black high school, which taught 60 students, to make room for 300 black primary school students. It promised to build a black high school as soon as it could afford one, but it neglected to mention that it had funded a high school for white girls and was in the process of constructing a high school for white boys. The plaintiff, Cumming, a taxpayer in Richmond County, sued to get relief from paying taxes. The Supreme Court ruled unanimously that there was no evidence that the school board intended to harm the black high school students; in fact, Justice John Marshall Harlan wrote for the Court that the school board had made the proper decision to make the space available for 300 students instead of 60. Although the plaintiffs attempted in the Court's oral arguments to build a case against segregated education, their failure to bring this issue up in the trial court made the point moot.

Daniel et al. v. Paul (U.S., 1969)

In *Daniel et al. v. Paul*, the Supreme Court clarified the definition of a "public accommodation" under the meaning of the Civil Rights Act of 1964. The Lake Nixon Club was an amusement and entertainment center, based in Little Rock, Arkansas. Although it advertised in magazines and distributed membership cards, it refused to serve black customers. Several black citizens sued the club to gain entry. The club countered that it was not a public accommodation under color of state action, but a private club, and so was not covered by the 1964 act. A district court, while agreeing that the club was not a private club, and deciding that the plaintiffs had been denied access because of the color of their skin, nonetheless held that under the constrictions of the 1964 act, the club could not properly be called a public accommodation within the meaning of the law. The Eighth Circuit Court of Appeals upheld the verdict, and the plaintiffs sued to the U.S. Supreme Court. The Court ruled on 2 June 1969 that, under its interpretation of the Civil Rights Act of 1964, the club was a public accommodation. Speaking for the Court, Justice William Brennan wrote, "The Lake Nixon Club's snack bar is a place of public accommodation under section 201 (b) (2) of the Act since it is 'principally engaged in selling food for consumption on the premises' ... the operations of the bar 'affect commerce' under section 201 (c) (2) of the Act ... the club is a covered accommodation under sections 201 (b) (3) and 201 (c) (3) of the Act as it is a 'place of entertainment,' which, in the light of the overriding purpose of Title II [of the Act] to remove discriminatory denials of access to public facilities, includes recreational areas and is not, as respondent argues, limited to spectator entertainment."

Davis v. County School Board of Prince Edward County, Virginia (U.S., 1954)

Davis, a companion case to *Brown v. Board of Education*, involved several black schoolchildren in Prince Edward County, Virginia, who sued in the Court for the Eastern District of Virginia to stop the enforcement of the sections of the Virginia Constitution that mandated separate schools for blacks and whites. Although the court ruled that the black schools were inferior in all areas (site, curriculum, and transportation), it held that the sections of the constitution mandating separate educational facilities were constitutional. The plaintiffs sued to the U.S. Supreme Court. When the *Brown* decision came down, the Court found in all other related cases that segregated schools were unconstitutional and set arguments for the following year to determine a proper course in ending the practice.

See also Briggs v. Elliott; Brown v. Board of Education.

Dayton Board of Education v. Brinkman (U.S., 1977)

In *Dayton Board of Education* the Supreme Court struck down the use of "optional attendance zones," which caused segregation in schools. Several black schoolchildren and their parents filed suit in the District Court for the Southern District of Ohio in 1972 to end what they termed "attendance zones," in which white children had the option of going or not going to racially mixed schools. In 1973, the court found that these zones were violative of the equal protection clause of the

Fourteenth Amendment and ordered a remedy of options across the entire school system. The Dayton Board of Education appealed, and the case was finally heard by the Supreme Court in April 1977. Ruling against the lower court's findings, Justice William Rehnquist, writing for a unanimous U.S. Supreme Court, said, "The District Court's findings of constitutional violations did not suffice to justify the systemwide remedy . . . it was thus not demonstrated that the systemwide remedy, in effect imposed by the court of appeals, was necessary to 'eliminate all vestiges of the state-imposed school segregation.'"

Dees, Morris Seligman (1936–)

Morris S. Dees, a white civil rights activist, is best known for his establishment of KlanWatch, an advocacy group opposing the Ku Klux Klan. Dees was born in Mount Meigs, Alabama, the son of a farmer. He learned about racism at an early age. When he called a black man a nigger, his father gave him a brutal whipping. Racially tolerant, the Dees family invited blacks into their home. Although Morris wanted to be a farmer, his father pushed him into becoming a lawyer. While getting his law degree, he was the partner in a cake delivery enterprise.

Disgusted after a black client was convicted on baseless charges, Dees set out to change a justice system he felt was unfair to blacks. Further agitated by the growing civil rights movement, he took part in the march on Selma with Reverend Dr. Martin Luther King, Jr. Later, as an attorney for the American Civil Liberties Union, Dees helped to open a YMCA in Montgomery to blacks.

In 1971, Dees cofounded the Southern Poverty Law Center, a nonprofit foundation that supplies lawyers to people of all races who cannot afford expensive attorneys. After being intimidated by the Ku Klux Klan and finding out his name was on a Klan "hit list," Dees founded Klan-Watch, which brought to public attention

facts and cases involving the Klan. In 1981, Dees took on the case of Beulah Mae Donald, whose son Michael had been lynched by the Klan. Using new legal tactics, Dees sued the Klan for Donald's wrongful death. Five years later, an all-white jury found for Donald's mother and awarded her $7 million in damages, effectively bankrupting the Klan nationwide. Dees continues to battle the Klan, and remains to this day an effective spokesman in the defense of civil rights.

DeFunis v. Odegaard (U.S., 1974)

DeFunis preceded the landmark Supreme Court decision in Bakke, and is perhaps best known for the high court's failure to rule on the validity of race-conscious affirmative action programs in colleges when such programs may infringe on the rights of others. The case involved Marco DeFunis, Jr., a Jew of Spanish-Portuguese descent whose family had been in America for several generations. In 1970 and again in 1971, the University of Washington Law School (UWLS) turned down DeFunis for a place in the law school, even though his test scores were higher than some minority applicants. DeFunis sued the school to enroll. A trial court ruled in DeFunis's favor; the Washington State Supreme Court overturned the decision. In 1974, the U.S. Supreme Court granted certiorari, or the right to bring the case. The Court's ultimate ruling, however, did not clear up the basic question. A majority of the justices ruled that since the original trial court had ordered DeFunis's admission into the school, and he had been attending for almost two full years, the question of whether or not he had been discriminated against earlier was moot. Justices William Brennan, Thurgood Marshall, and Byron White attacked the majority for "straining to rid itself of this dispute." Justice William O. Douglas, a dissenter in this case, went farther. He wrote out a full opinion in which he discussed why he would have ruled against the UWLS's admissions policy. "All races can compete fairly at all professional levels," he wrote. "So far as race is concerned, any state sponsored preference to one race over another in that competition is in my view 'invidious' and violative of the equal protection clause."

See also University of California Regents v. Bakke.

De Large, Robert Carlos (1842–1874)

Robert Carlos De Large was a black Freedmen's Bureau agent and organizer of the South Carolina state Republican Party, who served one controversial term in the U.S. House of Representatives, De Large was born a slave on 15 March 1842, near Aiken, South Carolina, and received a limited education at the Wood High School in Charleston. For a period of time he worked as a farmer and Freedmen's Bureau agent in South Carolina. Following the Civil War, De Large was instrumental in helping to organize the state Republican Party. He was the chairman of the credentials committee at the Colored People's Convention in Charleston in 1865 and chairman of the platform committee at the Republican state convention in 1867. In 1868, De Large was elected to the state House of Representatives and was named to the Ways and Means Committee. He later served as state land commissioner.

In 1870, De Large was elected to the Forty-second Congress, beating another Republican, Christopher C. Bowen, who challenged the results. In the meantime, De Large took his seat. He spent much of the term defending Southerners who sympathized with the Union and calling for funding of an orphanage whose nuns had cared for Union troops during the Civil War. De Large did not seek reelection in 1872, and Alonzo Ransier, another black, succeeded him. In 1873, shortly before De Large left office, the elections committee found that there had been so many irregularities in the 1870 election that the seat was declared vacant. While

Robert Carlos De Large

the point was moot, the decision recorded that De Large had, in fact, illegitimately served his term.

Robert Carlos De Large lived only a year after he left Congress. In 1873, he was appointed by Republican Governor Robert K. Scott of South Carolina as a magistrate for the City of Charleston. In early 1874, he contracted tuberculosis and died a month later on 14 February 1874, at the age of 31.

De Priest, Oscar Stanton (1871–1951)

The first black from a northern state (Illinois) to sit in the U.S. House of Representatives, De Priest was born the free son of former slaves, on 9 March 1871, in Florence, Alabama. The family moved to Salina, Kansas, when the child was seven. De Priest ran away from home with two white friends at the age of 17 and ended up in Chicago. There, over the next several years, he did odd jobs to earn a living. One of these jobs led to a successful real estate business. By 1904, De Priest's power in the black community in Chicago got him elected to a seat on the Cook County Board of Commissioners.

By 1914, De Priest felt that he had achieved enough popularity to run for a seat on the Chicago City Council. He was elected and served from 1915 to 1917. In that latter year, a scandal involving protection money drove him from office, but he was represented by Clarence Darrow in a criminal trial and acquitted. In 1918 and 1919, De Priest tried to regain his seat on the city council, but he was defeated by the regular Republican candidate, another black. In 1924, De Priest was finally elected Third Ward alderman, a post that put him high up on the list as a possible congressional candidate. For a time it seemed that in the 1928 election, he would be passed over for incumbent Congressman Martin Madden, but Madden's death in April 1928 left De Priest as his successor. De Priest was elected, and served in the Seventy-first to the Seventy-third Congresses, 1929–1935. In his three terms, De Priest, as the first black ever sent to the U.S. House of Representatives from a northern state, worked to pass antilynching legislation, sought to have Abraham Lincoln's birthday declared a national holiday, and called for an end to race discrimination in criminal trials. He spent a considerable amount of time unsuccessfully lobbying President Franklin D. Roosevelt on behalf of activist Marcus Garvey to get Garvey readmitted into the United States, following a fraud conviction and expulsion from the country. De Priest was defeated by a black New Deal Democrat, Arthur W. Mitchell, in the 1934 elections. Mitchell's victory made him the first black Democrat to serve in Congress. In 1936, De Priest challenged Mitchell for the seat, but was again defeated. He later served as the Third Ward alderman, as well as on the Chicago City Council. Before his death, De Priest re-turned to a lucrative real estate business. He died in Chicago on 12 May 1951.

Dixiecrats
See States' Rights Party.

Douglass, Frederick (1817?–1895)

Frederick Douglass was a journalist, orator, and nineteenth-century civil rights activist. The precise date and place of Douglass's birth remain a mystery; what is known is that he was born a slave in Tuckahoe, Maryland, about 1817. In 1825 he was sent to Baltimore as a houseboy, and here he learned the rudimentary skills of reading and writing. He never formally received an education. In 1838, Douglass escaped, settling as a freeman in New Bedford, Massachusetts, with his wife, whom he had met in New York.

Douglass soon began to agitate as an abolitionist and writer on slavery. He later became a speaker for the Massachusetts Anti-Slavery Society, where he was an associate of white abolitionists Wendell Phillips and William Lloyd

Frederick Douglass

Garrison. In 1845, he authored *Narrative of the Life of Frederick Douglass*, in which he described his experiences as a slave. In 1847 he began the publication of the *North Star*, an abolitionist weekly newspaper. In 1851 he changed the name to *Frederick Douglass's Paper*; then, in 1860, until its closing three years later, *Douglass's Monthly*. During the Civil War, he visited the White House and urged President Abraham Lincoln to free the slaves.

Following the war, Douglass remained a staunch supporter of the Republican Party. In 1870 he spoke out in favor of the Fifteenth Amendment's passage and was named marshal of the District of Columbia in 1877. In 1881, he was named recorder of deeds for the district. He went on the stump for the national Republican ticket in 1888 and was appointed by President Benjamin Harrison minister and consul-general to Haiti and chargé d'affairs to the Dominican Republic. In all, Douglass received four appointments, all from Republican presidents.

In his final years, Douglass remained interested not only in the advancement of the black people but in other groups as well. On 20 February 1895, he spoke before a session of the National Council of Women in support of women's suffrage. That night, he suffered a fatal heart attack and died at his home in Washington, D.C.

Dred Scott v. Sandford (U.S., 1857)

Dred Scott was undoubtedly the most important Supreme Court case dealing with slavery, although Scott himself probably did not realize it and did not live to see the repercussions. He was born in slavery sometime around 1798 and died in freedom less than a year after his famous case reached the Supreme Court. Scott was born the slave of a man named Peter Blow. In 1827, Blow moved to St. Louis from Virginia, but he died in 1831. Blow's daughter Elizabeth inherited Scott. Two years later, however, she sold him to Dr. John Emerson, a surgeon. Emerson

Plaintiff Dred Scott

treated Scott more as a manservant than a slave during his travels to various military posts, but this relationship ended with Emerson's death around 1838. Emerson's widow inherited Scott, but she loaned him to two men, Henry and Taylor Blow, sons of Scott's original owner. Things had changed for the Blow family. Henry Blow, an attorney, was an antislavery Whig (later he would help found the Free Soil movement in Missouri and become a Republican), and he set Scott free, suing Mrs. Emerson, an opponent of slavery herself, for Scott's complete freedom.

The lawsuit, originally called *Scott, a Man of Color, v. Emerson*, argued one basic point: that when Peter Blow and John Emerson moved Scott from slave soil to free soil, Scott essentially became free. Although a lower court ruled for Scott, the Missouri Supreme Court struck down the decision, arguing that as property of a citizen of the state of Missouri, a slave state, Scott was still a slave. Following this court ruling in 1852, it took five years for the appeal to come before the U.S. Supreme Court. By this time, Mrs. Emerson had remarried and had given ownership of Dred Scott to her brother, John F. A. Sanford. Sanford wanted Scott as his slave. He sued Scott's lawyers to return him. By 1857, the suit had reached the Supreme Court. A court clerk accidentally entered the name of the case as *Dred Scott v. Sandford*, by which it is known today.

The Supreme Court at the time included some of the most interesting men in the court's history. The four Southerners who sat on the Court—John Archibald Campbell of Alabama, John Catron of Tennessee, Peter Vivian Daniel of Virginia, and James Moore Wayne of Georgia—were all supporters of slaveowners' rights. Of the three Northerners—Benjamin R. Curtis of Massachusetts, Robert C. Grier of Pennsylvania, and Samuel Nelson of New York—there was a proslavery tilt, although Curtis was personally against slavery on its face. Justice John McLean of Ohio was a staunch antislavery advocate, but he was 72 years old and would only live four more years. Chief Justice Roger B. Taney of Maryland, almost 80 years old and in his twenty-second year on the Court, was bound to shift to a proslavery position. The decision that came down on 6 March 1857, two days after proslavery President James Buchanan took office, shook the nation to its foundations. Taney read the 7–2 decision, which ruled that even if Scott were free, the Constitution did not consider blacks as "citizens" with the right to sue for anything. Slaves were considered "altogether unfit to associate with the white race and so far inferior, that they have no rights which the white man is bound to respect; and might justly and lawfully be reduced to slavery for his benefit," Taney wrote in the majority opinion. The chief justice reiterated that the right to own slaves was a fundamental right secured to slaveown-

ers in the Constitution, and that no entity, even the federal government, had the power to take that right away. Justices McLean and Curtis dissented, calling Scott a "citizen" and claiming that his movement into antislavery territory constituted him as a freeman. Further, they supported the restrictions against slavery in the Missouri Compromise of 1850. The radical nature of the majority decision has not been lost on Constitutional scholars. In *Dred Scott*, the court held that any congressional legislation aimed at correcting a judicial wrong was an unconstitutional blow at the separation of powers.

Despite the decision, Scott was freed by his masters, but he did not live long to enjoy his freedom. He died in obscurity in St. Louis on 17 September 1858. Chief Justice Charles Evans Hughes later called the Dred Scott decision a "self-inflicted wound" the Court brought on itself.

Drew, Charles Richard (1904–1950)

Dr. Charles R. Drew was a black physician whose pioneering work in the field of blood storage paved the way for the treatment and conquering of previously fatal diseases. Drew was born one of five children in Washington, D.C., on 3 June 1904. In school, he was a noted athlete, and he attended Amherst University on an athletic scholarship. A sports-related injury finished his dreams of a career in sports. Instead, he decided on the field of medicine. His application to Howard University Medical School denied, Drew enrolled at McGill Medical College in Montreal, Quebec. He earned a master of surgery degree and graduated with honors in 1933. He interned for a year at the Royal Victoria Hospital, then served at Montreal Hospital. In 1935, Howard University Medical School, which had once turned down his application, hired him as a member of the school faculty. After working at several hospitals, Drew was awarded a fellowship from the Rockefeller Institute, did postgraduate work at Columbia University's College of

Physicians and Surgeons, and completed a period of residency at Presbyterian Hospital in New York.

It was at Presbyterian that Drew met and worked with Dr. John Scudder, who, for many years, had been studying the storage of blood products. Drew joined him on delicate work that tried to solve the problem of how blood could be stored for a period of time without clotting or going bad. After two years, Drew completed his thesis on blood banks and received the degree of doctor of science in surgery from Columbia—the first black man in America to be so honored.

World War II created an unprecedented need for blood supplies. Drew was named as the medical supervisor of an experimental committee, the Blood for Britain Project. Under Drew's leadership, some 14,000 donations were made and shipped to England. After the committee disbanded, Drew was named head of the department of surgery at Howard University. He received several awards, including the NAACP's distinguished Spingarn Award, for his work in blood projects.

Drew was in constant demand for speaking engagements. In April 1950, he traveled to Alabama with three other black doctors to speak at Tuskegee University. On the night of 1 April, as the four men drove to Tuskegee, their car turned over, and Drew was severely injured. Later reports said that Drew was denied access to a white hospital. In fact, all four men were taken to a black hospital that was closer to the scene of the accident. For Dr. Charles Drew, however, it was too late. The man who had shown the world how to utilize blood products properly bled to death. He was 45 years old.

Drexel, Reverend Mother Mary Katherine (1858–1955)

A nun who founded the Sisters of the Blessed Sacrament for the Indians and Colored People, Mary Katherine Drexel was born in Philadelphia, Pennsylvania, on 26 November 1858. She was the daughter of Francis Anthony Drexel, a rich Austrian emigrant banker and intimate of J. P. Morgan, who was heavily involved in philanthropic causes, and Hannah Langstroth Drexel, a Quaker of German descent. Hannah Drexel died when Mary was five weeks old, and she was raised by a stepmother to whom her father was married in 1860. In 1883, and then two years later, Mary Drexel was jolted by the deaths first of her stepmother, then of her wealthy father, who left Mary and her sister several million dollars. Determined to use the money for worthy causes, Mary joined the Sisters of Mercy in Pittsburgh in 1889. Two years later, with the blessing of Pope Leo XIII, she founded the Sisters of the Blessed Sacrament for the Indians and Colored People, a religious order that worked exclusively with Native Americans and blacks. She helped found Xavier University in New Orleans, the only Catholic college in the United States for blacks. Over a 60-year period, Drexel attracted 51 sisters and, by the time of her death, had contributed some $12 million of her own funds to build 49 houses. In 1935, she suffered a serious heart attack and retired to St. Elizabeth's Convent in Cornwell's Heights near Philadelphia. She lived there until her death on 3 March 1955, at the age of 96. She was beatified in 1964, and, in 1973, her writings were approved by the Church, opening the way for her canonization.

DuBois, William Edward Burghardt (1868–1963)

One of the most influential leaders of the nascent civil rights movement, a key founder of the National Association for the Advancement of Colored People (NAACP) and the first editor of its journal, *The Crisis*, William Edward Burghardt DuBois was born on 23 February 1868, in Great Barrington, Massachusetts. His father was a mulatto. When William

William Edward Burghardt DuBois

DuBois was 18, he saved for a year to enter Harvard University, but instead enrolled at Fisk University in Nashville, Tennessee.While there, he served as editor of the Fisk *Herald*, the college newspaper. He graduated in 1888 and entered Harvard, where he earned a degree in sociology. He did several years of graduate study, during which he had a chance to travel to Europe. When he returned, in 1894, he took a job as a professor at Wilberforce University in Ohio. Two years later, he moved to the University of Pennsylvania. It was at this time that he began to write not only articles, like the several he did for the *Atlantic Monthly*, but an entire encyclopedia on race relations and the American Negro. Following this work, he went through a period of transition that lasted five years, 1903–1908. DuBois was in conflict with Booker T. Washington, who preached that hard work and moral living would earn the black an equal place in American society. DuBois saw matters differently. He called for educational enlightenment, reaching out to the so-called "Talented Tenth" of American black society. He put his ideas into a book, *The Souls of Black Folk* (1903).

The rift with Washington grew. After the arrest of a pro-DuBois heckler, who antagonized Washington at a Boston speech, DuBois gathered together his forces in a small town near Buffalo, New York, where the Niagara Movement was born. The group had eight goals, which included the right to vote for black men and the end of all laws based on color. The group met again in Virginia in 1906, but it was without national strength. In 1909, the group met for a third conference. This time, they formed the NAACP. DuBois was named the group's director of publications and research. He immediately started a journal, *The Crisis*, which carried in it for the first time in the history of the black press articles on the problems in American black life. For the next several decades, DuBois the reformer worked to improve the black man's lot.

Work in a Pan-African Congress and travels to Africa convinced DuBois that blacks needed to work harder for their rights. He parted company with the NAACP as his program became more radical. In 1961, at the age of 93, he turned his back on his country and moved to the African country of Ghana, where he renounced his American citizenship and joined the Communist party. He died on 27 August 1963, at the age of 95.

See also The Crisis; McGhee, Frederick Lamar; National Association for the Advancement of Colored People; Niagara Movement.

Dunn, Oscar James (1820? or 1821?–1871)

Oscar J. Dunn was the black lieutenant governor of Louisiana whose promising political career was cut short by his mysterious death. According to some disputed accounts, Dunn was born into slavery, although his mother was free and operated a lodging house in New Orleans. Nothing is known of his father, but his mother married a man named Dunn and her son took that name as his.

While young, he was apprenticed to a plasterer. He soon ran away and was the subject of an intense but unsuccessful hunt. His education was minimal at best, although he later became an accomplished violin player.

There is no record of what Dunn did between 1845 and the start of the Civil War in 1861, although he may have worked as a plasterer and as a violin teacher. When General Benjamin Butler's troops entered New Orleans in 1863, Dunn was made a captain of the colored division. He later resigned his commission over the promotion of a white man he felt was inferior. During Reconstruction, however, General Philip Sheridan named him to the New Orleans City Council. In this post, he gathered political experience and became a leader in the Louisiana state Republican Party. In 1868, the Republicans nominated Henry Clay Warmoth, a young, white, Civil War veteran, for governor, and Dunn for lieutenant governor. When they were elected over a more radical Republican ticket, Dunn became the first black in America to be elected to a major state office.

During the next three years, Dunn became embroiled in a factional dispute with Warmoth and other leaders in the state Republican Party, including P. B. S. Pinchback, a leading black state senator. At the Republican state convention in 1870, he took a leading role, and many people presumed that he would be the Republican nominee for governor in 1872. Even the most disillusioned whites considered Dunn to be the most honest politician in the state. His star was rising rapidly. All that ended in early November 1871, when Dunn came down with an illness that rapidly sapped his strength. Doctors were called, but to no avail. Dunn succumbed to his mystery illness on 22 November, at the presumed age of 50 or 51.

Many speculated that the Warmoth-Pinchback wing of the party had poisoned Dunn; signs of arsenic poisoning were evident. Yet there was no autopsy, and when Warmoth was removed from power, it was not Oscar Dunn but P. B. S. Pinchback who became the first black man in America to become the governor of a state. Dunn's accomplishments remain, to this day, obscure.

Durr, Clifford Judkins (1899–1975)

Few whites took prominent roles in the movement to gain civil rights for black Americans. Clifford Durr and his wife Virginia Foster Durr were exceptions. Clifford Durr was born in Montgomery, Alabama, and attended the University of Alabama, earning his law degree in 1919. Before graduating, he served for a year in the armed forces during the First World War. In 1925, he married Virginia Foster, whose sister was married to future Supreme Court Justice Hugo Black.

During the 1930s and 1940s, Clifford Durr served in the government, working as assistant general counsel to the Reconstruction Finance Corporation. He also served as general counsel to, and director of, the Defense Plant Corporation, which helped American industry build up for the Second World War. From 1941 until 1948, Durr was a commissioner on the Federal Communications Commission. As a private attorney in Washington, he handled the controversial cases of several well-known figures, including scientist Robert J. Oppenheimer.

When Durr and his wife returned to Montgomery in 1951, he became the only white attorney in town who would represent black clients. A friend of seamstress Rosa Parks, it was Durr who worked with Edgar Daniel Nixon of the Alabama chapter of the National Association for the Advancement of Colored People (NAACP) to raise her bail after she was arrested, following her refusal to move to the back of a segregated city bus. During the ensuing Montgomery Bus Boycott, Clifford and Virginia Durr, among other whites, backed the action. Clifford Durr was later called "a moral giant to a generation of young Southerners" for his stand against segregation. A leader in the fight to overturn Jim Crow, in which he and his wife allowed Freedom Riders to use their house as a way station, Durr was awarded the Civil Liberties Award in 1966 from the New York Civil Liberties Union. He died on 12 May 1975. His wife, now almost 90, remains an avid agitator for civil rights. In 1985, her autobiography, *Outside the Magic Circle*, was published by the University of Alabama Press.

Durr, Virginia Foster
See Durr, Clifford Judkins.

Dyer, Leonidas Carstarphen (1871–1957)

A Republican congressman from Missouri, Dyer was one of the leaders in the early part of the twentieth century in pushing for the enactment of federal antilynching legislation. Dyer was born in Warren County, Missouri, on 11 June 1871. He attended local schools and graduated from Washington University in St. Louis. He studied law and was admitted to the Missouri bar. Dyer was a veteran of the Spanish-American War. Elected to the U.S. House of Representatives in 1911, he served a single term but was defeated two years later. In 1914, he ran for his old seat, was elected, and served until 1933. In his 11 terms, he was known as the father of the Dyer Motor Vehicle Theft Act of 1919 and the China Trade Act of 1922. It was, however, his work in the area of antilynching legislation that was his passion. During the 1920s, Dyer became agitated over the serious number of lynchings taking place, particularly in his native South. The Dyer Anti-Lynching Bill, which came up for a vote several times before Congress but was voted down by the Democrat-controlled House every time except one, would have made the crime of lynching a federal offense. In 1922, the antilynching bill passed the House but was defeated in the Senate. Dyer spent the rest of his career trying to revive it, with no success. In 1932, he was defeated for reelection and resumed the practice of law. Dyer died of old age in St. Louis on 15 December 1957, at the age of 86.

See also Antilynching Laws.

Elliott, Robert Brown (1842?–1884)

Few historians have taken note of Robert Brown Elliott, an apparently British-born black, who served two terms in the U.S. House of Representatives, and later was speaker of the South Carolina General Assembly. Robert Elliott's beginnings are shrouded in mystery. One source says that he was born in Boston of West Indian parents on 11 August 1842; Russell Adams, in his *Great Negroes: Past and Present* (1964), reports that Elliott's parents were South Carolinian and that he was born somewhere in the United States on 15 March 1842; a third source concludes that Elliott was born in Liverpool, England, sometime in 1842. This final source most likely is correct, as it is noted by contemporaries that Elliott had a British accent. Although there is no formal evidence, he apparently received some semblance of an education, and served for some interval an apprenticeship in the typesetter's trade. If the third story of his life is true, then reports that he spent some time in the British Royal Navy and emigrated to Boston in 1867 are consistent. A fourth source, however, says that he spent time in the Union navy during the Civil War and was injured in an accident that left him lame.

The multitude of stories seem to agree on the events in Elliott's life after 1867. That year, he moved to Charleston, South Carolina, where he practiced law and became the assistant editor of the South Carolina *Leader*, under the tutelage of Richard Harvey Cain, a black minister and future U.S. congressman.

Elliott was a delegate to the South Carolina Constitutional Convention in 1868. That year, he was elected to the state House of Representatives. During his single term, he was appointed by the governor to be the head of the militia, which was being utilized by the state to battle the Ku Klux Klan. In 1870, Elliott was nominated by the Republicans and elected to the U.S. House of Representatives. He served in the Forty-second and Forty-third Congresses, from 1871 to 1874. His most famous act in his two terms was the two-hour speech he gave on the floor of the House in favor of the Civil Rights Act of 1875. Following the speech, he resigned his seat and won a seat in the South Carolina state general assembly. In 1874, Elliott was elected speaker of the assembly, the first black man to be so honored. In 1876, he was elected as South Carolina state attorney general, again a first. With the end of Reconstruction the following year, however, Elliott was forced from his job when the Democrats re-established their power in the state government.

Elliott's last years were spent in private law practice, serving as a special customs inspector to the Treasury Department, and acting as manager for John Sherman's black delegation in Sherman's ill-fated 1880 presidential campaign. In 1881, Elliott was transferred to New Orleans, but the move from South Carolina disagreed with him, and he resigned. He remained in New Orleans, trying to resurrect his law practice. In New Orleans, he contracted malaria, which, added to his lapse into poverty, contributed to his death. Elliott died on 9 August 1884. Not knowing that he had died, a Washington, D.C., commission appointed him the day after his death as the United States agent for affairs in the Congo Free State.

Enforcement Act of 31 May 1870

The Enforcement Act of 31 May 1870 (16 Stat. 140) was the congressional action taken to "enforce" the provisions of the Fifteenth Amendment and the right to vote. The act stated, in part, that "citizens otherwise qualified to vote shall be entitled to vote, without distinction to race"; that poll taxes, literacy tests, and other "prerequisites" could not be used on the basis of race; and it discussed penalties if such prerequisites on the basis of race were used. Further, the act dictated punishment for those who intimidated any person, regardless of color, from voting or into voting a certain way. This last section was aimed specifically at the Ku Klux Klan. Lastly, the violator of any part of the act would be subject not to federal jurisdiction but to control in the state where the crime was committed.

In all, there were 22 sections to the act. Many involved the discussion of officers who were elected through voter fraud. These were called the "corrupt practices" sections. Almost immediately after passage, there was a challenge to the act. The case of *United States v. Souders*, in which a white man intimidated black voters who later voted anyway, called into question whether the Enforcement Act's language forbade intimidation that stopped voting altogether or any intimidation at all. Judge John T. Nixon of the District Court of New Jersey ruled that the act outlawed any intimidation related to voting.

Enforcement Act of 28 February 1871

This was the congressional action taken to strengthen the Enforcement Act of 31 May 1870. The weakness of the first act was that although its aim was to protect the voting rights of blacks in the South, it failed to provide official oversight to protect these rights. The Enforcement Act of 28 February 1871, also known as the Second Enforcement Act, or Supplementary Enforcement Act, set up a system of supervisors to oversee state and local elections. Any interference with these officers would constitute a federal offense, subject to a fine and imprisonment. This second act did little to curb the power of the Ku Klux Klan, leading the way to the passage of the Third Enforcement Act, also known as the Ku Klux Klan Act.

Enforcement Act of 20 April 1871

Also known as the Third Enforcement Act or the Ku Klux Klan Act, the Enforcement Act of 20 April 1871 was based on hearings before a Senate select committee empaneled to hear evidence regarding Ku Klux Klan activities in the South. The committee hearings closed before the end of the 41st Congress, but when the 42nd convened, a Republican representative introduced H.R. 320, the Ku Klux Klan Enforcement Bill. When passed, the act stipulated, in part, that "any person, regardless of any law, statute, ordinance, regulation, custom, or usage of a State, shall not subject, or cause to be subjected, any person in the jurisdiction of the United States to be deprived of rights, privileges, or immunities available to that person under the existing laws of the United States." Violators of the act were to be liable for criminal as well as civil action to remedy the injustice. The act further stated that if two or more persons conspired to overthrow the government of the United States, or seize property of the United States, or if force, intimidation, or threats were utilized against someone testifying in court, or against any person for having testified in court, these persons would be subject to criminal penalties. The act is currently Title 42, section 1983, of the U.S. Code.

Equal Employment Opportunity Commission (EEOC)

The EEOC is the governmental body that oversees attempts to eliminate discrimination in hiring based on race, color, religion, sex, national origin, or age. The commission was created under

Title VII of the Civil Rights Act of 1964 (now 42 U.S.C. 2000e) and began its work on 2 July 1965. Under several congressional acts, authority for expanded oversight of discrimination in several areas, such as pregnancy, sex-based pay, and federal agencies, has been delegated to the commission. The latest legislation, the Americans with Disabilities Act of 1990, gives the commission new powers in the area of discrimination based on handicap. Since its inception, there have been 10 Chairmen of the Commission: Stephen Shulman, 1965–1967; Clifford L. Alexander, Jr., 1968–1969; William H. Brown III, 1969–1975; John H. Powell, Jr., 1975–1976; Ethel Bent Walsh, 1976–1977; Lowell W. Perry, 1977–1978; Eleanor Holmes Norton, 1979–1981; Cathie Shattuck, 1982–1983; Clarence Thomas, 1983–1989; and Evan J. Kemp, Jr., 1989–.

Evans v. Newton (U.S., 1966)

Evans v. Newton was the Supreme Court case in which the Court held that states that are deeded land by private individuals on condition that the land be segregated are, if they enforce the segregation, in violation of the equal protection clause of the Fourteenth Amendment requiring government agencies to follow nonsegregationist policies on public lands. Senator Augustus O. Bacon, in his 1911 will, deeded a tract of land in Macon, Georgia, to the mayor and the city council, which, after the death of his wife and daughters, would be used as "a park and pleasure ground" for all of the white citizens to utilize. Bacon wrote in his will that while he liked blacks, he felt that the black and white races should be "forever separate." For some time after it took control of the land, the City of Macon segregated it; later, however, as a matter of sound public policy, it began to let blacks use the park on a limited basis. Upon this move, several members of the board of managers of the park and some of Bacon's heirs interceded, claiming that allowing blacks to use the park was contrary to

Bacon's will, and asking that the park be taken from the city's ownership and given to a private individual. The city then gave up ownership to three trustees, who resegregated it according to Bacon's will. Several black Macon citizens then sued, claiming that the removal of the city as trustee was a violation of their Fourteenth Amendment rights. The trial court accepted the city's resignation as trustee, and approved the three new trustees.

The Georgia Supreme Court upheld the order, holding that as owner, Bacon had the right to deed his land as he wanted it used. The black litigants then sued to the U.S. Supreme Court. On 17 January 1966, the Court found that the use of Bacon's land as a public park was a governmental action, and any segregation was a violation of the equal protection clause of the Fourteenth Amendment. Justice William O. Douglas wrote the Court's 8–1 opinion, with Justice John Marshall Harlan dissenting.

Evers, Medgar Wiley (1925–1963)

Among the martyrs of the civil rights movement stands Medgar Evers, the field director for the National Association for the Advancement of Colored People (NAACP) in Mississippi, who was assassinated in 1963. His death touched off a firestorm of controversy that, to this day, has not subsided. Evers was born on 2 July 1925 in Decatur, Mississippi. He attended local schools, then enlisted in the army in 1943. Following the Second World War, he attended Alcorn A & M College in Mississippi. After graduating, he worked as an insurance salesman. In 1952, he joined the NAACP, and became a working member of its cadre in Mississippi. In 1951, he married Myrlie Beasley.

From the time Evers enlisted with the NAACP in a segregated state such as Mississippi, he was never far from the possibility that he would be killed. In a 1962 interview, he told of anonymous calls in the middle of the night warning him that his house would be blown up. "I

Medgar Wiley Evers

have only a few hours to live," he recalled thinking. In June 1963, he was spearheading a drive for Jackson, Mississippi, to hire more black policemen. On the night of 11 June 1963, after a heated meeting with other civil rights advocates to discuss options for the drive, Evers returned to his home. As he stepped out of his car in the early morning hours, someone shot at him, and the bullet hit him just below his right shoulder blade. A neighbor drove Evers to a nearby hospital, but the civil rights leader died of his injuries soon after. His death sent a shockwave across the nation. The next day, demonstrations broke out in Jackson.

To this day, Evers's murder officially remains unsolved. For the past few years, however, Mississippi prosecutors, who were children when Evers was murdered, have been trying to convict Byron de la Beckwith, a member of the Ku Klux Klan, for the murder. Much of the evidence is circumstantial but incriminating: the murder weapon belonged to Beckwith, his fingerprints were found on

it, and his alibi remains shaky. Two all-white juries have been unable to reach verdicts. In 1991, new attempts to put Beckwith on trial were initiated, with prosecutors claiming that new witnesses put him at the scene.

Executive Order 8802 (25 June 1941)

Executive Order 8802, signed by President Franklin Delano Roosevelt, was intended to eliminate discrimination in the defense industry during World War II. The directive established the Fair Employment Practices Commission (FEPC), which over the next five years attempted to end discrimination in the hiring and training of black workers in the government. Roosevelt signed 8802 under intense pressure from civil rights leaders, most notably A. Philip Randolph of the Brotherhood of Sleeping Car Porters, who promised that 50,000 to 100,000 African Americans would march in Washington if something was not done to end such discrimination.

See also Committee on Fair Employment Practices.

Executive Order 9808 (5 December 1946)

President Harry S Truman signed this order on 5 December 1946, creating the President's Committee on Civil Rights.

Executive Orders 9980 and 9981 (26 July 1948)

President Harry S Truman signed both orders on 26 July after elaborating his civil rights platform in his 2 February 1948 speech to Congress. In that speech, he promised presidential action on a number of civil rights issues; these two executive orders fulfilled this promise. Executive Order 9980 established the Fair Employment Board in the Civil Service Commission, which allowed for the fairer hiring of blacks in government civil service positions. Executive Order 9981 created the President's Committee on Equality of Treatment and Opportunity in the Armed Forces.

See also President's Committee on Equality of Treatment and Opportunity in the Armed Forces.

Executive Order 11063
(20 November 1962)

Executive Order 11063 was signed by President John F. Kennedy to remedy racial discrimination in housing. The order contained six parts: Part I, which discussed the prevention of housing discrimination; Part II, which covered the use of governmental agencies to remedy such discrimination; Part III, which explained enforcement of the order; Part IV, which established a Presidential Committee on Equal Opportunity in Housing (this part was rescinded by Executive Order 12259, signed by President Jimmy Carter on 31 December 1980); Part V, which outlined the duties of the President's Committee on Equality in Housing; and Part VI, containing definitions.

Ex Parte Siebold (U.S., 1880)

Although not a civil rights case, *Ex Parte Siebold* was an important litigation involving the issue of whether the federal government had the jurisdiction over state and local elections. In many cases, local authorities kept blacks from voting and claimed that only they had control over such elections. The case involved one Albert Siebold, a judge, who was caught with five other judges stuffing ballot boxes in Baltimore during the congressional election of 1878. Siebold and the other judges were prosecuted under federal law. Siebold sued, claiming that the federal government had no jurisdiction over the way state and local races were conducted. Justice Joseph P. Bradley read the 7–2 decision, in which the Court found that the government had the right to prosecute the men and oversee local

and congressional elections. Wrote Bradley, "Whilst the states are really sovereign as to all matters which have not been granted to the jurisdiction and control of the United States, the Constitution and constitutional laws of the latter are the supreme laws of the land; and when they are in conflict with the laws of the states, they are of paramount authority and obligation."

Ex Parte Virginia (U.S., 1880)

The Supreme Court ruled in *Ex Parte Virginia* that unless a state dictated that blacks be excluded from juries or from testifying, the mere fact that blacks did not serve on a particular jury or testify on their own behalf did not constitute a denial of due process. The case originally involved Burwell and Lee Reynolds, two black brothers who were indicted for murdering Aaron Shelton, a white man, in 1877. When they went to trial, no blacks were picked for the jury, even though the defendants demanded a jury with at least one-third black representation. Both men were convicted of murder. On two occasions, their convictions were set aside by Judge Alexander Rives of the District Court for Western Virginia on the grounds that the all-white juries that convicted the men denied them due process. The Commonwealth of Virginia sued Rives in the U.S. Supreme Court, demanding that the grounds Rives used to overturn the men's convictions be ruled unconstitutional. The case, fully named *Ex Parte: In the Matter of the Commonwealth of Virginia, Petitioner v. Rives*, appeared to rest on the narrow grounds of whether the absence of blacks on the grand and trial juries reflected the population of the state or state discrimination.

Justice William Strong delivered the unanimous judgment of the Supreme Court, which upheld the convictions of the men and dismissed Judge Rives's objection to the process by which they were convicted. In the case of *Strauder v. West Virginia*, which had recently been decided, the Court had found that the state had deliberately acted to prevent blacks from serving on the jury, and so found against the state. In *Ex Parte Virginia*, the Court ruled that the state of Virginia did not bar black jurors from serving; further, the Court found that the men had received a fair trial.

See also Strauder v. West Virginia.

Ex Parte Yarbrough (U.S., 1884)

In *Ex Parte Yarbrough*, the Supreme Court held that infringements of the voting rights of blacks violate the Fifteenth Amendment to the Constitution. On 25 July 1883, eight men, including Jasper, James, and Dilmus Yarbrough, beat Berry Saunders, a black man, for trying to vote. In the charges against the men, they were accused of "conspiracy to beat, bruise, wound and otherwise maltreat" Saunders. As the allegations against the men discuss the "disguises" they had adopted, there is reason to believe they were dressed as Ku Klux Klansmen. All eight were convicted on both counts: the assault itself and the conspiracy to deprive Saunders of his civil rights. They sued on a writ of error to the U.S. Supreme Court, claiming that the states had no right to protect who could vote. Justice Samuel Freeman Miller, a founder of the Republican Party in Iowa who had been Abraham Lincoln's first nominee to the Court, wrote the unanimous opinion, which upheld the plaintiffs' convictions. Miller wrote, "If the recurrence of such acts as these prisoners stand convicted of are too common in one quarter of the country, and give omen of danger from lawless violence, the free use of money in elections, arising from the vast growth of recent wealth in other quarters, presents equal cause for anxiety. If the government of the United States has within its constitutional domain no authority to provide against these evils, if the very sources of power may be poisoned by corruption or controlled by violence or outrage, without legal restraint, then, indeed, is the country in danger, and its best powers, its highest purposes, the hopes which it inspires, and the love which enshrines it, are at the mercy of combinations of those who respect no right but brute force, on one hand, and unprincipled corruptionists on the other."

Fair Employment Practices Committee (FEPC)

The Fair Employment Practices Committee (FEPC) was the first federal agency created to put into place a governmentwide policy of ending discrimination in federal hiring, employment, and training. The committee was authorized by President Franklin D. Roosevelt's Executive Order 8802 of 25 June 1941, which was the result of pressure brought by black activists, mainly A. Philip Randolph, head of the Brotherhood of Sleeping Car Porters. Randolph threatened Roosevelt with a march on the nation's capital if such an antidiscrimination order was not issued immediately. Randolph claimed that, if the order had not been issued, 50,000 to 100,000 blacks would have marched.

The FEPC lasted from its inception in 1941 until 1946, when it released its final report to President Harry S Truman. From 1941 until 1943, the panel had toured the country, holding hearings to investigate hiring complaints and issue recommendations. On 30 July 1943, President Roosevelt placed the FEPC under the jurisdiction of the War Manpower Commission (WMC), which, under the guise of national security, postponed all future public hearings. Angered, many civil rights leaders again went to the president, who, in his Executive Order 9346, again asserted the independence of the FEPC. By 1946, state fair employment practices (FEP) laws were in place in several states. When the FEPC went out of existence, it had settled peacefully some 40 racial strikes, resolved about 5,000 cases, and had held 15 national public hearings.

Fair Housing Act of 1968

The Fair Housing Act of 1968 was the landmark civil rights legislation passed by Congress and signed by President Johnson that ended all discriminatory practices in the selling and renting of land to blacks.

Farmer, James (1920–)

James Farmer is the noted civil rights leader who was active in the Fellowship of Reconciliation (FOR) and was the head of the Congress of Racial Equality (CORE) from 1961 to 1966. Farmer was born in 1920 in Marshall, Texas, where his father was a Methodist minister and his mother a teacher. He graduated from Wiley College in Marshall, then went on to study theology at Howard University in Washington, D.C. After receiving his degree from Howard, Farmer went to Chicago to help found the Fellowship of Reconciliation, based on the Gandhian principles of nonviolent protest against discrimination. In 1942, Farmer helped found the Congress of Racial Equality, which in many ways emulated but was more moderate than the Fellowship of Reconciliation. In 1947, FOR was sponsoring the first "freedom rides" of white and black civil rights workers in the South. Freedom rides became a key portion of CORE's program, testing segregation on buses in the South. In 1961, Farmer was named as the head of CORE. In 1963, he was jailed in Louisiana and missed the historic March on Washington for Jobs and Freedom.

By the late 1960s, CORE was riddled with strife among radicals and moderates in the civil rights movement. Farmer resigned and began teaching at Lincoln University in Pennsylvania and New York University. In 1968 he ran for Congress but lost to Shirley Chisholm. He served two years as assistant secretary of health, education and welfare in the Nixon administration.

The author of *Lay Bare the Heart: The Autobiography of the Civil Rights Movement*, Farmer began to lose his sight in the mid-1980s. Now totally blind, he teaches civil rights history at Mary Washington College in Fredericksburg, Virginia.

See also Congress of Racial Equality.

Fellowship of Reconciliation (FOR)
See Congress of Racial Equality.

Fifteenth Amendment (1870)
Enacted on 30 March 1870, the Fifteenth Amendment reads in part:

> The right of citizens of the United States to vote shall not be denied or abridged by the United States or by any state on account of race, color, or previous condition of servitude.

The amendment was enacted in response to many people's fears that, with former Confederates once again allowed in the Southern states to vote and to hold office, such rights would be denied to freed slaves. The amendment started out as a joint resolution, the intention of which was to provide for passage of an act protecting these rights for blacks.

Fifth Circuit Court of Appeals
The Fifth Circuit Court was, with the Supreme Court, the judicial bulwark against racial discrimination in the South. Originally based in Atlanta, the Court is now situated in New Orleans. From 1951, when Richard T. Rives was put on the Court, until 1979, when Joseph W. Hatchett became the first African American to serve on a court of appeals, the Fifth Circuit was a key battleground in the fight for civil rights.

Richard Taylor Rives (1895–1982), a native of Alabama and friend of Supreme Court Justice and former Ku Klux Klansman Hugo Black, was named to the Court by President Truman in 1951. Rives was from the old school of Southern politics, but his son, Richard T. Rives, Jr., a veteran of the Second World War, introduced his father to Gunnar Myrdal's *An American Dilemma*, which chronicled the injustice in the Jim Crow South through the eyes of a foreigner. One of Rives's first cases was *Beal v. Holcombe*, in which a black litigant sought to desegregate whites-only golf courses in Houston, Texas. Rives voted with the majority in opening up the courses. In other cases involving the "white primary" and desegregation of historically white schools, Rives was a champion of civil rights. He paid a heavy price for this opinion, however. His former preacher damned him from the pulpit, and his son's grave was vandalized. Rives retired from the Court in 1966. He died in 1982.

Elbert Parr Tuttle (1897–) was a native of California and Hawaii who moved to Atlanta in 1926 to open a law practice there. A combat hero in World War Two, he opposed segregation and Jim Crow, and so worked to reorganize the shattered Republican Party of Georgia. Although Democrats ruled the state, and a political office was out of the question, in 1954 Tuttle was named by President Eisenhower to the Fifth Circuit Court in Atlanta. Along with fellow Fifth Circuit Judges John Robert Brown (1909–), John Minor Wisdom (1905–), and Rives, the Fifth Circuit had four clear votes out of seven to overturn segregationist laws. This was done en masse in the late 1950s and early 1960s in dozens of cases—from school desegregation to the opening up of public accommodations. Said Claude Sitton, a *New York Times* reporter, "Those who think Martin Luther King desegregated the South don't know Elbert Tuttle and the record of the Fifth Circuit Court of Appeals."

In 1961, Griffin Boyette Bell joined the Fifth Circuit. Later Jimmy Carter's attorney general, Bell was more moderate in his civil rights views. He wrote several controversial decisions, including a refusal to order busing to achieve desegregation and upholding the right of the Georgia legislature to refuse to seat Julian Bond over his views on the Vietnam War. Over the next two decades, the Fifth Circuit Court included such jurists as William Homer Thornberry, who was denied a seat on the U.S. Supreme Court; James Plemon Coleman, a former governor of Mississippi with a spotty civil rights record; and Frank Minis Johnson, Jr.

Frank Johnson (1918–) was a judge of the Federal District Court for the Middle District of Alabama from 1955 to 1979. In 1955 he wrote the decision ruling that the Montgomery, Alabama, bus system, which had been featured in the Rosa Parks case, was in violation of the Fourteenth Amendment by having a segregated seating policy. Over the next two decades, Johnson wrote many civil rights opinions. A law school friend of George Wallace, the fiery segregationist governor of Alabama, Johnson faced down his former friend on more than one occasion. When he ordered Wallace to submit state voting records for inspection, Wallace turned them in through a third party, thus claiming that he had not buckled to Johnson. Years later, Wallace angrily called Johnson a "carpetbagging, scalawagging, integrating, baldfaced liar" for saying Wallace had been forced to submit the records to Johnson anyway. In 1977, President Carter tried to nominate Johnson to head the FBI, but health problems precluded Johnson's accepting the appointment. Two years later, however, Carter elevated Johnson to the Fifth Circuit. One of the court's most respected members, Johnson retired from his seat in 1993.

In 1979, Carter elevated Joseph W. Hatchett, the first black man on the Florida Supreme Court, to the Fifth Circuit. A volunteer for the National Association for the Advancement of Colored People (NAACP) Legal Defense Fund, as well as a U.S. attorney, Hatchett became one of the highest-ranking blacks in the American judiciary. In 1981, the Fifth Circuit was reorganized and moved to New Orleans, with one half becoming the Eleventh Circuit in Atlanta.

See also Bell, Griffin Boyette; Coleman, James Plemon; Johnson, Frank Minis, Jr.

Fleming, Harold Curtis (1922–1992)

Harold C. Fleming was a noted white civil rights activist who, as the leader of the Southern Regional Council (SRC), was called "one of the great figures of the New South." Fleming was born in Atlanta on 27 July 1922. In the late 1930s he enrolled at Harvard University, and for a time worked on the college paper, *The Crimson*. Fleming first learned of racial hatred during the Second World War, when he commanded an all-black regiment on Okinawa. He later said the experience "shocked" him. After the war, he graduated magna cum laude from Harvard. A year later he returned to Atlanta, where he became friends with Atlanta *Constitution* editor Ralph McGill. McGill told Fleming that the best place to direct his anger at segregation was in the Southern Regional Council. The council, a biracial research group that collected and disseminated data on civil rights, was at the time that Fleming joined it a moderate and at times meek organization. In his 14 years at the SRC, Fleming was key in its transformation into a radical voice in the call for civil rights legislation. Fleming's idea of a broad-based voter registration drive gave birth to the SRC's Voter Education Project (VEP). Fanning out all over the South, the VEP compiled statistics on blacks registering to vote and gave evidence in hundreds of voting rights lawsuits.

As well as his work at the SRC, Fleming was involved in the founding of the National Urban Coalition, and he served as deputy director of the United States Community Relations Service during the Johnson administration. In 1962, he founded the Potomac Institute, a non-profit research group that gave advice on combating racism to government agencies and private organizations. Fleming was the author of *Integration: North and South*, which, two years after the historic *Brown* decision, predicted a smooth road toward desegregated schools in the nation. Harold C. Fleming died at his home in Washington, D.C., on 4 September 1992, at the age of 70.

Florida

Florida was one of the 11 states of the Confederacy. Segregation of the schools was established by the 1885 state constitution, which stipulated that "white and colored children shall not be taught in the same school, but impartial provision shall be made for both." Florida's governors have been more tolerant of civil rights than their Southern counterparts. The beginning of the modern civil rights movement saw Fuller Warren (1905–1973) in office. He served from 1949 until 1953. Warren's key accomplishment in the field of civil rights was to send to the legislature a bill to unmask the Ku Klux Klan. His successor, Daniel Thomas McCarty (1912–1953), only served a single year in office, 1953, and never had a chance to make much of an imprint before dying of a heart attack. His replacement, State Senate President Charley Eugene Johns (1905–1990), could only finish McCarty's term before he was unseated. It was the next governor, Thomas LeRoy Collins (1909–1991), who broke the mold for Southern governors standing for segregation. At the height of the civil rights tumult enveloping the South, he asked the citizens of Florida to accept integration for the good of the state. In March 1960, during a vicious strike in Tallahassee, Collins went on television to deride white storeowners who segregated black customers in one part of their stores while allowing them to shop freely in others. After Collins, Cecil Farris Bryant (1914–) decried integration, but did nothing to stop its implementation statewide. His successors, Haydon Williams Burns (1912–) and Claude Roy Kirk (1926–) did little to stop or advance integration. The last governor of the civil rights era, Reuben O'Donovan Askew (1928–), appointed the first black man, Joseph W. Hatchett, to the Florida Supreme Court. According to the 1990 census, Florida had 10,749,285 whites, 1,759,534 blacks, and 429,107 people of other races.

See also Collins, Thomas LeRoy.

Ford, James William (1893–1957)

A black Communist leader during the 1920s and 1930s, Ford was the vice presidential candidate of the Communist party in 1932, 1936, and 1940. Ford was born James William Fourche in Pratt City, Alabama, a suburb of Birmingham, on 22 December 1893. He was the son of Lyman Fourche, a steelworker and coalminer, and Nancy Reynolds Fourche. Lyman Fourche's father was apparently lynched when James was a young boy; his grandfather's violent death made a great impression on him. According to Ford, the family name was changed when a white policeman stopped his father and, encountering difficulty in spelling his last name, said, "How do you spell it? Oh, never mind—we'll just make it a name you can pronounce, like F-O-R-D."

The newly named James Ford went to work on the railroad when he was 13 and continued to do odd jobs during his high school years. In 1913, he enrolled at Fisk University in Nashville, where he was noted for his athletic ability. Friends years later remembered Ford more as "Rabbit" Ford than for his political stands. In 1917, just short of his degree, he entered the army in order to fight in Europe. He was a member of the Signal Corps as a radio engineer in the 92nd Division, a segregated unit, and earned high praise for his work. Discharged honorably, he returned to Fisk and in 1920 earned his bachelor's degree.

After graduating, Ford landed in Chicago and found a job as a parcel post dispatcher when the government refused to hire him. He was later fired from the job because he tried to unionize his coworkers. In 1925, now a radical, he formed the American Negro Labor Congress, and joined the Communist party in 1926. In 1928, he was selected as a delegate to a party conference in Moscow and, as one of a handful of blacks in the party, was given wide recognition. He organized a conference of black workers in Germany, and edited *The Negro Worker* for a year. He returned to the United States in 1931, and a year later, at the Communist National Convention, was nominated for vice president of the United States, the first black to be so honored. (Frederick Douglass was nominated for vice president by the Equal Rights party in 1872, but he never accepted the nomination or campaigned.) He was also selected as the party's vice-presidential candidate in 1936 and 1940. In all, he earned some 210,000 votes.

In Harlem, Ford was involved as an organizer of boycotts against stores that refused to hire black workers. In 1933, he spoke out in favor of the Scottsboro Boys. As a friend of A. Philip Randolph, he dealt with the labor leader on matters relating to unions, including Randolph's Brotherhood of Sleeping Car Porters. In essence, he was a civil rights advocate before the start of the modern civil rights era.

James William Ford died on 21 July 1957, just a few years before Freedom Riders would travel into his native Alabama agitating for equality. Few histories of the civil rights movement mention his name.

Forrest, Nathan Bedford (1821–1877)

Nathan Bedford Forrest was a founder of the first rising of the Ku Klux Klan following the end of the Civil War. Forrest was born in Bedford County (now Marshall County), Tennessee, the son of a blacksmith. His father's death when he was 16 led Forrest to take charge of his large family. By slowly investing in land, and later in horses and slaves, he was a millionaire by 1845. In 1861, he enlisted in the Confederate army as a private but, because he paid for his own troops, he was commissioned as a lieutenant colonel. He saw action at the battles of Fort Donelson and Shiloh, where he was severely wounded. He was later promoted to major general. In April 1864 he commanded a force that captured Fort Pillow, Tennessee. After the fort's capture, his troops proceeded to murder some 250 black soldiers of the garrison. His report stated, "We bust the fort at ninerclock and scattered the niggers. The men are still killenem in the woods." After the war's conclusion, President Andrew Johnson, once governor of Tennessee, granted Forrest an unconditional pardon.

Just two years after the war, Forrest took the lead in organizing the nascent Exalted Knights of the Ku Klux Klan. He was eventually to become the Klan's Grand Wizard. Although some biographies have endeavored to gloss over Forrest's influence in the Klan, it is clear that he was the group's leader, and thus stood with its policy of harassing and killing freed slaves. In 1871, Forrest testified before a congressional committee investigating the Klan, telling them that the group "grew out of Southern insecurity. There was no political intention at all." His appearance before the committee ensured his freedom from jail. Later, Forrest claimed he had "lied like a gentleman" before the committee. After the Klan, he was involved in the construction and operation of the Selma, Marion & Memphis Railroad, a venture that, when it collapsed, precipitated his own financial ruin. Forrest died in Memphis on 29 October 1877, aged 56.

Fortune, Timothy Thomas (1856–1928)

T. Thomas Fortune was the first black journalist in the United States with a national following. Born into slavery in Marianna, Florida, he started his career by delivering newspapers and by training as a printer. After attending Howard University in Washington, D.C., Fortune went to New York, where, in 1880, he began work on the black tabloid *Rumor*. Later that year, the owner, George Parker, renamed the paper the New York *Globe*. Fortune, who with W. Walter Sampson made up the printing crew as well as Parker's partners, worked to turn the *Globe* into a money-maker. In 1884, though, he left to found the New York *Freeman*. In 1887, he renamed it the New York *Age*, and it became the first daily black newspaper in America. Fortune worked on the *Age* until he sold it in 1907. He later became a supporter of Marcus Garvey's Back to Africa program, and for a time wrote for Garvey's journal, *Negro World*. Fortune himself founded the National Afro-American League, a forerunner of the National Association for the Advancement of Colored People (NAACP) as a black protest organization, in 1890. In his later years, he suffered from mental illness. He died in obscurity in 1928. Today his name is barely recognized among scholars as the founder of the modern black press in America.

See also Black Newspapers.

Fourteenth Amendment (1868)

Enacted in July 1868, the Fourteenth Amendment was the second of the so-called "Reconstruction Amendments" passed by Congress in the years following the Civil War that enforced the end of slavery and protected the rights of free blacks. The amendment's first section, the one dealing with the enforcement of rights for freed slaves, reads:

> All persons born or naturalized in the United States and subject to the jurisdiction thereof, are citizens of the United States and of the state wherein they reside. No State shall make or enforce any law which shall abridge the privileges or immunities of citizens of the United States; nor shall any State deprive any person of life, liberty, or property, without due process of law; nor deny to any person within its jurisdiction the equal protection of the laws.

The other sections of the amendment deal with representation in Congress following the Southern rebellion and the validity of the debt incurred during the Civil War.

Frank v. Mangum (U.S., 1915)

Frank v. Mangum was the Supreme Court case in which Leo Frank, accused in the notorious murder of Mary Phagan, was refused a new trial. Frank, who was Jewish, was found guilty of the 1913 murder of Phagan, a young girl who worked at his pencil factory in Atlanta, Georgia. Although the evidence against him was sparse at best, a court found him guilty and sentenced him to death. Frank appealed his conviction on the grounds that the trial was conducted by mob rule, that his rights under the Fourteenth Amendment were violated, and that he was refused the right to be present when the verdict was read. Frank sued Mangum, the sheriff of Fulton County, Georgia. A state court held that all of Frank's appeal grounds contained no evidence, and refused him relief. Frank appealed to a district court that the conditions in the courtroom amounted to mob rule over law. The appeal was denied, and the Supreme Court granted *certiorari.* The Court ruled that in each of Frank's arguments, there were no grounds to reverse his conviction. Mob rule must be proven throughout a trial, not just at certain intervals, the Court said. Further, the Fourteenth Amendment did not preclude a state from denying a defendant the right to hear the verdict in his case. Frank was later granted a pardon by the governor of Georgia, but a terrorist group dubbed "The Knights of Mary Phagan," abducted him from jail and lynched him. These "Knights" later became the second rising of the Ku Klux Klan.

See also Ku Klux Klan; Watson, Thomas Edward.

Freedom Rides and Riders

Freedom rides were organized by civil rights activists to send white and black students throughout the South to fight against segregation on public transportation. The first freedom ride was a little-known affair arranged by the Fellowship of Reconciliation (FOR) in 1947. It drew little attention, and was quickly forgotten.

Following the Supreme Court's 1960 *Boynton* decision, which opened up segregated bus terminals, James Farmer issued a call for another freedom ride, this one to go through the South and end at New Orleans, marking the seventh anniversary of *Brown v. Board of Education.* Thirteen riders, black and white, left Washington, D.C., on 4 May. They encountered little resistance until they reached Alabama. In three cities there—Anniston, Birmingham, and Montgomery—the buses and their occupants were verbally abused, attacked by crowds, and firebombed. On 20 May, after the riders were attacked and beaten by a thousand rioting whites, President John F. Kennedy sent 350 federal marshals to protect the group as interstate travelers. The next day, while meeting in the Reverend Dr. Ralph

David Abernathy's church in Montgomery, they were for a time besieged by white protestors outside. On 23 May, the group arrived in Jackson, Mississippi, where the riders (including James Farmer) and several marshals were arrested for using a white restroom. There the ride ended. On 26 May, CORE announced that more freedom rides would take place. Throughout the rest of that summer, freedom rides took place along with freedom trains and freedom flights. Their goal, the desegregation of public transportation, was attained with passage of the 1964 Civil Rights Act.

See also Farmer, James.

Freeman et al. v. Pitts et al. (U.S., 1992)

In the *Freeman* case, the Supreme Court ruled that where school districts have made a complete, good-faith effort to undo segregation in schools with busing, but are still stymied by segregation in residential patterns, those school districts have no obligation to continue busing to correct the *de facto* segregation. Justice Anthony Kennedy wrote for a unanimous Court (on an 8–0 vote, as Justice Clarence Thomas did not participate), "With respect to those areas where compliance had been achieved, the District Court [of the Northern District of Georgia, which oversaw the desegregation of Georgia schools] did not find that DCSS [the Dekalb County, Georgia, School System] had acted in bad faith or engaged in further acts of discrimination since the desegregation plan went into effect."

Fullilove v. Klutznick (U.S., 1980)

Fullilove was the Supreme Court case in which the Court decided that Congress had the power to pass laws that made limited use of racial quotas to remedy past discrimination. The law, section 103(f)(2) of the Public Works Employment Act of 1977, stated, "No grant shall be made under this Act for any local public works project unless the applicant gives satisfactory assurance to the Secretary [of Commerce] that at least ten per centum of the amount of each grant shall be expended for minority business enterprises [MBE's]." Later in 1977, Fullilove, a New York contractor, sued to get relief from the act, which he claimed was discrimination in reverse. Two lower courts upheld the constitutionality of 103(f)(2), to which the Supreme Court granted review. The Court ruled, 6–3, that 103(f)(2) was constitutional on its face. Chief Justice Warren Burger delivered the majority opinion of the Court. "Any preference based on racial or ethnic criteria must necessarily receive a most searching examination to make sure that its does not conflict with constitutional guarantees. This case is one which requires, and which has received, that kind of examination. This opinion does not adopt, either expressly or implicitly, the formulas of analysis articulated in such cases as *University of California Regents v. Bakke* (1978). However, our analysis demonstrates that the MBE provision would survive judicial review under either 'test' articulated in the several Bakke opinions. The MBE provision does not violate the Constitution."

Garner et al. v. Louisiana (U.S., 1961)

The Supreme Court's ruling in *Garner et al. v. Louisiana* struck down the convictions of several sit-down protestors for "disturbing the peace." *Garner* was actually three cases combined into one: *Garner et al. v. Louisiana*, *Briscoe et al. v. Louisiana*, and *Hoston et al. v. Louisiana*. All three cases dealt with sit-down protests at the food counters at a Kress department store and a Sitman's drugstore in Baton Rouge, Louisiana, in March 1960. The facts of the case are these: In both sit-downs, the plaintiffs entered the establishments and sat down at segregated, whites-only food counters. They did not hold up placards, made no speeches, and did nothing to attract attention to themselves except sit quietly in their seats. The proprietors of both stores did not ask them to leave, but the police were called, and when the protestors refused their requests to leave, they were arrested. At trial, they were quickly convicted of "disturbing the peace," which the state defined as "the doing of specified violent, boisterous or disruptive acts and any other act in such a manner as to unreasonably disturb or alarm the public." Plaintiffs asked the state supreme court for relief, but were denied. They then sued to the U.S. Supreme Court. On 11 December 1961, the Court unanimously overturned the convictions. Chief Justice Earl Warren, writing for the Court, called the convictions "so totally devoid of evidentiary support as to violate the Due Process Clause of the Fourteenth Amendment."

Garvey, Marcus Mosiah (1887–1940)

Marcus Garvey was the Jamaican activist and founder of the Back to Africa movement, and the initiator of the Pan-Africanist Congress. Garvey was born on 17 August 1887, in St. Ann's Bay, on the northern coast of the island of Jamaica. His parents were of mixed African heritage, and his father was a poor stone mason. Garvey received some schooling in Jamaica, possibly including instruction at an Anglican grammar school. In 1901, he became a printer's apprentice and, three years later, was plying his trade in the slums of Kingston, the capital.

After an unsuccessful printer's strike disillusioned him with the impact black unions would have, Garvey traveled to Costa Rica, where he worked for a time for the United Fruit Company, then to Panama, where he worked for several newspapers. Upset at the treatment black workers received, he went to London, where he was educated at Birkbeck College. He was indoctrinated into the black rights movement while working for Egyptian nationalist Duse Mohammed Ali's Africa *Times* and reading Booker T. Washington's *Up From Slavery*. Fired up, Garvey returned home to Jamaica and founded, on 1 August 1914, the Universal Negro Improvement and Conservation Association and African Communities League (better known as the Universal Negro Improvement Association, or the UNIA). The group's aims were to encourage black racial pride, to discuss ways to improve black self-worth, to create new opportunities to enrich black education, and to encourage recognition of Africa as the homeland of black people everywhere and urge a return to the continent.

Garvey's first foray into the education area, a trade school in Jamaica modeled after Booker T. Washington's Tuskegee Institute, failed miserably. Garvey then brought his message to the United States. Unfortunately, he arrived just months after the death of Washington and was

Marcus Mosiah Garvey

forced to travel the nation alone. He started publishing *The Negro World* in 1918, as a way to advance his views. From his headquarters in Liberty Hall in Harlem, New York, Garvey saw the UNIA movement grow to several hundred thousand members in the United States and abroad in just a few years. His Black Star Line, a fleet of ships that would link blacks worldwide with Africa, and his Negro Factories Corporation, which raised capital for struggling black businesses, were minor successes but raised the hopes of Garvey's followers. In 1920, a UNIA conference held in New York named Garvey president of all of Africa in exile.

Garvey's world fell apart in 1923. He was arrested for mailing fraudulent advertisements for the Black Star Line, which had become a financial boondoggle. Convicted of fraud, he was sentenced to prison. Originally released pending appeal, he entered federal prison in Atlanta in 1925, when the appeal failed. In November 1927, President Calvin Coolidge pardoned Garvey, but he was

deported to Jamaica. Over the next 13 years, Garvey's followers in the United States tried to have his deportation order nullified so that he could reenter the country, but without success. His most strident supporter in this effort was black congressman Oscar Stanton De Priest of Illinois. Even with a Democrat, Franklin D. Roosevelt, in the White House, De Priest was unable to arrange for Garvey's return to the United States. De Priest was still working for Garvey's reentry when the Jamaican activist died after suffering a stroke in London, England, on 10 June 1940.

See also Universal Negro Improvement Association.

Georgia

One of the 11 Confederate states, Georgia was among the most staunch in its opposition to civil rights. In its state constitution, Georgia had a provision passed during Reconstruction that read, "separate schools shall be provided for white and colored." The modern civil rights period in Georgia's government started with Herman Eugene Talmadge (1913–), whose father, Eugene, had also been governor. Talmadge, who was governor from 1947 to 1955, was a champion of the segregationist line. He was a strong leader as governor and, later, as a noted U.S. senator, in the fight against civil rights. His successor, Melvin Ernest Thompson (1903–), was one of the more liberal Southern governors of his era, yet he never pushed for civil rights legislation to be passed. Following Thompson, however, was a succession of segregationist governors: Samuel Marvin Griffin (1907–1990), Samuel Ernest Vandiver (1918–), Carl E. Sanders (1925–), and Lester Garfield Maddox (1915–)—the last three particularly noted as radical Southern spokesmen for the continuance of segregation. It was Lester Maddox, owner of a barbecue restaurant, who chased blacks from his establishment with an axe in 1964, when they tried to sit down. He

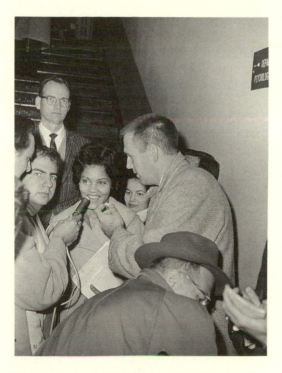

The press interviews University of Georgia student Charlayne Hunter, the first black student to enroll, 11 January 1961.

later closed the business rather than admit black customers.

It took the inauguration of James Earl "Jimmy" Carter in 1971 to change Georgia's attitude and laws. Carter, from rural Georgia, had grown up segregated from black people but reached out to the black community by attending black churches and meeting black voters. As governor, he supported the legislature in passing civil rights legislation that brought the state in line with the rest of the country. According to the 1990 census, Georgia had 4,600,148 whites, 1,746,565 blacks, and 131,503 people of other races.

Georgia v. Stanton (U.S., 1868)

The second Supreme Court challenge to the Reconstruction Acts passed by Congress, *Georgia v. Stanton* was dismissed by the Court on the grounds that the argument was a political question, not one of constitutionality. Justice Samuel

Nelson wrote for a unanimous Court (Chief Justice Salmon Portland Chase wrote a separate, but concurring, opinion) when he struck down the state of Georgia's argument that Reconstruction would deprive the state the use of public buildings, insisting that to deprive meant to destroy, not take over for a limited period of time. A third challenge to the Reconstruction Acts, *Ex Parte McCardle*, dealt with a publisher printing what some military authorities considered libelous matter in Reconstruction areas.

See also Mississippi v. Johnson.

Gibson v. Mississippi (U.S., 1896)

The Supreme Court decision in *Gibson*, while holding that a lack of blacks on a jury did not taint a conviction, also held that preventing blacks from serving on a jury strictly because of their race was a violation of the Fourteenth Amendment. Plaintiff John Gibson, a black man, was indicted in Washington County, Mississippi, for murder. Under Mississippi law, jurors had to be male, freeholders, citizens, of a certain age, and with certain educational attainments. Gibson requested a mixed jury of white and black, but he received an all-white panel. He was convicted of murder and sentenced to death. He and his lawyers appealed on the grounds that his rights were violated by not having any blacks on the jury. When the Supreme Court of Mississippi affirmed the judgment, Gibson sued to the U.S. Supreme Court. The Court held, on 13 April 1896, that if blacks had been excluded from Gibson's trial by law, then his conviction must not stand. However, as Justice John Marshall Harlan, who wrote the dissenting opinion in *Plessy v. Ferguson*, opined: "We recognize the possession of all these rights by the defendant; but upon a careful consideration of all the points of which we can take cognizance ... we cannot find from the record before us that his rights secured by the supreme law of the land were violated by the trial court or disregarded by the highest court of Mississippi. . . . The judgment is, therefore, affirmed."

Gomillion v. Lightfoot (U.S., 1960)

Gomillion was a key Supreme Court case in which an act of the Alabama legislature that defined voting boundaries based on race was struck down as unconstitutional. In 1957, the Alabama legislature redrew the boundaries of the City of Tuskegee so that the city included whites but excluded blacks. Charles Gomillion sued Tuskegee Mayor Phil Lightfoot for relief from the act, labeled number 140. Both a district court and a federal appeals court dismissed Gomillion's suit, but the Supreme Court decided to review the statute. It ruled, unanimously, that the statute was unconstitutional. Justice Felix Frankfurter, writing for the Court, said: "Such state power . . . is met and overcome by the Fifteenth Amendment . . . which forbids a state from passing a law which deprives a citizen of his vote because of his race."

Gong Lum et al. v. Rice et al. (U.S., 1927)

Gong Lum is the little-known Supreme Court case in which the practice of sending Oriental children to segregated schools with black children was upheld as constitutional. Gong Lum was a Chinese mercantile businessman in Mississippi. He wanted to send his daughter, Martha, to school in the Rosedale Consolidated High School District. Upon learning that Martha was Chinese, the school board sent her to a segregated school attended by black students only. Gong Lum sued Rice, who was the school superintendent, and the school board for violating his daughter's rights of equal protection under the Fourteenth Amendment. A lower court agreed, ordering that Martha be allowed to attend school with whites. The Mississippi Supreme Court, however, ruled that section 207 of the state constitution—"Separate schools shall be maintained for children of the white and colored races"—dealt with Martha Lum, as she was of the "Mongolian, or yellow race." Gong Lum sued to the U.S. Supreme Court. On 21 November 1927, the Court held in a unanimous decision that classifying Martha as "of the yellow race," and thus "colored," allowed the school board to send her to a separate school. Chief Justice William Howard Taft wrote the Court's opinion.

Goodman, Andrew (1943–1964)

Andrew Goodman was one of three civil rights workers murdered by the Ku Klux Klan near Philadelphia, Mississippi, in 1964. Goodman was born in New York City on 23 November 1943, the son of well-to-do liberal Jewish parents. From the time he was three until he was 18, Goodman attended an exclusive Jewish private educational institution, the Walden School.

In December 1958, Andrew Goodman got his first taste of social activism, when he and a friend traveled in some poorer sections of West Virginia. After a short stint at the University of Wisconsin, Goodman dropped out, only to enroll at Queens College in New York. It was at this time, 1963, that he became involved heavily in the civil rights movement. The events of the time shaped this move. Activist William Moore was murdered in Alabama. Medgar Evers was assassinated in Mississippi. And in November, President Kennedy was cut down in Dallas. In early 1964, Goodman joined the Mississippi Summer Project (MSP). Headquartered in Jackson, Mississippi, the MSP sent thousands of northern college students to perform civil rights work in Southern states. The project grouped together Goodman with 21-year-old James Earl Chaney, a black youth from Mississippi, and 24-year-old Michael Henry Schwerner of New York. Like Goodman, Schwerner was Jewish.

Andrew Goodman

Chaney and Schwerner were based in Meridian, Mississippi. Goodman joined them there on 20 June 1964. The next day, in nearby Neshoba County, a group of black parishioners was attacked and their church burned down by a group of Klansmen. Returning to Meridian following the investigation, the three men vanished somewhere near the town of Philadelphia, Mississippi. Two days later, their car was found in a canal, but the three men were missing. An intensive search followed, which culminated in the discovery of their bodies on 4 August. The three had been shot and their bodies dumped in a pit next to an earthen dam.

The murders of Goodman, Schwerner, and Chaney shocked the nation. Their murderers were later brought to justice and convicted. Today, the names of the three civil rights workers stand next to those of other martyrs of the civil rights movement.

See also Chaney, James Earl; Schwerner, Michael Henry.

Goss et al. v. Board of Education of Knoxville, Tennessee, et al. (U.S., 1963)

Goss was the Supreme Court case in which "voluntary student transfer plans" were held to be unconstitutional. Black students and their parents brought suit against the Knoxville, Tennessee, School Board, after the board's desegregation plan allowed for white students to stay in segregated schools if they chose. These so-called "voluntary student transfer plans" were approved by the trial court that looked at the desegregation plan, as well as the Court of Appeals for the Sixth Circuit. The black students appealed to the U.S. Supreme Court. The high court held that such transfer plans were unconstitutional. Writing for the Court, Justice Tom Clark opined: "Insofar as they approve such transfer provisions, the judgments of the Court of Appeals are reversed, since such transfer plans are based on racial factors which inevitably would lead towards segregation of students by race, contrary to this Court's admonition in *Brown v. Board of Education.*"

Granger, Lester Blackwell (1896–1976)

The third executive secretary of the National Urban League was the noted social worker and civil rights activist Lester Granger. Granger was born on 16 September 1896 in Newport News, Virginia, the son of William Randolph Granger, a native of Barbados, and Mary Turpin, a school teacher. William Granger was a former cabin boy who jumped ship, came to America, enrolled in Bucknell University and the University of Vermont, and emerged from college with a degree in medicine. Five of his six sons (Lester Granger excluded) later followed in their father's footsteps and went on to earn medical degrees and to practice medicine. When the eldest Granger son had finished seventh grade—the highest grade a black child could legally reach in Newport News schools—the family moved to Newark, New Jersey. Lester Granger followed five of his brothers and enrolled in Dartmouth University. After graduating with a bachelor's degree, he decided to become a lawyer, and applied at Harvard University Law School. America entered the First World War at this time, and Granger volunteered for the army. While most black troops were in service or support units, Granger was at the battlefront, serving as a field artillery sergeant in the American Expeditionary Force's 92nd Division in France.

When he returned from overseas, Granger gave up on his plans for law school and instead took a job in the industrial relations department of the Newark chapter of the National Urban League. "I didn't know what it was all about," he later confessed in an interview, "and after seven months I resigned—to the politely concealed relief of my superior." He spent the next two years teaching at two North Carolina schools (Slater Normal School in Winston and St. Augustine College in Raleigh), before taking some graduate courses at New York University. In 1922, Granger was hired as an extension worker (a type of counselor and teacher) at the State Manual Training School in Bordentown, New Jersey. For the next 12 years, he was the school's counselor, organizer, and athletic coach. While at the school he met Harriett Lane, who worked as the school bookkeeper, and they married in 1923. At Bordentown, Granger became interested in social work. He took some courses at the New York School for Social Work. Then, in 1930, he took a year's leave and organized the Urban League chapter in Los Angeles. In 1934, he left Bordentown to join the staff of the National Urban League in New York as the business manager of the league's organ, *Opportunity*.

Granger headed up the Workers' Education Bureau for four years, then took a two-year leave of absence from the National Urban League in 1938 to serve as secretary of the New York City Welfare Council. In 1940, he returned to the league and was appointed assistant executive secretary. In 1941, when the league's executive secretary, Eugene Jones, retired, Granger was chosen as his successor. Granger served as head of the league from 1941 until his retirement in October 1961. In those 20 years, he spearheaded the movement to end racial segregation in the armed forces. He joined with A. Philip Randolph of the Brotherhood of Railroad Porters, as well as other black leaders, to demand that President Franklin D. Roosevelt end segregation in the workplace. Roosevelt complied and issued Executive Order 8802 in 1941, which created the Fair Employment Practices Committee (FEPC).

In 1945, Granger was made an assistant to Navy Secretary James Forrestal to combat racial discrimination in the military. "Our most important work lies in two fields: community relations and industrial relations," Granger told the New York *Post* on 8 May 1945. The National Urban League's Department of Industrial Relations developed a program in 1949 that placed blacks in jobs once closed to them.

Granger retired as head of the National Urban League in October 1961. He was named president of the International Conference of Social Work, the first American to hold that post. In 1965, he began a series of professorships at several universities, ending with a stint as the first Edgar B. Stern professor at Dillard University in New Orleans, Louisiana. It was in Alexandria, Louisiana, that Granger was felled by a fatal heart attack on 9 January 1976. He was 71 years old.

See also Fair Employment Practices Committee; National Urban League.

Green v. New Kent County School Board (U.S., 1968)

Green was the Supreme Court case that struck down Freedom of Choice attendance plans as unconstitutional. Freedom of Choice, hailed by some as an answer to the locking in of students to a particular neighborhood school, was seen by Green, the plaintiff, as causing segregation. The Supreme Court struck down the school board's order as violating the equal protection clause of the Fourteenth Amendment. For the first time, the Court looked not at what the school board intended but at what effect its actions created. Justice William Brennan wrote for the majority, "The burden on the school board today is to come forward with a plan that promises realistically to work now." *Green* and *Alexander v. Holmes County Board of Education* were the last of the historic school desegregation cases to be decided by the Warren Court.

Griffin et al. v. Breckinridge et al. (U.S., 1971)

Griffin et al. was the Supreme Court case in which the high court determined that individuals can be prosecuted for violating civil rights laws even if they act independently of "state action." The plaintiffs were two black men, Eugene Griffin and R. G. Grady, who were traveling through Mississippi in their automobile. James Calvin Breckinridge, a white Mississippian, and his cohorts in this suit attacked the black men, believing that they were civil rights workers. According to the complaint, the two black men were forced from the road, threatened at gunpoint, and severely beaten. Later, they asked a court to find their attackers guilty under 42 U.S.C. section 1985(3), which reads: "If two or more persons conspire or go in disguise on the highway or on the premises of another, for the purposes of depriving any person or class of persons the equal protection of the laws, or of equal privileges and immunities under the laws the party so injured or deprived may have a cause of action against the conspirators."

The District Court in Mississippi dismissed the complaint against Breckinridge et al. on the grounds that there was "a failure to state a cause of action." The court relied on *Collins v. Hardyman* (U.S., 1951), in which the Supreme Court ruled that an action had to be backed by the state, or to have been commanded by a state official, to sustain a charge of conspiracy to deprive another of equal protection of the laws. The plaintiffs sought relief from the Fifth Circuit Court of Appeals, which affirmed the lower court ruling. Griffin sued to the U.S. Supreme Court. On 7 June 1971, the Court in effect overruled its decision in *Collins* and found that violence could be perpetrated without the color of state action. In his opinion, Justice Potter Stewart found that under section 2 of the Thirteenth Amendment, as well as under its power to protect interstate travel, Congress was within its jurisdiction to pass 42 U.S.C. 1985(3).

Griffin v. County School Board of Prince Edward County (U.S., 1964)

The *Griffin* case tested the power of the Court to open schools closed by a school board intent on disobeying a desegregation order. This case started in 1951, when the plaintiffs began their lawsuit, and ended in 1964. When the order came down from the Supreme Court in 1954 in the *Brown* decision that the schools of Prince Edward County, Virginia, were to be desegregated, the school board refused to appropriate any monies to operate the public schools, even though a private foundation was funding whites-only schools. Other schools in the state remained open. This situation lasted until 1961, when a court ordered the private foundation to cease funding the whites-only schools. The Fourth Circuit Court of Appeals reversed on narrow grounds, claiming that the funding should stop only when the desegregation matter was settled in the state courts. The plaintiffs, black school children, sued to the U.S. Supreme Court. The Court ruled that because the school board's action was based on race, it was violating the equal protection clause of the Fourteenth Amendment and, further, that the district court had the right to try to stop this violation.

Griggs v. Duke Power Company (U.S., 1971)

In the case of *Griggs v. Duke Power Company* the Supreme Court rejected racial preferences in employment and hiring through the use of personnel testing.

The plaintiff in *Griggs* was a black employee of the Duke Power Company's Dan River Steam Station near Draper, North Carolina. As a condition of employment or to transfer to another job at the station, all employees, white and black, were required to have a high school education and to take a standardized employment test. Griggs sued under Title VII of the 1964 Civil Rights Act, which prohibits discrimination against employees because of their race, to have these conditions removed, as they discriminated against blacks. The District Court found that although there had been discrimination at the plant before the passage of the 1964 Civil Rights Act, such discrimination had been removed. It found that Title VII did not preclude an employer from using tests as a condition of employment. The Court of Appeals upheld the judgment that Title VII did not cover testing. The Supreme Court granted *certiorari*. On 8 March 1971, the Court held 8-0 (Justice William Brennan did not participate) that such personnel tests, unless reasonably demonstrated by an employer to be "substantially related to job performance," violated Title VII of the 1964 Civil Rights Act.

See also Civil Rights Act of 1964.

Grovey v. Townsend (U.S., 1935)

Grovey was the Supreme Court case in which the high court upheld the so-called "white primary," a primary election in which only whites were allowed to vote. Plaintiff Grovey, a black man, wished to vote in the Democratic primary held in Texas on 28 July 1934. Townsend, a county voting clerk, refused him a ballot because "he was of the negro race." Grovey immediately demanded a fine of $10 because of the violation of his rights; later he sued in a justice's court. The court found no action for his fine; the Texas Supreme Court further found that the Democratic Party was a separate body from the state, and as such could hold elections and allow whomever it wished to vote in them. Grovey sued to the U.S. Supreme Court. Justice Owen Roberts wrote for the Court, which upheld the Democratic primary as lacking in state action. "In Texas, [while] nomination by the Democratic Party is equivalent to election, and exclusion from the primary virtually disenfranchises the voter ... [this] does not ... make out a forbidden discrimination in this case."

Guinn and Beal v. United States (U.S., 1915)

Guinn was one of two companion Supreme Court cases in 1915 that struck down grandfather clauses as unconstitutional. Under section 1, article 3 of the Oklahoma constitution, suffrage was guaranteed; however, in an amendment passed in 1910, all those whose grandfathers had voted in 1865 could vote—others could not. This made it possible for blacks, whose suffrage was guaranteed by the Fifteenth Amendment in 1866, to be refused the right to vote. Guinn and Beal were state elections officers who, in 1910, put into effect this amendment and refused all blacks the right to vote. The United States sued the two men under what is now 42 U.S.C. 1985(3), under which conspiracies to deprive others of their civil rights were violations punishable by fines. The Supreme Court heard this case in 1913 but did not issue an opinion until two years later. Chief Justice Edward Douglass White, a former Confederate officer, wrote in the Court's decision upholding Guinn and Beal's conviction: "While the Fifteenth Amendment gives no right of suffrage, as its command is self-executing, rights of suffrage may be enjoyed by reason of the striking out of discriminations against the exercise of the right .The so-called Grandfather Clause of the amendment to the constitution of Oklahoma of 1910 is void because it violates the Fifteenth Amendment to the Constitution of the United States."

See also Lane v. Wilson et al.; Myers and Others v. Anderson.

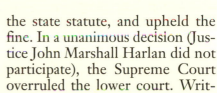

Hale v. Commonwealth of Kentucky (U.S., 1938)

In the case of *Hale v. Commonwealth of Kentucky*, the Supreme Court held the systematic exclusion of blacks from jury lists because of their race to be a denial of a defendant's, as well as a potential juror's, rights under the equal protection clause of the Fourteenth Amendment. The case involved Hale, a black man, who was indicted in McCracken County, Kentucky, on the charge of murder. Hale's attorney moved to have the indictment dismissed because, of the approximately 600 names put in a tumbler for selection of grand jurors, none were of blacks, although blacks made up one-eighth of the county's citizenry. The court hearing the trial rejected Hale's motion, proceeded with the trial, found him guilty, and sentenced him to death. The Kentucky Court of Appeals upheld the sentence. Charles H. Houston, the noted black attorney, represented Hale before the U.S. Supreme Court. On 11 April 1938, the Court unanimously found that there was a systematic exclusion of blacks from the grand jury. The Court ruled that this taint demanded that Hale's conviction be set aside.

Hall v. DeCuir (U.S., 1878)

In the case of *Hall v. DeCuir*, the Supreme Court struck down a state statute that called for "equal rights and privileges" for all races in public travel. When a black man was segregated on a steamboat traveling between New Orleans, Louisiana, and Vicksburg, Mississippi, the state of Louisiana fined the steamboat line for breaking its antisegregation law. The line sued to a Louisiana state court, which found that the action of the line violated the state statute, and upheld the fine. In a unanimous decision (Justice John Marshall Harlan did not participate), the Supreme Court overruled the lower court. Writing for the Court, Chief Justice Morrison Remick Waite wrote that interstate travel could be regulated only by Congress, and it must make such rules binding to all states, not selected ones. "Commerce cannot flourish in the midst of such embarrassments," Waite wrote. Twelve years later, however, in *Louisville, New Orleans & Texas Railway v. Mississippi*, the Court would allow a state to act without Congress in enforcing a prosegregation statute.

See also Louisville, New Orleans & Texas Railway v. Mississippi.

Hamer, Fannie Lou Townsend (1917–1977)

An outspoken female black civil rights activist who worked to register black voters in Mississippi, Fannie Lou Hamer was a heroine in the ranks of those who strove for equal rights. Born in poverty as the youngest of 20 children of a sharecropper who was formerly a slave, Fannie Lou Townsend started working on her family's farm when she turned six. She received a total of six years of formal education, then, in 1945, married Perry "Pap" Hamer, a young black man who at one time worked on the same plantation as the Townsends. Fannie and Pap adopted two children, one of whom died of malnutrition, a victim of the poverty that held that section of the nation in its grasp.

Fannie Lou Hamer became politicized in 1961, when she entered a hospital to have a uterine tumor removed. Upon awakening from what should have been a minor operation, she was told that she had accidentally been given a hysterectomy. The next year, she complied with the request that she register to vote, but failed the state literacy test and was denied the right to vote. Angered at being denied the vote, she attended a freedom rally in her home town and joined the Student Nonviolent Coordinating Committee (SNCC) to register black voters in Sunflower County, Mississippi. During the course of the next several years, she was beaten and jailed for standing in a whites-only line at a bus station and became one of the founding members of the Mississippi Freedom Democratic Party, an offshoot of the national Democratic Party. The Freedom Democratic Party was used unsuccessfully by civil rights workers as a vehicle to deny recognition to the regular all-white state delegation to the Democratic National Convention in 1964; however, they succeeded in replacing the state delegation at the 1968 convention in Chicago.

As a black woman, Fannie Lou Hamer was a standout in a field dominated by men. She remained close to her roots, never leaving rural Ruleville, Mississippi, where she rented a small apartment. Hamer was considered a leading voice in the civil rights movement during the 15 years she struggled to reform the South. She succumbed to breast cancer on 14 March 1977.

Haralson, Jeremiah (1846–1916?)

Jeremiah Haralson, a former slave, served as Alabama's first black member in the U.S. House of Representatives. Few records of his life exist. Born into slavery on a plantation near Columbus, in Muscogee County, Georgia, on 1 April 1846, Haralson was self-educated. There is no record of his original owner; however, historical evidence shows that, in 1859, he was sold to one John Haralson and taken to Alabama, where he remained as

Haralson's property until emancipation in 1865. What little is recorded about Jeremiah Haralson's early life shows that after the Civil War, he became a farmer and may have been ordained a minister.

In 1868, as a former slave with little education living in a former slave state, Haralson made his first try at elected office, the U.S. House of Representatives. He failed in this first attempt, but in 1870 ran as an independent candidate for the Alabama House of Representatives and defeated the Republican incumbent. Two years later, Haralson was elected by the citizens of the Twenty-first Alabama District as their state senator. During his years in the state House of Representatives and senate, Haralson moved from independent to Republican. In 1872, he called on Liberal Republicans to repudiate their breakaway nomination of Horace Greeley for president and to instead support Ulysses S. Grant. In 1874, Haralson ran for a seat in the U.S. House of Representatives as a regular Republican against incumbent Liberal Republican Frederick G. Bromberg, and won. Although Bromberg contested the election, a House committee sided with Haralson.

Jeremiah Haralson served only a single term in the House, the Forty-fourth Congress, from 1875 until 1877. He called for amnesty for all former Confederate officers and soldiers, for federal financial relief of a medical college in his home state, and for the use of funds from the sale of public lands to enhance educational funding. In 1876, he ran as an independent in a three-way race against the black former Representative James Thomas Rapier, who had won the Republican nomination, and Charles M. Shelley, a white Democrat. The split in the Republican vote gave the election to Shelley. Two years later, Haralson challenged Shelley alone, but was defeated.

In 1878, Haralson was appointed as a United States customs inspector in Baltimore, a post he held until 1882. He was then named as a clerk in the Interior Department, and later to a position in the Pension Bureau in Washington. Haralson left these governmental jobs in 1884. He moved to Louisiana, where he went back to farming, and then to Arkansas in 1904, where he served for a short time as a pension agent. He returned to Alabama in 1912, then wandered west to Oklahoma and Colorado. His death is shrouded in mystery. In 1916, while working as a miner near Denver, he was supposedly killed by wild beasts, although there were no witnesses and his body was never found. Whether or not this did in fact happen, Jeremiah Haralson vanished, never to be heard from again.

Harlan, John Marshall (1833–1911)

John Marshall Harlan is best noted for his strongly worded dissent from the Supreme Court's majority opinion in the 1883 Civil Rights Cases, as well as his dissent in *Plessy v. Ferguson* in 1896. He is sometimes identified as "the Elder" to distinguish him from his grandson, also named John Marshall Harlan, who served on the Supreme Court from 1957 to 1971. Harlan was born in Boyle County, Kentucky, on 1 June 1833, and was named by his father after the great jurist and Supreme Court chief justice John Marshall. Although at one time a conservative on matters such as the right to own slaves (which he did at one time), during the first 30 years of his life Harlan seemed to move away from a slaveowners' rights stance. In the final turn from his youth, Harlan served in the Union army during the Civil War. From 1863 until 1867, he served as the attorney general of Kentucky. Twice, in 1871 and 1875, he was the Republican nominee for governor of Kentucky. In 1872, his name was presented before the Republican National Convention as a candidate for the vice presidency, although he received few votes. In 1877, because of his support of

Republican Rutherford B. Hayes for president, Harlan was appointed an associate justice of the U.S. Supreme Court, to succeed the retiring David Davis. In his 34 years on the Court, Harlan was a vigorous dissenter, as exemplified by his caustic protests against the striking down of the 1875 Civil Rights Act, and the upholding of the doctrine of "separate but equal" in the infamous *Plessy v. Ferguson* decision in 1896. In 1908, in the last strong dissent before his death, he dissented in the *Berea College v. Commonwealth of Kentucky* case, in which the Court upheld the right of states to segregate educational institutions. Harlan once remarked, "Let it be said that I am right rather than consistent." He died of bronchitis at his Washington, D.C., home on 14 October 1911.

See also Berea College v. Commonwealth of Kentucky; "Civil Rights Cases"; Plessy v. Ferguson.

Harman v. Forssenius (U.S., 1965)

One of the Warren Court's lesser-known decisions in the area of civil rights was the ruling in which a state government's attempt to impose a poll tax before passage of the Twenty-fourth Amendment to the Constitution, which eventually prohibited such fees, was held to be unconstitutional. The case, coming just two years before passage of the Twenty-fourth Amendment, was a closely watched litigation. The case was actually three different Virginia cases melded into one; in the chief case, plaintiff Harman, a black voter, sued Forssenius, a state elections worker, to get relief from paying a poll tax that was obviously going to become illegal under the pending Twenty-fourth Amendment. A district court found that several issues involved in the state attempt to impose a poll tax made the law illegal; on 27 April 1965, the Supreme Court affirmed that decision. Writing for the Court, Chief Justice Earl Warren wrote simply: "The poll tax is abolished absolutely as a prerequisite for voting in federal elections, and no equivalent or milder substitute may be imposed."

See also Harper et al. v. Virginia State Board of Elections et al.

Harper et al. v. Virginia State Board of Elections et al. (U.S., 1966)

Less than a year after the Supreme Court held the poll tax to be unconstitutional in *Harman v. Forssenius*, the Court was faced with a similar case in *Harper*. The appellants in this matter, black Virginia residents, asked a state district court to strike down a state poll tax as discriminatory. The lower court refused. The Supreme Court on review ruled 8–1 (Justice Hugo Black dissenting) that the poll tax violated the equal protection clause of the Fourteenth Amendment. The Court's opinion declared: "Fee payments or wealth, like race, creed and color, are unrelated to the citizen's ability to participate intelligently in the electoral process .Once the franchise is granted to the electorate, lines which determine who may vote may not be drawn so as to cause invidious discrimination."

See also Harman v. Forssenius.

George Edmund Haynes

Haynes, George Edmund (1880–1960)

The first executive secretary of the National Urban League was a sociologist who was the first African American to earn a doctorate from Columbia University. Haynes was born in Pine Bluff, Arkansas, on 11 May 1880. He attended local schools, then enrolled at Fisk University in Tennessee, from which he received his bachelor's degree. He then went to Yale University on a scholarship, where he earned his master's degree. After Yale, he served as the student secretary to the Colored Men's Department of the International Committee of the YMCA, then spent the summers of 1906 and 1907 studying sociology at the Uni-

versity of Chicago. His interest in that work led him to New York, where in 1910 he graduated from the New York School of Social Work. In 1912, Haynes made black history when he earned a doctorate of philosophy from Columbia University.

Concern about the social conditions that blacks were experiencing led Haynes to cofound the National Committee on Urban Conditions Among Negroes (CUCAN) in 1910 with Mrs. Ruth Standish Baldwin, the widow of the founder of the Long Island Railroad, and Dr. Edwin R. A. Seligman, Haynes's professor of economics at Columbia. Haynes was named as the committee's first executive secretary, a post he held until 1911. He also served as chairman of the Department of Economics and Sociology at Fisk University. In his service to CUCAN, which later became the National Urban League, Haynes provided social workers to aid in black migration and settlement, established, in the area of education, goals for black children with the founding of the Association of Colleges for Negro Youth, and worked to create the Fisk University Bethlehem Training Center, which aided blacks in social service training.

In 1918, Haynes left the Urban League to head the United States Department of Labor's Division of Negro Economics. In 1920, he took on additional duties in helping the Department of Labor's Children's Bureau stop child labor. In 1921, he was also named to the President's Unemployment Conference. In 1922, he took a post as executive secretary of the Department of Race Relations of the Federal Council of Churches of Christ in America, a job he held until 1947. He then took a job teaching at New York College. He retired in 1956, due to poor health. George Edmund Haynes died four years later on 8 January 1960. He was 79 years old.

See also National Urban League; Seligman, Edwin Robert Anderson.

Heard v. Georgia Railroad Company (1888)

Heard was one of the Interstate Commerce Commission's (ICC) first cases dealing with discrimination on the basis of race in interstate travel. William H. Heard, a black man, purchased a first-class ticket on the Georgia Railroad Company for passage from Cincinnati, Ohio, to Charleston, South Carolina. When he went to board the train in Cincinnati, he was told by a conductor that the railroad did not allow blacks in the first class car, and Heard was asked to ride in what was called the "Jim Crow car." This compartment was in fact the smoking car. According to Heard's complaint, the car was "dirty, and dirty railroad hands with their tools and baggage" were allowed to ride in the car. Heard later filed a complaint with the ICC, asking that such separate

accommodation rules be set aside as being in violation of section 3 of the Interstate Commerce Act of 4 February 1887.

After a hearing, the ICC ruled that such separate and unequal accommodations were a violation of section 3. Wrote the commission: "Passengers paying the same fare upon the same railroad train, whether white or colored, are entitled to equality of transportation, in respect to the character of the cars in which they travel, and the comforts and conveniences supplied . . . by requiring the petitioner who had paid a first class fare to ride in a half car set aside for colored passengers, with accommodations and comforts inferior to the car for white passengers in the same train who paid the same fare. . . . The Georgia Railroad Company subjected him to undue and unreasonable prejudice and disadvantage, in violation of the third section of the Act to Regulate Commerce."

Heart of Atlanta Motel v. United States (U.S., 1964)

The right of interstate travel as guaranteed by the Constitution was the subject of this controversial case, in which it was held that the public accommodations clause of the 1964 Civil Rights Act, making interstate travel a constitutional right, was itself constitutional. The owners of the Heart of Atlanta Motel on Peachtree Street in Atlanta, Georgia, were ordered by the U.S. government under Title II of the 1964 Civil Rights Act to admit black guests to the hotel, which they refused to do. The owners then sued the government to obtain relief from carrying out the order. Title II of the act prohibited racial discrimination in places of public accommodation in which interstate travelers were served. The owners argued that such a clause in the 1875 Civil Rights Act had been struck down by the Court in 1883 as being an infringement of the commerce clause, article 1, section 8, of the Constitution. Justice Tom Clark read the opinion of a unanimous Court in upholding Title II of the 1964 Civil Rights Act. He denied that the section was a denial of due process of law, and that it did not violate the commerce clause. He closed his opinion by arguing: "It is doubtful if in the long run appellant will suffer economic loss as a result of the Act."

Henderson v. United States et al. (U.S., 1950)

In ruling on *Henderson*, the Supreme Court held that separate accommodations in dining cars on railways doing interstate travel violated section 3 of the Interstate Commerce Act of 1887. Plaintiff Elmer W. Henderson traveled on the Southern Railroad Company's train from Washington, D.C., to Atlanta, Georgia, through Birmingham, Alabama, in 1942. When the train passed into Virginia, dinner was served. In the dining car, the railway set up ten tables for whites in the front of the car for every two tables for blacks at the back. Further, curtains were drawn to divide the two races. If whites needed those two black tables, the black patrons would be forced to eat dinner at a later hour. Henderson entered the car to see all of the tables occupied save one seat, which he took. He was then asked to leave, and an offer was made to call him when the white passengers were finished. Henderson acceded to this demand, but he was never called, and the dining car was closed. Henderson later filed a complaint with the Interstate Commerce Commission (ICC), which refused to hear his case.

Henderson sued in district court to have the government give a fair hearing to his grievance. The United States District Court for the Eastern District of Maryland held that the railway's policy violated section 3(1) of the Interstate Commerce Act. The railway changed its rules, giving blacks four tables to ten for whites. Henderson again sued. The same district court ruled that the modified

rules were constitutional. Henderson sued to the U.S. Supreme Court. Eight years after the original incident, on 5 June 1950, the Court ruled unanimously that the new dining car rules were still in violation of section 3(1) of the Interstate Commerce Act. Justice Harold H. Burton, writing for the Court, opined that "the right to be free from unreasonable discriminations belongs, under sec. 3(1), to each particular person."

Hills (Secretary of Housing and Urban Development) v. Gautreaux et al. (U.S., 1976)

Gautreaux and several other black applicants for low-cost housing in the Chicago area brought separate suits against the Chicago Housing Authority (CHA) and Carla Hills, secretary of Housing and Urban Development (HUD) in the Ford administration, charging that both groups had built low-cost housing, targeted for blacks, in areas devoid of whites. This, they claimed, created state-sponsored segregation and thus was in violation of the Fourteenth Amendment's equal protection clause. A district court found against the CHA, but dismissed the suit against Hills and HUD. An appeals court reinstated the suit against Hills and HUD by ruling that HUD's policies had led the CHA to create its programs, which had been found to be discriminatory. Hills and HUD sued to the Supreme Court. The Court, by an 8–0 vote (Justice John Paul Stevens did not participate) reinstated the suit against Hills and HUD, ruling that HUD's policies were discriminatory. The case was thus remanded back to the Illinois courts for further hearings.

Holden, William Woods (1818–1892)

As governor of North Carolina during Reconstruction, William Woods Holden faced down the Ku Klux Klan with force during his administration (1868–1870) and was impeached because of his stand.

Holden was born on 24 November 1818, near Hillsborough, Orange County, North Carolina, the eleventh child of a miller. Barely educated, he left home at age ten and became an apprentice printer. Before his twentieth birthday, he had worked at several North Carolina newspapers. In 1837, he became a writer for the Raleigh *Star.* At the same time, he took up the study of law; in 1841, he was admitted to the state bar. Two years later Holden became the editor of the North Carolina *Standard* and turned that paper into the most radical in favor of secession in the state. He served as a member of the state House of Commons from 1846–1847, but was defeated in the next two years for the Democratic nomination for governor and for a U.S. Senate seat.

In 1861, Holden was a delegate to the North Carolina Secession Convention, which voted for an end to the Union. At first, Holden argued for the state to remain in the Union, then flipped and argued for secession. Holden came to despise the Civil War, and by 1864 he was a Peace Democrat, calling for an end to the conflict. That year he ran for governor, calling for North Carolina to secede from the Confederacy, but he was badly defeated. Instead, he joined a third party, Heroes of America, also known as the Red Strings because they aided Southerners who sided against the Confederacy. With the end of the war, Holden was appointed by President Andrew Johnson as provisional governor of the state. Holden then held a state convention where slavery was outlawed, secession was repealed, and new elections were scheduled. In those elections, Holden was badly defeated in his bid to remain governor. He was chosen as minister to San Salvador, but the Senate refused to confirm him. Instead, he took up newspaper writing again. Once an opponent of black suffrage, he now called for its immediate passage in the form of the Fourteenth Amendment. He was now the leading pro-Reconstruction politician in the state. In 1867, he helped form

North Carolina's Republican Party. The next year, he was easily elected governor, but mainly by free black votes.

Holden's administration is best remembered for his call for the state legislature to enact tough laws against the Ku Klux Klan. Part of the law allowed the governor to declare an insurrection in counties where Klan violence was out of control. Klan activities in 1869 and early 1870 led Holden to send the militia to Caswell and Alamance counties under the command of a former Union officer, George W. Kirk. Upwards of 100 Klansmen were arrested; Holden then suspended the writ of habeas corpus and allowed military trials to proceed. Democrats took Holden to federal court, which ordered the governor to submit to its will. The local courts were reopened, and the Klansmen were released. The Democrats then won control of the legislature in 1870 and impeached Holden for high crimes and misdemeanors. Holden was removed from the governorship, the last elected state post he could legally hold.

In his later years, Holden served as the editor of the Washington *Standard* and as postmaster of Raleigh, North Carolina. In his last act, he quit the Republican Party because he felt it had gone too far in the quest for black equality. Holden died in Raleigh on 1 March 1892, and was buried there.

Holland, William H. (1841? or 1849?–1907)

A barely known black educator who opened the nation's first school for blind and deaf black children, Holland was born a slave in Marshall, Texas, sometime in either 1841 or 1849. Details about his youth are contradictory. One source says that he was the illegitimate son of Bird (or Byrd) Holland, Texas's secretary of state, while others say that Bird Holland bought William and his brothers Milton and James at a slave auction. His middle name is unknown, thus the "H." Before the Civil War started, Bird Holland sent his three "sons," adopted or otherwise, to Ohio where William and Milton were enrolled at the Albany Enterprise Academy, the first black-owned and operated institution of learning in the United States. Bird Holland was a soldier in the Confederate Army and was killed at the Battle of the Sabine Cross Roads.

In 1864, William Holland entered the war on the Union side, enlisting and serving with merit in the 16th Colored Troops regiment at the battles of Nashville and Overton Hill. Milton Holland later won the Congressional Medal of Honor for bravery at the battle of New Market Heights in 1864. After the war, William Holland returned to Ohio and spent two years at Oberlin College, although he did not graduate. In 1869, he returned to Texas. As a Republican, he was named to a position in the Dallas post office, a job he held for several years. In 1876, he was elected to a seat in the Texas legislature.

In 1887, Holland introduced a bill that created the Prairie View Normal School for black students in Texas. With the help of fellow legislator Norris Wright Cuney, he helped pass a bill that led to the construction of the Texas Institute for Deaf, Dumb and Blind Colored Youth near Austin. Following its completion, Governor L. S. Ross appointed Holland as the school's first superintendent. Holland served in this post until 1897. In the last 10 years of his life, Holland initiated an organization called Friend In Need, which, acting as a type of precursor to the United Negro College Fund, supplied needed funds to worthy black students unable to afford college. In 1904, he was reappointed superintendent of the D. D. & B. Institute, a post he held until his death in Mineral Wells, Texas, on 27 May 1907.

Hollins v. State of Oklahoma (U.S., 1935)

Hollins was the landmark Supreme Court case in which the Court declared that the exclusion of blacks from a jury solely on account of their race was a violation of the Fourteenth Amendment to the Constitution. Plaintiff Hollins, a black man, was convicted in a district court in Okmulgee County, Oklahoma, on the charge of rape. Hollins's attorney charged during the trial that the past and present exclusion of blacks from juries in Okmulgee County was a violation of Hollins's Fourteenth Amendment rights. After he was convicted, a criminal court of appeals denied his assertion and upheld the sentence. Hollins sued for relief to the U.S. Supreme Court. Noted black attorney Charles Hamilton Houston represented Hollins before the high court. On 13 May 1935, the Court unanimously struck down Hollins's conviction as a violation of the Fourteenth Amendment. In its short opinion, the Court upheld the principles it set down in *Norris v. Alabama*.

See also Houston, Charles Hamilton; Norris v. Alabama.

Hooks, Benjamin Lawson (1925–)

Benjamin Hooks was the first black member of the Federal Communications Commission (FCC) from 1972 to 1979, and the head of the National Association for the Advancement of Colored People (NAACP) from 1979 until 1993. He was born on 31 January 1925 in Memphis, Tennessee. His father and uncle ran Hooks Brothers Photography on Beale Street, one of the most successful black businesses in the city at that time. Hooks attended local schools, then enrolled at LeMoyne College in Memphis. After two years, he was inducted into the 92nd Infantry of the United States Army, where, while serving eight months in Italy, he found himself guarding Italian prisoners of war who were allowed to eat in the "whites only" restaurants he was forbidden to enter. After his military service, he enrolled at the De Paul University Law School because no Tennessee law institution would admit blacks. In

1948, Hooks was awarded a juris doctor degree.

When he returned to Memphis, Hooks became caught up in the voter registration movement. In 1954 he ran unsuccessfully for a seat in the state legislature. In 1959, he ran unsuccessfully for a seat on the juvenile court, then, in 1961, was named assistant public defender of Shelby County, which encompasses Memphis. Six years later, he was appointed a criminal court judge by Governor Frank Clement, making him the first black to hold such a post since Reconstruction. Hooks retained that position from 1965 until 1969, when he left the bench to join with two partners in a fried chicken business that ultimately failed in 1972.

During the presidential campaign of 1968, Richard Nixon promised to name a black to the FCC, a seven-member group that oversees licensing of radio and television stations, as well as regulating satellite and telephone communications. On 12 April 1972, upon the resignation of Robert T. Barkley, Nixon named Hooks to the vacant seat. The new commissioner was a liberal advocate, speaking in favor of and voting for a racist politician being allowed to voice his views on the public airwaves.

On 6 November 1976, the NAACP board of directors voted for Hooks to succeed Roy Wilkins, who was retiring that year, as executive director of the organization. On 1 August 1977, Hooks assumed control of the NAACP. He left the organization in 1993. In his 16 years as head of the NAACP, the nation's largest civil rights organization, Hooks fought for home rule for the District of Columbia and against the antibusing bill before Congress and the Supreme Court nomination of Justice Clarence Thomas.

Houston, Charles Hamilton
(1895–1950)

Charles Hamilton Houston was the special counsel for the NAACP who led the judicial fight for civil rights from 1929 until his untimely death just four years before the historic Brown decision. Born in Washington, D.C., the grandson of slaves and the son of a lawyer, Houston earned a bachelor of arts degree from Amherst College, before serving two years in the American Expeditionary Force during the First World War. After his return to the United States, he entered Harvard Law School, where he became a student of future Supreme Court Justice Felix Frankfurter. He was the first black to sit on the editorial board of the *Harvard Law Review.* Following his graduation, Houston returned to Washington, D.C., to work with his attorney father and serve as a professor at Howard University. In 1929, he became the first black dean of that institution. Eventually, he became caught up in the ongoing fight for civil rights.

Starting in 1933, he took up several cases and, in 1935, argued the case of *Hollins v. State of Oklahoma* before the Supreme Court, in which a black man was sentenced to death for assaulting a white woman. This was the first instance in which a civil rights case before the Court was argued by all-black counsel. As with the *Strauder* decision some 50 years earlier, the Court overturned the death sentence of Houston's client because the jury lacked any black representation. Houston was the full-time special counsel for the NAACP from 1935 until 1939. Following that, he became the counsel for the Association of Colored Railway Trainmen and Locomotive Firemen, as well as the International Association of Railway Employees, until his death in 1950. In 1944, President Franklin D. Roosevelt appointed Houston to the Fair Employment Practices Committee (FEPC), but he resigned a year later when he felt that President Truman was sabotaging the federal commission. In his last years, Houston fought two important cases before the Supreme Court, *Hurd v. Hodge* and *Shelley v. Kraemer,* which the

Court used to strike down restrictive covenants. Houston died suddenly on 22 April 1950, at the age of 54.

See also Hollins v. State of Oklahoma; Hurd v. Hodge; Shelley v. Kraemer.

Hurd v. Hodge (U.S., 1948)

Destined to be one of two famous Supreme Court cases in which restrictive covenants—those housing contracts in which racial or religious minorities are sometimes disallowed from owning or renting certain properties—were struck down as unconstitutional, *Hurd* was a landmark in constitutional law. This case, actually three lawsuits melded into one, came from the District of Columbia, where Hurd, a black, purchased property from a landowner on Bryant Street in Washington, D.C. In 1906, 100 land-owners had signed a covenant that their properties would not be rented or sold to blacks. Hodge, a neighbor, sued Hurd to stop him from taking possession of the property. A district court held that the covenant was legal; the District of Columbia Court of Appeals affirmed this judgment. The Supreme Court, upon granting *certiorari*, held that such restrictions violated section 1978 of the Revised Statutes, which guarantees to all citizens of the United States equal treatment in the right to hold, sell, inherit, or rent real and personal property.

See also Houston, Charles Hamilton; Shelley v. Kraemer.

Hyman, John Adams (1840–1891)

The first black to represent North Carolina in the U.S. House of Representatives was a former slave who could barely read and write. Hyman was born into slavery on 23 July 1840, near Warrenton, North Carolina. His early life remains bathed in mystery. Apparently, in 1861, he belonged to a jeweler named King who taught Hyman how to read and write. When locals became enraged at the education of a slave, Hyman was sold to another master in Alabama. There is no record of what he did during the Civil War, although after the war ended, he returned to Warrenton and opened a country store. Blacks in North Carolina called for a Freed-men's Convention to fight for freedmen's rights. Hyman was a delegate to this convention. He joined the Republican Party in 1867, and that year was elected to the North Carolina Republican State Executive Committee. In 1868, Hyman was one of 15 black delegates chosen for the state constitutional convention. Following the convention, he was elected to the North Carolina state senate. He spent both terms as a state senator denying charges from Democrats that he had been bribed by the railroads.

In 1872, Hyman ran for a seat in the U.S. House of Representatives but lost by a narrow margin. Two years later, he again ran for Congress and was elected. He served a single term, in the Forty-fourth Congress, from 1875 to 1877. Unfortunately, he spent much of the time fighting his Democratic opponent, who claimed that Hyman had been fraudulently elected. Although a congressional committee later settled the issue in Hyman's favor, it was too late in the term to do much work. Although he did not officially speak on the House floor, he did introduce several bills, one of which was to reimburse creditors of the failed Freedman's Bank for losses incurred by the bank's failure. In 1876, Hyman lost his reelection bid.

In his final years, Hyman again returned to North Carolina, where he became a farmer and the owner of a liquor store. In 1879, he traveled to Maryland to work as a mail clerk's assistant. After a decade in this job, he went to Washington, D.C., where he was a worker in the seed dispensary of the Agriculture Department. John Adams Hyman died of a paralytic stroke in Washington, D.C., on 14 September 1891, at the age of 51.

"I Have A Dream" Speech

The speech delivered by the Reverend Dr. Martin Luther King in front of the Lincoln Memorial, during the March on Washington for Jobs and Freedom in August 1963, marked one of the most moving events in the struggle for civil rights. The exact text reads:

I am happy to join with you today in what will go down in history as the greatest demonstration for freedom in the history of our nation.

Fivescore years ago, a great American, in whose symbolic shadow we stand today, signed the Emancipation Proclamation. This momentous decree came as a great beacon light of hope to millions of Negro slaves who had been seared in the flames of withering injustice. It came as a joyous daybreak to end the long night of their captivity.

But one hundred years later, the Negro still is not free; one hundred years later, the life of the Negro is still sadly crippled by the manacles of segregation and the chains of discrimination; one hundred years later, the Negro lives on a lonely island of poverty in the midst of a vast ocean of material prosperity; one hundred years later, the Negro is still languished in the corners of American society and finds himself in exile in his own land.

So we've come here today to dramatize a shameful condition. In a sense we've come to our nation's capital to cash a check. When the architects of our republic wrote the magnificent words of the Constitution and the Declaration of Independence, they were signing a promissory note to which every American was to fall heir. This note was the promise that all men, yes, black men as well as white men, would be guaranteed the unalienable rights of life, liberty, and the pursuit of happiness.

It is obvious today that America has defaulted on this promissory note insofar as her citizens of color are concerned. Instead of honoring this sacred obligation, America has given the Negro people a bad check; a check which has come back marked 'insufficient funds.' We refuse to believe that there are insufficient funds in the great vaults of opportunity of this nation. And so we've come to cash this check, a check that will give us upon demand the riches of freedom and the security of justice.

We have also come to this hallowed spot to remind America of the fierce urgency of now. This is no time to engage in the luxury of cooling off or to take the tranquilizing drug of gradualism. Now is the time to make real the promises of democracy; now is the time to rise from the dark and desolate valley of segregation to the sunlit path of racial justice; now is the time to lift our nation from the quicksands of racial injustice to the solid rock of brotherhood; now is the time to make justice a reality for all God's children. It would be fatal for the nation to overlook the urgency of the moment. The sweltering summer of the Negro's legitimate discontent will not pass until there is an invigorating autumn of freedom and equality.

Nineteen sixty-three is not an end, but a beginning. And those who

Martin Luther King, Jr. at the Lincoln Memorial, 19 August 1963

hope that the Negro needed to blow off steam and will now be content will have a rude awakening if the nation returns to business as usual.

There will be neither rest nor tranquility in America until the Negro is granted his citizenship rights. The whirlwinds of revolt will continue to shake the foundations of our nation until the bright day of justice emerges.

But there is something that I must say to my people who stand on the warm threshold which leads into the palace of justice. In the process of gaining our rightful place we must not be guilty of wrongful deeds.

Let us not seek to satisfy our thirst for freedom by drinking from the cup of bitterness and hatred. We must forever conduct our struggle on the high plane of dignity and discipline. We must not allow our creative protest to degenerate into physical violence. Again and again we must rise to the majestic heights of meeting physical force with soul force.

The marvelous new militancy which has engulfed the Negro community must not lead us to a distrust of all white people, for many of our white brothers, as evidenced by their presence here today, have come to realize that their destiny is tied up with our destiny and they have come to realize that their freedom is inextricably bound to our freedom. This offense we share mounted to storm the battlements of injustice must be carried forth by a biracial army. We cannot walk alone.

And as we walk, we must make the pledge that we shall always march ahead. We cannot turn back. There are those who are asking the devotees of civil rights, 'When will you be satisfied?' We can never be satisfied as long as the Negro is the victim of the unspeakable horrors of police brutality.

We can never be satisfied as long as our bodies, heavy with fatigue of travel, cannot gain lodging in the motels of the highways and the hotels of the cities. We cannot be satisfied as long as the Negro's basic mobility is from a smaller ghetto to a larger one.

We can never be satisfied as long as our children are stripped of their selfhood and robbed of their dignity by signs stating 'for whites only.' We cannot be satisfied as long as a Negro in Mississippi cannot vote and a Negro in New York believes he has nothing for which to vote. No, we are not satisfied, and we will not be satisfied until justice rolls down like waters and righteousness like a mighty stream.

I am not unmindful that some of you come here out of excessive trials and tribulation. Some of you have come fresh from narrow jail cells. Some of you have come from areas where your quest for freedom left you battered by the storms of persecution and staggered by the winds of police brutality. You have been the veterans of creative suffering. Continue to work with the faith that unearned suffering is redemptive.

Go back to Mississippi; go back to Alabama; go back to South Carolina; go back to Georgia; go back to Louisiana; go back to the slums and ghettoes of the northern cities, knowing that somehow this situation can, and will be changed. Let us not wallow in the valley of despair.

So I say to you, my friends, that even though we must face the difficulties of today and tomorrow, I still have a dream. It is a dream deeply rooted in the American dream that one day this nation will rise up and live out the true meaning of its creed—we hold these truths to be self-evident, that all men are created equal.

I have a dream that one day on the red hills of Georgia, sons of former slaves and sons of former slave-owners will be able to sit down together at the table of brotherhood.

I have a dream that one day, even the state of Mississippi, a state sweltering with the heat of injustice, sweltering with the heat of oppression, will be transformed into an oasis of freedom and justice.

I have a dream my four little children will one day live in a nation where they will not be judged by the color of their skin but by the content of their character. I have a dream today!

I have a dream that one day, down in Alabama, with its vicious racists, with its governor having his lips dripping with the words of interposition and nullification, that one day, right there in Alabama, little black boys and black girls will be able to join hands with little white boys and white girls as sisters and brothers. I have a dream today!

I have a dream that one day every valley shall be exalted, every hill and mountain shall be made low, the rough places shall be made plain, and the crooked places shall be made straight and the glory of the Lord will be revealed and all flesh shall see it together.

This is our hope. This is the faith that I go back to the South with.

With this faith we will be able to work together, to pray together, to struggle together, to go to jail together, to stand up to freedom together, knowing that we will be free one day. This will be the day when all of God's children will be able to sing with new meaning—"my country 'tis of thee; sweet land of liberty; of thee I sing; land where my fathers died, land of the pilgrim's pride, from every mountain side, let freedom ring"—and if America is to be a great nation, this must become true.

So let freedom ring from the prodigious hilltops of New Hampshire.

Let freedom ring from the mighty mountains of New York.

Let freedom ring from the heightening Alleghenies of Pennsylvania.

Let freedom ring from the snow-capped Rockies of Colorado.

Let freedom ring from the curvaceous slopes of California.

But not only that.

Let freedom ring from Stone Mountain of Georgia.

Let freedom ring from Lookout Mountain of Tennessee.

Let freedom ring from every hill and molehill of Mississippi, from every mountainside, let freedom ring.

And when we allow freedom to ring, when we let it ring from every village and hamlet, from every state and city, we will be able to speed up that day when all of God's children—black men and white men, Jews and Gentiles, Catholics and Protestants—will be able to join hands and to sing in the words of the old Negro spiritual, "Free at last, free at last, thank God Almighty, we are free at last."

In Re Turner (1867)

The first key test to the constitutionality of the Civil Rights Act of 9 April 1866 was *In Re Turner*, simply meaning "in regard to Turner." Although Maryland drafted its new constitution in 1864, prohibiting slavery, plaintiff Elizabeth Turner, a black girl, was "apprenticed" to her former owner to work as his servant until she reached the age of 18 in 1874. Two antislavery lawyers, Nathan Pusey and Henry Stockbridge, sued on her behalf that the "apprenticeship" violated the Thirteenth Amendment's prohibition against involuntary servitude and was outlawed by the 1866 Civil Rights Act. Chief Justice Salmon P. Chase of the U.S. Supreme Court heard the petition for habeas corpus. He ruled that Turner's "apprenticeship" was a violation of her rights under the Civil Rights Act and the Thirteenth Amendment. At the same time, the case of *United States v. Rhodes*, a second test of the 1866 Civil Rights Act, was being heard by Justice Noah H. Swayne on circuit in Kentucky.

See also United States v. Rhodes.

Innis, Roy (1934–)

The outspoken head of the Congress of Racial Equality (CORE), a leading civil rights group, Roy Innis remains one of America's leading voices for tolerance and equality. He was born in St. Croix, Virgin Islands, on 6 June 1934. His father, a policeman, died when Innis was a child, forcing the widowed mother and her young son to move to New York. Innis dropped out of high school to join the U.S. Army, where he encountered for the first time the stinging effects of American segregation. After leaving military service, Innis completed high school and studied for a time at the City College of New York. For several years after college he worked as a chemical engineer, and also in a union local at a hospital.

In 1963, Innis became a member of CORE. He was considered a radical who called for immediate but peaceful action to "break down the walls" of segregation.

Appointed chairman of CORE's Harlem Education Committee in 1964, Innis pushed for local control of the educational curriculum to break the stranglehold of segregation in New York City schools. In 1965, he was named head of CORE's Harlem organization and later became a member of the Metropolitan Applied Research Center, a think tank designed to study urban problems. In 1967, he was named second national vice chairman of CORE, and then associate national director. He was, in effect, being groomed to head the group. In 1968, CORE's director, Floyd McKissick, left the organization for reasons of ill health and was replaced by Innis. Roy Innis has headed CORE since that time. Now considered a moderate in the civil rights community, his has been a voice of calm and reason during episodes of racial strife nationwide.

See also Congress of Racial Equality.

Jackson, Jesse Louis (1941–)

The Reverend Jesse Jackson, activist, noted clergyman, civil rights leader, and, more recently, talk show host, ran two distinctive campaigns for the U.S. presidency in 1984 and 1988. Born Jesse Burns, in Greenville, South Carolina, on 8 October 1941, his name was soon changed to his adopted father's, Jackson. Although granted an athletic scholarship to the all-white University of Illinois, Jackson spent only a year there before transferring to North Carolina Agricultural & Technical College in Greensboro, where he started on the road to becoming a civil rights activist. He eventually graduated with a bachelor's degree in sociology. While at North Carolina A & T, he decided to become a minister and later studied at the Chicago Theological Seminary, although he never earned a degree. At this time, he became involved with the charismatic leadership of the Reverend Dr. Martin Luther King, Jr., whom Jackson met in Selma, Alabama, in 1965. The next year, King appointed him director of the Southern Christian Leadership Conference's (SCLC) Operation Breadbasket, a food program for poor blacks. Jackson served in this post from 1966 to 1971. Jackson was in Memphis with King when the civil rights leader was assassinated in 1968. His claim that he was standing next to King when the fatal shot was fired, as well as his wearing a shirt with King's blood on it, angered many of King's associates, who felt that Jackson was capitalizing on the tragedy.

In 1972, Jackson broke from the SCLC and founded Operation PUSH (People United to Save Humanity), which was intended to be an all-encompassing civil rights organization. Joseph Califano, a member of the Carter administration who worked with Jackson and PUSH, claimed that without the civil rights advocate, the organization had little or no power.

In 1984, Jackson ran for president, the first black to run with a nationwide campaign. He formed a "Rainbow Coalition" of poor blacks, Hispanics, women, and pacifists. Jackson won about 3.25 million votes in the primaries. With the 1984 campaign, however, came charges of blatant anti-Semitism on Jackson's part. He angrily referred to New York City, the home of many of the nation's Jews, as "Hymietown," and Jews as "Hymies." Further, he defended his meetings with Palestinian Liberation Organization leader Yasser Arafat and his support for a Palestinian homeland in Israel. In 1988, Jackson again ran for president and received 7 million votes. In the 1992 election, he refused a third run for the presidency, but demanded that he be considered for the Democratic nomination for vice president. He later endorsed the Clinton-Gore Democratic ticket, which went on to win the election in November.

Jacob, John Edward (1934–)

John Edward Jacob has been the president of the National Urban League (NUL) since 1982. He was born in Trout, Louisiana, on 16 December 1934, one of five sons of a Baptist minister. When Jacob was young, the family moved to Houston, Texas. On a scholarship, he entered Howard University in Washington, D.C., and in 1957 earned his bachelor's degree in economics. After a short stint in the United States Army, he earned a master's degree in social work from Howard in 1963. For the next two years,

John Edward Jacob

he served as a case supervisor for the Department of Public Welfare in Baltimore, Maryland.

In 1965, Jacob joined the Washington, D.C., chapter of the NUL as that branch's director of education and youth incentives. Three years later, he was named executive director of the D.C. chapter. Under his leadership, NUL initiated several innovative programs to combat poverty in the nation's capital. For a short period in 1970, Jacob directed the community organizing and training program for the league's eastern division. That same year, he was transferred to become the head of NUL's San Diego branch. He remained in San Diego until 1975, then returned as director of the Washington, D.C., chapter.

In 1979, Jacob was appointed as NUL's executive vice president, in effect the number two man in that organization. When the president, Vernon Jordan, was wounded in an assassination attempt in 1980, John Jacob stepped into place as the league's spokesman. After recuperating, Jordan stepped down in 1982, and the league's officers named Jacob as his successor. In his 10 years as president, Jacob has advanced self-help programs, attending to such issues as teenage pregnancies in the black community. He has also called for a large governmental "Marshall Plan" to aid U.S. cities.

Jenkins, David (1811–1877)

A black activist and agitator for civil rights before and after the Civil War, Jenkins was born in Lynchburg, Virginia, in 1811. He was educated mainly through the efforts of his father, who hired a private tutor. In 1837, Jenkins moved to Columbus, Ohio, where he worked as a painter and glazier. He purchased several pieces of real estate and thereby amassed a small fortune.

On 27 December 1843, Jenkins began publication of *The Palladium of Liberty*, a weekly antislavery newspaper. The *Palladium* lasted only a year, but it was the first black newspaper published in Ohio. It carried a strong abolitionist message, but also preached for temperance and the franchise for all black citizens. During the rest of the 1840s and the entire decade of the 1850s, Jenkins toured the state of Ohio, delivering antislavery speeches in many towns. He was also a founding member of the Ohio State Anti-Slavery Society, as well as being active in the Underground Railroad.

During the Civil War, Jenkins toured Ohio asking for funds for the Union cause and espousing the right of black soldiers to fight. At the end of the war, Jenkins was active in the Republican Party in Franklin County, Ohio, and served as a delegate to the county Republican convention. In 1873, he left Ohio for Canton, Mississippi, where he taught in a freedmen's school there. In 1875, he was elected to a single term in the Mississippi legislature. Jenkins became ill on

1 September 1877, and died four days later, on 5 September, at the age of 66.

Jim Crow Laws

Jim Crow was the name given to the laws designed to segregate blacks from whites and to disenfranchise black voters. The term came from a white minstrel dance show that appeared in the northern part of the country around 1928, entitled "Jump Jim Crow," which was first performed by entertainer Thomas Dartmouth "Daddy" Rice. Rice was later billed as "Jim Crow" Rice because of the popularity of his act. He appeared in blackface and danced around, singing spirituals in such a way that the show was derogatory to blacks. Jim Crow laws, by informal extension, were laws designed to denigrate black people socially and to separate them physically from white people in almost all areas of daily life.

Such laws, however, appeared long before Thomas Rice did his show. They were enacted following the end of Reconstruction, about 1877, when Southern legislatures, free from the federal intervention of Reconstruction, worked to impede black voting and social rights without resorting to a return to outright slavery. By 1885, every former Confederate state had passed some type of restrictive law, encompassing many areas that were to be segregated. Bathrooms, railcars, dining facilities, schools, hotels (as well as other types of living quarters), theaters, steamships, cemeteries, parks, and beaches were by law to have "separate but equal" facilities. The U.S. Supreme Court, in 1896's infamous *Plessy v. Ferguson* decision, put its stamp of approval on such state action. There were bans on intermarriage, a poll tax for every black person who wanted to vote, and literacy tests for those who could afford to pay the tax. Lynchings occurred where blacks had few judicial rights.

Jim Crow laws began to unravel in the 1940s, with civil rights legislation gaining favor among many whites. By the 1950s, the tide was turning, with the Supreme Court's *Brown* decision striking down segregated educational facilities. In the 1960s, such legislation as the Civil Rights Act of 1964, the Voting Rights Act of 1965, and the Fair Housing Act of 1968 were passed to do away with as many inequalities as government could fight.

Johnson, Charles Spurgeon (1893–1956)

A black sociologist, Charles S. Johnson served on the commission that investigated the Chicago riots of 1919 and became the first director of research at the National Urban League (NUL). Johnson was born in Bristol, Virginia, on 24 July 1893, the eldest of five children of a former slave. In 1909, he was sent to the Wayland Academy, an all-black Baptist school in Richmond. In 1913, he entered the Virginia Union University. A member of the student council and editor of the college newspaper, Johnson was also a member of the Lyceum Club and an active debater. He graduated in 1916, with a bachelor's degree in sociology. He earned his Ph.D. in 1917.

In 1918, Johnson enlisted in the United States Army and served with merit during the Meuse-Argonnes offensive in France. In 1919, he was discharged and returned to Chicago to complete his studies under sociologist Robert E. Park. A week after Johnson returned home, the great Chicago Riot of 1919 broke out. Triggered by the stoning and drowning of a black youth, Eugene Williams, at a whites-only beach, the riot shook the foundations of America in ways not seen since the draft riots that engulfed New York during the Civil War. More than 500 people—both black and white—were killed or injured in the insurrection. Governor Frank O. Lowden appointed a panel, the Chicago Commission on Race Relations, to examine the riot and see what could be done to prevent it from happening again. It was an early twentieth-century version of the Kerner Commission. Johnson was appointed as the commission's associate executive secretary. He spent the next three years of his life looking at why he felt the "Great Migration" of Southern blacks to northern cities had been an underlying cause of the riot. The commission report, *The Negro in Chicago: A Study of Race Relations and the Race Riot*, largely written by Johnson, was a classic work on the issue of race relations. Charles Johnson became an instant authority on the matter.

In 1921, Johnson was named director of the NUL's Department of Research and Investigations. For the next seven years, until 1928, he initiated several studies of black urban life, including "Negro Membership in American Labor Unions." During the last five years of his tenure at the league, he founded and edited its official organ, *Opportunity: A Journal of Negro Life*. In 1928, Johnson resigned from NUL to become head of the Department of Social Sciences at Fisk University in Nashville, Tennessee. At Fisk, he later created a Department of Race Relations. As the nation's leading sociologist, Johnson's many studies of black life became and remain to this day unique. In 1947, Johnson became Fisk University's first black president.

Following the historic Supreme Court ruling on *Brown* in 1954, which outlawed school segregation, Johnson and several educators formed the Southern Educational Reporting Service (SERS), a foundation that reported on the national goal of desegregating schools. Johnson was an integral part of SERS until his death of a massive heart attack two years later, on 27 October 1956. He was 63 years old.

See also Chicago Riot of 1919; Kerner Commission.

Johnson, Frank Minis, Jr. (1918–)

Frank Johnson remains unheralded in American history, despite handing down several key decisions as a federal judge during the civil rights era. He was born the eldest of seven children to Frank Johnson, Sr. and Alabama Long Johnson, in the small town of Haleyville, Alabama, on 30 October 1918. The elder Johnson, a high school teacher and farmer, also served as the only Republican member of the state legislature. Frank Johnson attended local schools, the Gulf Coast Military Academy at Gulfport, Mississippi, and several small colleges before entering the University of Alabama, where he received his law degree in 1943.

Johnson enlisted in the U.S. Army and was wounded in action during the invasion of Normandy in 1944. He served as a military aide in England for the rest of the war. Returning to the United States in 1945, he cofounded a law firm with two friends in Jasper, Alabama. In 1952, he was a leading voice in the organization Alabama Veterans for Eisenhower, an advocacy group for the Republican presidential nominee. With Eisenhower's victory came an appointment for Johnson, in August 1953, as U.S. attorney for the Northern District of Alabama. On 7 November 1955, Eisenhower elevated Johnson to judge of the U.S. district court for the Middle District of Alabama. At 37, Johnson was the youngest man ever to sit on a federal bench.

Johnson's first major civil rights case was the appeal by Rosa Parks of her conviction for illegally sitting in the white section of a Montgomery, Alabama, public bus. With Johnson siding with fellow judge Richard Taylor Rives, the court ruled 2–1 that Montgomery's system of segregated public transportation was unconstitutional. Until 1979, Johnson, on the district court, struck down many of the segregationist laws in Alabama as unconstitutional, making that state one of the first in the South to integrate by law. Johnson was opposed by Alabama governors, including George C. Wallace, who ironically had been a close friend of Johnson's in law school. In 1959, the two men clashed over Wallace's withholding of documents related to the state's voting records from the U.S. Civil Rights Commission. In a duel of clashing interests and cultures, Johnson won out when he gave Wallace the opportunity to save face and hand the records over through a third party. In 1965, Johnson again made headlines when he ruled that the Reverend Dr. Martin Luther King, Jr., had a right to march through Alabama to petition Wallace for voting rights.

Frank Johnson's name stands out among those in the civil rights community. In 1969, there was speculation that he would replace retiring justice Abe Fortas on the U.S. Supreme Court, but his name was blocked by angry segregationists. On 17 August 1977, President Jimmy Carter nominated Johnson to become the director of the Federal Bureau of Investigation (FBI), but Johnson withdrew his name for reasons of ill health. On 19 June 1979, however, Carter elevated Johnson to the Fifth Circuit Court of Appeals in New Orleans, Louisiana. Johnson announced his retirement in 1992 and left the bench in 1993.

See also Fifth Circuit Court of Appeals; Wallace, George Corley.

Jones, Eugene Kinckle (1885–1954)

Eugene Jones, the second executive secretary of the National Urban League (NUL), was born on 30 July 1885, in Richmond, Virginia, the son of a former slave and one of Virginia's first black college graduates. He earned his bachelor's degree from Virginia Union University in 1906, and his master's degree in social science from Cornell University in New York in 1908. At Cornell, Jones was one of the founding members of Alpha Phi Alpha, the nation's first black fraternity.

Jones was a protégé of NUL's first executive secretary, George Edmund Haynes. Jones joined the league in 1911 as the organization's field secretary after resigning as an instructor at the Central High School in Louisville, Kentucky. NUL was at that time called the Committee on Urban Conditions Among Negroes. Under the leadership of Haynes and Jones, the organization soon merged with the National League for the Protection of Colored Women and the Committee for Improving the Industrial Conditions for Negroes to become the NUL. When Haynes left the league in 1911 to become a professor at Fisk University, Jones was made his successor and served from 1911 until 1941. In those three decades, he made the league a national organization of equality and civil rights. *Opportunity: A Journal of Negro Life*, the league's official organ, began publication in 1923 under the direction of Dr. Charles S. Johnson. In 1926, the Arthur Schomburg collection of black history came up for sale, and Jones pursuaded the Carnegie Foundation to purchase the collection and donate it to the people, where it can now be found at the Schomburg Center for Research in Black Culture at the New York Public Library.

Jones resigned as executive director in 1941 and was replaced by Lester Blackwell Granger. Jones was so highly thought of as a civil rights leader that he was asked to stay on as NUL's general secretary, which he did until 1950. He died four years later, on 11 January 1954, at the age of 68.

See also Granger, Lester Blackwell; Haynes, George Edmund; National Urban League.

Jones v. Alfred H. Mayer Co. (U.S., 1968)

Jones was the classic Supreme Court case in which the Court ruled that restrictive covenants in the purchase of land and/or property were unconstitutional. The petitioner, Joseph Lee Jones, a black man, attempted to purchase a home from the respondents in St. Louis County, Missouri. Jones was refused because of his race. He sued in the District Court for the Eastern District of Missouri for relief from the covenant. The district court dismissed the complaint, and the Eighth Circuit Court of Appeals affirmed the decision. Jones took the case to the

Supreme Court. The Court ruled 7–2 that under section 1982 of the U.S. Code, Congress had the right to ban racial discrimination in the sale or rental of real estate.

See also Hurd v. Hodge; Shelley v. Kraemer.

Jones v. Jones (U.S., 1914)

Although not a civil rights case, *Jones v. Jones* did mark the first time the high court ruled that former slaves could not inherit property that had not been willed to them. The Tennessee state statute under review firmly prohibited the unwilled estate of a deceased person from going to a former slave. Justice Horace Harmon Lurton, on his final day as a Supreme Court justice, spoke for a unanimous Court in upholding the Tennessee statute as lawful under the Fourteenth Amendment.

Barbara Charline Jordan

Jordan, Barbara Charline (1936–)

A towering personality on the American political scene, Barbara Jordan was the first black United States representative from Texas, as well as the first black woman to deliver the keynote address at a major political convention. She was born in Houston on 21 February 1936, the daughter of the Reverend Benjamin Jordan, a Baptist minister. She was educated in the public schools of Houston, then enrolled at Texas Southern University, an all-black school, where she majored in political science and history. She received her bachelor of arts degree in 1956, graduating magna cum laude in both subjects. She entered Boston University and earned her law degree in 1959, that year being admitted to the Texas and Massachusetts bars. Returning to Houston, she opened her law office in her parents' dining room and worked there until she could afford her own law office three years later.

In the meantime, Jordan had entered politics and had been defeated in a race for a seat in the Texas House of Representatives in 1962. She suffered a similar loss in 1964. In 1966, however, she ran for the state senate and defeated a white liberal to become the first black woman to serve in the state senate, as well as the first black to serve in that body since 1883. In 1968, Jordan was reelected to the state senate for a four-year term. In that post, she championed fair employment legislation, improved workman's compensation measures, and helped the state government draft an antidiscrimination clause to be included in its business contracts. In 1972, Jordan was elected to the U.S. House of Representatives and was named to the prestigious Judiciary Committee. In 1973–1974, she was a leader on that panel when she spoke out in favor of voting for all five articles of impeachment against President Richard M. Nixon. In 1976, she became the first black woman to deliver the keynote address at a major national convention, when she spoke before the Democratic National Convention.

In 1977, Jordan announced that she would not be a candidate for reelection the following year. In 1979, she was named professor at the Lyndon B. Johnson School of Public Affairs at the University of Texas at Austin. In 1990, she nearly accidentally drowned in her home swimming pool in Houston. Suffering from multiple sclerosis and confined to a wheelchair, she delivered one of three keynote addresses before the Democratic National Convention in 1992.

Jordan, Vernon Eulion, Jr. (1935–)

Jordan, a noted civil rights leader, was executive director of the National Urban League (NUL) from 1972 until his near assassination in 1980. He was born in Atlanta, Georgia, on 15 August 1935. He received a public school education, and, as the only black in his class, graduated from DePauw University in Indiana in 1957, with a bachelor's degree in political science. He then attended Howard University Law School, earned his law degree in 1960, and began work soon after as a law clerk in the Atlanta law office of civil rights attorney Donald Hollowell. In 1961, Hollowell defended two black students who sought to enter the University of Georgia. The federal district court ordered the two students to be admitted, and, in perhaps his greatest moment, Jordan used his body as a shield to escort one of the students, Charlayne Hunter, through a white mob into the university. Later a reporter for the *New York Times*, Charlayne Hunter-Gault is now a television reporter and presenter for the McNeil/Lehrer News Hour.

In 1962, Jordan was hired as the field secretary for the Georgia branch of the National Association for the Advancement of Colored People (NAACP). In this post, he led a boycott of Augusta, Georgia, stores that refused to hire black workers. Two years later, he became the director of the Southern Regional Council's Voter Education Project. In March 1970, he was appointed executive director of the United Negro College Fund, a post he held for a little more than a year. In March 1971, Whitney M. Young, Jr., executive secretary of NUL, drowned in Lagos, Nigeria. Two months later, the NUL executive board unanimously chose Jordan as Young's successor. Under Jordan's tenure, the league began publication of *The State of Black America*, a yearly compendium of the condition of blacks in the United States. Taking a cue from his days as head of the Voter Education Project, where he helped register some 2 million new black voters, Jordan instituted a voter registration program which brought out more than 30,000 new black voters in 10 cities. Fundraising goals were raised, and Jordan attempted to introduce NUL into areas of black unemployment and underemployment.

A white supremacist attempted to murder Jordan on 29 May 1980, while the NUL leader was in Indiana. Although he later recovered from his gunshot wounds, he resigned his position at the league and returned to his private law practice in Washington, D.C. Although he continues his civil rights work, he is mostly involved in the law. In 1992 and 1993, he served on the Clinton transition team.

Jordan v. Massachusetts (U.S., 1912)

Jordan, while not dealing specifically with civil rights, was a Supreme Court case that was later used as a guide in deciding future civil rights cases. The case involved Jordan, a Massachusetts black man, who was found guilty by a jury of committing murder and sentenced to death. Jordan later discovered that one of the jury was insane, and that the prosecution knew it during *voir dire*, the jury selection process. He appealed to the Superior Court of the Commonwealth of Massachusetts to have his murder conviction set aside. The superior court ruled against him, so Jordan asked the U.S. Supreme Court to review the case. Justice Horace Harmon Lurton ruled for the Court by upholding

Jordan's conviction. Lurton argued that at the time, according to the trial judge and fellow jurors, the one insane juror was found to be mentally competent to the point that he could reasonably judge Jordan's guilt or innocence. Further, Lurton found that Jordan's right to due process was not violated by the superior court's action of not setting aside the verdict. This case was used in later Supreme Court decisions as a guide in determining what constituted a fair and impartial jury, and whether or not black defendants received the due process of the laws.

Katzenbach v. McClung (U.S., 1964)

Katzenbach was one of two 1964 Supreme Court decisions (the other was *Heart of Atlanta Motel v. United States*) that upheld the constitutionality of Title II of the Civil Rights Act of 1964. The case involved the owner of Ollie's Barbecue in Birmingham, Alabama, who had a take-out service for blacks but refused to serve them in the restaurant. Under the auspices of the Justice Department and Attorney General Nicholas Katzenbach, the United States sued to have the restaurant comply with Title II, which outlawed segregation in dining facilities that did interstate commerce. Although Ollie's Barbecue admitted that it fell under the jurisdiction of Title II, it declared that it was being forced to admit patrons, and thus was denied due process in commerce under Article I of the Constitution. The Court ruled unanimously that Title II did not interfere with the commerce clause, and therefore was constitutional. Justice Tom Clark wrote the majority opinion for the Court. "We must conclude that it [the Congress] had a rational basis for finding that racial discrimination in restaurants had a direct and adverse effect on the free flow of interstate commerce . We think that in doing so that Congress acted well within its power to protect and foster commerce in extending the coverage of Title II only to those restaurants offering to serve interstate travelers ."

See also Heart of Atlanta Motel v. United States.

Katzenbach v. Morgan (U.S., 1966)

In *Katzenbach v. Morgan*, the Supreme Court held that Congress had the power to prohibit the use of literacy tests for voting, although the Court had ruled that such tests did not inherently violate the Equal Protection clause of the Fourteenth Amendment.

The 1965 Voting Rights Act specified that persons educated in Puerto Rican schools where they learned a language other than English could not be denied the right to vote in the United States proper because they did not speak English. Morgan, a voter in New York City, sued Attorney General Nicholas Katzenbach to stop non-English speaking Puerto Ricans from voting. The Court found 7–2 (with Justice William Brennan writing the majority opinion, and Justices John Marshall Harlan and Potter Stewart dissenting) that Congress had the right to legislate voting procedures and methods within the scope of its powers under the Fourteenth Amendment.

Kennedy, Stetson (1916–)

A noted writer and civil rights activist, Stetson Kennedy was born in Jacksonville, Florida, in 1916, the son of a furniture store owner. His ancestors include signers of the Declaration of Independence, a Confederate officer, and an early member of the Ku Klux Klan. Kennedy graduated from a local high school and attended the University of Florida before joining Franklin D. Roosevelt's Works Progress Administration (WPA) in 1937 to conduct ethnic and cultural studies in Florida. Working with African-American author Zora Neale Hurston, Kennedy roamed the state conducting interviews for the WPA's *Florida Guide*. It was, however, an article in the area of civil rights that led to Kennedy's early success as a writer.

The article, a short piece on a lynching in Key West, Florida, caught the eye of Southern folklorist Erskine Caldwell, who approached Kennedy about writing a book about Florida. The result was *Palmetto Country*, a collection of anecdotes about Florida life. In 1942, curious about white supremacist activities in the South, Kennedy infiltrated the Klan, using the alias John S. Perkins. Working undercover for such groups as B'nai B'rith, Kennedy was able to penetrate the Atlanta Klavern of the Association of Georgia Klans, led by Grand Dragon Sam Green. Gradually collecting evidence on Klan activities, Kennedy began sending reports to columnist Drew Pearson and the Federal Bureau of Investigation (FBI). When once-secret information began appearing in Pearson's column, Green, aware that his organization had been infiltrated, offered $1,000 a pound for "the traitor's ass, F.O.B. Atlanta." Pearson later called Kennedy "the nation's No. 1 Klan buster" in an exposé of the undercover investigation. Kennedy wrote two books based on his experiences inside the Klan: *The Klan Unmasked* and *The Jim Crow Guide*. In 1950, he ran unsuccessfully for the U.S. Senate as a "color-blind" candidate.

Perhaps Kennedy's most important investigation was his research into the murders of Harry and Harriette Moore, slain by a bomb blast in their Florida home on Christmas night, 1951. The case was taken up by Kennedy, who accused local law enforcement officials, whom he sensed were secret Klan members, of either complicity in the crime or the covering up of its details. Kennedy pieced together enough information to convince Florida governor Lawton Chiles to reopen the murder investigation in 1990. Stetson Kennedy remains today a deeply respected advocate for human and civil rights.

See also Moore, Harry Tyson.

Kerner, Otto, Jr. (1908–1976)

Although his name graces the commission report that urgently warned Americans that the nation "was moving toward separate societies, one black, one white—separate and unequal," Otto Kerner, who was once the respected governor of Illinois but ended his days in disgrace, is not well known. Kerner was born on 15 August 1908, in Chicago, Illinois, the son of Otto Kerner, Sr., a noted leader in Chicago's Czech community, a lawyer, and judge on the Seventh Circuit Court. Otto Kerner, Jr., was sent to prestigious schools in the wealthy suburb of River Forrest and enrolled in Brown University, from which he graduated in 1930. He attended Trinity College, Cambridge University, England, from 1930 to 1931, then received a law degree from Northwestern University in 1934. For a 10-year period, starting in 1936, he was a member of the Black Horse Troop of the Illinois National Guard. By the time he left the national guard in 1946, Kerner was a major general in the field artillery.

Following his service for the national guard, Kerner decided to enter politics. As a Democrat, he had close connections with the Cook County (Chicago) government "machine." In 1947, he was appointed a U.S. attorney for the Northern District of Illinois, a post he held until 1954. In that year, Kerner was elected as a county judge for Cook County. He was reelected in 1958 but left the bench in 1960, when he ran for governor. He was elected over the Republican incumbent, William G. Stratton, in a closely run race. He won a second term in 1964. Kerner was not particularly known as a firm advocate of civil rights, although as governor he did champion a state fair employment practices law. He was, however, considered an honest and efficient administrator. On 27 July 1967, following a series of riots in Newark and Detroit, President Lyndon B. Johnson named Kerner as the head of the National Commission on Civil Disorders, which, for the next seven months, investigated the riots and their root causes and made wide-ranging recommendations. The commission to this day is known as the Kerner Commission.

Otto Kerner resigned the governorship on 22 May 1968 to accept an appointment from President Johnson to sit on the U.S. Court of Appeals for the Seventh Circuit, the same court his father had sat on. In 1972, however, Kerner was indicted, and in 1973 found guilty, on charges that during his first term as governor he had legislated favorable racing dates for the state's race tracks in exchange for low-cost stock in the tracks. He appealed his conviction, but on 28 July 1974 entered prison for a three-year sentence. While in prison, his wife died, he suffered a heart attack, and it was found only seven months into his sentence that he was dying of incurable lung cancer. Paroled, he returned home, and died on 9 May 1976, at the age of 67.

See also Kerner Commission.

Kerner Commission

Officially known as the National Commission on Civil Disorders, this panel of distinguished Americans assembled by President Lyndon B. Johnson on 27 July 1967, following racial riots in Newark and Detroit, was a ten-man, one-woman panel chaired by Governor Otto Kerner of Illinois. Besides Kerner, the commission's members were: Roy Wilkins, executive director of the National Association for the Advancement of Colored People (NAACP); Mayor John V. Lindsay of New York; Sen. Edward W. Brooke of Massachusetts; Iorwith Wilbur ("I. W.") Abel, president of the United Steelworkers; Charles Thornton, president and chairman of the board of Litton Industries; Sen. Fred Harris, Democrat of Oklahoma; Rep. William M. McCulloch, Republican of Ohio; Rep. James C. Corman, Democrat of California; Katherine Graham Peden, commerce commissioner of the state of Kentucky; and Herbert Jenkins, chief of police, Atlanta, Georgia.

The commission's report, released on 2 March 1968, started with one dramatic conclusion: "Our nation is moving toward two separate societies, one black, one white—separate and unequal." In a multisectioned report, the commission 1) studied the 1967 riots; 2) looked into whether each riot followed a distinct pattern; 3) investigated whether there was planning or organization in the riots; 4) addressed the causes of the riots; 5) traced the history of the "Negro protest"; 6) examined the reasons why ghettoes persisted; 7) discussed the problems of unemployment, family structure, and social disorganization in the ghettoes; 8) focused on life in the ghettoes; 9) compared the experiences of natural immigrants and blacks; 10) explained how the community's response to pressures that build up would cause or head off riots; 11) considered responses from the police that would serve to diffuse crises; 12) recommended a plan by which only experienced police would cover ghetto areas; 13) called for the creation of an emergency justice system to handle arrests during a riot or similar crisis; 14) plotted the federal government's role in cleaning up the rioted areas; and 15) praised the news and other media for a balanced and factual handling of the riots. There was a further description of the future of the American city without reforms, as well as commission recommendations for national action.

See also Kerner, Otto, Jr.

Keyes v. School District No. 1 of Denver, Colorado (U.S., 1973)

The matter of segregated schools in the northern part of the United States was addressed for the first time in this little-known but landmark Supreme Court decision. Although there was no legal segregation in Denver—in fact, Colorado had an antisegregation law—the plaintiff Keyes sued on the grounds that certain decisions made by the school board of District No. 1 created "a segregated atmosphere." The Court found that Denver had no special obligation to remedy segregation through law. The Court, through the majority opinion written by

Justice William Brennan, defined the differences between *de jure* segregation (segregation that is constituted by law) and *de facto* segregation (segregation created by housing patterns, community equations, and other factors not having the backing of law or state action). Justice William Rehnquist dissented from the entire opinion, and Justice Lewis Powell, Jr., concurred in part and dissented in part, calling for the end of what he called "the *de facto–de jure* distinction."

King, Chevene Bowers (1923–1988)

C. B. King was a little-known civil rights lawyer in the deep South during the turbulent 1960s who played a key role in the civil rights movement when he served for a time as the personal attorney for the Reverend Dr. Martin Luther King, Jr., and the Reverend Ralph David Abernathy. Chevene King, who was not related to Martin Luther King, was born in Albany, Georgia, on 12 October 1923. He attended local schools, served in the U.S. Navy, then received a degree from Fisk University in Nashville and a law degree from Case Western Reserve University in Ohio.

In 1962, King and Atlanta attorney Donald L. Hollowell represented Reverend Dr. Martin Luther King and Reverend Ralph David Abernathy when the two men were arrested during a civil rights march. King was also the lawyer for a group of students who conducted a sit-in in Albany. When King went to the Albany courthouse to visit a group of demonstrators who were under arrest, he was hit on the head by a blunt instrument. He later accused a sheriff of committing the act, but could not prove the allegation. Outside of his law practice, he ran for a congressional seat in 1964, but was defeated. King later ran for governor of Georgia in 1970, the first black to do so since Reconstruction. He came in third in the Democratic primary with 8 percent of the vote. Known as "C. B.," King died of cancer in San Diego, California, on 15 March 1988, at 65 years of age.

King, Martin Luther, Jr. (1929–1968)

The Reverend Dr. Martin Luther King remains the best-known and most revered of the civil rights leaders our nation has produced. He was born on 15 January 1929, in Atlanta, Georgia, the son of the Reverend Martin Luther King, Sr., later known as "Daddy King," whose own father, James Albert King, had been a poor sharecropper. Martin Luther King, Jr., was of a mixed heritage of African, Irish, and American Indian.

In 1940, after skipping a year of high school, King entered Morehouse College, an all-black school in Atlanta. Although at first he majored in sociology, by his senior year he had decided to follow in his father's footsteps and enter the ministry. In 1947, he was ordained as a Baptist minister and made assistant pastor at the Ebenezer Baptist Church in Atlanta. After graduating from Morehouse in 1948, he entered the Crozer Theological Seminary to finish his religious training. While at Crozer in 1950, he heard a lecture on the pacifist teachings of Mohandas Gandhi, the Indian civil rights leader who, in 1948, had led a successful peaceful revolt against British rule in India. In 1951, King graduated from Crozer with the highest grade point average in his class. He then enrolled at Boston University to earn a doctorate in philosophy. It was there that he fell in love with, and later married, Coretta Scott, a native of Alabama. In June 1952, King and his wife, who had completed her studies at the prestigious New England Conservatory of Music, returned to the racially divided South, where King in 1954 was named pastor of the Dexter Avenue Church in Montgomery, Alabama. He accepted the pastorate and took control of the church in May 1954.

Just seven months later Montgomery exploded, following the decision by a white bus driver to have black seamstress

Martin Luther King, Jr.

Rosa Parks arrested for refusing to leave the white section of a city bus. Four days later, at a meeting at the Holt Street Baptist Church, the Montgomery Improvement Association (MIA) was created, with King as the organization's president. As its first act, the MIA issued an order to all black patrons of the city bus system to boycott the system immediately. Over the next year, until the buses were desegregated in December 1956, King and his followers suffered threats, abuse, arrest, and trial for their support of the boycott. On 30 January 1955, while King was in jail on a speeding charge, someone attempted to bomb his home, leaving his wife and child stunned but uninjured. Tried on a state charge that his city bus boycott was blocking the operation of a lawful business, King was found guilty but released on appeal. In November 1956, the U.S. Supreme Court overturned Montgomery's segregated bus system as a violation of the Constitution. In December, it was King along with other MIA intimates who rode the first desegregated bus in Montgomery.

With the end of the boycott, King became the most famous civil rights leader in the country. In January 1957, he was one of 60 civil rights leaders who created the Southern Christian Leadership Conference (SCLC), which was the first civil rights organization of the modern civil rights era. Installed as president of the SCLC, King led the group in the Prayer Pilgrimage to Washington, D.C., on the third anniversary of the Supreme Court's historic *Brown* decision, which had desegregated the nation's schools. That year, after visiting the African nation of Ghana, he published his first book, *Stride Toward Freedom*, a work about the Montgomery bus boycott. Over the next three years he was jailed, heckled, and almost assassinated in New York. Nevertheless, he persevered, but in 1959 he was forced to resign from the Dexter Avenue Church in Montgomery.

In the early 1960s, King oversaw the rising struggle for civil rights. Following a sit-in demonstration in Atlanta, he was arrested for violating probation. Sent to prison, it took calls from Sen. John F. Kennedy, then running for president, and his brother Robert, to get King out of jail. Their commitment to him led King, as well as multitudes of black voters, to support Kennedy's run for president. Kennedy's presidency, however, was a disappointment to King. Nothing was done on the federal front in the fight for civil rights until the 1963 clash in Birmingham with Sheriff Eugene "Bull" Connor was seen by a shocked nation. Kennedy called segregation immoral and stepped up the fight to get federal civil rights legislation passed.

It was at this time, during the drive in Birmingham to desegregate dining and other facilities, that King was arrested again. While incarcerated, he wrote his now famous *Letter from Birmingham Jail*, one of the most important documents of the civil rights movement. Written on 16 April 1963, the letter called attention to the demands of blacks in Birmingham. In it, he wrote: "There can be no gainsaying the fact that racial injustice engulfs this community. Birmingham is probably the most thoroughly segregated city in the United States. Its ugly record of brutality is widely known. Negroes have experienced grossly unjust treatment in the courts. There have been more unsolved bombings of Negro homes and churches in Birmingham than in any other city in the nation. These are the hard, brutal facts of the case." On 10 May, just three weeks later, Birmingham officials met most of the SCLC's demands dealing with desegregating public facilities. On 28 August 1963, King participated in the historic March on Washington, in which 250,000 people, both black and white, came to the nation's capital to protest segregation. During the march, King delivered his "I Have a Dream" speech, in which he laid out his vision for a society free of racism.

Over the next five years, King worked to improve American society's attitudes toward racial matters. Several times he participated in SCLC campaigns for voter registration and against segregation. In 1963 he was *Time* magazine's Man of the Year. In 1964, he was awarded the Nobel Peace Prize. In 1965, he led the famous Selma to Montgomery march, which culminated in the passage of the 1965 Voting Rights Act.

King was always under threat of assassination. Yet he never flinched from what he saw as his responsibility to fight for civil rights. This same mission brought him to Memphis on 3 April 1968 to participate in a sanitation workers' strike. The next day, while King stood on a balcony at the Lorraine Motel, Memphis, shots rang out, striking King and wounding him fatally. James Earl Ray, a career criminal, was later arrested and pleaded guilty to the murder. King's body was brought back to Atlanta, where he was laid to rest. On his tomb are the words of his famous speech during the March on Washington: "Free at last! Free at last! Thank God almighty, we are free at last."

See also "I Have A Dream" Speech; March on Washington for Jobs and Freedom.

Ku Klux Klan

The Ku Klux Klan is the ultra-racist organization that sprang up following the Civil War to harass freed slaves. The first two words of the name come from the Greek *kuklos*, or "band"; *Klan* is simply a variation on *clan*. The group was founded sometime in May or June 1866, in Judge Thomas M. Jones's law office in Pulaski, Tennessee. Six men, all former Confederate soldiers, are credited with being the founding members of the Klan: Major James R. Crowe; Captain John C. Lester, later a lawyer and member of the Tennessee legislature; Calvin Jones, son of Judge Jones; John B. Kennedy; Frank O. McCord, editor of a weekly newspaper, the Pulaski *Citizen;* and Richard R. Reed. Positions in the group were laid out: the head was the Grand Cyclops (today the Grand Wizard), the second in command the Grand Magi, the third in command the Grand Turk, and others called Lictors, or guardians. Frank O. McCord was the first Grand Cyclops, and there is evidence that Kennedy, who came up with the name Ku Klux Klan, was the first Grand Magi. The group's original costume included such devices as a cap with colorful feathers, but eventually evolved into the frightening white robe and hood. The Klan grew in numbers as successive meetings were held in Pulaski to plot strategies. At a meeting in the Maxwell House Hotel in Nashville in 1867, a middle-aged man joined the Klan with great fervor. His name was Nathan Bedford Forrest, and he would eventually become the Grand Wizard of the entire Ku Klux Klan.

At the Nashville meeting, the group was structurally formulated: each group, or den, would consist of a Grand Cyclops, sustained by two Night Hawks. A county den was to be led by the Grand Giant of the Province and four Goblins. Each

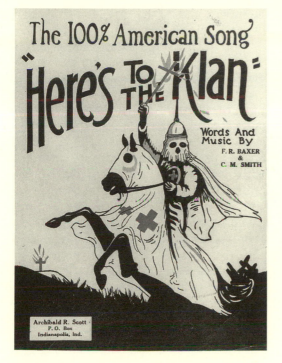

Ku Klux Klan sheet music from the 1920s

congressional district was to be under the command of the Grand Titan of the Dominion and six Furies. The state group was led by the Grand Dragon of the Realm and eight Hydras. The entire nation was to be commanded by the Grand Wizard of the Empire and his ten Genii. Further, each member had to swear the following pledge: "This is an institution of Chivalry, Humanity, Mercy, and Patriotism; embodying in its genius and its principles all that is chivalric in conduct, noble in sentiment, generous in manhood, and patriotic in purpose." Over the next several years, the Klan utilized terror, intimidation, and murder to stop black suffrage and intimidate former slaves.

In 1871, the House of Representatives created a Joint Select Committee on the Condition of Affairs in the Late Insurrectionary States, the so-called Ku Klux Klan Committee. On it sat seven senators and 14 representatives. The group's goal was simple: to examine the condition in the former Confederate states and see what impact the Ku Klux Klan was having on efforts to improve the lot of the freed slaves. Such witnesses as Gen. John B. Gordon of Georgia, a Klan member, and Forrest testified before the committee. In response to a question on the Klan's motives, Gordon said: "The organization was simply this—nothing more and nothing less; it was an organization, a brotherhood of the property-holders, the peaceable, law-abiding citizens of the state, for self-protection." For the Klan, however, its reputation as a "fraternal organization" committed to the superiority of whites soon was dirtied by reports of the abuse and murder of black citizens in the South. By the 1880s, most Klan members were jailed or had given up their fight.

In 1915, an event occurred that gave birth to the "second rising" of the Klan. It was the release of silent film *Birth of a Nation*, based on Thomas Dixon's epic book *The Clansmen*, which had created great controversy when first published. Director David Wark (D. W.) Griffith, a great innovator in moviemaking at the time, took Dixon's book and created an expansive view of the South after the Civil War, as seen through the eyes of white Southerners. Viewers were treated to a white woman being attacked by newly freed slaves, to scenes of black "savages" who had been elected to state legislatures acting like buffoons, and to images of the noble Ku Klux Klan coming to the aid of a family harrassed by blacks. In the South, *Birth of a Nation* was seen as a vindication of their "lost cause" in the Civil War. Although a generation had passed since the first Klan, Griffith's portrayal of the group as one of respect and white power gave it new life.

Additional impetus for the Klan's second rising came from the case of Leo M. Frank, a Jewish pencil factory owner in Atlanta, Georgia. Sentenced to death for the rape and murder of Mary Phagan, a young girl, Frank was kidnapped and lynched by a group calling itself "The Knights of Mary Phagan." This group, headed by Spanish–American War veteran William Joseph Simmons, later converged atop Stone Mountain outside Atlanta and proclaimed themselves the new Ku Klux Klan. Within 10 years, many parts of the country were ruled by officials who had been elected either as Klan members or with Klan backing. One of the key controversies of the 1924 Democratic National Convention was the insertion of an anti-Klan plank in the party platform.

Eventually, several factors nearly drove the Klan to a second extinction. Violence by some Klansmen earned them unflattering headlines, and the overall message of the Klan turned off many voters. Federal authorities prosecuted Klan members, and by the early 1940s the grip of the Klan was broken.

The third rising of the Klan, one that continues today, came with the emergence of the modern civil rights movement. Their tactics in opposing Southern desegregation included murder, bombing, and other terrorist acts. Nevertheless, this third Klan, never more than a few thousand members strong, dwindled with civil rights victories, widespread public disapprobation, and federal prosecution. By the 1970s, the Klan was outpaced in violence and savagery by white supremacist groups, such as The Order and the White Aryan Resistance. Although still a threat, the Klan today is but a shell of its former self.

See also Birth of a Nation; Dees, Morris Seligman, Jr.; Forrest, Nathan Bedford.

Lane v. Wilson et al.
(U.S., 1939)

Lane was the Supreme Court case in which the "Grandfather Clause" was ruled unconstitutional. Plaintiff Lane, a black man, sued Wilson and two other unnamed Oklahoma state elections officials. Under election laws, only those voters who voted in 1914 could legally vote in the 1934 election. In 1915, the Supreme Court held in *Guinn and Beal v. United States* that any such "Grandfather Clause," which, in 1914, had prohibited from voting any person who had not voted in 1866, was unconstitutional. Because many blacks had been prohibited from voting in 1914, they were ineligible to vote in 1934. Lane sued for $5,000 in damages and took his case to a district court, which ruled against him, and an appeals court, which affirmed the lower court's decision. The Supreme Court granted *certiorari*, and on 22 May 1939 struck down the Oklahoma law as "repugnant" to Lane's rights under the Fifteenth Amendment. Wrote Justice Felix Frankfurter: "A negro who is denied by state registration officials the right of registration, prerequisite to the right to vote, under color of a state registration statute which, in violation of the Fifteenth Amendment, works discrimination against the colored race, has a right of action against such officials ."

Langston, John Mercer (1829–1897)

John Langston was, in 1855, the first black elected to a public office; he later served a single term in the U.S. House of Representatives. Langston was born in Lousa, Virginia, on 14 December 1829, the son of a white plantation owner, Ralph Quarles, and a free black mother, Lucy Langston. John Langston was never a slave; when his parents died in 1834, he was sent to live with a family friend. He received his college education from Oberlin College in Ohio, which awarded him a bachelor's degree in 1849 and a master's three years later. Denied admission to several law schools because he was half-black, Langston instead studied under a local judge in Elyria, Ohio. In 1854, he was admitted to the Ohio bar.

In 1855, while handling a private law practice in Brownhelm, Ohio, Langston was elected clerk of the township on the Liberty party ticket, thereby becoming the first black in America to be elected to public office. Frederick Douglass, in his *Frederick Douglass's Paper* of 20 April 1855, reported Langston's election in a letter from the newly elected clerk: "They [the Liberty Party] put upon their ticket the name of a colored man, who was elected clerk of Brownhelm Township, by a very handsome majority indeed. Since I am the only colored man who lives in this township, you can easily guess the name of the man who was so fortunate to secure this election. To my knowledge, the like has not been known in Ohio before. It argues the steady march of the Anti-Slavery sentiment, and augurs the inevitable destruction and annihilation of American prejudice against colored men."

In 1856, Langston moved to Oberlin, where he served on that town's board of education. During the Civil War, Langston recruited black soldiers to fight for the Union army. In 1864, he became the head of the National Equal Rights League. Following the war, he served as a member of the Oberlin City Council and was reelected to the town board of education. In 1867, he was hired by the Freedmen's Bureau to tour the South and speak on the need for former slaves to get an education. The following year, Langston founded the Howard University Law School, of which he was dean from 1868 until 1875.

From 1871 until 1874, Langston was a member of the District of Columbia Board of Health, and from 1874–1875 he served as vice president of Howard University. In 1877, President Rutherford B. Hayes appointed Langston as Minister to Haiti and chargé d'affairs to Santo Domingo. Langston served eight years in this post. In 1885 he resigned and settled in Virginia, where he became the head of the Virginia Normal and Collegiate Institute in Petersburg, which had been founded by a Republican administration in the state. In 1888, Langston was forced to resign from the school when the state elected a Democratic governor. Instead, he ran for a seat representing the Fourth Congressional District in the U.S. House of Representatives. Initial results showed that he had lost by some 300 votes, but he challenged the election in the House. In a committee hearing that was boycotted by Democrats, the House declared Langston the winner. The challenge had taken all of the two years of the term. A week later, Langston ran for "reelection" and lost. He returned to Washington to serve what was left of his term. When he left Congress in March 1891, he had served a total of four months. The Republicans tried to recruit him to run again in 1892, but Langston refused. Instead, he published his memoirs, *From the Virginia Plantation to the National Capitol,* in 1894. John Mercer Langston died in Washington, D.C., on 15 November 1897.

Lee, Bernard Scott (1935–1991)

A civil rights leader who was an associate of the Reverend Dr. Martin Luther King, Jr., and a founding member of the Student Nonviolent Coordinating Committee (SNCC), the Reverend Bernard Scott Lee was born in Norfolk, Virginia,

in 1935. He attended local schools and later served in the U.S. Air Force. He was a student at Alabama State College in Montgomery in 1960, when he became a founding member of the SNCC. Lee also organized Freedom Rides in the South, as well as civil rights protests in such places as Albany, Georgia. He later received both his bachelor's degree and divinity degree from Howard University. In 1965, Lee marched with Reverend Dr. Martin Luther King, whom he had known since 1955, in the famous Selma to Montgomery march to urge Congress to pass the 1965 Voting Rights Act. In the 1960s, in the years leading up to King's assassination, Lee served as a vice president of the Southern Christian Leadership Conference (SCLC) in Atlanta. When King was murdered in Memphis in April 1968, Lee was about to join him in his hotel room and was in a courtyard below when the fatal shots rang out.

Following King's death, Lee was less visible in the civil rights movement. In 1976 he was named by President Jimmy Carter as a special assistant to the Environmental Protection Agency (EPA) administrator. In 1980, Lee served as the deputy campaign chairman in Mississippi for Carter's reelection effort.

In his final years, Lee worked with inmates at the Lorton Correctional Complex in Washington, D.C. In 1990, he underwent triple bypass surgery, but succumbed to heart disease on 10 February 1991. He was 55 years old.

Leibowitz, Samuel Simon (1893–1978)

Samuel Leibowitz was the noted attorney who defended the Scottsboro Boys during their trials in the 1930s and 1940s. Leibowitz was born Samuel LeBeau in Jasey, Romania, on 14 August 1893, and immigrated with his parents to the United States when he was four. His father, a poor pushcart peddler on New York's Lower East Side, changed the family name. After attending local schools in New York, Leibowitz enrolled at Cornell University, from which he received his law degree in 1916. Although his law practice started out slow at first, he gradually built a reputation as a fiery orator in the courtroom. In the 1920s, he earned the emnity of prosecutors with his successful defenses of gangsters and racketeers, such as Al Capone. In all, he defended 140 clients and bragged later that he lost only one to the electric chair. Leibowitz's real fame came in 1931, with the Scottsboro Boys case. After the nine young men involved in the alleged rape in Alabama had been convicted and sentenced to death, Leibowitz gave up his lucrative law practice in New York and headed down south. This was a strange and dangerous place for a Jewish liberal hell-bent on defending the nine black "fiends" accused of raping two white women. Yet Leibowitz handled the case with grace and aplomb, refusing to succumb to the taunts of segregationists who attended the trial. Even though, on appeal, Leibowitz got the Supreme Court to overturn all of the death sentences, they were eventually reimposed on all but one of the youths by an Alabama court. Leibowitz worked tirelessly throughout the rest of the decade and into the 1940s, until all of the charges against the Scottsboro nine were dropped and they were all freed. Following his work for the Scottsboro Boys, Leibowitz was named to a seat on New York's Criminal Court in 1941, a post he held for 28 years. Although still a liberal, he was noted for the harshness of the sentences he imposed on convicted criminals. From 1949 to 1951, he conducted a wide-scale investigation of organized crime in New York. Leibowitz retired in 1969, at the age of 76. In an interview that year he said: "If there's anything else I can take to my grave, it's that I got the first black man on a jury in the South in the history of the United States." Leibowitz died eight years later, on 11 January 1978.

See also Scottsboro Boys.

Lewis, John (1940–)

John Lewis was one of the founders of the Student Nonviolent Coordinating Committee (SNCC) in the 1960s. Noted as a tireless worker in the pursuit of equality, he was later elected to a seat in the U.S. House of Representatives. Lewis was born on 21 February 1940, in Troy, Alabama, the son of a sharecropper. He attended local schools, then enrolled at the American Baptist Theological Seminary in Nashville. It was at the seminary that Lewis began to agitate for civil rights. With fellow student Diane Nash and others, he helped found the Nashville Student Movement. The movement organized student sit-ins and other demonstrations on behalf of civil rights. He was a founding member of the SNCC and served as the group's chairman from 1963 until 1966. As head of SNCC and a Freedom Rider in the 1960s, Lewis spearheaded a drive during the Mississippi Summer in 1964 to register black voters. In 1965, he was a visible participant in the march from Selma to Montgomery. After leaving SNCC, he served with the Southern Regional Council and the Voter Education Project, both voter registration organizations.

In the 1970s, Lewis became involved in politics. Named to a federal agency by President Jimmy Carter in 1977, Lewis later was elected to the Atlanta City Council. In 1986, he was elected to a seat in the U.S. House of Representatives, a seat he still holds.

See also Student Nonviolent Coordinating Committee.

Little, Malcolm
See Malcolm X.

Lombard et al. v. Louisiana (U.S., 1963)

Lombard was a Supreme Court case in which the Court ruled that the intent by government officials to uphold segregationist practices, even in the absence of specific segregationist laws, was contrary to the Fourteenth Amendment. The plaintiffs were three black students and one white student who staged a sit-in demonstration at a McCrory Five and Ten in New Orleans on 17 September 1960. After being refused service, they were asked by the store manager to leave. Although there was no state or city statute requiring segregation in dining facilities, the mayor and police chief had announced that such demonstrations would not be tolerated; the four were thus arrested and convicted of "criminal mischief." They were ordered to pay a fine of $350 each and to serve 60 days in jail. If the fine went unpaid, an additional term of 60 days was to be served. On appeal, the Louisiana Supreme Court upheld the sentences. The Supreme Court granted *certiorari*, and ruled, on 20 May 1963, that the convictions of the four violated the equal protection clause of the Fourteenth Amendment. Wrote Justice Earl Warren: "As we interpret the New Orleans city officials' statements, they were determined that the city would not permit Negroes to seek desegregated service in restaurants. Consequently, the city must be treated exactly as if it had an ordinance prohibiting such conduct."

Long, Jefferson Franklin (1836–1900? or 1901?)

Jefferson Franklin Long was the first black congressman from Georgia and the first black to speak on the floor of the House of Representatives. He was born a slave in the small hamlet of Knoxville, in western Georgia, on 3 March 1836, the son of a slave mother and a white father. Little is known about Long's early years; however, he did receive some semblance of an education and became a tailor, settling in Macon, Georgia.

A tailor and prosperous merchant, Long was soon connected to Republican politics. In December 1870, the state held elections to fill seats in the U.S. House of Representatives for a short session of the Forty-first Congress, January–March 1871. Long was elected to the seat in the Fourth Georgia District. He took his seat on 16 January 1871 and served until 3 March 1871. Long was the second black in the House after Joseph Hayne Rainey of South Carolina. In the short time of his tenure, Long became the first black member to make an address from the House floor. He called for opposition to a House bill that would have restored the rights of former Confederates before they pledged allegiance to the Union. He further supported ratification of the Fifteenth Amendment and called for the suffrage of all persons in the District of Columbia.

After Long left office, he became disillusioned with the Republican Party, which he felt treated blacks unfairly, and with politics in general, as he saw blacks disenfranchised, their rights whittled away after all they had fought for in the Civil War. Eventually he returned to his tailoring business. The date of his death remains in dispute. Some sources say he died in Macon on 5 February 1900, while others claim 4 February 1901.

Louisiana Ex Rel. Gremillion, Attorney General, et al. v. NAACP et al. (U.S., 1961)

Gremillion, like *Bryant v. Zimmerman* and *NAACP v. Alabama Ex Rel. Patterson, Attorney General*, revolved around the issue of an organization defying a state demand to see the group's membership lists. Like *Patterson* in 1958, this 1961 Supreme Court decision was crucial to allowing the NAACP to work in a state free from harassment. Jack P. F. Gremillion, attorney general of the state of Louisiana, sued in 1956 to force the Louisiana NAACP to release its membership lists under a state law in which organizations had to file with the state a list of the organization's officers and members. The NAACP sued to stop enforcement of the law. A district court enjoined, or stopped, the state from enforcing the law. The state of Louisiana, represented by Attorney General Gremillion, sued to the U.S. Supreme Court. On 22 May 1961, the Court ruled 9-0 to uphold the lower court's judgment. Justice William O. Douglas wrote the Court's opinion, in which he said, "If it be shown that disclosure of the Association's membership lists results in reprisals and hostility to members, such disclosure may not be required consistently with the First Amendment, made applicable to the states by the Due Process Clause of the Fourteenth Amendment."

See also Bryant v. Zimmerman; NAACP v. Alabama Ex Rel. Patterson, Attorney General.

Louisville, New Orleans & Texas Railway v. Mississippi (U.S., 1890)

Louisville was the first Supreme Court case that dealt with segregation in railway travel. The plaintiff, the Louisville, New Orleans & Texas Railway Company, was ordered by a Mississippi statute to provide a segregated car on all of its trains traveling through the state of Mississippi. The railroad sued to stop enforcement of the statute as an infringement of interstate commerce. In the earlier case of *Hall v. DeCuir*, the Court had ruled that the regulation of interstate travel was the exclusive province of the Congress. In that case, a state law desegregating public transport was struck down. In *Louisville* the Court ruled just the opposite. Justice David Brewer wrote the 7–2 decision of the Court, which upheld the Mississippi statute. Justice John Marshall Harlan was incredulous at the difference in the Court's attitude toward statutes of similar nature from different states. Harlan angrily wrote in his stinging dissent that he "found it difficult to understand how a state enactment, requiring the separation of the white and black races on interstate

carriers of passengers, is [not] a regulation of commerce among the states, while a similar enactment forbidding such separation is a regulation of the character."

See also Hall v. DeCuir.

Loving v. Virginia (U.S., 1967)

Loving was the landmark Supreme Court case in which state bans on intermarriage between whites and blacks were held to be unconstitutional. In 1958, two Virginia residents, Mildred Jeter, a black woman, and Richard Loving, a white man, were married in Washington, D.C. They then returned home to Virginia, where a ban on such intermarriages existed. A grand jury indicted the pair for violating the state antimiscegenation statute, and in January 1959 they pleaded guilty to the charge. Each received a one-year jail term, but the judge offered to suspend the sentences if the two left the state and did not return for a period of 25 years; after that period, they might return, but only divorced. They followed this dictate and left the state, taking up residence in the District of Columbia.

In 1963, they asked a trial court to set aside the convictions so that they might return as a couple to Virginia. When the court refused, they asked the United States District Court for the Eastern District of Virginia in October 1964 to set aside the convictions. The court upheld the verdicts, as well as the constitutionality of the state law, and on 12 December 1966 the Supreme Court granted *certiorari*. On 12 June 1967, the Court unanimously struck down the Virginia ban. Writing for the Court, Chief Justice Earl Warren held that the ban violated the equal protection and due process clause of the Fourteenth Amendment. Concurring in the judgment, Justice Potter Stewart said: "It is simply not possible for state law to be valid under our Constitution which makes the criminality of an act depend upon the race of the actor."

Lowery, Joseph Echols (1924–)

A noted civil rights leader, the Reverend Joseph E. Lowery has been the head of Southern Christian Leadership Conference (SCLC) since 1977. He was born in Huntsville, Alabama, on 6 October 1924, the grandson of a noted pastor. His early education included periods at Knoxville College, Payne College, and Wayne University. He received his divinity degrees from the Payne Theological Seminary and Chicago Ecumenical Institute. In 1948, a year after preaching his first sermon at the Lakeside United Methodist Church in Huntsville, where his grandfather had a pastorate (he was the first black pastor in Huntsville), Lowery was given his own pastorate at the St. James Church in Montgomery, Alabama. A year later, he was sent to a church in Alexander City, Alabama. It was here that Lowery first became involved in the civil rights struggle, serving for a time as president of the Interdenominational Ministerial Alliance, an early civil rights group. In the early 1950s, he was among four ministers sued in the landmark *Sullivan v. New York Times* lawsuit, which was decided by the U.S. Supreme Court.

In 1952, Lowery became head of Alabama's second largest church, the Warren Street Church, in Mobile, Alabama. While at Mobile, he was again named head of the Interdenominational Ministerial Alliance and, as president of the organization, gave financial support to the Montgomery Bus Boycott going on nearby. As head of the Alabama Civic Affairs Association, based in Mobile, Lowery led the black citizens of that city in calling for desegregated busing in Mobile. In 1957, Lowery, Reverend Dr. Martin Luther King, Jr., Reverend Fred Shuttlesworth, and Reverend Ralph David Abernathy founded the SCLC as a vehicle for civil rights agitation. Lowery became the SCLC's first secretary. In 1967, King asked him to become chairman of the SCLC national board of directors, a post he held for 10 years.

In the 1960s, as head of the Nashville Inter-Civic Coordinating Council, Lowery was responsible for civil rights crusades in Nashville, Tennessee, and for leading the drive to hire black policemen in Birmingham. After the assassination of Reverend Dr. Martin Luther King in 1968, Lowery remained one of the leaders in the SCLC. In 1977, he was unanimously elected the organization's third president, succeeding the Reverend Abernathy. As SCLC president, Lowery has been just as outspoken as he was during his years on the front lines of the civil rights battle. In 1982, he led a 2,700-mile march through five states and 70 cities that heightened the awareness for an extension of the Voting Rights Act. New programs such as "Wings of Hope," an antidrug effort, and the "Stop the Killing!" campaign against guns, are examples of Lowery's leadership. He remains, as of this writing, one of the last surviving leaders of the early years of the civil rights struggles.

See also Southern Christian Leadership Conference.

Lynch, John Roy (1847–1939)

Known as the first black to serve as the temporary chairman of a national political convention and as a three-term congressman from Mississippi, John Lynch was born a slave on the Tacony Plantation near Vidalia, or Vadalia, in Concordia Parish, Louisiana, on 10 September 1847. He was the son of Catherine White, a slave, and Patrick Lynch, a white plantation owner. Lynch's father died before he could buy Lynch's mother and their three sons, and all four were sold to a planter who moved them to Natchez, Mississippi. Freed when Union troops entered Mississippi in 1863, Lynch joined an Illinois regiment as a cook. After the war, he was apprenticed as a photographer and, for a while, owned his own studio. In his spare time, he would study books. For a period, he attended an all-white chil-

John Roy Lynch

dren's school during the day and an all-black school at night.

In 1868, Lynch was recruited by the Republican Club of Natchez to lobby for political appointments from the military governor, Adelbert Ames. Lynch related in his autobiography, *Reminiscences of an Active Life*, that Ames treated him with cordiality and respect. The governor was so impressed with the former slave that he appointed him justice of the peace of Adams County, which included Natchez. Lynch served in this post from April to December 1869, leaving it after his election to a seat in the state House of Representatives. Lynch served on the prestigious Judiciary Committee and the Committee on Elections and Education in his first term. Reelected in 1871, Lynch was made speaker of the House, and he utilized this post to gerrymander all of Mississippi House districts into majority Republican districts. For his work, the Republicans nominated Lynch for a seat in the U.S. House of Representatives in 1872. He was easily elected over his Democratic opponent. At 25, Lynch was sworn into the Forty-third Congress in March 1873. Eight days after Congress convened he made his first speech, denouncing pay increases, on the House floor. Later, he spoke in favor of the passage of the Civil Rights Act of 1875.

In 1874, Lynch was reelected, but in 1876, Republican governor James L. Alcorn requested federal troops because Democrats had set up a White League to stop blacks from voting. Lynch returned to Mississippi and canvassed the state with Senator-elect Blanche K. Bruce, the second black in the U.S. Senate. Lynch was defeated in the election by James Chalmers, a former Confederate general. Although there was a protest that blacks were prohibited from voting, Chalmers was seated. Lynch ran against Chalmers in 1880. Even though there was a 15,000-vote Republican majority in the district, Chalmers again won. Again, Lynch challenged Chalmers for fraud. After a lengthy investigation, the House seated Lynch. It was nearly the end of the term, however, and Lynch lost reelection in 1882. His congressional career ended on 3 March 1883. His career in politics, however, was not over. From 1881 until 1883, he was the chairman of the Mississippi state Republican executive committee. In 1884, he was the temporary chairman and keynote speaker at the Republican National Convention, the first black to be so honored. President Benjamin Harrison appointed him as the fourth auditor of the United States Treasury, a post Lynch held from 1889 until 1893. In 1896, he was admitted to the Mississippi bar and opened a private law practice there. During the Spanish–American War, he served as the paymaster to the United States Army, with the rank of captain. He was promoted to the rank of major in 1906 and retired from the military in 1911.

In 1912, Lynch moved to Chicago, where he continued his law practice. He published *The Facts of Reconstruction* (1913), which dealt with his role in that period of history. He contributed articles to the *Journal of Negro History* and finished his memoirs in the 1930s, although they were not published until 1970. John Roy Lynch died in Chicago on 2 November 1939 and was buried with full military honors in Arlington National Cemetery. In an obituary, the *New York Times* said that Lynch was "one of the most fluent and forceful speakers in the politics of the Seventies and Eighties."

Malcolm X (1925–1965)

Malcolm X, also known by his birthname Malcolm Little, and his religious name El-Hajj Malik El-Shabazz, was a minister in the Nation of Islam who was assassinated by Muslim extremists in 1965. Malcolm X was born Malcolm Little on 19 May 1925, in Omaha, Nebraska, the son of the Reverend Earl Little, a Baptist minister. When Malcolm was young, the family moved to Lansing, Michigan, where the family home was burned down by the Ku Klux Klan. When his son was six years old, Reverend Little was killed in an accident when he fell under the wheels of a streetcar, but to the end of his life, Malcolm X believed his father had been murdered.

Malcolm dropped out of school in the eighth grade and took a bus to Boston to live with his sister. There, he was caught up in the seamier side of urban life: he ran numbers, hustled and sold drugs, and pimped for both black and white prostitutes. To satisfy his $20-a-day cocaine habit, he committed a series of burglaries, which culminated in his arrest in a Boston suburb in 1946. He was sentenced to a term of eight to ten years, but served only six before being paroled in 1952. In prison, however, Malcolm came under the influence of the teachings of Elijah Muhammad, who led the Nation of Islam, a radical black religious sect. Elijah Muhammad, formerly Elijah Poole, taught that black men were the superior race and that whites were "devils." Before his release, Malcolm shed his "slave name," Little, changed it to "X," and began to educate himself about the workings of Islam. Soon after his release from prison, he went to Chicago, Muhammad's headquarters, and was ordained a minister. Over the next 12 years, as Muhammad's spokesman, Malcolm X toured the country and opened several Muslim mosques.

He is credited with building the Nation of Islam's following in the United States from about 1,000 in 1952 to more than 10,000 by 1963.

Following President John F. Kennedy's assassination in November 1963, Malcolm X called the president's murder "a case of chickens coming home to roost," which led Elijah Muhammad to suspend him from the Nation of Islam. In March 1964, Malcolm X quit the sect altogether and set up his own religious group in Harlem, first calling it the Muslim Mosque, Inc., then the Organization of Afro-American Unity. He collided with Muhammad when he called his former leader a "racist" and a "religious faker." Muhammad responded by issuing a notice that Malcolm X was "worthy of death." On 14 February 1965, Malcolm X's home in Queens, New York, was fire-bombed, but he and his family were unhurt. Just a week later, on 21 February 1965, he was scheduled to speak to a crowd at the Audubon Ballroom in Washington Heights, in upper Manhattan. As he approached the podium to speak, shots rang out and Malcolm X was fatally wounded. Three Muslims—Talmadge X Hayer, Norman 3X Butler, and Thomas 15X Johnson—were eventually convicted of the murder and served various prison terms. Hayer later said that he was behind the killing and that Butler and Johnson were innocent. In an article written in the year before his death, Malcolm X wrote prophetically: "Some of the followers of Elijah Muhammad would still consider it a first-rank honor to kill me."

Malcolm X

Black director Spike Lee's 1992 film *Malcolm X* was the first cinematic treatment of this civil rights advocate.

The controversial film and the subsequent national discussion of Malcolm X's place in civil rights history have led many

Americans, both black and white, to re-examine his life.

March on Washington for Jobs and Freedom (1963)

In August 1963, several hundred thousand people of all races, led by leading civil rights advocates, marched to Washington, D.C., to demonstrate for civil rights and against segregation in the United States. The procession has become symbolic for the shift in attitudes in the American public it demonstrated. Known more formally as the March on Washington, the demonstration was arranged to push for a comprehensive civil rights bill in Congress, to call for national desegregation of schools in 1963, and to demand a higher minimum wage. Ten civil rights and religious leaders led the march: Mathew Ahmann, executive director of the National Catholic Conference for Interracial Justice; Dr. Eugene Carson Blake, chief executive officer of the United Presbyterian Church in the United States; Rabbi Joachim Prinz, president of the American Jewish Congress; Whitney M. Young, Jr., executive director of the National Urban League; Walter P. Reuther, president of the United Automobile Workers; John Lewis, chairman of the Student Nonviolent Coordinating Committee; A. Philip Randolph, executive director of the Negro American Labor Congress and organizer of the march; Roy Wilkins, executive director of the National Association for the Advancement of Colored People; Floyd McKissick, national chairman of the Congress of Racial Equality (who was substituting for executive director James Farmer, who was imprisoned in Louisiana); and the Reverend Dr. Martin Luther King, Jr., president of the Southern Christian Leadership Conference. In all, some 200,000 people marched to the reflecting pool in front of the Lincoln Memorial, where King delivered his famous "I Have A Dream" speech. The pro-cession gave a new and fresh impetus to the growing civil rights movement and showed the government, which had been dragging its feet on litigation in this area, that action was needed quickly.

See also "I Have A Dream" Speech.

Marshall, Thurgood (1908–1993)

When Supreme Court Justice Thurgood Marshall died in early 1993, the *New York Times* wrote of him that he was a "pillar of the civil rights revolution, architect of the legal strategy that ended the era of official segregation, and the first black Justice of the U.S. Supreme Court"; many legal scholars, however, simply remember Thurgood Marshall as a judicial giant.

Marshall was born in Baltimore, Maryland, on 2 July 1908, the great-grandson of a slave and the son of a Pullman car porter and waiter. Marshall graduated with honors from Douglas High School in Baltimore, then attended Lincoln University in Pennsylvania, working his way through college by doing odd jobs such as clerking. When he graduated from Lincoln, he tried to enroll at the University of Maryland, but the school barred blacks, and he was turned away. Instead, he entered the Howard University Law School in Washington. Marshall graduated magna cum laude from Howard in 1933. Immediately, he opened a private practice but signed on as counsel to the Baltimore branch of the National Association for the Advancement of Colored People (NAACP). From 1933 until 1938, Marshall's chief specialty was civil rights cases. He became an assistant to Charles Hamilton Houston, special counsel to the NAACP. In 1938, upon Houston's retirement, Marshall succeeded him at the NAACP headquarters in New York City.

Marshall's first case as special counsel was to prepare the brief in the case of *Missouri Ex Rel. Gaines v. Canada*, in which a black man, Lloyd Gaines, was refused admission to the University of Missouri. Over the next several years, Marshall was the chief attorney in the nation dealing with civil rights. Said Federal Judge William H. Hastie of the Third Circuit Court of Appeals, in 1951: "Certainly no lawyer, and practically no member of the bench, has Thurgood Marshall's grasp of the doctrine of law as it affects civil rights." In 1947, Marshall handled the case of Heman Sweatt, a black man who wished to enter the University of Texas Law School but was denied because of his race. In 1954, Marshall paved the way for the end of legal segregation in schools, when he acted as chief counsel in the case of *Brown v. Board of Education of Topeka, Kansas.* Overall, Marshall won 29 of the 32 cases he personally handled for the NAACP.

In 1962, President John F. Kennedy appointed Marshall as a judge on the Second District Court of Appeals. The appointment was a lifetime one; however, in 1965, when President Lyndon B. Johnson offered Marshall the post of solicitor general—the individual who is charged with arguing the administration's cases before the Supreme Court—Marshall accepted. Two years later, upon the retirement of Justice Tom Clark, Johnson appointed Marshall to the Supreme Court. Although there was heavy Southern opposition to his appointment, Marshall was confirmed easily 69–11.

In his 23 years on the Court, Marshall, more than any other man, stood by his liberal principles. He supported busing and affirmative action, opposed the death penalty, and generally sided with what he called "the little man." As the 1980s wore on, however, and fellow justices from the Earl Warren era left the Court, Marshall was increasingly in the minority on many issues. He held out as long as he could for the day when he could be replaced by another liberal justice. In 1991, however, as he approached his 83rd birthday, age and failing health brought him to resign from the Court. Ironically, this first black man on the Court was replaced by

another African American, Clarence Thomas, whose upbringing was similar but whose ideology is very different.

Marshall lived only a year and a half after resigning from the Court. Ill health led to his hospitalization at the Bethesda Naval Medical Center in January 1993, where he died on 24 January at the age of 84.

See also Thomas, Clarence.

McCabe v. Atchison, Topeka & Santa Fe Railway (U.S., 1914)

McCabe was the first Supreme Court case that dealt with the constitutionality of state Jim Crow laws. The case involved a 1907 Oklahoma statute that required the railroads to "provide separate coaches or compartments, for the accommodation of the white and negro races equal in all points of comfort and convenience." McCabe and four other black plaintiffs sued the railroad line for relief from the statute just days before it went into effect. The Eighth Circuit Court of Appeals denied the plaintiff's request to strike down the law, and the five men appealed to the U.S. Supreme Court. Justice Charles Evans Hughes was prepared, along with four other justices, to strike down the Oklahoma law; however, to be eligible for relief, plaintiffs must have suffered under the offending statute. Since McCabe and the others sued to stop the law before it went into effect, the Court had no choice but to uphold the court of appeals verdict. In his opinion, however, Justice Hughes indicated that the era of Supreme Court sanction of Jim Crow and other discriminatory laws would end if the proper case came before the justices.

McGhee, Frederick Lamar (1861–1912)

Frederick L. McGhee was one of the 29 men who oversaw the first Niagara Conference of 1905, which eventually led to the creation of the National Association for the Advancement of Colored People (NAACP). He was born in 1861, in Aberdeen, Mississippi, the son of slaves. His father, a self-educated Baptist preacher, and his mother died soon after emancipation. Frederick McGhee received his education from missionaries. He later studied the law in Chicago and was admitted to the Illinois bar in 1885.

Four years later, McGhee moved to St. Paul, Minnesota, then a virtually all-white area. According to the glowing obituary written by his intimate and fellow Niagara Movement activist W. E. B. DuBois, McGhee "was not simply a lawyer—he stood like a wall against the encroachment of color caste in the Northwest." A member of the National Afro-American League and its successor, the National Afro-American Council, McGhee was one of the leaders of the movement to establish an all-encompassing national civil rights organization. In 1905 he became friendly with DuBois, who was organizing the Niagara Movement. McGhee became the organization's legal mind, giving his time to fighting discrimination cases, such as the one against the Pullman Company in 1907.

A year after the founding of the NAACP, McGhee helped organize the group's first branch in St. Paul. Just two years later, however, on 9 September 1912, in the midst of his work, he succumbed to pleurisy. Today he is all but unknown to students of the early twentieth-century civil rights movement.

See also DuBois, William Edward Burghardt; National Association for the Advancement of Colored People; Niagara Movement.

McKissick, Floyd Bixler (1922–1991)

Floyd Bixler McKissick was the chairman and director of the Congress of Racial Equality (CORE) who worked to build an all-black city in North Carolina. His support of Richard Nixon for president at the end of his life led to his being appointed as a state district judge by a Re-

publican governor. McKissick was born in Asheville, North Carolina, on 9 March 1922. He was infused with hatred of oppression at an early age when, at an athletic event, he was assaulted because of his race. McKissick performed odd jobs in his youth. After graduating from high school, he enlisted in the U.S. Army and served as a sergeant in Europe during World War Two, earning the Purple Heart for bravery. When he returned to the United States, he entered Morehouse College in Atlanta, Georgia. He went on to earn his bachelor's degree from North Carolina College in 1951. He applied to the all-white University of North Carolina Law School at Chapel Hill, but was denied because of his race. Thurgood Marshall, then the lead attorney for the National Association for the Advancement of Colored People (NAACP), took on McKissick's case and sued to an appeals court, which ordered the school to admit McKissick. He received his law degree in 1952 and was admitted to the North Carolina bar.

For several years prior to 1952, Floyd McKissick had served as youth chairman of the North Carolina branch of the NAACP as well as a worker for the Congress of Racial Equality (CORE), a pacifist group set up by black activist James Farmer and others in the early 1940s. McKissick was a member of the Journey of Reconciliation, which toured the deep South in 1947. In the 1950s, he was a partner in a law firm in Durham, North Carolina. Some of his cases included defending black demonstrators at sit-ins, as well as his daughter, who sought to enroll at an all-white high school. As the civil rights movement became more heated, McKissick was first named as CORE's leading legal counsel, then, on 29 June 1963, the organization's national chairman, the first black to hold the post. He was one of the featured speakers at the March on Washington that August. On 3 January 1966, McKissick was named director of CORE, a post he held for less than two years. As director of CORE, he gradually began to distance himself from Reverend Dr. Martin Luther King, who called for national civil disobedience. McKissick instead said that CORE's job would be to promote social and economic programs that help blacks. In September 1967, he resigned from CORE to head up a program created by the Ford Foundation to give blacks training in leadership positions.

In 1972, McKissick shocked many members of the civil rights community by switching his registration from Democrat to Republican and supporting President Richard Nixon's reelection efforts that year. The former CORE director countered the criticism by claiming that the Democratic Party took black votes for granted. After the campaign, McKissick spent the next decade trying to build Soul City, an all-black community 60 miles northeast of Raleigh, North Carolina. He envisioned a city with some 45,000 black residents by the year 2000 and received $18 million in federal aid toward his goal. Unfortunately, the community was not supportable. Five years into the project, only 135 people lived there, 30 of them white. When the government cut off funding for the city, it became a ghost town. Less than 400 people live there today.

In June 1990, North Carolina Governor James Martin, a Republican, appointed McKissick to fill a vacancy on the Ninth North Carolina Judicial District. McKissick had served only a few months on the bench when he was stricken with lung cancer, which claimed his life on 28 April 1991.

McLaurin v. Oklahoma State Regents for Higher Education (U.S., 1950)

The Supreme Court ruled in *McLaurin* that any segregation, in any form, in a public educational institution, such as a college or university, was a violation of the equal protection clause of the Fourteenth Amendment to the Constitution. Plaintiff McLaurin was a black citizen of Oklahoma, who was denied entry to the University of Oklahoma to earn a doctorate in education. He sued to the U.S. Supreme Court to be allowed to enroll, but a new law passed by the Oklahoma legislature called for "segregated facilities." Thus, although McLaurin was allowed to attend classes with white students, he was forced to sit in a "negro section" of his classes and to sit separately in the library and lunchroom. Citing these actions as a denial of his Fourteenth Amendment rights, he went to court again to have the law overruled. First a district court, then an appeals court, refused to hear his case. As a final resort, McLaurin appealed to the U.S. Supreme Court. On 5 June 1950, the Court ruled unanimously that the segregation in the school violated McLaurin's Fourteenth Amendment rights. Chief Justice Fred Vinson wrote the Court's opinion.

Menard, John Willis (1838–1893)

John Menard was the first black to be elected to Congress, although he was denied his seat by a fraudulent election investigation. Menard was born in Kaskaskia, Illinois, on 3 April 1838, of French-Creole ancestry. An ancestor, Michel Branamour Menard, was the founder of Galveston, Texas. Further, Menard counties in Illinois and Texas were founded by relatives of John Willis Menard. Menard himself attended schools in Sparta, Illinois, and enrolled in Iberia (Ohio) College when he was 21.

In 1862, in the midst of the Civil War, Menard was appointed to the post of clerk in the Bureau of Emigration at the Interior Department. This was the first time that a black was named to a federal clerkship. In 1863, he traveled to British Honduras (now Guyana) to search for a spot for a colored emigrants colony. When the Civil War ended, he went to New Orleans and was appointed customs inspector. He eventually served as a street commissioner of the city. He also published two Republican newspapers, *The Free South* and *The Radical Standard.*

In 1868, Menard was nominated for the U.S. House of Representatives by the Republicans. His opponent was Democrat Caleb S. Hunt. Although Menard won easily, the election was thrown into the House, where a committee heard the evidence. During the controversy, Menard was allowed to speak on the House floor, the first black to do so. The New York *Herald* declared that Menard "delivered what he had to say with a cool readiness and clearness that surprised everybody." Eventually, the committee ruled that the election be declared null and void, with the salary to be divided between the two men and the seat left vacant for the rest of the term. Menard did not run for the seat again.

John Menard went to Florida in 1871, where he published *The Sun.* He was hired as a clerk in the post office in Jacksonville. He was also elected to a single term in the Florida state legislature. Later, he served as an Internal Revenue Service collector and a justice of the peace. In 1876, he was a Florida delegate to the Republican National Convention in Cincinnati. Eventually, he purchased a Key West paper, *The Island City News,* and moved it to Jacksonville in 1885 as a black paper. John Willis Menard died in Washington, D.C., on 8 October 1893 at the age of 55.

Meredith, James Howard (1933–)

James Meredith was the first black student to attend the University of Mississippi. Meredith was born near the small town of Kosciusko, Mississippi, on 25 June 1933. After graduating from high school, he enlisted in the U.S. Air Force and served until 1960. On his return, he enrolled at the all-black Jackson State College for a year. In 1961, wishing to enter the all-white bastion of the University of Mississippi, "Ole Miss," he asked Medgar Evers, the president of the Mississippi branch of the National Associa-

tion for the Advancement of Colored People (NAACP), to help him in his case. Evers directed Meredith to Thurgood Marshall, the leading civil rights attorney in the nation. Marshall took up Meredith's case in the courts.

On 3 September 1962, the Fifth Circuit Court of Appeals ordered Mississippi governor Ross Barnett to allow Meredith to enroll at Ole Miss. That night, Barnett went on television to stand tall against the court order. "There is no case in history where the Caucasian race has survived total integration . We must either submit to the awful dictate of the federal government or stand up like men and tell them, 'Never.' " When Barnett refused to allow Meredith to enroll, President John F. Kennedy called in the National Guard to facilitate Meredith's entry to the college. Meredith attended class and graduated with a political science degree on 18 August 1963.

After graduation, Meredith attended Columbia University Law School, then returned to the South to participate in civil rights demonstrations. On 5 June 1966, he was shot by an unknown gunman. Fortunately, the wound was not serious, and he recovered fully. He returned to Columbia and earned his law degree in 1968. In 1972, he ran for the Republican nomination for the U.S. Senate from Mississippi, but lost in the primary. In 1990, Meredith backed former Ku Klux Klan leader David Duke in Duke's controversial campaign for the governorship of Louisiana. Presently living in Mississippi, he is the author of several works, including *Three Years in Mississippi* (1966).

Miller, Thomas Ezekiel (1849–1938)

Thomas E. Miller served a single term in Congress and was the chairman of the South Carolina state Republican Party. He was born in freedom in the small town of Ferrebeeville, South Carolina, a town founded by his mother's family, on 17 June 1849. In 1851, he and his family moved to nearby Charleston, where Miller attended all-black schools. There is no record of his activities during the Civil War, but it is known that after the conflict ended he attended Lincoln University in Chester County, Pennsylvania, on a scholarship. After graduation, he returned to Charleston and took a law course and read law under two attorneys. In 1875, Miller was admitted to the South Carolina state bar and began a private practice.

With his entry into law, Miller also became involved in local politics as a Republican. As a member of the Beaufort County Republican Party, he was elected school commissioner in 1872, then to a seat in the state general assembly, where he served from 1874 until 1880. In that year, he was elected to the state senate and would have been the Republican nominee for lieutenant governor had not the Democrats objected to a black man serving as the number two official in the state. Miller served a single two-year term in the state senate, then became the state party chairman in 1884. He was re-elected to the state general assembly two years later. In 1888, he was the Republican nominee to the U.S. House of Representatives, representing South Carolina's Seventh Congressional District. After the vote count, Miller was declared the loser by a slim margin, but he protested to the House Committee on Elections and was eventually seated due to election irregularities.

Miller served in Congress less than four months before the challenge to the election was settled, in September 1890, near what would have been the end of the term. In the election of November 1890, Miller was the apparent victor over his 1888 opponent, but the South Carolina Supreme Court threw out overturned the result on the basis of ballot irregularities. Refused his seat, he left the Congress.

Miller lived nearly 50 years after his congressional experience. He served again in the state general assembly, from 1894

to 1896, and played a prominent role in the South Carolina Constitutional Convention in 1895. He was a founder of the State Negro College at Orangeburg, serving as the college's first president from 1896 to 1911. After retirement, he took up residence in Philadelphia, where he delivered a series of speeches on black life in the South during Reconstruction. In 1934, he returned to Charleston and died there on 8 April 1938, at the age of 88. On his gravestone is the epitaph, "Not having loved the white man less, but having felt the Negro needed me more."

Milliken v. Bradley I (U.S., 1974)

Milliken I was the Supreme Court case that examined issues surrounding white flight and its impact on urban schools. The case subsumed two other actions: *Allen Park Public Schools v. Bradley* and *Grosse Point Public School System v. Bradley*. The Detroit city schools were ordered to be desegregated, but because the overwhelming majority of the students attending the schools were black, integration was impossible to achieve within the city school system. First a district court, then an appeals court, ordered several forms of relief, including busing to suburban schools, to achieve desegregation. The Supreme Court decided to review the case in 1974, four years after the actions were ordered. The Court ruled 5–4 that since the suburban schools did not practice *de jure* segregation—that is, segregation by law—the courts had no constitutional basis on which to order desegregation methods.

Milliken v. Bradley II (U.S., 1977)

Milliken II was the second case from Detroit to deal with the desegregation of schools. After the Supreme Court overturned the original trial court findings, the case was remanded, or sent back, to a lower court for a new trial. In this action, the trial court ordered the institution of remedial or compensatory education programs, new training mechanisms for teachers in urban schools, and improved guidance programs and testing procedures. The plaintiffs in *Milliken I* appealed the order to a court of appeals, which upheld the new order. The Supreme Court again looked at the case. The Court ruled that the lower court's order requiring compensatory programs was legally permissible.

Mississippi

The Magnolia State was one of the most staunchly segregationist states, led by a series of governors opposed to civil rights. Opposition to the modern civil rights movement was spearheaded by Fielding Wright (1895–1956), who won the governorship in 1946. In addition to his segregationist stance, Wright led the walkout at the 1948 Democratic National Convention over President Harry Truman's inclusion of a strong civil rights plank in the party platform. Wright later joined South Carolina governor Strom Thurmond as the vice-presidential candidate of the States' Rights, or "Dixiecrat," party, which carried four states in the 1948 election.

Wright was governor of Mississippi from 1946 until 1952. His successor, former governor Hugh Lawson White (1882–1965), who served from 1952 until 1956, supported a state law that fined any white student who chose to go to any state-supported school where blacks were taught. Following White was James Plemon Coleman (1914–1991), who, among Mississippi governors of this period, was perhaps the least strident in his opposition to civil rights. Coleman opposed an effort to ban the National Association for the Advancement of Colored People (NAACP) from the state and supported the construction of a Veteran's Administration hospital that became the first integrated hospital in the state. Although he was a founding member of the racist Mississippi Sovereignty Commis-

sion, Coleman was rewarded for his moderation in the area of civil rights when President Lyndon B. Johnson named him to the Fifth Circuit Court of Appeals in 1965.

The man who followed Coleman as governor of Mississippi, Ross Robert Barnett (1898–1987), was among the most vocal opponents of civil rights in the nation. It was Barnett who stood against the courts and the federal government's efforts to integrate the state's schools when James Meredith tried to enter the University of Mississippi in 1962. In 1963, Barnett went so far as to call for a group of Southern states to band together as a unit to resist desegregation.

Barnett lost his reelection bid in 1964 and was succeeded by Paul Burney Johnson, Jr. (1916–), who came into office at the height of civil rights demonstrations in Mississippi and worked to change the state's stance on segregation. He asked for redistricting measures to conform to the Supreme Court's "one man, one vote" formula and signed a voting rights law that replaced a state ban on black suffrage passed in 1908. By the late 1960s, civil rights were guaranteed by a growing body of law, so the next two governors, John Bell Williams (1918–), who named blacks as delegates to represent Mississippi at the Democratic National Convention, and William Lowe Waller (1926–), were able to reduce the state government's focus on the civil rights conflict. According to the 1990 census, Mississippi had 1,633,461 whites, 915,057 blacks, and 24,668 American Indian, Asian, or peoples of other races.

See also Barnett, Ross Robert; Coleman, James Plemon; Mississippi Sovereignty Commission; States' Rights Party.

Mississippi Sovereignty Commission

The Mississippi Sovereignty Commission was the bureau of the Mississippi state government that was created with the sole purpose of stopping civil rights progress in the state and as a means of keeping track of civil rights workers. The commission was the creation of Governor James Plemon Coleman during his administration (1956–1960), but was strengthened and reinforced under the leadership of Governor Ross Robert Barnett (1960–1964), who served as the group's chairman. The commission was a force to be reckoned with in the racial politics of Mississippi until it was disbanded in 1973.

Mississippi v. Johnson (U.S., 1867)

Mississippi was the Supreme Court case in which the Court was asked to rule on the constitutionality of Reconstruction. The state of Mississippi sued President Andrew Johnson, as well as General Edward Otho Cresap Ord, the military commander in Arkansas and Tennessee, asking the Court to enjoin, or stop, the two men from enforcing the Reconstruction acts passed by Congress on 2 and 23 March 1867. Attorney General Henry Stanbery, representing the Johnson administration, argued that the Court could not stop the president from carrying out his constitutional duties. Chief Justice Salmon P. Chase spoke for a unanimous Court in ruling that Stanbery's motion was correct, and that Mississippi was not entitled to relief from the Court. The state of Georgia then used other tactics in the courts to end Reconstruction. For this companion case, see *Georgia v. Stanton*.

See also Georgia v. Stanton.

Missouri Ex Rel. Gaines v. Canada (U.S., 1938)

The decision in the Supreme Court case *Missouri Ex Rel. Gaines v. Canada* led to the first crack in the wall of segregated education in America. Although the Court did not specifically examine the doctrine of "separate but equal," it did decide in *Gaines* that where there were separate white and black schools, the

black school must be equal to the white institution. Lloyd Gaines, a black honor student from Lincoln University in Jefferson City, Missouri, sought entry to the University of Missouri Law School. He was denied admission because of his race, but the university offered to pay his tuition at any other school. Gaines brought suit against Canada, the registrar, to be allowed to enroll at Missouri. A district court found that the admission policy was valid, and the judgment was upheld by an appeals court. Gaines took the case to the U.S. Supreme Court. The Court ruled that either the university must admit Gaines or find him an equal school in the state. The state decided to build a law school for Gaines, which opened up on the campus of Lincoln University. Gaines never attended the new school; he went to a law school in Michigan and later disappeared.

Mitchell, Charles Lewis (1829–1912)

Charles Lewis Mitchell, one of the first blacks elected to a legislative seat in the United States, was born on 10 November 1829, in Hartford, Connecticut, of a well-known black family. Little is known about what education, if any, he received. In 1853, he went to Boston, where he found employment as a printer working on abolitionist William Lloyd Garrison's *Liberator*. Mitchell apparently worked for Garrison until 1863, when he enlisted with the 54th Massachusetts Infantry Regiment, the black regiment led by Robert Gould Shaw and immortalized in the movie *Glory*. Mitchell served with honor, was wounded and lost his right foot at the Battle of Honey Hill, North Carolina, and left the service in 1865.

After the war, Mitchell entered Massachusetts politics as a Republican. In 1866, he was elected to the Massachusetts State House; he and fellow legislator Edward G. Walker became the first blacks elected to a state legislature. Mitchell only served one term. In 1867, he left the legislature.

He later became the first black customs inspector in Boston, a post he held the last 40 years of his life. As a former leader in the abolitionist movement, he served as a pallbearer at the funeral of mentor William Lloyd Garrison. Before Mitchell retired in 1909, he helped to organize Company L, the black regiment that served in the Spanish–American War. Mitchell died on 13 April 1912, at the age of 82.

See also Walker, Edward Garrison.

Mitchell v. United States et al. (U.S., 1941)

Mitchell was the Supreme Court case involving Congressman Arthur Wergs Mitchell (D-Illinois) in which the Court upheld the right of blacks to sue for discrimination in interstate travel, over the objections of the Interstate Commerce Commission (ICC). Mitchell, a highly respected black member of Congress, booked passage on the Illinois Central Railroad to travel to Memphis, Tennessee, then transferred to the Chicago,

Congressman Arthur Wergs Mitchell

Rock Island, & Pacific Railway from Memphis to his ultimate destination, Hot Springs, Arkansas. While on the Illinois Central Railroad, Mitchell did not have any problems. When he transferred to the Rock Island line, however, he was first asked and then ordered to move from his first-class Pullman car to a lesser one reserved for blacks only. This was in accordance with Arkansas law, which called for "equal, but separate and sufficient accommodations" for white and black passengers. Later, Mitchell filed a complaint with the ICC, alleging discrimination in interstate commerce. After a hearing, the commission dismissed Mitchell's complaint, so he appealed to the U.S. Supreme Court for relief. As the ICC was an agency of the federal government, the United States was named as the defendant. Chief Justice Charles Evans Hughes delivered the Court's unanimous judgment on 28 April 1941, ruling that Mitchell was discriminated against by the Rock Island line, and that the ICC was out of line to dismiss Mitchell's complaint on the grounds that "there was comparatively little colored traffic on the line."

Mobile v. Bolden (U.S., 1980)

Mobile v. Bolden was the Supreme Court case in which the Court upheld the constitutionality of municipal at-large elections. The case involved the election process in the city of Mobile, Alabama, where a "winner-take-all" process, instead of a single-member district system, was in place. A district court found the system violated the equal protection clause of the Fourteenth Amendment. The City of Mobile appealed to the Supreme Court for relief from the district court order to hold new elections. The Court ruled 6–3 (with Justices William Brennan, Thurgood Marshall, and Byron White dissenting) that the Mobile election plan was valid. While the Court had previously struck down such processes in cases such as *Baker v.*

Carr, where obvious voting discrimination patterns existed, in *Mobile* the Court found that a "winner-take-all" system did not violate the Fourteenth Amendment.

See also Baker v. Carr; Reynolds, a Judge, et al. v. Sims et al.

Monroe v. Pape (U.S., 1961)

Monroe was the Supreme Court case in which the Court deemed police brutality to be state action under the meaning of Title 42, section 1983 of the U.S. Code, which speaks of civil action for the deprivation of civil rights.

Monroe, a black man, was suspected of murder by the Chicago police. In the middle of the night, they entered his home without a warrant, conducted a search, arrested Monroe, and detained him for 10 hours without a lawyer being called. Monroe sued under Revised Statutes section 1979 (originally section 1 of the Enforcement Act, or Ku Klux Klan Act, of 20 April 1871) that the police had infringed on his "rights, privileges and immunities secured by the Constitution." The city of Chicago asked the district court to dismiss the suit on the grounds that the city could not be held liable under section 1979 for actions performed as part of "normal" governmental duties. The court dismissed Monroe's complaint, and an appeals court upheld the judgment. Monroe sued to the U.S. Supreme Court. The Court ruled 8-1 (Justice Felix Frankfurter dissented) that while the city was not liable under section 1979, the police, as a separate entity, were. Justice William O. Douglas wrote for the majority that the "allegation of the facts constituting a deprivation under color of state authority against unreasonable searches and seizures, contained in the Fourth Amendment and made applicable to the States by the Due Process Clause of the Fourteenth Amendment, satisfies to that extent the requirement of section 1979." This case was the basis for later decisions, such as that in *United States v. Price*, that allowed for lawsuits

against police officers for brutality under the color of state authority.

See also United States v. Price et al.

Montgomery Bus Boycott (1955–1956)

The Montgomery Bus Boycott was the first major event of the modern civil rights era. It lasted from 5 December 1955 to 21 December 1956, when the Montgomery, Alabama, city bus lines were forced to integrate. The bus boycott was instituted by the Montgomery Improvement Association (MIA), which called for the action after Rosa Parks, a black seamstress, was arrested for refusing to move to the colored section of a city bus on 1 December 1955.

More than a year before, in May 1954, Mrs. Jo Ann Gibson Robinson, a black English professor at Alabama State College in Montgomery and head of the Women's Political Caucus, a black women's group that had been denied entry into the League of Women Voters, wrote to Montgomery mayor W. A. Gayle protesting segregation on the city bus system. The city's subsequent failure to alleviate the situation paved the way for the founding of the MIA.

The Reverend Dr. Martin Luther King and other members of the MIA were pleasantly surprised that patrons of the bus system were willing to inconvenience themselves in order to back the bus boycott. Many white riders, in deference to their black neighbors, joined the boycott. The city bus system, which depended heavily on black ridership, soon found itself in serious financial straits. The bus owners met some of the MIA's demands: black bus drivers would be provided on routes where blacks were prevalent, and name-calling by white drivers would cease. This was a start, but the MIA did not end the boycott. At the same time, a backlash against the boycott began. The white mayor of Montgomery advocated a "get tough" policy toward the boycotters, and a White Citizen's

Council called for a violent reaction. King was arrested in January 1956 for going 30 miles per hour in a 25 miles-per-hour zone. That same month, a bomb exploded outside his house, leaving his family shaken but unhurt. On 21 February 1956, a Montgomery grand jury, utilizing an old anti-union law that outlawed conspiracies to block a lawful business, indicted Dr. King and 100 others for their part in the boycott. King was found guilty on 22 March, but his $1,000 fine was suspended pending appeal. On 13 November 1956, the U.S. Supreme Court upheld a lower court order that struck down Montgomery's segregated bus system as illegal and ruled that, as soon as Montgomery city officials were presented with the Court's order, integration must begin. On 21 December, the day after the order was delivered, Dr. King, the Reverend Dr. Ralph David Abernathy, Edgar Nixon, and David Smiley, a white minister, boarded a city bus and took the seats of their choosing. Although there was scattered violence aimed at undoing integration, the court order held and the boycott ended.

See also King, Martin Luther, Jr.; Montgomery Improvement Association.

Montgomery Improvement Association (MIA)

The Montgomery Improvement Association (MIA) was established during a meeting at the Holt Street Baptist Church in Montgomery, Alabama, on 5 December 1955, just four days after Rosa Parks's arrest for refusing to move to the colored section of a city bus. The association was founded, in the words of one of the leaders of the Montgomery Bus Boycott, Jo Ann Gibson Robinson, "to protect, defend, encourage, enlighten, and assist the members of the black community against unfair treatment, prejudice, and unacceptable subordination." The Reverend Dr. Martin Luther King, Jr., was chosen as MIA president, with the Reverend L. Roy Bennett

as vice president. Edgar Daniel Nixon, a former president of the state National Association for the Advancement of Colored People (NAACP) and the man who helped pay for Rosa Parks's appeal bond, was named treasurer. Although Dr. King was the pastor of the Dexter Avenue Church, he was not widely known outside the close-knit black community of Montgomery. The first action of the MIA was to organize a boycott of the Montgomery city bus system. It further called for an end to discrimination in the hiring of city bus drivers, and for the fair allocation of seating on a first-come, first-served basis.

During the course of the boycott, which ran 381 days, the MIA was the organizational backbone of the integration movement. The Supreme Court ordered the city bus system to integrate in November 1956, and the boycott ended a month later. The MIA was later melded into the Southern Christian Leadership Conference, of which it is still part.

See also King, Martin Luther, Jr.; Montgomery Bus Boycott; Parks, Rosa McCauley.

Moore, Harry Tyson (1906–1951)

Harry and Harriette Simms Moore (1905–1952) were the first martyrs of the modern civil rights movement in the United States. Few people remember their names, as they died several years before civil rights emerged as a key national issue. Their murders happened 13 years before Medgar Evers was killed in Mississippi and 27 years before the Reverend Dr. Martin Luther King was cut down in Memphis.

Harry Tyson Moore grew up in rural Florida, at a time when black Americans in the South had virtually been stripped of their civil rights. Born in Houston, Suwannee County, to uneducated parents who nonetheless instilled in him a desire to attain an education, Moore attended the High School Department of the Florida Baptist Institute in Cocoa Beach and graduated from there in 1924.

Harry Tyson Moore

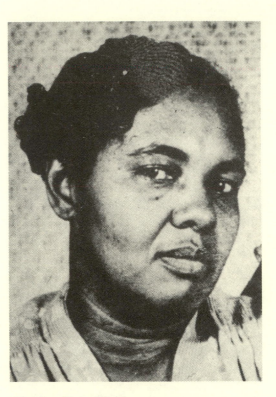

Harriette Simms Moore

That same year he began teaching at the institute. In 1951, through summer studies work, he received his bachelor's degree from Bethune-Cookman College. It was at this time that a cousin of Moore's called his attention to some pamphlets from the National Association for the Advancement of Colored People (NAACP). With his wife, Harriette Simms Moore, he began to work for civil rights. In 1935, he founded the Brevard County branch of the NAACP, a daring act in those days of Ku Klux Klan power and segregation. In 1938, he initiated a lawsuit to establish an equal pay system for black and white teachers. Later, Moore traveled across the state, distributing NAACP literature and founding NAACP branches. He was named president of the Florida NAACP in 1941.

Harry Moore was aware that what he was doing might cost him his life. Much like Medgar Evers, he would say to intimates, "I know they'll eventually try to kill me, but I have to do what I'm doing."

In 1944, Moore and Edward D. Davis of Howard University founded the Progressive Voters' League of Florida, which helped black voters cast ballots in primaries that had once been only for whites. There were threats from the Ku Klux Klan, but nothing came of them until December 1951.

On Christmas night, Moore and his wife went to sleep in the bedroom of their small home in Mims, near Cape Canaveral. At about 10:20 P.M., neighbors heard an explosion. A bomb had gone off under the Moores' bed. The bed was thrown through the roof before crashing down. Harry Moore was found unconscious under a pile of furniture. His wife was lying next to him, writhing in pain. Neighbors rushed them to a hospital, but Harry was dead on arrival. Harriette lived for nine days before succumbing to her injuries.

Since their deaths, the Federal Bureau of Investigation (FBI) has conducted an intensive search for the killers. Although there were several suspects, there was not enough evidence to bring charges. Author and activist Stetson Kennedy has followed the case for 40 years. It was his diligence that brought the case to light again in 1990, when it was reopened by Florida governor Lawton Chiles.

See also Kennedy, Stetson.

Moore v. Charlotte-Mecklenburg Board of Education (U.S., 1971)

Moore was a companion case to *Swann v. Charlotte-Mecklenburg Board of Education* and *North Carolina Board of Education v. Swann.* Originally heard in 1970, the Court delayed the *Moore* decision until the other two cases could be heard. Moore involved a plaintiff who, with the blessings of the North Carolina Board of Education, sought to have North Carolina's antibusing law upheld. When the U.S. District Court for the Western District of North Carolina struck it down as unconstitutional, the Supreme Court granted *certiorari* to hear the appeal. The Court held, on 20 April 1971, that because it had decided in the other two cases that the antibusing law was unconstitutional, and that both plaintiff and defendant were essentially on the same side, the *Moore* case was moot and dismissed it.

Moore v. Dempsey (U.S., 1923)

Moore was the Supreme Court case in which the Court recognized that mob rule over a court of justice precluded any conviction from being affirmed. The case involved black sharecroppers in Elaine, Phillips County, Arkansas. When the sharecroppers tried to improve conditions on their farms, whites in the area established mob rule. More than 200 black men, women, and children were lynched. When a white man was killed, 79 black farmers were indicted for murder and, in a mob setting, were all convicted. Twelve of them were sentenced to death. The National Association for the Advancement of Colored People (NAACP) brought the case before several courts, which upheld the sentences. The Supreme Court granted *certiorari* to hear the case, which was argued by three NAACP attorneys: U. S. Bratton, Moorfield Storey, and Scipio Africanus Jones. The Court ruled that the defendants were unjustly convicted. Justice Oliver Wendell Holmes wrote the majority opinion. He said: "In *Frank v. Mangum,* it was recognized of course that if in fact a trial is dominated by a mob so that there is an actual interference with the course of justice, there is a departure from due process of law; and that 'if the State, supplying no corrective process, carries into execution a judgment of death or imprisonment based upon a verdict thus produced by mob domination, the State deprives the accused of his life or liberty without due process of law.' "

See also Frank v. Mangum.

Moose Lodge #107 of Harrisburg v. Irvis (U.S., 1972)

Moose Lodge was the Supreme Court case in which the Court ruled that private clubs with no connection to the state could not be sued for discriminatory policies. The case involved K. Leroy Irvis, the black minority leader of the Pennsylvania House of Representatives, who sought admission to Moose Lodge #107 in Harrisburg, Pennsylvania, but was denied access and service because of his race. Irvis sued in the federal courts under Title 42, section 1983 of the U.S. Code, seeking to have the club's liquor license lifted until its policy of discrimination ended. He argued that since the club possessed a state liquor license, the discrimination was in essence "state action." The district court hearing the case ruled that the club's policies were illegal, and that the state must take back the club's liquor license to force compliance with antidiscrimination laws. The Moose Lodge appealed the verdict to the Supreme Court. The Court ruled 6–3 that the Moose Lodge, as a private club, had no duty to admit Irvis, and that their possession of a liquor license could not be based on their admittance policies. Speaking for the majority, Justice William H. Rehnquist wrote: "Our holdings indicate that where the impetus for the discrimination is private, the State must have 'significantly involved itself with invidious discriminations,' in order for the discriminatory action to fall within the ambit of the constitutional prohibition."

Murray, George Washington (1853–1926)

George Washington Murray was the black Republican orator and voting rights agitator who served two terms in the U.S. House of Representatives. Murray was born a slave near Rembert, in Sumter County, South Carolina, on 22 September 1853, and orphaned at an early age. He attended local schools, then enrolled at the University of South Carolina and the State Normal Institute at Columbia. After he graduated, he became a farmer, a teacher, and a lecturer for the Colored Farmers' Alliance. He was at one time known as the "most intellectual negro in the county." A staunch Republican, his work for President Benjamin Harrison in 1888 led to his appointment as a customs inspector at the Port of Charleston in 1890. That year he ran as the Republican candidate for Congress but was defeated. Two years later, in 1892, he ran again and this time was elected. From 1893 until he left Congress in 1897, Murray was the only black in Congress.

In his two terms in the House, Murray worked to protect Reconstruction laws designed to aid black voters. In addition, he proposed the building of a system of Southern normal schools for black students. Murray's other demand was that an exhibit at the Cotton States Exhibition in Atlanta devoted solely to the accomplishments of blacks be federally funded. As a demonstration, he included

George Washington Murray

in the *Congressional Record* a list of 92 patents awarded to American blacks, including eight by Murray himself.

Although reelected in 1894, Murray spent much of his second term battling South Carolina Governor Ben Tillman's efforts to prevent "Negro rule" through the repeal of the franchise for blacks. Although he fought hard against such measures, poll taxes and literacy tests were instituted statewide for black voters. In 1896, Murray was undercut by a division in the state Republican Party between the "Black and Tan" faction and the "Lily White" faction and lost in his bid for a third term. He challenged his Democratic opponent, William Elliott, in 1898, but again was defeated.

After leaving Congress, Murray returned to farming and real estate investment. In 1905, he had to flee South Carolina to avoid going to jail after being convicted of forging a contract with a tenant farmer. Murray eventually settled in Chicago. He later served as a delegate to several Republican conventions, but his main job was as a writer on race relations, as evidenced by his *Race Ideals: Effects, Cause and Remedy for Afro-American Race Troubles* (1910). George Washington Murray died in Chicago on 21 June 1926, at the age of 73.

Myers and Others v. Anderson (U.S., 1915)

Myers was one of three companion Supreme Court cases in which the high court struck down the notorious "grandfather" clauses as unconstitutional. The state of Oklahoma had instituted a tough literacy test designed to keep blacks from voting. The state exempted from taking the test anyone who had been a registered voter in 1866 or 1867 (before free blacks had their right to vote guaranteed by the Fifteenth Amendment in 1870). The other cases were *Myers and Others v. Howard* and *Myers and Others v. Brown*. All were consolidated as *Myers and Others v. Anderson*. Chief Justice Edward Douglass White, a former Confederate officer, spoke for a unanimous Court when he wrote that the 1866 act was null and void from its inception. "The 1866 standard never took life, since it was void from the beginning because of the operation upon it of the prohibitions of the Fifteenth Amendment," White wrote.

See also Guinn and Beal v. United States.

Myrdal, Karl Gunnar (1898–1987)

Gunnar Myrdal was the Swedish economist whose 1944 analysis of American race relations, *An American Dilemma*, served as a key document in the effort to dismantle legal segregation in the United States. Myrdal was born on 6 December 1898, in the small village of Gustafs Parish in the Kopparberg region of central Sweden. He entered Stockholm University at age 21 and, during his studies in economics and law, so impressed his professors that at graduation he was hired as a member of the school faculty.

In 1924, a year after earning his law degree, he married Alva Reimer, a fellow student. Gunnar and Alva Myrdal would become the only husband-and-wife team to win Nobel Prizes.

After marriage, Myrdal opened a law practice, but the law did not excite him, and he returned to Stockholm University, where he was awarded a doctorate in economics in 1927. In the late 1920s, he toured England, France, and, during the period immediately following the Wall Street crash, the United States. When he returned to Sweden, he served first as a professor in economics, then in political economy and science. In 1934, he and his wife published *Crisis in the Population Question*, which discussed Sweden's declining birth rate. The Myrdals were catalysts in changing much of the social policy of the Swedish government.

By 1938, Gunnar Myrdal was considered an international authority on the social problems of nations. In that year, the Carnegie Corporation awarded him $250,000 to study racial problems in the United States. The result was the 1944 work *An American Dilemma: The Negro Problem and Modern Democracy*, which he wrote with the aid of such American black leaders as Dr. Ralph Bunche and Dr. Kenneth B. Clark. Other leaders in the nation were impressed by the work. In footnote 11 of the Supreme Court's historic decision in *Brown v. Board of Education*, Chief Justice Earl Warren cited *An American Dilemma* as a source of information. Myrdal's main point in his work was that racism and the American Constitution were incompatible, and right-thinking people would destroy the remnants of racism once segregation in society was dismantled. Years later, during the explosive riots that enveloped urban ghettoes in the 1960s, Myrdal suggested that poverty was perhaps an even more important factor than segregation in the continued survival of racism.

After the Second World War, Myrdal served as Swedish commerce minister from 1945 to 1947 and, from 1947 to 1957, as secretary general of the United Nations Economic Commission for Europe. In this latter post, he came under criticism when he advocated trade with the Soviet Union, and it was this stand that some observers felt led to Myrdal being passed over for the post of United Nations secretary general to succeed Trygve Lie. When he resigned from the United Nations in 1957, he and his wife moved to Asia, where she had been appointed the Swedish ambassador to India, and Myrdal begin a massive study of that region's economic policies. The result was his *Asian Drama: An Inquiry into the Poverty of Nations* (1968), the first study of its kind.

Toward the end of their lives, Gunnar and Alva Myrdal won numerous accolades from their peers. In 1974, Gunnar Myrdal was awarded the Nobel Prize for Economic Science, sharing the honor with Friedrich von Hayek, a conservative Austrian economist. In 1982, Alva Myrdal was awarded the Nobel Peace Prize for her work toward disarmament. Alva Myrdal lived only four years after winning the Nobel Prize, dying in 1986. Gunnar Myrdal lived a year longer, dying in Stockholm on 17 May 1987, at the age of 88.

Nabrit, James Madison, Jr. (1900–)

James Nabrit is the noted black attorney whose briefs in the cases of *Lane v. Wilson, Nixon v. Herndon*, and *Bolling v. Sharpe* made him a leading civil rights lawyer. Nabrit was born in Atlanta, Georgia, on 4 September 1900. He earned his law degree at Northwestern University in Evanston, Illinois, in 1927, then went on to teach at Leland College in Louisiana. In 1928, he began a two-year stint as dean of the Arkansas Agricultural, Mechanical and Normal College at Pine Bluff. In 1930, he went into private law practice in Houston, Texas, for six years. It was during this time that he handled cases dealing with the white primary and voting rights.

In 1936, Nabrit was named assistant professor at Howard University's School of Law. He taught at Howard for 24 years, until his retirement, alternating between teaching civil rights and constitutional law and handling noted civil rights cases before the nation's courts. His most famous cases include *Lane v. Wilson*, in which Oklahoma's "Grandfather Clause" was struck down; *Bolling v. Sharpe*, which held segregated education in the District of Columbia to be unconstitutional; *Elmer v. Rice*, in which blacks were excluded from voting in South Carolina; and *Nixon v. Herndon*, the landmark case that found the white primary in Texas to be a violation of the Fifteenth Amendment.

In 1960, Nabrit succeeded Dr. Mordecai W. Johnson, who had been president of Howard for 34 years, as head of the school. Nabrit held this position until 1965, when he was asked to serve as deputy U.S. representative to the United Nations Security Council under President Lyndon B. Johnson. In 1968, Nabrit returned to Howard, only to retire the following year. Along with Thurgood Marshall, Nabrit is considered to be one of the "deans" of civil rights law. He is now in his nineties.

See also Bolling v. Sharpe; Lane v. Wilson et al.; Nixon v. Herndon.

Nash, Charles Edmund (1844–1913)

Charles Edmund Nash was the first black to represent Louisiana in the U.S. House of Representatives, serving a single term during the Forty-fourth Congress (1875–1877). Nash was born in Opelousas, in St. Landry Parish, Louisiana, on 23 May 1844. He attended local schools, then went to work as a bricklayer. In July 1863, he enlisted in the 82nd Regiment of the United States Volunteers, seeing action in several Civil War battles. He was wounded and lost part of his right leg at the battle of Fort Blakely, Alabama, in April 1865.

Considered a Republican before the war, Nash was appointed to a position in the New Orleans Custom House in 1869. Local Republicans saw Nash as a possible candidate for the U.S. House of Representatives. In 1874, he was elected to the House, representing the Sixth Louisiana District. He delivered only a few speeches on the House floor, one of which he asked not be included in the *Congressional Record*. One of these contained laudatory remarks for the Republican Party and what Nash claimed it had done for him and other blacks. A clash between two segments of the party in Louisiana led to his renomination in 1876, but defeat in the general election. Nash retired, never to hold public office again. He returned to the bricklayer's trade, but eventually his war injury drove him to work as a cigarmaker in New Orleans. Nash died there on 21 June 1913, less than a month after his sixty-ninth birthday.

Nashville Movement

The Nashville Movement was the group of civil rights activists that, led by black divinity student James Lawson, used sit-in protests at segregated Nashville dining facilities to call attention to Jim Crow laws in the South. Lawson, a pacifist and member of the Fellowship of Reconciliation (FOR), founded the Nashville Movement in Nashville, Tennessee in 1959. He had been hired by the Nashville Christian Leadership Council, a branch of the Southern Christian Leadership Conference, to create programs to help desegregate Nashville using nonviolent methods. Lawson in turn took on young black students to be trained in these techniques. These students included John Lewis, Marion Barry, Diane Nash, James Bevel, and Bernard Lafayette. Although a small sit-in took place in November 1959, it was little noticed. The real push of the group came on 13 February 1960, after such protests became successful in Greensboro, North Carolina. They hit three stores on that day: Kress, Woolworth's, and McLellan's. Casually, wearing nice suits and ties, they occupied the lunch counters of the three stores. Over the next several days, the group also took over W. T. Grant's and Walgreens. Eighty-one demonstrators were arrested on 27 February. White protestors beat some of the black students, earning enmity even from some staunchly segregationist newspapers. By the third week in April, however, faced with a "Don't Buy Downtown" campaign against white businesses, the white lead-

ership in Nashville sat down with the Nashville Movement's leaders to reach a compromise.

National Association for the Advancement of Colored People (NAACP)

One of the oldest civil rights organizations still in existence, the National Association for the Advancement of Colored People (NAACP) was founded on the one-hundredth anniversary of Abraham Lincoln's birthday, 12 February 1909. The NAACP was formed from a small committee of signers to a proclamation decrying the way American blacks were treated socially and legally in the United States. It had its roots in the historic Niagara Conference of 1905, which was held in upstate New York to discuss the treatment of black Americans. At that time, a powerful civil rights organization working successfully toward equal treatment for blacks seemed far off, although there were several attempts in the next four years to formulate such a group. Then, in May 1908, a convention was called to discuss the condition of the Negro in America. Such notables as Joel Spingarn, Dr. Henry Moskowitz, Moorfield Storey, Frederick Lamar McGhee, and William Edward Burghardt DuBois attended this convention. The outcome of the work at the convention produced an organization called the National Negro Committee (NNC). On 12 February 1909, the NNC, together with delegates from the Niagara Movement, formed the NAACP.

Over the following decades, with leadership supplied by such notables as W. E. B. DuBois and Thurgood Marshall, the NAACP took the lead in attacking racial barriers, building black voter registration, and working for economic opportunity and political justice for African Americans. It remains today the leading civil rights organization in the United States.

See also DuBois, William Edward Burghardt; Hooks, Benjamin Lawson; McGhee, Frederick Lamar; Niagara Movement.

NAACP v. Alabama Ex Rel. Patterson, Attorney General (U.S., 1958)

In this little-known but highly important Supreme Court case, the high court struck down a state's power to require disclosure of a controversial organization's membership lists and contributors. To combat the growing power of the National Association for the Advancement of Colored People (NAACP), the state of Alabama passed a law requiring organizations or corporations chartered in another state to file with the state the company's charter, to indicate where in the state the company did its business, and to recognize the agent in the state who was carrying out the organization's business. The NAACP refused to comply with the law. Alabama Attorney General John Patterson took the group to court, where a judge ordered the NAACP to cease doing business in Alabama until it complied with the law. Further, the judge set a date for the group to turn over pertinent records to the state. When the NAACP initially refused, they were given a $10,000 fine. The judge promised to increase it to $100,000 if the NAACP had not complied with the order at the end of five days. Five days later, the NAACP attorneys turned over all of the group's records except for the membership lists, which, if released, they argued, would infringe on their First Amendment right to free speech. The judge duly increased the fine to $100,000. The NAACP appealed to the Alabama Supreme Court, which affirmed the lower court ruling to turn over the records, as well as the fine. The NAACP appealed to the U.S. Supreme Court, which found, in a unanimous decision, that the Alabama statute was unconstitutional and voided the fine. Justice John Marshall Harlan II wrote the opinion of the Court, which found that: "It is beyond debate that freedom to engage in association for the advancement of beliefs and ideas is an inseparable aspect of the 'liberty' assured by the Due Process Clause of the Fourteenth Amendment which embraces freedom of speech . Of course, it is immaterial whether the beliefs sought to be advanced by association pertain to political, economic, religious, or cultural matters, and state action which may have the effect of curtailing the freedom to associate is subject to the closest scrutiny."

See also Bryant v. Zimmerman; Louisiana Ex Rel. Gremillion, Attorney General, et al. v. NAACP et al.

NAACP et al. v. St. Louis–San Francisco Railway Company et al. (1955)

The Interstate Commerce Commission (ICC) found in the St. Louis–San Francisco Railway Company dispute that separate waiting rooms for white and nonwhite train passengers constituted a violation of the Interstate Commerce Act of 1887. The National Association for the Advancement of Colored People (NAACP), as the principal plaintiff, filed a motion against several railroad companies, chief among them the St. Louis–San Francisco Railway Company, which separated white and black travelers in its railway coach, train, and station waiting rooms. The Interstate Commerce Commission held its hearing and, on 7 November 1955, found that such discrimination was in violation of section 3(1) of the Interstate Commerce Act of 1887. It also found, though, that segregated lunchrooms operated by a separate company at a station in Richmond were not under the jurisdiction of the ICC, as they were not involved in interstate commerce per se.

National Urban League (NUL)

The National Urban League is a national civil rights organization that assists blacks in the struggle for economic and social equality. The league has its origins in the first years of the twentieth century, when black migration to the North created urban tensions and economic hardships for the new arrivals. There were several agencies in New York City in par-

1911–1948

1968 to present

1948–1967

ticular that strove to alleviate the situation. Among the contributors to these agencies were William H. Baldwin, Jr., and his wife, Ruth Standish Baldwin, owners of the Long Island Railroad; Edwin Robert Anderson Seligman, a Columbia University economics professor; and George Edmund Haynes, a student of Seligman's and the first black to earn a doctorate degree from Columbia University. William H. Baldwin, Jr., died in 1905.

On 20 January 1910, Baldwin's widow held an interracial conference at her home in New York City with the idea of founding an all-encompassing organization to help migrating blacks. One of the attendees was white writer Ray Stannard Baker, whose article on Alonzo Bailey, the poor Alabama sharecropper, led to national exposure for Bailey's landmark case before the Supreme Court, *Bailey v. Alabama*. Baker reported on conditions in the North and in the Southern states, where Jim Crow laws and racial segregation had imposed a harsh life on the former slaves. The meeting broke up without any further discussion, but the group regathered the following 29 September to found the Committee on Urban Conditions Among Negroes (CUCAN). George Edmund Haynes was made the group's first executive director, and a budget of $2,500 with a staff of only two people was allocated. As the first chairman of CUCAN, Seligman encouraged such men as John D. Rockefeller and Julius Rosenwald, among others, to contribute funds to the organization.

In 1911, Haynes stepped down as CUCAN executive director and was replaced by Eugene Kinckle Jones, CUCAN's field secretary and founder of the nation's first black fraternity. Jones served as executive secretary from 1911 until 1918 and executive director from 1918 until 1941. In those years, he continued the work of Haynes and Baldwin and expanded the group's goals. Soon after becoming director, he merged CUCAN with the National League for the Protection of Colored Women, which had been founded in 1905, and the Committee for Improving the Industrial Relations for Negroes. The new group Jones headed was called the National League on Urban Conditions Among Negroes (NLUCAN), later shortened to the National Urban League (NUL). In his 30 years of work, Jones expanded the league from one small office to 58 affiliates nationwide, with a budget, in 1941, of $2.5 million.

In 1941, Jones stepped down and was replaced by Lester Blackwell Granger, a noted social worker in the area of race relations and civil rights. Granger saw the league through the Second World War and attempts by civil rights leaders to end discrimination in employment and hiring. The efforts led to Executive Order 8802, signed by President Franklin Delano Roosevelt on 25 June 1941. By the time of Granger's retirement in 1961, there were affiliates in 53 cities with an annual budget of $4.5 million. Granger's successor was Whitney Moore Young, Jr., a charismatic veteran of World War Two who had served as executive director of NUL in Omaha, Nebraska, in the 1950s. Young's vision of an urban renewal program—a national "Marshall Plan"—was his greatest accomplishment. Further, he used the league to create several programs dealing with social, educational and economic empowerment. Young drowned in 1971 during a visit to Lagos, Nigeria.

Vernon Eulion Jordan, Jr., who had headed up the United Negro College Fund, succeeded Young as head of the NUL. Jordan differed from his predecessors at NUL in that, while they were all social workers, he was a noted attorney.

During his decade as executive secretary, Jordan worked at increasing black voter registration. He found new sources of support in funding and, under his leadership, the league began publication of *The State of Black America*, a yearly examination of the goals of and challenges to the black community. In 1980, a white supremacist attempted to assassinate Jordan, and two years later he stepped down in favor of John Edward Jacob. Jacob had been Jordan's right-hand man and had directed the league's national office in the days following the assassination attempt. Jacob allocated NUL resources to four main areas: solving the problems associated with teenage pregnancies in the black community; conquering voter apathy and getting individuals involved with voter registration; researching the issue of crime and how it affects black Americans; and studying the problems and challenges of single-parent households. Under Jacob's leadership, the league reached an affiliate total of 114 in 1990, with offices in 34 states and the District of Columbia, and a budget of nearly $24 million.

See also Granger, Lester Blackwell; Haynes, George Edmund; Jacob, John Edward; Jones, Eugene Kinckle; Jordan, Vernon Eulion, Jr.; Seligman, Edwin Robert Anderson; Young, Whitney Moore, Jr.

Niagara Movement

The Niagara Movement was a series of conferences on racial questions and problems in the United States, largely organized by writer and activist W. E. B. DuBois, together with activists William Monroe Trotter and Frederick L. McGhee, starting in July 1905. Its aims were to secure the freedom of speech, suffrage for all black citizens, the "abolition of caste distinctions based simply on race and color," and "a belief in the dignity of labor." Civil rights were to be espoused, Negro history was to be discussed, Negro businesses were to be established, and the education of blacks to be productive members of society was to be encouraged. In 1906, a second Niagara Conference was held at Harper's Ferry, Virginia, where some of the delegates made a pilgrimage to the site where John Brown had been executed. At a third conference, held in New York in 1909, many of the delegates, including DuBois and white civil rights activists Mary White Ovington, Oswald Villard, Joel Spingarn, Moorfield Storey, and educator John Dewey, among others, saw the need for a permanent organization, which was then established as the National Association for the Advancement of Colored People (NAACP).

See also DuBois, William Edward Burghardt; National Association for the Advancement of Colored People; Ovington, Mary White; Spingarn, Joel Elias.

Nixon v. Condon (U.S., 1932)

Nixon v. Condon was a Supreme Court case in which the Court struck down a Texas law allowing political parties to limit the qualifications of voters. This law was set up by the state to circumvent the Court's earlier decision in *Nixon v. Herndon.* Justice Benjamin Cardozo wrote the 5–4 decision, in which Justices James Clarke McReynolds, George Sutherland, Pierce Butler, and Willis Van Devanter dissented.

See also Grovey v. Townsend; Nixon v. Herndon; Smith v. Allwright.

Nixon v. Herndon (U.S., 1927)

Nixon v. Herndon was the Supreme Court case in which the Court found that Texas primaries closed to blacks, based on their race, were unconstitutional. This case was the first in a series that struck down so-called "white primaries" set up by the state to disenfranchise black voters. After the decision, the Texas legislature tried to give the power of selecting the "qualifi-

cations" of voters to the state Democratic Party, but this was struck down five years later in *Nixon v. Condon.*

See also Grovey v. Townsend; Nabrit, James Madison, Jr.; Nixon v. Condon; Smith v. Allwright.

Norris v. Alabama (U.S., 1935)
See Scottsboro Boys.

North Carolina

One of 11 former Confederate states, North Carolina embraced segregation throughout much of the era of modern civil rights and was one of the main targets of the civil rights movement. Racial segregation, at least in the public schools of North Carolina, was required by Article 9, Section 2 of the 1868 state constitution, which read: " And the children of the white race and the children of the colored race shall be taught in separate public schools, but there shall be no discrimination in favor or to the prejudice of either race." Beginning in the 1940s, though, North Carolina was led by a series of governors who, although not integrationist in thought, made some small but historic steps to advance civil rights.

In 1945, Robert Gregg Cherry (1891–1957) assumed the governorship and served a single four-year term. Cherry was noted for his refusal to join the walkout of Southern delegates at the 1948 Democratic National Convention, in response to President Truman's inclusion of a strong civil rights plank in the party platform. Cherry was among a courageous few of the South's leaders who stuck by Truman during that election instead of joining the segregationist States' Rights, or "Dixiecrat," party. Cherry's successor, William Kerr Scott (1896–1958), appointed the first black to the state board of education. The next governor, William

Bradley Umstead (1895–1954), who served from 1953 until his death, criticized the 1954 *Brown* decision as an invasion of state sovereignty; he did, however, cooperate with the decision and appointed a biracial commission to make recommendations on how state schools could comply with the Court's decision to dismantle segregation. With Umstead's untimely death in 1954, Luther Hartwell Hodges (1898–1974) took over the governorship. Although he worked to integrate the schools, Hodges supported a plan to give local school boards the option of integrating black students. He also favored tuition grants to students who preferred not to attend integrated schools. Hodges's successor, Terry Sanford (1917–), defeated a Democratic segregationist in the primaries. During his term, he made strides toward ending discrimination and segregation in the South by instigating the Good Neighbor Council, an organization that encouraged equal opportunity in hiring and education. According to the 1990 census, North Carolina had 5,008,491 whites, 1,456,323 blacks, and 163,823 people of other backgrounds.

See also States' Rights Party.

North Carolina State Board of Education v. Swann (U.S., 1971)

North Carolina State Board of Education was the Supreme Court case that struck down a state "antibusing" law as unconstitutional. The opinion in this case came down the same day as another historic decision, *Swann v. Charlotte-Mecklenburg Board of Education*. Both cases involved the right of students to attend "neighborhood schools," in effect, allowing patterns of housing to affect desegregation methods. In *Swann*, the Court held that busing students to schools (no more than a few miles or 15 minutes' travel) was legal to create desegregated schools. In *North Carolina*, the Court held that a state law that read: "No students shall be assigned or compelled to attend school on account of race, creed, color or national origin, or for the purpose of creating a balance or ratio of race, religion or national origins. Involuntary busing of students in contravention of this article is prohibited, and public funds shall not be used for any such bussing," violated the Fourteenth Amendment.

See also Swann v. Charlotte-Mecklenburg Board of Education.

O'Hara, James Edward (1844–1905)

James Edward O'Hara was the black son of an Irish father and a West Indian mother who represented North Carolina in the U.S. House of Representatives from 1883 until 1887. O'Hara was apparently born free in New York City on 26 February 1844, although the *Congressional Record* states that he was born in the West Indies. By 1850, the family were citizens of the United States. By the end of the Civil War, they were living in North Carolina. Before the move south, James O'Hara received an education in the New York schools and was trained as a schoolteacher. In North Carolina, he studied law, and later attended, but did not graduate from, Howard University. In 1871 he was admitted to the North Carolina bar, and two years later opened his own law practice.

O'Hara got his start in politics in 1867, when he served both as a delegate and secretary to the Republican state convention. In 1873, he was elected chairman of the Halifax Board of Commissioners. Two years later, O'Hara was named to the state constitutional convention.

Although he lost a congressional race in 1878, he won the race in 1882 and was elected. He was reelected in 1884, but lost in 1886. In those two congressional terms, O'Hara tried to have antidiscrimination provisions inserted into several bills dealing with interstate commerce and public accommodations in the area of dining. He proposed undoing the Supreme Court's nullification of the Civil Rights Act of 1875 by calling for a ban on discrimination in all forms of public accommodations. He spoke forcefully on the horrors of lynching in Mississippi.

Following his defeat in 1886, James O'Hara resumed the practice of law in Enfield, North Carolina. He died from a stroke on 15 September 1905.

Ovington, Mary White (1865–1951)

Mary Ovington White, a white civil rights advocate, was a noted author on civil rights and a founding member of the National Association for the Advancement of Colored People (NAACP). White was born in Brooklyn, New York, the daughter of Theodore Ovington, the owner of Ovington's, a large department store on Fifth Avenue in New York City. Mary White Ovington attended the prestigious Brackett School and Parker Institute. Indoctrinated by the family minister on issues of racial equality, she attended Radcliffe College and became a devout socialist. In 1891, after her family lost their fortune, she returned to New York and lived in several "settlements" for black migratory families from the South, at times the only white person there. In 1904, she joined the Greenwich Committee on Social Investigations and began researching the lives of migrating black families. Her report, *Half a Man: The Status of the Negro* (1911), was a landmark work on racial thought for a white writer.

It was at this time that Ovington met and began to work with W. E. B. DuBois, the noted black writer and activist. In 1908, following the bloody Springfield, Illinois, racial riots, DuBois asked Ovington to join his Niagara Movement, a group of mainly black intellectuals who came together at several conventions to discuss ways of combating racism. In 1909, with DuBois, Ovington was one of the founding members of the NAACP, the organization that was a natural outgrowth of the Niagara Movement.

During the next 38 years, she served for a time as chairman of the NAACP and as the organization's treasurer, and also traveled and lectured nationally. The NAACP, in this period, achieved only limited success in removing racial barriers for black Americans; but, before her retirement in 1947, Ovington persuaded the organization to focus its efforts on dismantling segregation in education. The group was finally successful in this area in 1954, when the Supreme Court's *Brown* decision struck down segregated education as unconstitutional. Sadly, Mary White Ovington did not live to see the decision. She died at her sister's home in Auburndale, outside Boston, Massachusetts, on 15 July 1951, at the age of 86. Her last work, *The Walls Came Tumbling Down*, is an autobiographical look at her six decades of civil rights work.

Pace v. Alabama (U.S., 1883)

Pace was the Supreme Court case in which the Court upheld the right of states to ban intermarriage between blacks and whites. Tony Pace, a black man, and Mary Cox, a white woman, were indicted in 1881 under section 4189 of the Alabama Code, which read: "if any white person and any negro, or the descendent of a negro to the third generation, intermarry or live in adultery or fornication with each other, each of them must, on conviction, be imprisoned in the penitentiary or sentenced to hard labor for the county for not less than two nor more than seven years." On appeal, the Alabama Supreme Court upheld the convictions, so Pace took his appeal to the U.S. Supreme Court. Justice Stephen J. Field read the unanimous decision of the Court to uphold the convictions. Wrote Field: "Section 4189 applies the same punishment to both offenders, the white and the black. Indeed, the offense against which this section is aimed cannot be committed without involving the persons of both races in the same punishment. Whatever discrimination is made in the punishment described is directed against the offense designated and not against the person of any particular color or race. The punishment of each offending person, whether white or black, is the same."

Palmer et al. v. Thompson (U.S., 1971)

In *Palmer et al. v. Thompson* the Supreme Court found on narrow grounds that segregated facilities closed to all persons did not constitute a denial of equal protection to black citizens. Following a district court ruling that all Jackson, Mississippi, city public facilities must be open to all races, the city, claiming a lack of security, sold off ownership in four city pools, and handed the lease on a fifth pool to the YMCA, which continued to operate it for whites only. Plaintiffs Palmer and several other black citizens of Jackson sued Thompson, the mayor of Jackson, on the grounds that closing the pools denied them the equal protection of the laws. A district court found for Thompson; an appeals court upheld the judgment. Palmer appealed to the U.S. Supreme Court. On 14 June 1971, the Court ruled 5–4 that by closing the pools to *all* citizens of Jackson, there was no discrimination per se against Palmer. Justice Hugo Black, writing for the majority, argued that since there was no state action in operating a segregated facility—in other words, finding it not illegal *not* to operate a segregated facility—Palmer could not argue that there was a denial of equal protection.

Palmore v. Sidoti (U.S., 1984)

Palmore was a key test of the Supreme Court's 1967 opinion in *Loving v. Virginia*, in which the Court had invalidated a state ban against racial intermarriage. The case involved Anthony and Linda Sidoti, a Florida couple. After their divorce, Mrs. Sidoti met and moved in with Clarence Palmore, Jr., a black man. Anthony Sidoti filed suit against his wife, charging that the presence of a black man in the house caused trauma to their daughter, and demanding custody of the child. A court in Florida sided with the father, and the Second District Court of Appeals affirmed the decision, while denying the Florida Supreme Court the right to review. Palmore and Mrs. Sidoti appealed the case to the U.S. Supreme Court. Chief Justice Warren Burger wrote the unanimous decision for the Court, holding that while Sidoti may be correct that social pressures from living with an interracial couple were hard on the Sidoti child, they were not acceptable challenges to Mrs. Sidoti's custody. Burger cited *Buchanan v. Warley*, a 1917 Supreme Court case in which a Kentucky law mandating separate homes for blacks was struck down. The argument for the Kentucky law, Burger said, was to preserve racial peace and social harmony. Sidoti's challenge to his ex-wife's custody, if allowed to stand, would do exactly the same thing and deny his wife equal protection.

See also Loving v. Virginia.

Parks, Rosa McCauley (1913–)

Rosa Parks, a seamstress from Montgomery, Alabama, refused to move from the white section of a city bus to the col-ored section in 1954, thereby precipitating the Montgomery Bus Boycott, which heralded the start of the modern civil rights movement. Born Rosa McCauley in 1913 in Tuskegee, Alabama, to a carpenter and his wife, Rosa attended a poor, ramshackle, all-black school. Eventually, when she turned 11, her parents saved some money for her to go to a private school in Montgomery. She attended school there and eventually took some classes at the Alabama State College for Negroes. In 1932, she married Raymond Parks, a local barber. From 1932 until her fateful collision with history in 1954, Rosa Parks worked as a clerk, a seamstress, and as a volunteer for the Montgomery Voters League.

On 1 December 1955, Parks was returning home at night from her seamstress job. Tired, she boarded a city bus

A Montgomery, Alabama, deputy sheriff fingerprints Rosa Parks.

and took one of the seats that was up front. Soon the bus started to get crowded and, according to Alabama law, blacks had to move toward the back to make room for white passengers. The driver stopped the bus and asked Parks and three other blacks to make room for whites. The others complied, but Rosa Parks refused. "I was just plain tired," she said later, "and my feet hurt." When the driver insisted she move, she told him no. It was an answer heard around the world. Rosa Parks was arrested, only to be bailed out by black activist Edgar Daniel Nixon and white attorney Clifford Judkins Durr that night.

As word of Rosa Parks's arrest spread, anger built up in the black community about this final indignity. Eventually, with the help of other Montgomery civil rights activists and outside speakers, such as the Reverend Dr. Martin Luther King, Jr., the Montgomery Improvement Association (MIA) was formed. The association organized a boycott of city buses that lasted for a year, until segregation on city buses was ruled illegal by the Supreme Court. The modern civil rights era had begun. Today, Rosa Parks lives in Detroit, Michigan, having retired there after working for black Congressman John Conyers. She remains "the mother of the civil rights movement."

See also Durr, Clifford Judkins; Montgomery Bus Boycott; Montgomery Improvement Association; King, Martin Luther, Jr.

Pasadena City Board of Education v. Spangler (U.S., 1976)

In 1968, a number of black students sued the Pasadena, California, school board for maintaining a segregated school system. A district court found the board to be in violation of the Fourteenth Amendment and ordered it to submit a desegregation plan at once. This plan, called the "Pasadena Plan," required that there would be no "minority–majority schools" and was accepted by the court. In 1974,

however, new officials on the school board felt that the "no minority-majority" part of the plan was vague, and asked the district court to modify this part of the plan. The district court refused, holding that although the school board was not directly liable for segregation due to housing patterns, it was still under court order to remedy the situation. The school board members sued to the Ninth Circuit Court of Appeals, which upheld the judgment, but expressed concern that the district court not hold endless jurisdiction over the school board. The school board sued to the U.S. Supreme Court. The Court held 6–2 (Justices Thurgood Marshall and William Brennan dissenting) that the district court could not oversee the school board for its "lifetime" just because housing patterns continued some segregation. Justice William Rehnquist wrote the majority opinion.

Patterson, Frederick Douglass (1901–1988)

Frederick Douglass Patterson was the founder of the United Negro College Fund in 1944. Patterson was born in Washington, D.C., on 10 October 1901, and named after the great abolitionist Frederick Douglass. Orphaned at age two, he was raised by his older sister, Wilhelmina, a schoolteacher in Texas. Patterson attended the Prairie View State College in Prairie View, Texas, until he transferred to Iowa State College, where he took up the study of veterinary science. He received his doctorate in that field in 1923 and a master of science degree in 1927. In 1932, Cornell University awarded him a second doctorate in veterinary science.

Patterson taught veterinary science at Virginia State College for several years, starting in 1924, and advancing to director of the college's agriculture program. He was then hired by the prestigious Tuskegee Institute in Alabama to head up that school's veterinary program and to teach bacteriology. In 1933, Tuskegee named Patterson director of its School of Agriculture. Two years later, he was made the head of Tuskegee itself, succeeding the school's second president, Dr. Robert R. Moton. (The first president was Booker T. Washington.) Patterson was the president of Tuskegee from 1935 until his retirement in 1953.

In 1943, Patterson wrote an article in the Pittsburgh *Courier* that called for a conference of the heads of black colleges to find new ways to fund the institutions. The conference led to the creation, in 1944, of the United Negro College Fund (UNCF). Beginning with 27 member colleges (which in 1945 increased to 32), covering some 12,000 students across the nation and creating a pool of about $765,000, the UNCF, with its catchy slogan, "A mind is a terrible thing to waste," began to fund the educations of needy black college students. Before his retirement from Tuskegee, Patterson served on President Harry S Truman's Commission of Higher Education, which advocated a system of federal aid to colleges.

After retiring from Tuskegee, Patterson was known as the grandfather of fundraising for black colleges. In the 1970s, he established a second organization, the College Endowment Funding Plan, which solicited donations from corporate sponsors, with the possibility of matching federal funds. In 1987, he was awarded the Presidential Medal of Freedom by President Ronald Reagan. Frederick Douglass Patterson died at his home in New Rochelle, New York, on 26 April 1988, at the age of 86.

Patton v. Mississippi (U.S., 1947)

Patton was the Supreme Court case in which it was held that the systematic exclusion of blacks from grand and/or petit juries allowed for the dismissal of convictions against defendants. Plaintiff Patton, a black man, was indicted in Lauderdale County, Mississippi, for the murder of a white man, by an all-white grand jury. At trial, his lawyer attempted to show that although blacks make up a certain percentage of the population of the county, there had been no blacks on grand or petit juries in more than 30 years. With this information, he attempted to quash, or dismiss, the indictment. The court refused to hear his evidence, proceeded with the trial (by an all-white jury), and convicted Patton of first-degree murder. The Mississippi Supreme Court affirmed the conviction and overruled any attempt to get the indictment quashed on the grounds that the juries' exclusion of blacks was a violation of the Fourteenth Amendment. The U.S. Supreme Court granted *certiorari*, and on 8 December 1947 ruled that this type of exclusion of blacks on juries was evidence of violations of equal protection rights under the Fourteenth Amendment. Justice Hugo Black, a former Ku Klux Klansman, wrote the majority opinion, in which he stated that "the fact that no Negro had served on a criminal court grand or petit jury for a period of 30 years created a strong presumption that Negroes were systematically excluded from jury service because of race."

Pendleton, Clarence McLane (1930–1988)

Charles McLane Pendleton was the first black chairman of the U.S. Civil Rights Commission. Pendleton was born in Louisville, Kentucky, on 10 November 1930, but moved with his family to Washington, D.C., soon after. He followed family tradition and enrolled in Howard University, where he was awarded a bachelor of science degree in 1954. For a short time after graduation Pendleton worked for the District of Columbia's recreation department. Soon after, he entered the U.S. Army. He was discharged in 1957 and joined the faculty of Howard

University as a swimming coach while he earned a master's degree in education. In the next 11 years, Pendleton coached 10 swimming championship teams. He moved on to Baltimore, where he served as that city's recreation coordinator. After two years at the post, he joined the National Recreation and Parks Association as the head of its Urban Affairs Department. In 1972, he was named as the director of San Diego's Model Cities Program. In 1975, Pendleton became the executive director of San Diego's National Urban League (NUL) chapter.

While in California, Pendleton began to change his liberal views and became a conscious conservative. In 1980 he bucked the tide and became the only one of more than 150 NUL officers nationwide to endorse Ronald Reagan for the presidency. Reagan was impressed by Pendleton's credentials and conservative leanings. On taking office, President Reagan forced Arthur Fletcher, the head of the U.S. Civil Rights Commission, to resign and, on 16 November 1981, appointed Pendleton as the commission's first black chairman. As chairman, Pendleton angered many civil rights leaders by his outspoken support of Reagan's "color-blind society." He opposed desegregation in busing as an infringement of the rights of parents to choose neighborhood schools. He mocked the notion of "comparable worth"—the idea that persons in similar jobs should be paid a roughly equal wages—as the "looniest idea since 'Looney Tunes.'" Further, he demanded that black leaders lead blacks away from the Democratic Party, which he called a "plantation." Pendleton was in San Diego on 5 June 1988 when he collapsed and died of a heart attack. He was 57 years old. Equal Employment Opportunity Commission Chairman and future Supreme Court Justice Clarence Thomas, a black who shared Pendleton's ideology and convictions, said of Pendleton: "He was just trying to tell the world

that there was a different point of view, that not all blacks thought alike. What he would say privately he would also say publicly. That's a rare thing."

See also United States Civil Rights Commission.

Peonage Abolition Act of 2 March 1867

The Peonage Abolition Act was passed by the thirty-ninth Congress, which was ruled by radical Republicans. Peonage, a practice in which a person can be forced to labor to discharge a debt, was used by former slaveowners as a way of holding onto their slaves as workers. The Peonage Abolition Act made such work illegal. The act was later tested before the Supreme Court in the cases of *Bailey v. Alabama* and *United States v. Reynolds.*

See also Bailey v. Alabama; Clyatt v. United States; Pollock v. Williams; United States v. Reynolds.

Peonage Cases

See Bailey v. Alabama; Clyatt v. United States; Pollock v. Williams; United States v. Reynolds.

Peterson v. City of Greenville (U.S., 1963)

In *Peterson*, the Supreme Court ruled that when black patrons protested segregation in dining facilities, they could not be arrested for trespass if the city had such segregationist laws on its books. The case involved Peterson, a black man, who, along with other black diners, was ordered from a Greenville, South Carolina, restaurant and, when they refused to leave, were arrested for trespassing. The Court ruled 8–1 that there was no reasonable basis to uphold the trespass conviction when the prosecution of the protestors was based on a segregationist statute.

Pinchback, Pinckney Benton Stewart (1837–1921)

P. B. S. Pinchback was the charismatic Mississippian who became the first black man to serve as both lieutenant governor and governor of a state, although he was not elected to either post. Born in Holmes County, Mississippi, Pinchback was sent with his slave mother to Ohio to get an education. He earned a living by plying the boat trade. At the start of the Civil War, he returned to his native South and assembled two regiments of black troops to fight for the Union but was refused the right to fight himself. Instead, at the end of the war, he joined the Republican Party in Louisiana and worked his way up the electoral ladder, first as a state Republican committee member, then as a state senator (he served as president pro tempore in 1871). That same year, he was elevated to the lieutenant governor's seat upon the death of the incumbent, Oscar Dunn, who was the first black lieutenant governor in American history. In 1872, Mississippi Governor Henry Clay Warmoth was removed from power, and Pinchback took over the governorship for four months. Warmoth's term expired before he could face impeachment, and a new governor, William Pitt Kellogg, was sworn in. In late 1872, Pinchback was elected to the U.S. House of Representatives, but the Democrats contested the seat and Pinchback was removed. In 1873, the legislature elected him to the U.S. Senate, but again the Democrats had him removed. Eventually, he served as the New Orleans surveyor of customs. In 1890, he moved to Washington, D.C., and spent the remainder of his life there. He practiced law until he died at the age of 84 in 1921.

See also Dunn, Oscar James.

Plessy v. Ferguson (U.S., 1896)

Plessy v. Ferguson was the famous Supreme Court case that upheld the right of states to impose "separate but equal" facilities on blacks. The case involved Homer Plessy, a black man, who attempted to sit in the whites-only section of a passenger train. The Louisiana state legislature in 1890 had passed a law that "separate but equal" train facilities would be created for both races. There was a fine imposed if any individual of one race tried to sit in another race's section. Following his arrest, Plessy sued the trial judge, John Ferguson, and tried to get a higher court to set aside any proceedings against him. The Louisiana Supreme Court heard the case, but ruled against Plessy. Plessy and his attorney, Albion Tourgee, took the case to the U.S. Supreme Court. On May 18, 1896, the Court handed down its decision. By a 7–1 majority (Justice David Brewer did not participate), the justices upheld the Louisiana statute. Wrote Justice Henry Billings Brown for the majority: "A statute which implies merely a legal distinction between the white and colored races has no tendency to destroy the legal equality of the two races, or re-establish a state of involuntary servitude. The argument [of the plaintiff] also assumes that social prejudices may be overcome by legislation, and that equal rights cannot be secured to the Negro except by an enforced commingling of the two races. We cannot accept this proposition. If the two races are to meet upon terms of social equality it must be the result of natural affinities, a mutual appreciation of each other's merits, and a voluntary consent of individuals." Justice John Marshall Harlan, serving his nineteenth year on the Court, was the lone dissenter. In a sometimes angry and bitter opinion, he said: "The present decision, it may well be apprehended, will not only stimulate aggressions, more or less brutal and irritating, upon the admitted rights of colored citizens, but will encourage the belief that it is possible, by means of state enactments, to defeat the beneficent purposes which the people of the United States had in view when they adopted the recent amendments to the Constitution." Fifty-eight years later, when the *Brown* decision, which overruled Plessy, came down, the *New York Times* made a point of remembering Justice Harlan's dissent.

See also Harlan, John Marshall.

Poll Taxes

The fees incurred by poor and usually black voters as a way to keep them from exercising the franchise have been a bone of contention since the end of the Civil War, when the Thirteenth, Fourteenth, and Fifteenth amendments to the Constitution gave blacks equal rights. Southern politicians, in an attempt to keep blacks and poor whites from voting, instituted a "poll tax," or assessment of sorts, to pay for the privilege of voting. Although in most cases less than $2 or $3, the tax nonetheless was too burdensome for many, who found it easier not to vote. William Brewer, in his article "The Poll Tax and the Poll Taxers," lays out how Southern congressmen used the poll tax to strip voting totals to less than 1 percent of their voting constituencies. He also proves how, in the 1942 elections, one of the last in which a poll tax was legally used, less than 5 percent of the public voted in poll tax states, while in others, mostly northern states, the average was about 25 percent. Brewer also points out that in that 1942 campaign alone, in just seven Southern states (Alabama, Arkansas, Georgia, Mississippi, South Carolina, Texas, and Virginia), almost 7 million poor whites were disenfranchised, while slightly more than 4 milion blacks were denied the right to vote—a total of nearly 11 million people.

Pollock v. Williams (U.S., 1944)

While not a civil rights case, in *Pollock* the Supreme Court upheld the right of Congress to outlaw peonage, a form of wage slavery. Plaintiff Pollock was hired out to an employer to perform work for an advance wage of $5.00. Pollock did not do the work and was subsequently arrested. Admitting before the court that he had taken the money but had not performed the service, he was found guilty and sent to jail. He then sued Williams, the jailkeeper, for holding him contrary to the Supreme Court's decision in *Bailey v. Alabama*, which outlawed peonage. A circuit court reversed Pollock's conviction, but the Florida Supreme Court reversed this judgment. Pollock sued to the U.S. Supreme Court. Justice Robert H. Jackson wrote for the Court, which struck down Pollock's conviction: "A statute which makes guilty of a misdemeanor any person who, with intent to defraud, obtains an advance upon an agreement to render services, and which provides further that failure to perform the services for which the advance was obtained shall be prima facie evidence of intent to defraud, [is] held violative of the Thirteenth Amendment and the federal Antipeonage Act."

See also Bailey v. Alabama.

Powell, Adam Clayton, Jr.
(1908–1972)

Adam Clayton Powell, Jr., was the charismatic black minister who served in the U.S. House of Representatives from 1945 until 1971. Powell was born in New Haven, Connecticut, on 29 November 1908, the son of the Reverend Adam Clayton Powell. In early 1909, Reverend Powell moved his family to New York, where he bacame the pastor of the Abyssinian Baptist Church. The younger Powell attended the public schools of New York City and the City College of New York, before earning a bachelor's degree from Colgate University in 1930 and a master's degree in religious education from Columbia University in 1932.

Beginning in 1930, as assistant manager of the Abyssinian Baptist Church, he began to protest racism by demanding the rehiring of five black doctors fired because of their race. During the Depression, he organized food drives and demanded reforms in the hiring of blacks by local businesses. In 1936, he succeeded his father as pastor of the Abyssinian Baptist Church. During this period, he evolved into the charismatic religious and civil rights leader who was to later gain fame.

Elected as a member of the New York City Council in 1941, he demanded that blacks be allowed to serve on the front lines during World War II, not only as foot soldiers but "on the decks and into the seats of planes." In 1942, he outlined a manifesto of 63 areas of improvement for black citizens. In 1944, he was elected to a seat in the U.S. House of Representatives as a Democrat, and served until 1971.

During his time in Washington, he led the fight to integrate dining facilities on Capitol Hill, which were at that time still completely segregated. He fought for legislation outlawing the poll tax and lynching and demanded reforms in the armed forces regarding discrimination in hiring and duty.

Over the years, several controversial matters dogged Powell, such as unneeded trips, mismanagement of budgets, and a refusal to go back to his home district where he was wanted for not paying a slander judgment. These transgressions led the House of Representatives to unseat him in March 1967. That April, he won the special election held to fill the vacancy, but the House refused to seat him. Powell won reelection in 1968, but when he was stripped of seniority, he refused to take the seat. In June 1969, the Supreme Court ruled that the House had the right to strip Powell of his seniority, and Powell took the seat as a freshman congressman. In 1970, he was denied renomination in the Democratic primary. Failing to win as an independent, Powell's career in politics ended. Just a few months after retiring as pastor of the Abyssinian Baptist Church, he suffered a heart attack while visiting Miami and died on 2 April 1972. He was 67 years old.

Powell, Colin Luther (1937–)

General Colin Powell was the first black American to serve as chairman of the joint chiefs of staff of the U.S. military. Powell was born in the Bronx, New York City, on 5 April 1937, the son of Jamaican immigrants. He received his bachelor's degree from City College in New York, and his master's degree in business administration from George Washington University. In 1958, Powell was commissioned as a second lieutenant in the U.S. Army. He served through two tours of duty in Vietnam (1962 and 1968) before being made commander of the Second Brigade of the 101st Airborne Division at Fort Campbell, Kentucky, 1976–1977. In 1983, President Ronald Reagan named Powell military assistant to the secretary of defense, a post he held until 1986, when he became commander of V Corps in Europe. The following year, Reagan named Powell deputy national security adviser, then national security adviser—the first black to hold those posts. In October 1989, President George Bush appointed General Powell as chairman of the joint chiefs of staff, the second most powerful position in the nation's military after the president. During the Persian Gulf War in 1991, General Colin Powell was the president's point man on strategy and logistics. He left the joint chiefs in September 1993.

Powell v. Alabama
See Scottsboro Boys.

President's Committee on Equality of Treatment and Opportunity in the Armed Forces

The committee, established by President Harry S Truman under his Executive Order 9981 of 29 July 1948, was created to examine the armed forces to determine what could be done to alleviate and end discrimination based on race. The members of the committee were: Chairman Charles H. Fahy, an appeals court judge in Washington, D.C., and a former solicitor general; Lester Blackwell Granger, executive secretary of the National Urban League; John H. Sengstacke, editor of the black newspaper the Chicago *Defender*; Alphonsus J. Donahue, president of the Donahue Sales Corporation; Dwight R. G. Palmer, president of the General Cable Corporation; William E. Stevenson, president of Oberlin (Ohio) College; and Charles Luckman, president of the Lever Brothers Company. The panel was better known as the Fahy Committee.

It met for the first time on 12 January 1949 and published its final report, *Freedom to Serve: Equality of Treatment and Opportunity in the Armed Forces; A Report by the President's Committee*, on 22 May 1950. In the year and a half it existed, the committee convened in 40 sessions, toured 25 military bases, heard almost 70 witnesses, and listened to several officials at the Pentagon. While the committee met, the U.S. Air Force drew up a plan that later moved about 25,000 black pilots from segregated units to mixed units. The air force plan was a model for all the armed forces. By the time of the committee's final report, all quotas and segregated units in the navy and army had been abolished.

Prigg, Plaintiff in Error, v. The Commonwealth of Pennsylvania (U.S., 1842)

Prigg was the landmark Supreme Court case in which state laws barring the return of fugitive slaves were held to be unconstitutional. Edward Prigg, a native of Maryland, was hired in April 1837, along with Nathan S. Benis, Jacob Forward, and Stephen Lewis, Jr., to retrieve a slave named Margaret Morgan, who had fled to Pennsylvania. Pennsylvania law denied slaveowners the right to retrieve slaves who had fled to the state. When Prigg and his compatriots seized Margaret Morgan, they were arrested and indicted by a grand jury there. Although they pleaded not guilty, they were all convicted. The Supreme Court heard the case and struck down Prigg's conviction. Writing for the Court, Chief Justice Roger Taney, who later wrote the opinion in the *Dred Scott* case, said: "On consideration whereof, it is the opinion of this court, that the act of the commonwealth of Pennsylvania, upon which the indictment in this case is founded, is repugnant to the constitution and laws of the United States, and therefore, void."

Protest Collaboration Movement

The Protest Collaboration (or Accommodation) Movement was started and led primarily by Booker T. Washington and William H. Councill of Alabama. The movement's central tenet was that it was best for blacks to live in peace with whites; it endorsed compromise and called for racial disputes to be settled peaceably. Protest collaboration was viewed by some as a practical approach to improving the lot of black Americans, but others, such as W. E. B. DuBois, regarded it as unnecessarily slow and submissive. The movement lost much of its force as the new NAACP began to forge its political program, and it effectively disintegrated with the death of Washington in November 1915.

See also Councill, William Hooper; Washington, Booker Taliaferro.

Rainey, Joseph Hayne (1832–1887)

Joseph Rainey was the first black man to be elected to the U.S. House of Representatives, serving in Congress from 1870 to 1879. Rainey was born a slave on 21 June 1832, in Georgetown, South Carolina. When he was an infant, his father, Edward, purchased his family's freedom from its master and moved to Charleston. When the Civil War broke out, Joseph Rainey was enlisted to work gathering food and building battlements for Charleston. In 1862, he and his wife, whom he met in Philadelphia and married in 1859, escaped by blockade runner to Bermuda. They settled in the capital, St. Georges, where Rainey became a barber. In 1866, Rainey returned to South Carolina and set up his barber shop in Georgetown. In 1867, he was named as a member of the executive committee of the South Carolina state Republican Party. The following year, he was a delegate to the state constitutional convention.

With the resignation of Congressman Benjamin Whittemore amid charges of selling military appointments, Rainey was nominated by the Republicans to fill his seat. Rainey defeated his Democratic opponent, C. W. Dudley, and went to Washington as a member of the Forty-first Congress. He supported Senator Charles Sumner's efforts to enact civil rights laws and endorsed a civil rights act that protected blacks from the threats of the Ku Klux Klan. In 1874, Rainey briefly sat as speaker of the house, due to the illness of James G. Blaine, thereby becoming the first black man to hold that post.

Rainey sat through the Forty-fifth Congress. Each time he stood for reelection, Democrats in the state contested his victories. In 1876, Democrat John S. Richardson had the backing of the Democratic governor, but lost a close race. Richardson asked the House to invalidate Rainey's victory, but, two years later, the House found Rainey to have been legally elected. In 1878, however, Richardson defeated Rainey when widespread intimidation kept blacks from the polls. Rainey left Washington in 1879, having served the longest of the post–Civil War black congressmen.

After his years in Congress, Rainey went on to become revenue agent for South Carolina. He sought an appointment as clerk of the House of Representatives, but the Democrats blocked it. Instead, he entered the field of banking in Washington, D.C. When that failed, he worked at a coal and wood yard before

Joseph Hayne Rainey

165

returning to his home state. Rainey died at his home in Georgetown on 2 August 1887.

Randolph, Asa Philip (1889–1979)

A. Philip Randolph was the labor leader and civil rights activist whose most noteworthy work took place in the early part of the twentieth century. Born in Crescent City, Florida, just outside Jacksonville, on 15 April 1889, Randolph was the son of a Methodist minister. With his older brother, Randolph attended the Cookman Institute, a Methodist missionary school in Jacksonville, graduating from the school in 1907. After a series of odd jobs, he headed north to New York City, where he got a job as a porter for $4 a month. Randolph worked during the day and at night attended classes in sociology and English literature at City College. At this time, Randolph met Chandler Owen, a black law student at Columbia University. Randolph and Owen founded a black employment agency in Harlem, which they called the Brotherhood of Labor, and tried to unionize black workers. In 1915, the two men established *The Messenger*, a black magazine with socialist aims, which angrily editorialized against President Woodrow Wilson. Enraged at the treatment black porters were receiving from the Pullman railroad company, in 1925 Randolph founded the Brotherhood of Sleeping Car Porters (BSCP), which fought for the next 12 years to get a fair contract for black porters from Pullman. In 1937, the company buckled under the pressure of the BSCP and signed a contract. The company president ended the strike with the words: "Gentlemen, the Pullman Company is ready to sign." Similar pressure on the White House, in the form of a threatened march on Washington by some 100,000 blacks, led President Franklin D. Roosevelt to sign Executive Order 8802, which created the Fair Employment Practices Committee (FEPC) in 1941. Randolph was also an architect of the 1963 March on Washington.

Randolph joined the AFL-CIO as a member of the executive council, when the two labor organizations merged in 1955. In 1957, he was appointed vice president of the AFL-CIO. This was not enough, however. In 1960, he formed the Negro American Labor Council, which spoke for blacks in organized labor. The AFL-CIO committee censured him, accusing him of driving a wedge between working whites and working blacks. Randolph was undaunted. In 1965, he founded the A. Philip Randolph Institute, a think tank created to study the working and living conditions of blacks. In his final years, as the civil rights movement became more militant and divided, he kept a low profile. A. Philip Randolph died in his home in New York City on 16 May 1979.

Ransier, Alonzo Jacob (1834–1882)

Alonzo Jacob Ransier was the Republican congressman who represented South Carolina in the U.S. House of Representatives from 1873 to 1875. Ransier was born in freedom in Charleston, South Carolina, on 3 January 1834. He attended school briefly and then became an apprentice shipping clerk, which afforded him an entry into white South Carolina society that few blacks were allowed (shipping was a profession off limits to blacks). At the end of the Civil War, when he was 31 years old, Ransier was able to capitalize on this advantage when General Daniel Sickles, the military governor of the Carolinas, chose Ransier as elections registrar for his state. In 1868, Ransier represented his home district in the state constitutional convention, worked as chairman of the Republican state central committee, and that year was a presidential elector for Republican Ulysses S. Grant. The same year, he was elected to a single term in the state House of Representatives, where he served until 1870, when he was elected lieutenant governor, the first black man to be so honored in the state. Two years later, he was elected to the U.S. House of Representatives, defeating in the process an independent Republican, former Union General William Gurney.

Ransier served in only the Forty-third Congress, which sat from 1873 until 1875. He played a key role in the House debate on the Civil Rights Act of 1875, as well as working behind the scenes to get $100,000 appropriated to rebuild Charleston harbor, which had been shattered during the Civil War. When he returned home for renomination, Ransier found his state party fractured between Grant Republicans, of which he was one, and independents, who had broken from the party in 1872. Ransier himself took a leading role in ending the career of Republican Governor Franklin Moses, Jr., whom Ransier saw as corrupt. The fight, however, cost Ransier the support of many Republicans, who then nominated Charles W. Buttz, a white Republican, for his House seat.

His congressional career over, Ransier was able to get work as a collector of internal revenue for the second South Carolina District, but soon after, his wife died during the birth of their eleventh child, Charles Sumner Ransier (named after the author of the 1875 Civil Rights Act). Although Ransier was moderately well off, he was overwhelmed by the death of his wife. He soon slid into poverty, and died, a broken man, on 17 August 1882 in Charleston at the age of 48.

Rapier, James Thomas (1837–1883)

James Thomas Rapier was one of three black Republicans (Jeremiah Haralson and Benjamin Sterling Turner being the other two) to represent Alabama in the U.S. House of Representatives. Rapier was born in freedom on 13 November 1837, the fourth son of a barber and his wife. At the age of five, however, he was sent to live with his slave uncle, James P. Thomas (for whom he was named), in Nashville, Tennessee, so that he could attend school. Later, he spent two years on a trading boat on the Mississippi. In 1856, he went to Canada, where he lived with another paternal uncle and studied at the King School, in the experimental former slave community of Buxton, Ontario. He went on to enroll at a normal school near Toronto. In 1863, licensed as a teacher, he taught for a time at his former school in Buxton.

Rapier returned to Nashville in 1864 and settled in Maury County, Tennessee, where he rented 200 acres of cotton fields. He began to agitate for the freedom of slaves while he worked as a reporter for a northern newspaper. In 1865, he was the keynote speaker at the Tennessee Negro Suffrage Convention. Discouraged by the failure of Tennessee to give blacks the right to vote, Rapier returned to Alabama, where he rented a small island in the Tennessee River, hired some poor black tenant farmers, and grew a rich bounty of cotton. He established a Republican newspaper in Alabama and entered politics soon after. He was elected as a delegate to the first state Republican convention in 1867, where he served on the platform committee. There, he called for full black suffrage, as well as the restoration of the citizenship of all former Confederates. Rapier worked hard for the Republican presidential ticket in 1868, but shortly thereafter was driven from his home and threatened by the Ku Klux Klan; he remained in hiding for a year. In 1869 he became a founding member of the National Negro Labor Union. In 1870, he was the Republican nominee for Alabama secretary of state; however, the Klan participated in his defeat.

In 1872, Rapier was nominated by the Republicans for the U.S. House of Representatives and was elected to represent the Second Alabama District. He served a single term in the Forty-third Congress

(1873–1875). Before he took his seat, he was Alabama's delegate in Vienna, Austria, to the Fifth International Exposition. When he returned, he spent much of his term pushing to make Montgomery, Alabama, a port of delivery, striving to get federal improvements in Southern normal schools, and debating the proposed Civil Rights Act of 1875. Despite his efforts, though, Democrats were not pleased about having a black represent them in Congress. After the Democrats retook control of the state, they used every means necessary, including intimidation of black voters and the destruction of Republican ballots, to defeat Rapier for reelection and elect Democrat Jeremiah Williams, a former Confederate major, in his place.

Although Rapier ran for his old seat in 1876 and was defeated, he continued to be a force in Republican politics. In 1880 he attended the Republican National Convention and, from 1877 to 1883, was the collector of internal revenue for the Second Alabama District, a plum patronage post. One of his last acts was to purchase land in Kansas for a black retreat from the racist South. Rapier did not live to see this dream, however. Stricken with tuberculosis in the late 1870s, he succumbed to the disease on 31 May 1883, at the age of 46.

Rauh, Joseph Louis, Jr. (1911–1992)

Joseph Rauh, Jr., was a noted civil rights attorney who served as general counsel for the Leadership Conference of Civil Rights for more than 40 years. Rauh was born in Cincinnati on 3 January 1911. He attended Harvard University, graduated magna cum laude with a degree in economics, then enrolled in Harvard Law School, from which he graduated in 1935. His first position was as a law clerk to Supreme Court justices Benjamin Cardozo and Felix Frankfurter. At the same time, Rauh also was the counsel to several New Deal agencies, as well as the Lend Lease Administration. During World War II he served in the Pacific as an aide to General Douglas MacArthur.

After the war, Rauh returned to Washington, D.C., where he went into private practice as an attorney representing clients involved in the ongoing battle over civil liberties. Among his clients were left-wing writers Lillian Hellman and Arthur Miller and United Mine Workers official Joseph A. ("Jock") Yablonski. He became involved in the fight for civil rights on a national level, acting as counsel to the Freedom Riders, the Mississippi Freedom Democratic Party (an offshoot of the Democratic Party that fought for greater black representation in the state's delegation to the 1964 Democratic National Convention), and, in the 1950s, to the Leadership Council on Civil Rights, an umbrella organization of civil rights groups. In 1948, it was Rauh who wrote the controversial civil rights plank to the Democratic Party platform that drove many Southerners to leave the party and form the States' Rights party. A founder of the radical group Americans for Democratic Action, Rauh testified during the 1980s against all the Supreme Court nominees of Presidents Reagan and Bush. Rauh died in Washington on 3 September 1992, at the age of 81.

Reconstruction

Reconstruction, the policy of the U.S. government toward the defeated Southern states and their readmission to the Union, lasted from 1865 until 1877. In 1866, Senator James Willis Nesmith of Oregon claimed that the defeated Southern states were not part of the United States, but instead were conquered territories and should suffer military occupation. This policy was upheld for the first and only time in our nation's history. There is some dispute as to whether Abraham Lincoln would have treated the defeated Southern states as harshly, had he lived. Regardless, his successor, Andrew Johnson, fought tooth and nail against the will of the radical Republi-

Nineteenth-century cartoonist Thomas Nast's interpretation of "Reconstruction and How It Works"

cans in Congress, who first passed the Thirteenth, Fourteenth, and Fifteenth amendments, the so-called Reconstruction Amendments, to the U.S. Constitution, and then imposed a harsh military occupation on the former Confederate states. The leaders of these radicals were Congressman Thaddeus Stevens of

Pennsylvania and Senator Charles Sumner of Massachusetts. These men and others, such as Senator Benjamin Wade of Michigan, Senator Henry Wilson of Massachusetts, Senator Lyman Trubull of Illinois (author of the Civil Rights Act of 1866 and the Freedmen's Bureau Act of 1866), Congressman George Washington Julian of Indiana, and Congressman James Ashley of Ohio, led the way in controlling the agenda following the Civil War.

On the first day of the Thirty-ninth Congress, the Joint Committee on Reconstruction was created to investigate conditions in the South. This was the first step in the admission that the South was considered to have broken away from the nation and was now under strict military occupation. President Johnson, a moderate Democrat, saw the makings of a Republican coup and began to rail against the proceedings in the Congress. The Republicans ignored him. Instead, Senator Trumbull introduced, and got passed, a positive congressional vote on the Civil Rights Act of 1866, which defined American citizenship and allowed all who had it to enjoy the "full and equal benefit of the laws and proceedings for the security of person and property." The bill further allowed for prosecution of violators of the act in federal courts. Trumbull's Freedmen's Bureau bill was also passed by Congress. President Johnson, on the other hand, vetoed both measures, arguing that the Freedmen's Bureau was a financial boondoggle and labeling the Civil Rights Act as unconstitutional. Congress overrode Johnson's veto of the Civil Rights Act, but failed to override the Freedmen's Bureau veto. With Congress and the president at loggerheads, the next year Congress passed the Reconstruction Act of 1867. It divided the 11 former Confederate states, with the exception of Tennessee, into five military districts controlled by military leaders. Many of the whites who had been former slaveowners, and who had fought for the South during the war, were now disen-

franchised completely. Blacks began to fill positions in the state legislatures. In Mississippi, Hiram Revels, a black man, was elected to the U.S. Senate seat once held by Jefferson Davis before he became the president of the Confederacy.

Reconstruction paved the way for blacks to be enfranchised for the first time; however, it generated enormous anger among whites. A radical antiblack organization, the Knights of the Ku Klux Klan, sprang up to terrorize and murder freed slaves. In 1868, the Democratic presidential ticket of New York Governor Horatio Seymour and former Senator Francis P. Blair called for the reinitiation of the "white man's rule." And then, in 1876, in order to gain the Southern votes needed to be elected, Republican Rutherford B. Hayes promised to end Reconstruction. After he was inaugurated, he did just that. Reconstruction lasted 12 short years. During that time, a president had been impeached for opposing Congress; however, the act allowed the nation to begin to come to grips with the horrendous civil war it had just fought and still attempt to gain for blacks the rights denied to them as citizens.

See also Bureau of Refugees, Freedmen, and Abandoned Lands; Civil Rights Act of 1866; Fifteenth Amendment; Fourteenth Amendment; Ku Klux Klan; Stevens, Thaddeus; Sumner, Charles; Thirteenth Amendment; Trumbull, Lyman.

Reitman v. Mulkey (U.S., 1967)

Reitman was the Supreme Court case in which a state statute protecting private discrimination in the rental and sale of property was held to be unconstitutional. The Mulkeys, a black couple, attempted to rent an apartment from the Reitmans. They were turned away solely because of their race. Under section 26 of the California constitution, a referendum passed by the people in 1964, as Proposition 14, read: "Neither the State nor any subdivision or agency thereof shall deny, limit or abridge, directly or indirectly, the right of any person, who is willing or desires to sell, lease or rent any part or all of his real property, to decline to sell, lease or rent such property to such person or persons as he, in his absolute discretion, chooses." The Mulkeys' suit alleged that section 26 was a violation of their Fourteenth Amendment rights, as well as articles 51 and 52 of the California Civil Code. The Reitmans countered that section 26 made sections 51 and 52 null and void. The trial court dismissed the Mulkeys' complaint, with the California Supreme Court finding that enforcement of section 21 was a violation of the equal protection clause of the Fourteenth Amendment. The Reitmans appealed to the U.S. Supreme Court, which held, unanimously, that section 21 did violate the Fourteenth Amendment and affirmed the California Supreme Court's decision. Justice Byron White delivered the opinion of the Court on 29 May 1967.

Hiram Rhodes Revels

Revels, Hiram Rhodes (1827–1901)

Hiram Revels was the first black man ever elected to serve in the U.S. Senate. Referred to by his contemporaries as a "quadroon" (someone who is one-fourth black), Revels was born to free parents in Fayetteville, North Carolina, on 27 September 1827, apparently of Croatan Indian, African, and white ancestry. He received a limited education in a school run by a black woman in Fayetteville, but later attended Knox College in Galesburg, Illinois. In 1845, Revels was ordained a minister by the African Methodist Church in Baltimore. He served at various pastorates in the years leading up to the Civil War. When war broke out, he was in Maryland, where he helped enlist the first all-black regiment in that state. During the war, he opened a school for freedmen in St. Louis, administered aid as a chaplain of a black unit in Mississippi, and, as a member of the Freedmen's Commission, was a provost-marshal in Vicksburg.

In 1868, after settling in Natchez, Mississippi, he was elected an alderman. In 1869, the Republican state convention nominated Revels for the state senate. Less than a year later, the state legislature met to fill the vacated U.S. Senate seat of former Confederate President Jefferson Davis. Many people favored John Roy Lynch, the charismatic black who had just become Mississippi secretary of state; yet Lynch's selection would have required a state election. Instead, as a compromise, the legislature chose Revels.

On 25 February 1870, a dignified Hiram Revels strode onto the floor of the U.S. Senate and was sworn in as the first black senator. He served little more than two years of the term before leaving. He called for abstinence from alcohol and high moral behavior as the best route for black emancipation. Unlike other Republicans, he demanded the restoration of voting rights for former Confederate soldiers and high officials. As a senator, he appointed a black man to go to West Point. As his term came to an end, Revels accepted a position as the first president of Alcorn University, an all-black school near Rodney, Mississippi. He served in this capacity from

1871 until 1875, when an argument with the Republican governor led to his dismissal. In 1876, the new governor reappointed Revels as president of Alcorn. Revels held the job until he voluntarily retired in 1882. He spent his final years as a minister in the African Methodist Church. Hiram Revels died in Aberdeen, Mississippi, on 16 January 1901.

Reynolds, a Judge, et al. v. Sims et al. (U.S., 1964)

Reynolds was the Supreme Court case in which it was held that any reapportionment of a state legislature that disenfranchises any citizen is unconstitutional, and that federal courts have the power to stop such reapportionment. *Reynolds* was in fact a number of cases considered together, all of them dealing with the reapportionment of Alabama legislative districts for the 1962 election. Several black citizens, observing that the new boundaries left them underrepresented, sued in the state courts to block the new elections. In 1962, a three-judge panel allowed for new plans to be created, but later decided these new plans did not alter the disenfranchisement of some citizens. State officials appealed, suing one of the judges, Reynolds. After hearing the case in late 1963, the Supreme Court ruled on 15 June 1964 (together with the similar cases of *Vann et al. v. Baggett, Secretary of State of Alabama* and *McConnell et al. v. Baggett, Secretary of State of Alabama*) that the district court was correct in ruling the two reapportionment plans in violation of the equal protection clause of the Fourteenth Amendment.

See also Baker v. Carr; Mobile v. Bolden.

Robinson et al. v. Florida (U.S., 1964)

Robinson was the Supreme Court case in which the absence of "state action" in segregation was held to be a nonmitigating factor in whether the discrimination was legal or not. Robinson and 17 other students staged a sit-in at a Shell's City Restaurant in Miami, Florida, a segregated dining facility. The manager asked the students to leave; when they refused, they were all arrested and charged with violating section 509.141 of the Florida Statutes, which allowed for the manager of a store to ask undesirable customers to leave the premises. At trial, the manager explained that while black patrons were welcome in other departments of the Shell's Department Store, the cafeteria was for whites only. The defendants argued that their removal constituted state action in support of racial discrimination, but to no avail. Although the students were convicted, the judge only sentenced them to probation. On appeal, the Florida Supreme Court affirmed the lower court's convictions. The students and their attorneys, including famed National Association for the Advancement of Colored People (NAACP) lawyer Jack Greenberg, sued to the U.S. Supreme Court. The Court ruled, on 22 June 1964, that section 509.141 was in fact state action in the area of private discrimination and struck down the convictions of Robinson and the other students.

Roots

Roots, the television miniseries that brought to the American mainstream the story of slavery in America, was among the most-watched programs in the history of television. It originally ran from 23 to 30 January 1977, a total of eight episodes. It was the genealogical story of black writer Alex Haley, who had coauthored a work in the early 1960s with Malcolm X. Haley traced his lineage back to Kunte Kinte, an African youth from Gambia who was sold into slavery and taken to America sometime in the late eighteenth century. The program created a whirlwind of interest in black genealogy and finally established in popular view that American blacks had a rich history before and during the dark days of slavery.

Rosenwald, Julius (1862–1932)

Julius Rosenwald was a Jewish philanthropist and businessman best known for his donations to black charities and causes. Rosenwald was born in Springfield, Illinois, on 12 August 1862, in somewhat poverty-stricken conditions. He started doing odd jobs at age 15; eventually, he moved to New York, where he worked for his two uncles until he could save some money. With the stipend he received, he and a partner opened up a retail clothing business. The firm, Rosenwald & Company, began to market clothing through its mail order business and to sell surplus to Sears, Roebuck. In 1895, Rosenwald purchased a percentage of the Sears company. In 30 years, this small investment accumulated into more than $100 million. In 1896, Rosenwald became vice president of Sears, Roebuck.

With his fortune growing, Rosenwald turned to charitable causes as the best way to leave a legacy. In 1910, he met and befriended Booker T. Washington, who convinced Rosenwald to help fund Washington's Tuskegee University. In addition, Rosenwald dispensed funds that led to the construction of some 4,138 schools designed exclusively for Southern blacks. In addition to employing more than 11,000 black teachers, in excess of 500,000 black children received their education in these schools between 1910 and 1932. In 1917, Rosenwald created the Rosenwald Fund, which doled out monies to aid in alleviating the injustices done to American blacks and European Jews. The total funds Rosenwald gave away from 1917 until his death in 1932 amount to more than $20 million. In 1927, Rosenwald was awarded the gold medal of the William E. Harmon Awards for Distinguished Achievements in Race Relations.

Julius Rosenwald died of arterial sclerosis on 6 January 1932. In his will, he left a subsidy of $2.5 million to construct housing for blacks in Chicago's poorer areas.

Runyon, Doing Business as Bobbe's School, v. McCrary (U.S., 1976)

Runyon was the Supreme Court case in which the right of black children to go to private schools was upheld. Russell and Katheryne Runyon ran the Bobbe's School, a private institution, in Arlington, Virginia. The parents of Michael McCrary, a black youngster, attempted to enroll him at the school after receiving a brochure from the Runyons. Told that the school was not integrated and would not accept their child, the McCrarys sued under 42 U.S.C. 1981, which states: "All persons within the jurisdiction of the United States shall have the same right in every State and Territory to make and enforce contracts, to sue, be parties, give evidence, and to the full and equal benefit of all laws and proceedings for the security of persons and property as is enjoyed by white citizens, and shall be subject to like punishment, pains, penalties, taxes, licenses, and exactions of every kind, and to no other." A district court found against the Runyons and awarded the McCrarys compensation for the discrimination. The Fourth Circuit Court of Appeals affirmed the decision, so the Runyons appealed to the U.S. Supreme Court. The Court held unanimously that section 1981 does prohibit private discrimination in schooling and other educational facilities within the law, and at the same time does not violate the doctrine of free association and privacy. Justice Potter Stewart delivered the Court's opinion.

Rustin, Bayard (1910–1987)

Bayard Rustin, a civil rights leader, was a close associate of A. Philip Randolph and one of the organizers of the 1963 March on Washington. Rustin was born on 17 March 1910, in West Chester, Pennsylvania, one of 12 children of a West Indian father and a Quaker mother. He experienced discrimination at an early age when he was refused service at a local

Bayard Rustin

restaurant while he was in high school. "I sat there quite a long time, and was eventually thrown out bodily," he said in an interview. "From that point on, I took the conviction that I would not accept segregation."

After graduating from high school, Rustin wandered the United States doing odd jobs. Eventually, he returned to Pennsylvania, where, for a time, he studied at Cheney State Teachers' College and Wilberforce University. Influenced by his mother's Quaker beliefs, which promoted pacifism, he joined the Young Communist League in 1936. By 1941, disillusioned with communism, Rustin turned to the newly formed Fellowship of Reconciliation (FOR), a group of white and black civil rights advocates committed to pacifism. During the next 12 years, culminating in 1953, he served as FOR's field secretary and race relations secretary. In 1941, he was an advisor to A. Philip Randolph in the planning of a proposed March on Washington to protest discrimination in the armed forces. In 1943, called to military service, Rustin refused to serve and was sentenced to prison, where he spent 28 months. In 1947, he was arrested for the first time for protesting bus seating laws in North Carolina. Convicted, he served 22 days on a chain gang. In 1953, he quit FOR and joined the War Resisters League, a radical pacifist organization.

In the mid 1950s, Rustin hopped on the bandwagon of the civil rights movement led by the Reverend Dr. Martin Luther King, Jr. He worked with Reverend Dr. King in Montgomery during the city bus boycott there, then acted as a key advisor to King when the Southern Christian Leadership Conference was created. In 1963, again working with A. Philip Randolph, Rustin was the organizer of the March on Washington, which drew some 200,000 protesters to the nation's capital. In 1964, Rustin was the founder of the A. Philip Randolph Institute, an organization that advocated civil rights programs.

Rustin spent his later years as head of the A. Philip Randolph Institute and chairman of the Executive Committee of the Leadership Conference on Civil Rights. He died on 24 August 1987 at the age of 77.

Sarah C. Roberts v. The City of Boston (1850)

Sarah C. Roberts was the landmark Massachusetts Supreme Court case in which the doctrine of "separate but equal" was upheld as constitutional. The case involved Sarah C. Roberts, a five-year-old black girl who attempted to enroll at a white public school in Boston, but was denied entry because of her race. Charles Sumner, a Boston attorney who later became famous as the author of the Civil Rights Act of 1875, and his black associate, Robert Morris, sued the city to get the girl into the school. They claimed that the distance she would have to travel to a blacks-only school was a great inconvenience. Further, the two men asked for an end to overall inequality in education. Massachusetts Supreme Court Chief Justice Lemuel Shaw wrote in his opinion that Sarah was not entitled to equality, noting that racial prejudice is "not created by law, and probably cannot be changed by law." This case, along with two others from Indiana and Ohio, was used by the U.S. Supreme Court in 1857 to decide *Plessy v. Ferguson*.

See also Plessy v. Ferguson; Sumner, Charles.

Scheuer, Administratrix, v. Rhodes, Governor of Ohio (U.S., 1974)

Scheuer, while not specifically a civil rights case, did broaden the meaning of "police brutality," which the Supreme Court defined in its *Monroe v. Pape* decision. *Scheuer* was one of three cases taken together; the others were *Miller v. Rhodes* and *Krause v. Rhodes*. Scheuer, Miller, and Krause were three students killed at Kent State University in 1970 by the Ohio National Guard monitoring anti-Vietnam War protests there. The estates of the three sued the governor of Ohio, the adjunct general of the state, and various officers of the Ohio National Guard for using undue force as described in the Civil Rights Act of 1871 (now 42 U.S.C. 1983). The district court dismissed the claims against the officers under the Eleventh Amendment, which prevents states from being sued. The Supreme Court granted *certiorari* to examine the district court's decision. The Court ruled 8-0 (Justice William O. Douglas did not participate) that the officers of the state were not immune to all liabilities. Chief Justice Warren Burger wrote the opinion, saying, "The immunity of officers of the executive branch of a state government for their acts is not absolute but qualified and of varying degree, depending upon the scope of discretion and responsibilities of the particular office and the circumstances at the time the challenged action was taken."

Schwerner, Michael Henry (1939–1964)

Michael Schwerner was one of three civil rights workers killed near Philadelphia, Mississippi, in June 1964. Schwerner was born on 6 November 1939, in New York City, the son of a wig manufacturer. He was sent to the prestigious Walden School, years before Andrew Goodman, and, later, to public schools in Pelham, New York. He attended Michigan State University for a year, then the School of Veterinary Medicine at Cornell University in Ithaca, upstate New York. He later graduated from Cornell with a degree in

Michael Henry Schwerner

rural sociology. His time at Cornell was marked by his insistence on having a black student pledge at his fraternity.

After his graduation in 1961, for a time Schwerner attended Columbia University to study social work; he soon dropped out, however, because he felt helping to end poverty meant attacking what he felt was its root cause: racism. In 1962, he began to work at a public housing project on Manhattan's poor Lower East Side. He also did volunteer work for the Congress of Racial Equality (CORE). In July 1963, Schwerner was arrested in Maryland at a CORE-sponsored rally. After the Sixteenth Street Baptist Church bombing in September 1963, which killed four black girls, Schwerner asked CORE to transfer him to a Southern state, where his work could be more productive. He was assigned as a field staff worker in Meridian, Mississippi.

Schwerner was teamed with James Earl Chaney, a native of Meridian and a CORE worker himself. Later, the two men were joined by Andrew Goodman of New York, like Schwerner a liberal Jew

who had been involved in civil rights since he was a child. On 21 June 1964, the three men responded to a call that a black church was burning in Longdale, another rural town in Neshoba County. While returning from Longdale, the three men were picked up by the police, held, then released. They then disappeared. After an intense, two-month search, their bodies were found in the remains of an earthen dam. All had been tortured and shot. Gunpowder on the men's clothing indicated they had been shot at close range.

The deaths of Chaney, Schwerner, and Goodman shocked the nation and resulted in a far-ranging FBI manhunt, which brought to justice several Neshoba County police officials. The deaths of Schwerner and his companions were the subject of the 1989 movie *Mississippi Burning*.

See also Chaney, James Earl; Goodman, Andrew; United States v. Price et al.

Scottsboro Boys

The "Scottsboro Boys" were nine young black men, aged 13 to 20, accused of rape who, without the international notoriety their case attracted, would have died in the electric chair. The matter began on 24 March 1931, when about a dozen black youths were riding a train bound for Memphis. Before it stopped in the small town of Paint Rock, Alabama, several whites came aboard and picked a fight. The blacks fought back and forced the whites off the train. The whites raced to Paint Rock and reported to the police that nine black youths had just raped two white women on the train. When the train stopped, the blacks were ordered off, and among them were found two white girls, Victoria Price, 19, and Ruby Bates, 17. Both backed up the white boys' story that they had been raped. Nine black youths were arrested and taken to the nearby town of Scottsboro for trial.

Twelve days later, the nine went before an all-white jury. The evidence for rape

The Scottsboro Boys meet with attorney Samuel Leibowitz prior to their retrial.

was flimsy at best; a doctor testified that the two women had had sexual relations well before the train ride, and no bruises were found on either of them to indicate that force had been used. Still, the two women testified that all nine had raped them, and Price claimed that they did it "without letting [her] up between rapes to spit snuff." The defense counsel was an alcoholic and remained drunk throughout the trial, and the prosecutor inflamed passions with his closing statement that "Guilty or not, let's get rid of these niggers." Eight were found guilty of rape and they were sentenced to death (the case of the ninth was declared a mistrial; he later received a life sentence). Their execution date was set for July 10.

With the imposition of the death sentences, the case of the Scottsboro Nine took on amazing dimensions. A Scottsboro Defense Committee was established, backed by such organizations as the American Civil Liberties Union, the Brotherhood of Sleeping Car Porters, the Fellowship of Reconciliation (the forerunner of the Congress of Racial Equality), the National Association for the Advancement of Colored People, the International Labor Defense (a group of radical left-wing of attorneys), and the Unitarian Fellowship for Social Justice, among others.

While the appeal of the sentence went on, it seemed for a time that the noted attorney Clarence Darrow would defend the nine. Instead, he clashed with a lawyer from the International Labor Defense and, unable to work with a communist attorney, bowed out of the case. To the rescue came Samuel S. Leibowitz, a fiery Jewish lawyer from New York. Leibowitz took full control of the case. He sued to have the convictions overturned because there were no blacks on the jury. The Alabama Supreme Court upheld the sentences, but on 7 November 1932 the U.S. Supreme Court ruled 7–2 (Justice James McReynolds and Pierce Butler dissenting) that the absence of blacks on the jury tainted the convictions, and it overturned them and ordered new trials. All eight men were retried, but they were reconvicted and once more sentenced to death. Again, on appeal, the Supreme Court struck down the convictions. Finally, in 1937, after Ruby Bates recanted her allegations, charges against five of the accused were dropped. In the early 1940s, charges against the four others were finally dismissed as well. Altogether, they had served a century in prison. The last survivor of the group, Clarence Willie Norris, passed away in the early 1980s.

See also Leibowitz, Samuel Simon.

Seligman, Edwin Robert Anderson (1861–1939)

Edwin Seligman was the Columbia University economics professor who was a founding member of the Committee on Urban Condition Among Negroes, the forerunner of the National Urban League. He was born in New York City on 25 April 1861 and named after the heroic Major Robert Anderson, the Union officer who defended Fort Sumter in the opening battle of the Civil War. Seligman was of German Jewish ancestry, and his father, Joseph, who had founded the banking interest of J. & W. Seligman & Company, was later offered the post of secretary of the treasury by President Ulysses S. Grant. Edwin Seligman attended city schools, then enrolled at Columbia University, where he came under the influence of Professor John W. Burgess, a noted political science and history scholar. After Columbia, Seligman spent a year at the University of Berlin and a year at the Sorbonne in Paris. He returned to New York, received his master's degree and doctorate, and, in 1891, was promoted to full professor of economics at Columbia. His special field was taxation.

Seligman was deeply involved in helping people. He was a leader in the creation of the Educational Alliance, an organization founded to help aid immigrant Russian Jews, and in forming, with educator John Dewey, in 1909, the National Negro Conference, which highlighted poor conditions among blacks.

With the help of one of his economics students, George Edmund Haynes, Seligman was one of the founding members of the Committee on Urban Conditions Among Negroes in 1911. Seligman was chosen as the committee's first chairman, a post he held from 1911 until 1914.

Edwin Seligman died of a coronary thrombosis on 18 July 1939, at the age of 78.

Selma to Montgomery March

The march from Selma to Montgomery was the historic demonstration that took place during 21–25 March 1965 to protest segregation in Alabama. The procession was actually the last of three marches from Selma that spring: the first on 7 March had been broken up by Selma police officers, and the second had ended peacefully but short of its destination two days later.

Civil rights protest had been brewing in Alabama for a long time. Rights workers were harassed and beaten; blacks were refused the right to vote; and public facilities stayed locked in the grip of segregation. On 2 January 1965, the Reverend Dr. Martin Luther King, Jr., and members of the Southern Christian Leadership Conference came to Selma to join in the voting registration canvass there. They were also in Selma to protest recent court action aimed at stopping their work. In July 1964, Alabama Circuit Judge James Hare had banned all public meetings of three or more people in Dallas County. This court order had effectively halted the efforts of the Dallas County Voters League (DCVL), under the leadership of such local rights workers as Amelia Platts Boynton, a long-time activist; Marie Foster, a Selma dental hygienist; and Samuel W. Boynton, former president of the Selma branch of the National Association for the Advancement of Colored People (NAACP).

On 2 January, after arriving in Selma, the Reverend Dr. King and the others with him defied Judge Hare's judgment and held a meeting at the Browns Chapel African Methodist Episcopal Church. There was no violence at the church meeting, but the open defiance of the court order paved the way for confrontation over the next several months.

On the night of 18 February, a crowd at the Zion Methodist Church in nearby Marion, Alabama, was attacked by state troopers. Some of the protestors sought refuge in a nearby diner. Police followed them inside the diner and confronted Viola Jackson and her son, Jimmie Lee. After beating Viola, they turned on Jimmie Lee, who had tried to protect his mother. Jackson was struck, then shot in the back when he resisted. He died seven days later in a Selma hospital of an infection resulting from his gunshot wound.

Plans were laid for an all-encompassing march from Selma to Montgomery to highlight the abysmal segregation in Alabama. On 7 March, some 600 marchers, led by activist Hosea Williams, began the trek from Selma to Montgomery. They got no farther than the Edmund Pettus Bridge. There, Alabama state troopers set upon them, striking the marchers with clubs and firing tear gas canisters into the crowd. The negative press coverage of the police action was tempered two days later when a second march was stopped and ended peacefully at the Pettus Bridge.

On that night of 9 March, three ministers from Boston, among them the Reverend James J. Reeb, who had come to Selma to join in marching for civil rights, stopped by the Silver Moon Cafe in Selma. There, they were attacked by a group of whites. Reeb was hit in the head with a pipe and lay on the ground for an undetermined period of time. Later, he was rushed to the hospital, but died two days later. His death, as well as the murder of Jimmie Lee Jackson and the assault on the marchers on 7 March, prompted President Lyndon B. Johnson to send to Congress on 15 March what would become the Voting Rights Act of 1965.

On 16 March, after the Reverend Dr. Martin Luther King and Student Nonviolent Coordinating Committee (SNCC) activist James Forman had been attacked during a voting rights rally, District Judge Frank M. Johnson issued an injunction barring the state or local police from hindering a third Selma to Montgomery march. Four days later, President Johnson mobilized 4,000 Alabama National Guard troops to guard the marchers and issued Executive Order 3645, which authorized any help necessary to secure the safety of the marchers.

The third march started in Selma on 21 March. Altogether, 3,200 people, white and black, began the 54-mile journey at 1:15 in the afternoon as they crossed the Edmund Pettus Bridge, this time under the watchful eye of the Alabama National Guard. They marched a total of seven miles that first day, erecting a campsite near David Hall's farmhouse outside the town of Casey. By 22 March, they had moved to the town of Petronia, in Lowndes County. The campsite for 23 March was just a few miles from the border of Montgomery County. On 24 March, the protestors stayed at the City of St. Jude, a Catholic hospital and school just outside the Montgomery city limits. On 25 March, accompanied by several thousand additional protestors, who had joined them at St. Jude, the 300 marchers who had traveled the entire route entered Montgomery and ended the journey at the Dexter Avenue Baptist Church, where Reverend Dr. Martin Luther King, Jr., had once preached. King stood on a platform and delivered some remarks to the crowd. "Our bodies are tired, and our feet are somewhat sore, but today as I stand before you and think back over that

great march, I can say as Sister Pollard said, a 70-year-old Negro woman who lived in this community during the bus boycott, and one day she was asked while walking if she wanted a ride and when she answered, 'No,' the person said, 'Well, aren't you tired?' And with her ungrammatical profundity, she said, 'My feets is tired, but my soul is rested.' And in a real sense this afternoon, we can say that our feet are tired, but our souls are rested."

The Selma march was over, but the outrages committed against the civil rights workers were not. That night, white Michigan housewife Viola Gregg Liuzzo and her black friend, Leroy Moton, drove from Selma to Montgomery to transport some of the marchers home. Along the route, near the town of Wright Chapel, a carload of Ku Klux Klan members drove up next to the car and opened fire, hitting Liuzzo twice in the face and killing her instantly. The car crashed, and Moton played dead while the murderers checked the car. A Federal Bureau of Investigation (FBI) informant in the Klan helped lead to the murderers' arrest the next day.

The Selma march and the Liuzzo murder helped speed the passage of the Voting Rights Act. On 26 May, the Senate approved the act by a vote of 77–19; the House passed it overwhelmingly on 9 July; and, on 6 August, President Lyndon B. Johnson signed it into law.

Shaw et al. v. Reno, Attorney General, et al. (U.S., 1993)

Shaw was the landmark Supreme Court case in which the high court ruled that states may not draw the boundaries of congressional districts on the basis of race. In the 1990 census, North Carolina became entitled to create a twelfth congressional district. Because North Carolina had not sent a black person to Congress this century, the state General

Assembly drew up plans for 12 seats, one of which was a so-called "majority-minority seat," in which a majority of the voters belonged to racial or ethnic minorities. Under the provisions of Title 5 of the Voting Rights Act of 1965 (now 42 U.S.C. Section 1973c), under which a state found to have discriminated in the past must submit their reapportionment plans to either the U.S. District Court for the District of Columbia or the attorney general, the original apportionment plan was thrown out by the Justice Department so that a second so-called "minority seat" could be created. The state general assembly went back and redrew the plans, making for a second "majority-minority" seat.

Ruth O. Shaw was among several white voters who felt that this second seat, which snaked along a highway to include concentrations of black voters, left them with no voting strength. These plaintiffs sued in the U.S. District Court for the Eastern District of North Carolina. Their original suit, against the governor of North Carolina, was dismissed by the district court. They then sued the attorney general, Janet Reno, to the U.S. Supreme Court. On 28 June 1993, the last day of the 1992–93 term, the Court ruled 5–4 that the districts formed on the basis of race were unconstitutional. Writing for the majority (Justices Byron White, Harry Blackmun, John Paul Stevens, and David Souter dissented), Justice Sandra Day O'Connor wrote, "Racial classifications of any sort pose the risk of lasting harm to our society. They reinforce the belief, held by too many for too much of our history, that individuals should be judged by the color of their skin. Racial classifications with respect to voting carry particular dangers. Racial gerrymandering, even for remedial purposes, may balkanize us into competing racial factions; it threatens to carry us further from the goal of a politi-cal system in which race no longer matters—a goal that the Fourteenth and Fifteenth Amendments embody, and to which the Nation continues to aspire. It is for these reasons that race-based districting by our state legislatures demands close judicial scrutiny."

Shelley v. Kraemer (U.S., 1948)

Shelley was one of two Supreme Court cases—the other was *Hurd v. Hodge*—in which restrictive covenants, those housing contracts in which racial and religious minorities are contractually ruled ineligible to own certain properties, were struck down as unconstitutional. The case concerned a black man named Shelley, who purchased a piece of property from Fitzgerald, a white man. Fitzgerald was unaware that three-fourths of the land in the neighborhood were bound by restrictive covenants barring "buyers of the Negro or Mongolian race." One Kraemer, the owner of an adjoining property, sued Shelley, asking a state court to stop the black man from taking possession of the land. The state court ruled that the covenant was illegal, but it was reversed on appeal by the Missouri Supreme Court. Shelley then appealed the case to the U.S. Supreme Court. The Court ruled, 6–0 (Justices Stanley Reed, Robert Jackson and Wiley Rutledge did not participate) that the covenants were unconstitutional. Chief Justice Fred M. Vinson read the opinion of the Court. "Section 1 of the Civil Rights Act of 1866, which was enacted by Congress while the Fourteenth Amendment was under consideration, provides: 'All citizens of the United States shall have the same right, in every state and Territory, as is enjoyed by white citizens thereof to inherit, purchase, lease, sell, hold, and convey real and personal property.' We (the members of the Court) hold that in granting judicial enforcement of the restrictive agreements in these cases, the states have denied petitioners the equal protection of the laws and that, therefore, cannot stand."

See also Houston, Charles Hamilton; Hurd v. Hodge; Jones v. Alfred H. Mayer Co.

Shuttlesworth, Fred Lee (1922–)

Fred Lee Shuttlesworth was an early civil rights leader active in the Southern Christian Leadership Conference and a founder of the Alabama Christian Movement for Human Rights. Shuttlesworth was born in Montgomery County, Alabama, on 18 March 1922. Educated in the segregated schools of rural Alabama, he graduated with a bachelor of arts degree from Selma College and a bachelor of science degree from Alabama State College.

Although in his early years Shuttlesworth was involved in education, he became a member of the Alabama National Association for the Advancement of Colored People (NAACP) and began to fight for civil rights in the early 1950s. In 1953, when the state closed down the Alabama NAACP, Shuttlesworth formed the Alabama Christian Movement for Human Rights (ACMHR) to coordinate civil rights activity in the state. A few weeks later, the Rosa Parks bus incident triggered the Montgomery Bus Boycott, and Shuttlesworth became a powerful voice in the movement to end segregation on city buses in the state. At the time, he was a minister at the Revelation Baptist Church in Cincinnati.

Although not a national figure, Shuttlesworth did make headlines. In September 1957, he made the front page of the New York Times when he was beaten by white segregationists, who were protesting his attempt to enroll his daughter in Phillips High School in Birmingham. The front page carried a dramatic photograph of Shuttlesworth being pummeled on the ground by whites. In 1960, Shut-

tlesworth was arrested twice for sit-ins, and his home was bombed once. In 1963, he began a "direct-action" campaign to end segregation in Birmingham. During the five-week action, Shuttlesworth would rise at nightly town meetings among his followers and say, "We're tired of waiting. We're telling Ol' Bull Connor right here tonight that we're on the march and we're not going to stop marching until we get our rights!" After working behind the scenes with an official from the Justice Department, Shuttlesworth was able to reach an agreement by which lunch counters would be desegregated in large downtown department stores, stores and businesses would hire and promote black workers, black civil rights demonstrators would be released from jail, and a biracial city commission would be created. The Reverend Dr. Martin Luther King, Jr., called the agreement "the most significant victory for justice that we have seen in the Deep South."

Following his dramatic work, Shuttlesworth returned to the ministry. He is now the minister at the Greater New Light Baptist Church in Cincinnati and remains on the board of the Southern Christian Leadership Conference.

Sipuel v. Board of Regents of the University of Oklahoma et al. (U.S., 1948)

Sipuel was the landmark Supreme Court case in which the Court held that the states must provide equal education for "qualified" black students. Ada Lois Sipuel attempted to enroll at the University of Oklahoma Law School, but was denied because of her race. She sued in a Oklahoma district court, but was refused review of her case. The Oklahoma Supreme Court affirmed the lower court ruling, and Sipuel, backed by attorney Thurgood Marshall, sued to the U.S. Supreme Court. On 12 January 1948, just four days after oral arguments in the case ended, the Court unanimously struck down Oklahoma's refusal to admit Sipuel as a violation of the equal protection clause of the Fourteenth Amendment. The Court cited its previous ruling in *Missouri Ex Rel. Gaines v. Canada*, which struck down unequal education standards as unconstitutional.

Sit-down Demonstration

Also known as a "sit-in" demonstration, this form of protest was widely employed by civil rights advocates fighting against segregated dining facilities. The tactic was apparently first used on 1 February 1960, when four black freshmen at the all-black North Carolina A & T College in Greensboro, North Carolina, entered a Woolworth's restaurant in Greensboro, sat down at a whites-only counter, and demanded service or arrest before they would leave. The four men were Greensboro natives Ezell Blair and David Richmond, Joseph McNeil of Wilmington, North Carolina, and Franklin McCain of Washington, D.C. Although that first protest failed (the students were not served, and the store closed before they were arrested), the protests spread to other segregated facilities in the city. Eventually, hundreds of civil rights workers, white and black, were arrested across the segregated South by using this new form of agitation. The sit-in remained during the entire civil rights struggle as a valuable weapon against the power of Jim Crow.

A sit-down demonstration in Jackson, Mississippi, 12 June 1963

Sixteenth Street Baptist Church Bombing

On 15 September 1963, the Sixteenth Street Baptist Church in Birmingham, Alabama, was the subject of a terrorist attack by the Ku Klux Klan. Four young black girls were killed.

The civil rights struggle in Birmingham had been intensely confrontational from the early days of 1963. Several sit-in protests were held to forward the desegregation of lunch counters and public facilities. Dozens of activists were arrested, including Martin Luther King, Jr., who used his time in a prison cell to write the famous "Letter from Birmingham Jail." An integration agreement was hammered out between the activists and the storeowners, but on 11 May the progress was shattered by a series of bombings. Among the targets were the home of King's brother, A. L. King, and the A. G. Gaston Motel, owned by a prominent black activist. A riot ensued, and President John F. Kennedy dispatched federal troops to restore order.

Four months later, on Sunday, 15 September 1963, four black girls—Addie Mae Collins, Denise McNair, Cynthia Wesley, and Carol Robertson—were killed when the Sixteenth Street Baptist Church was blown up. The explosion, which was timed to coincide with Sunday prayers, set off another riot in Birmingham. No one was immediately arrested for the crime, but in 1977 Robert Edward Chambliss, a member of the Ku Klux Klan, was arrested, tried, and convicted of the murder of Denise McNair. Sentenced to life imprisonment, he died in prison in 1985.

See also Chambliss, Robert Edward.

Smalls, Robert (1839–1915)

Robert Smalls was the black slave whose exploits for the Union during the Civil War won him national recognition. Smalls was later elected as a Republican to five nonconsecutive terms in the U.S. House of Representatives. He was born a slave in Beaufort, on the Sea Islands of South Carolina, on 5 April 1839. There is no record existing of schooling or, for that matter, any semblance of an education. When he was 12, Smalls was sent to Charleston to work as sailmaker and rigger before becoming an expert sailor. At the start of the Civil War, the Confederates forced him into service on the cotton trawler *Planter*. In 1862, Smalls took command of the ship, sailed it past Charleston harbor, and turned it over to the Union army.

Now known as a national black hero, he attended the 1864 Republican National Convention in a bid to win support for his Port Royal Experiment, which would house freed slaves after the war. He attended the 1868 Republican National Convention and, in that year, was elected to a single two-year term in the South Carolina state House of Representatives. From 1870 until 1874, he was a member of the state senate. In 1874, Smalls was elected to the U.S. House of Representatives from the Fifth South Carolina District. He served two terms, in the Forty-fourth and Forty-fifth Congresses. A staunch Republican, he called for federal troops to be kept in the South to safeguard the rights of newly freed slaves.

After winning reelection in 1876, Democrats in South Carolina, under the leadership of Governor William D. Simpson, strove to drive Smalls from his seat. In 1877, Smalls was convicted on trumped-up charges of taking a bribe when he was a state senator. In 1878, Simpson's goons made sure that white gangs kept black voters away from the polls, leading to Smalls's defeat. He returned in 1880, but again lost because of low black turnout. He successfully appealed the case to the House and was seated. In 1882, he lost the Republican nomination to Edmund W. M. Mackey, but Mackey's death allowed Smalls to reclaim the seat in a special election. In

1884, the Democrats again tried to defeat him, but he was victorious over Democrat William Elliott. In 1886, with the help of President Grover Cleveland, Elliott defeated Smalls, and an appeal to the House was unsuccessful. Smalls's political career was over. In the next few years he remained a tireless worker for the full enfranchisement of black citizens. In 1889, President Benjamin Harrison appointed Smalls as collector of revenue for the port of Beaufort. In 1913, opposition from segregationist elements in the state forced his resignation. Smalls died two years later, on 22 February 1915.

Smith v. Allwright (U.S., 1944)

Smith was a Supreme Court decision that overturned an earlier ruling, *Grovey v. Townsend* (U.S., 1935), in which the Court had upheld the right of political parties to limit the qualifications of voters. In *Smith*, the Court ruled that in primary elections, such limits amounted to state action, whether the state was involved or not. In 1932, the Texas Democratic Party allowed "all white citizens" to vote in state and national elections. Lonnie Smith, a black man, brought suit against Allwright, a state elections official, who refused him the right to vote because the Democratic Party felt he was not qualified. The Court ruled 8–1 that the elections were under state authority, and thus were subject to discrimination laws. Justice Stanley Reed wrote the majority opinion. "The privilege of membership in a party may be, as this Court said in *Grovey v. Townsend*, no concern of a state. But when, as here, that privilege is also the essential qualification for voting in a primary to select nominees for a general election, the state makes the action of the party the action of the state. Here we are applying, contrary to the recent decision in Grovey, the well established principle of the Fifteenth Amendment, forbidding the abridgement by a

state of a citizen's right to vote. *Grovey v. Townsend* is reversed."

See also Grovey v. Townsend; Nixon v. Condon; Nixon v. Herndon; Terry v. Adams.

South Carolina v. Katzenbach (U.S., 1966)

In *South Carolina v. Katzenbach*, the Supreme Court turned back a challenge to the constitutionality of the 1965 Voting Rights Act. Following passage of the act, the state of South Carolina filed suit against Attorney General Nicholas Katzenbach, asking the Court to enjoin, or stop, Katzenbach from enforcing the provisions of the act. South Carolina claimed that the provisions of the act that banned literacy tests violated the Tenth Amendment to the Constitution. Katzenbach argued that the act was clearly constitutional under the Fourteenth Amendment. Chief Justice Earl Warren read the 8–1 opinion of the Court (Justice Hugo Black concurred in part and dissented in part) in upholding Katzenbach's enforcement power. Wrote Warren: "The Voting Rights Act of 1965 reflects Congress' firm intention to rid the country of racial discrimination in voting. The heart of the Act is a complex scheme of strident remedies aimed at areas where discrimination has been most flagrant. We here hold that the portions of the Voting Rights Act properly before us are a valid means for carrying out the commands of the Fifteenth Amendment."

South Covington & Cincinnati Street Railway v. Kentucky (U.S., 1920)

This was the third in a series of Supreme Court cases dealing with segregation in public accommodations. Five percent of South Covington's passengers on the company's streetcars from Cincinnati to Covington, Kentucky, were black. The state of Kentucky charged the company with violating its 1915 Act, which required separate accommodations for blacks and whites. The company complained that since part of its route was in Ohio, where such discrimination was illegal, the line was being forced to operate under differing laws. Further, such regulation was illegal under interstate commerce laws. A Kentucky state court ruled against the company. The railway sued to the U.S. Supreme Court for relief. The Court ruled 6–3 that the line was a separate operation in the state of Kentucky, and thus had to obey the laws of that state. Writing for the majority (Justices Mahlon Pitney, Willis Van Devanter, and William R. Day dissented), Justice Joseph McKenna ruled that laws aimed at the segregation of white and black travelers were not an undue burden on interstate commerce.

Southern Christian Leadership Conference (SCLC)

The SCLC is the civil rights organization that grew out of the Montgomery Bus Boycott. Founded in 1957 by Reverend Dr. Martin Luther King, Jr., Reverend Joseph E. Lowery, Reverend Ralph David Abernathy, Reverend Fred Shuttlesworth, and other ministers in the South, the Southern Leadership Conference on Transportation and Nonviolent Integration, as it was originally known, set out as its mission the end of segregation using nonviolent means. The Reverend Dr. Martin Luther King, Jr., was the group's first president, serving from 1957 until his assassination in 1968. The Reverend Ralph David Abernathy served as president from 1968 until 1977. Joseph E. Lowery has been the president since 1977. In addition to its campaigns for civil and equal rights, the SCLC assists black Americans in the areas of employment discrimination and health care. Working out of an office on Auburn Avenue in Atlanta, down the street from the Martin Luther King Center for Nonviolent Change, its agenda includes "Wings of Hope," an antidrug program, and "Stop the Killing!," an attempt to

end the proliferation of guns in the hands of youngsters.

Southern Manifesto

The Southern Manifesto was the petition signed on 12 March 1956 by 96 Southern politicians in the U.S. House of Representatives and the U.S. Senate in support of segregation. On 12 March, 19 senators and 77 congressman affixed their signatures to a declaration of their intent to "use all lawful means" to overturn the Supreme Court's landmark *Brown* decision, which had outlawed school segregation two years earlier. Senator Walter Franklin George, Democrat of Georgia, opened the debate on the Senate floor when he said, "The increasing gravity of the situation following the decision of the Supreme Court in the so-called segregation cases, and the peculiar stress in sections of the country where this decision has created many difficulties, unknown and unappreciated, perhaps, by many people residing in other parts of the country, have led some senators and some members of the House of Representatives to prepare a statement of the position which they have felt and now feel to be imperative." He then read the Southern Manifesto aloud:

> The unwarranted decision of the Supreme Court in the public school cases is now bearing the fruit always produced when men substitute naked power for established law.
>
> The Founding Fathers gave us a Constitution of checks and balances because they realized the inescapable lesson of history that no man or group of men can be safely trusted with unlimited power. They framed this Constitution with its provision for change by amendment in order to secure the fundamentals of government against the dangers or temporary popular passion or the personal predilections of public officeholders.

We regard the decision of the Supreme Court in the school cases as a clear abuse of judicial power. It climaxes a trend in the Federal Judiciary undertaking to legislate, in derogation of the authority of Congress, and to encroach upon the reserved rights of the States and the people.

The original Constitution does not mention education. Neither does the 14th Amendment nor any other amendment. The debates proceeding the submission of the 14th Amendment clearly show that there was no intent that it should affect the system of education maintained by the States.

The very Congress which proposed the amendment subsequently provided for segregated schools in the District of Columbia.

When the amendment was adopted in 1868, there were 37 States of the Union. Every one of the 26 States that had any substantial racial differences among its people, either approved the operation of segregated schools already in existence or subsequently established such schools by action of the same lawmaking body which considered the 14th Amendment.

As admitted by the Supreme Court in the public school case [*Brown v. Board of Education*], the doctrine of separate but equal schools "apparently originated in *Roberts v. City of Boston* (1850), upholding school segregation against attack as being violative of a State constitutional guarantee of equality." This constitutional doctrine began in the North, not in the South, and it was followed not only in Massachusetts, but in Connecticut, New York, Illinois, Indiana, Michigan, Minnesota, New Jersey, Ohio, Pennsylvania and other northern States until they, exercising their rights as States through the constitutional processes of local self-government, changed their school systems.

In the case of *Plessy v. Ferguson* in 1896 the Supreme Court expressly declared that under the 14th Amendment no person was denied any of his rights if the States provided separate but equal facilities. This decision has been followed in many other cases. It is notable that the Supreme Court, speaking through Chief Justice Taft, a former President of the United States, unanimously declared in 1927 in *Lum v. Rice* that the "separate but equal" principle "is within the discretion of the State in regulating its public schools and does not conflict with the 14th Amendment."

This interpretation, restated time and again, became a part of the life of the people of many of the States and confirmed their habits, customs, traditions, and way of life. It is founded on elemental humanity and commonsense, for parents should not be deprived by Government of the right to direct the lives and education of their own children.

Though there has been no constitutional amendment or act of Congress changing this established legal principle almost a century old, the Supreme Court of the United States, with no legal basis for such action, undertook to exercise their naked judicial power and substituted their personal political and social ideas for the established law of the land.

This unwarranted exercise of power by the Court, contrary to the Constitution, is creating chaos and confusion in the States principally affected. It is destroying the amicable relations between the white and Negro races that have been created through 90 years of patient effort by the good people of both races. It has planted hatred and suspicion where there had been heretofore friendship and understanding.

Without regard to the consent of the governed, outside agitators are threatening immediate and revolutionary changes in our public-school systems. If done, this is certain to destroy the system of public education in some of the States.

With the greatest concern for the explosive and dangerous condition created by this decision and inflamed by outside meddlers:

We reaffirm our reliance on the Constitution as the fundamental law of the land.

We decry the Supreme Court's encroachments on rights reserved to the States and to the people, contrary to established law, and the Constitution.

We commend the motives of those States which have declared their intention to resist forced integration by lawful means.

We appeal to the States and people who are not directly affected by these decisions to consider the constitutional principles involved against the time when they too, on issues vital to them, may be the victims of judicial encroachment.

Even though we constitute a minority in the present Congress, we have full faith that a majority of the American people believe in the dual system of government which has enabled us to achieve our greatness and will in time demand that the reserved rights of the States and of the people be made secure against judicial usurpation.

We pledge ourselves to use all lawful means to bring about a reversal of this decision which is contrary to the Constitution and to prevent the use of force in its implementation.

In this trying period, as we all seek to right this wrong, we appeal to our people not to be provoked by the agitators and troublemakers invading our States and to scrupulously refrain from disorder and lawless acts.

The document was signed by 19 senators and 77 representatives.

Spingarn, Joel Elias (1875–1939)

J. E. Spingarn was the social reformer and founding member of the National Association for the Advancement of Colored People (NAACP) whose Spingarn Medal is awarded every year to the black person who contributes the most to his or her race. Spingarn was born in New York City on 17 May 1875, the son of an Austrian father and English mother. Affluent because of his father's prosperous tobacco business, he attended the Collegiate Institute under the direction of Dr. Julius Sachs, as well as the City College of New York and Columbia and Harvard universities. Spingarn earned his bachelor's degree from Columbia in 1895 and received his Ph.D. from that same institution in 1899. In that latter year he was named assistant professor of comparative literature at Columbia; in 1904 he became an adjunct professor, in 1909 a full professor, and in 1911 head of the department. In 1911 he was involved in a disagreement with Columbia president Nicholas Murray Butler, and was dismissed from the college.

Throughout the early years of the twentieth century, Spingarn became involved with the cause of equal rights for blacks. In 1909, he was a leading spirit in the founding of the NAACP. He served as the organization's chairman of the board from 1913 to 1919, as treasurer from 1919 to 1930, and as president of the organization from 1930 until his death. In 1913 he established the Spingarn Medal, which the NAACP awards annually to blacks who have contributed the most to the advancement of their race. During the First World War, Spingarn was a leading voice in the call for desegregated units to fight the conflict. Through his efforts, a training camp for black officers was built at Des Moines, Iowa. A Republican, Spingarn was an unsuccessful candidate for the U.S. House of Representatives in 1908.

Joel E. Spingarn succumbed to a lengthy illness on 26 July 1938 at the age of 64. He was succeeded as NAACP president by his brother, Arthur, another champion in the fight for equal rights.

States' Rights Party

Also known as the "Dixiecrat" Party because most of its members were Southern walkouts from the regular Democratic Party, the States' Rights Party ran a single campaign in 1948, on a platform mostly concerned with preserving segregation in the South. Until 1948, the issue of segregation had been of little importance within the Democratic Party. By late 1947, however, President Harry S Truman was pushing to have a civil rights plank added to the Democratic platform. In January 1948, Mississippi Governor Fielding Lewis Wright was inaugurated for a second term and told the assembled crowd that if such a plank were added to the platform, he and other Southern delegates to the party's national convention would walk out and form a third party. In July 1948, when the plank was endorsed at the Democratic National Convention, Wright led the Mississippi delegation in a walkout (several other Southern delegates followed). They assembled in Jackson, Mississippi, a "Jeffersonian Democrat" convention of segregationists. The group nominated South Carolina Governor Strom Thurmond for president and Wright for vice president.

At first, it seemed that the States' Rights ticket could carry all of the South, thus denying any one candidate in the presidential election the electoral votes necessary for victory. As the campaign wore on, however, several influential Southern Democratic politicians abandoned the Dixiecrats and silently went home to their old party. In the end, the Thurmond–Wright ticket carried only

South Carolina, Mississippi, Alabama, and Louisiana, plus one delegate from Tennessee, a total of 39 electoral votes. Unable to remove Truman from power and stem the tide of desegregation, the States' Rights party passed out of existence soon after the 1948 election.

Stell v. Savannah-Chatham County Board of Education (1963)

Stell was the famous Georgia litigation in which segregationists argued that desegregation would be harmful to both black and white children. Under the name of plaintiff Stell, several black and white children applied to the U.S. District Court in the Southern District of Georgia for the right to go to desegregated schools. The Savannah-Chatham County Board of Education answered the suit in court. The district court found that the evidence presented indicated that where black and white children commingled, "intergroup tensions and conflicts result," and, further, that black children, when in an atmosphere other than one segregated from whites, "would lose their right of achievement." A year later, the Fifth Circuit Court of Appeals overturned the district court's ruling. Circuit Judge Griffin Bell, who later served as Jimmy Carter's attorney general, wrote the opinion for a unanimous Court when he wrote, "There is no constitutional prohibition against an assignment of individual students to particular schools on [the] basis of intelligence, achievement, or other aptitudes upon a uniformly administered program, but race must not be a factor in making the assignments."

Stevens, Thaddeus (1792–1868)

Thaddeus Stevens was a radical Republican in Congress who supported Reconstruction, as well as the Freedmen's Bureau and the Civil Rights Act of 1866. Stevens was born in Danville, Vermont, on 4 April 1792, the son of a poor shoemaker who disappeared when Thaddeus

Thaddeus Stevens

was a young boy, leaving his wife with four sons to raise. The family moved to Peacham, Vermont, where Thaddeus attended the prestigious academy there. Eventually he spent some time at Dartmouth College and the University of Vermont.

About 1816, Stevens took the bar examination in Maryland, then set up a law practice in Pennsylvania. As he was just across the state line and was a constant witness to the brutality of slavery, Stevens became a rabid abolitionist, defending runaway slaves for free and using his money to purchase and then set free some slaves. In 1831, he was a speaker at the landmark Anti-Masonic Convention, which nominated the party's first presidential candidate. Two years later, Stevens won a seat in the Pennsylvania state House of Representatives on the Anti-Masonic ticket, a post he held until 1841. As a state representative, he spoke out against Masonry and slavery, even refusing to sign the state constitution because it did not extend suffrage to free blacks. After 1841, he returned to his law practice, which soon became lucrative.

In 1848, he was elected to the U.S. House of Representatives as a Whig, even though he was, in fact, a member of the antislavery Free Soil Party. He spent much of his time condemning Southern slaveowners and their lackeys in the North who did little to stop slavery. He opposed the Compromise of 1850, as well as the Fugitive Slave Act. In 1852, upset by his lack of progress, he refused to run for a third term, returning to Pennsylvania.

In 1854, Stevens was a key figure in the formation of the state and national Republican Party, which called for the end of slavery as its first platform plank. He spoke in support of Supreme Court justice John McLean for the presidency at the 1856 National Republican Convention in Pittsburgh, earning great praise from his peers. In 1858, at the age of 66, he was elected again to the U.S. House of Representatives, this time as a Republican. His constant speeches against the South earned him great respect among his northern colleagues but great enmity from his Southern critics. In 1860 he supported Lincoln for president and, in 1861, was named chairman of the House Ways and Means Committee, a powerful post in which he controlled most, if not all, of the government spending during the Civil War. During the war, he called for the arrest of Confederate leaders, the confiscation of Confederate property, and the unrestricted freedom of slaves. With the war over, Stevens pushed for an ambitious Reconstruction plan that would punish the South to the fullest.

Following Lincoln's assassination, Stevens helped pass both the Freedmen's Bureau bill and the Civil Rights Act of 1866 over President Andrew Johnson's vetoes. Angered by what he saw as the new president's meddling and incompetence, Stevens sought to have Johnson impeached. When the House impeached Johnson but the Senate failed to convict him, Stevens gave up the fight. Dispirited, he asked to be taken back to his home in Pennsylvania, but died in Washington on 11 August 1868, before he could be moved. He was buried in

Lancaster, near his home. The words "Equality of Man Before His Creator" are engraved upon his tombstone.

Strauder v. West Virginia (U.S., 1880)

Although little known, *Strauder* was a Supreme Court case in which the Court's decision set a precedent for the better treatment of black people by the state and federal judicial systems. The case concerned Taylor Strauder, a black man, who sought to have his murder trial moved from a West Virginia state court to federal court because West Virginia did not allow blacks on state court juries. The West Virginia statute read: "All white male persons who are twenty-one years of age and who are citizens of this State shall be liable to serve as jurors, except as herein provided." The high court ruled by a vote of 7–2 that Strauder's rights were being infringed in the state courts. Justice William Strong wrote for the majority, "The very fact that colored people are singled out and expressly denied by statute all right to participate in the administration of the law, as jurors, because of their color, though they are citizens, and may be in other respects fully qualified, is practically a brand upon them, affixed by law, an assertion of their inferiority, and a stimulant to that race prejudice which is an impediment to securing to individuals of that race that equal justice which the law aims to secure to all others." Justices Stephen J. Field and Nathan Clifford dissented.

See also Ex Parte Virginia.

Student Nonviolent Coordinating Committee (SNCC)

The Student Nonviolent Coordinating Committee (SNCC) was a biracial civil rights organization mostly made up of students. Activist Ella Baker of the Southern Christian Leadership Conference (SCLC) asked her organization to back a conference of students to be held at Shaw University in Raleigh, North Carolina, on Easter weekend, 1960. Such civil rights activists as John Lewis, Diane Nash, Bernard Scott Lee, and James Lawson attended the meeting. On 17 April, they founded the SNCC, which would synchronize all of the student protests for civil rights across the nation, particularly the South. Only two days later, on 19 April, dynamite destroyed the home of Z. Alexander Looby, a black Nashville councilman and attorney. The violence against Looby led to a march by 2,500 students on Nashville's city hall.

In November 1963, 40 members of SNCC met at Greenville, Mississippi, to organize the so-called Mississippi Summer Project, a plan that would blanket the South with civil rights and voter registration activists. As a result of the Greenville conference, some 1,000 volunteers—most of them white—helped the civil rights revolution proceed in the South. In its early years, the SNCC was a mainstream organization opposed to violence, and it made great strides for the civil rights movement. By the mid-1960s, however, the organization was increasingly dominated by radicals, and, without a broad base of support, the SNCC's membership and power were diminished. In 1969, H. Rap Brown became head of the organization and renamed the group the Student National Coordinating Committee. By then, however, SNCC was virtually finished, and became defunct soon after.

See also Baker, Ella Jo; Brown, H. Rap; Lee, Bernard Scott; Lewis, John.

Sumner, Charles (1811–1874)

Charles Sumner was the chief architect of black civil rights in the years before and after the Civil War. Sumner was born as one of premature twins on 6 January 1811. He attended the Boston Latin School and enrolled at Harvard University. Although he graduated, he felt he was immature educationally. In 1831, he entered Harvard Law School. At this time, he came under the influence of

Joseph Story, who was a professor of law at Harvard and at the same time an associate justice on the U.S. Supreme Court. Following his graduation, Sumner spent a summer in Washington, D.C. On his journey to the capital, he saw slave auctions in Maryland. Sumner became incensed at the inhumanity of slavery, and, despite being a white man himself, became one of the most vocal opponents of slavery and a spokesman for oppressed blacks.

After he was admitted to the Massachusetts bar in 1834, Sumner started a law practice with another student of Story's, George S. Hilliard. Unexcited by the practice, Sumner took advantage of an offer to teach Story's classes at Harvard. In 1837, he went to Europe, and stayed for three years. When he returned, he became ill with tuberculosis and for a time was near death. He later recovered, and returned to his private law practice. In 1850, he was the attorney in the landmark case of *Sarah C. Roberts v. The City of Boston*, in which segregated schools were upheld by the Massachusetts Supreme Court as constitutional. Sumner lobbied the Massachusetts state legislature, and, in 1853, segregated schools were made illegal.

In 1851, with the help of a coalition of Free-Soilers and antislavery Democrats, Sumner was elected to the U.S. Senate. He spent much of his first term trying to repeal the Fugitive Slave Law. In 1856, when Sumner condemned South Carolina Senator Andrew Butler for his proslavery views on the floor of the Senate, Butler's nephew, Congressman Preston Brooks, attacked Sumner on the Senate floor with a cane and nearly killed him. It was three years before Sumner could return to his Senate duties, and by that time the Civil War was just beginning. Sumner spent much of the war asking President Abraham Lincoln to emancipate the slaves. Lincoln heeded Sumner's advice and signed the Emancipation Proclamation in 1863. By the end of the war, Sumner was associated with

Charles Sumner

Congressman Thaddeus Stevens of Pennsylvania, one of the most radical of the radical Republicans. Sumner led the fight in the Senate for the imposition on the South of harsh Reconstruction terms, the impeachment of President Andrew Johnson, and the passage of the Thirteenth, Fourteenth, and Fifteenth amendments to the Constitution. His cry for universal suffrage for blacks was his greatest legacy.

By 1874, Sumner was increasingly isolated from the majority of Americans, who were tired of continuing to fight the battles of the Civil War. On 11 March 1874, he died of angina in his Washington home. He was 63 years old.

See also Civil Rights Act of 1875; Reconstruction; Sarah C. Roberts v. The City of Boston.

Swann v. Charlotte-Mecklenburg Board of Education (U.S., 1971)

Swann was the Supreme Court case that led to busing to achieve racial integration in schools. In Charlotte-Mecklenburg, South Carolina, the school board was composed of "antibusing" commissioners. James Swann, a black man, sued in district court to force the board to utilize busing to achieve integration in education. The district court ruled against the school board's plan, and laid out its own. The board members sued to the Supreme Court to get relief, but the Court sided unanimously with the district court. Chief Justice Warren Burger, writing for the Court, used his opinion to demarcate the constitutional boundaries of busing.

See also North Carolina State Board of Education v. Swann.

Sweatt v. Painter (U.S., 1950)

The Supreme Court's ruling in the case of *Sweatt v. Painter* was the first crack in the wall of educational segregation. Coming four years before the famous *Brown* decision, *Sweatt v. Painter* is little remembered. It concerned H. M. Sweatt, a black man, who, in 1950, applied for admission to the University of Texas Law School, but was denied on the grounds that he was black. Sweatt then sued the admissions officer, Theophilis Painter, as well as other school officials, to compel them to admit him to the all-white school. A lower Texas court ruled that Sweatt was not entitled to relief since, at the time, Texas was building a blacks-only law school. Sweatt refused to attend this segregated institution and took the case to higher courts, including the Texas Court of Appeals, which affirmed the lower court decision, and the Texas Supreme Court, which denied Sweatt's writ of error. Sweatt subsequently took the case to the U.S. Supreme Court. Chief Justice Frederick M. Vinson wrote the majority opinion for a unanimous Court. In the decision, which struck down the University of Texas's segregated school policy, Vinson compared the law school for whites and the one built for blacks and found them anything but equal. Thus, the Court found that, under the circumstances, Sweatt could not get an equal education, would be denied the right to earn a fair living by practicing law, which was a "highly learned profession," and decided that "We [the Court] hold that the equal protection clause of the Fourteenth Amendment requires that petitioner be admitted to the University of Texas Law School."

See also Brown v. Board of Education of Topeka, Kansas I.

Talbert, Mary Morris Burnett (1866–1923)

Mary Burnett Talbert was a noted black educator and civil rights advocate. She was born Mary Morris Burnett on 18 September 1866, in Oberlin, Ohio, where she attended local schools, graduating from Oberlin College in 1886, at the age of 19. That year, she began teaching algebra, geometry, history, and Latin at Bethel University in Little Rock, Arkansas. In 1887, Mary Burnett was named assistant principal of Little Rock High School, the first black to hold such a position in the United States.

In 1891, Burnett married William H. Talbert, a bookkeeper from Buffalo, New York, and moved there to be with him. In Buffalo, she began her activism on behalf of blacks by founding the Christian Culture Congress, a black social society. She was a member of the National Association of Colored Women (NACW), and president of that organization from 1916 to 1921. She also served on the board of directors of the National Association for the Advancement of Colored People (NAACP), once that group was founded in 1910. As president of the NACW, she headed an effort to preserve the Washington, D.C., home of Frederick Douglass.

In the 1920s, Talbert was a leading voice in the nation's fight against lynching. She lobbied Congress to enact the Dyer Anti-Lynching Bill, which ultimately failed passage. In 1922, before her death, the NAACP awarded Talbert its distinguished Spingarn medal for her work in the area of civil rights. Mary Burnett Talbert died 15 October 1923 at the age of 57. Opined *The Crisis*, the

NAACP's official journal, "Overwork, the unstinted giving of herself to the Negro cause, led to her death in her prime."

Terry v. Adams (U.S., 1953)

Terry was the Supreme Court case in which the use of private clubs to restrict blacks from voting in, and being elected to office in, state primaries was held to be unconstitutional. The case concerned Terry, a black voter, who alleged that the Jaybird Association of Fort Bend County, Texas, allowed only white voters to be members and not blacks, thus denying blacks equal opportunity to be candidates in the Democratic primary for offices that the Jaybird Association selected. A Texas district court ruled that the association's actions were state actions and struck down the club's exclusionary practices. The Fifth Circuit Court of Appeals reversed the lower court, calling the association a "private club," within its rights to bar anyone. Terry took his case to the U.S. Supreme Court. The Court ruled, 8–1, that the association was not in fact a private club but an "auxiliary" of the Democratic Party, and that its denial of blacks to be members and thus hold office was a violation of the equal protection clause of the Fifteenth Amendment.

See also Smith v. Allwright.

Thirteenth Amendment (1865)

As the Civil War drew to a close, some members of Congress saw the immediate need for the constitutional protection for certain rights that freed blacks had just won. In 1864, Senator Lyman Trumbull of Illinois submitted the draft of the Thirteenth Amendment to the Judiciary

Committee, of which he was chairman. It was the first of the so-called "Reconstruction Amendments." The amendment reads:

Neither slavery nor involuntary servitude, except as the punishment for crime whereof the party shall have been duly convicted, shall exist within the United States, or any place subject to their jurisdiction.

The amendment further holds that Congress has the power to enforce the amendment with proper legislation. This it did the following year, with the passage of the Civil Rights Act of 1866.

See also Civil Rights Act of 1866; Trumbull, Lyman.

Thomas, Clarence (1948–)

Supreme Court Justice Clarence Thomas is the second black man to sit on the U.S. Supreme Court. He succeeded the first black justice, Thurgood Marshall, in 1991. Thomas was born into poverty in

Clarence Thomas

Pinpoint, Georgia, on 23 June 1948. His mother, Leola, who already had an infant daughter and was only 18 at the time of her son's birth, lived in a house that had no plumbing. His father left for Philadelphia when Clarence was only two; his parents later divorced. Leola's work as a housekeeper kept the family going. She later had a second son. When Clarence was seven, the family house burned down; Leola and her daughter went to Savannah to stay with an aunt, while Clarence and his brother moved in with Leola's parents: Christine and Myers Anderson. Clarence Thomas credits Myers Anderson with forcing him to get an education and make something of himself. Thomas said in an interview in 1991, "The most compassionate thing [my grandparents] did for us was to teach us to fend for ourselves and to do that in an openly hostile environment." His grandfather sent him to an all-black school run by white nuns, to an all-black high school, and then to an all-white Catholic seminary in rural Georgia.

With thoughts of becoming a priest, Thomas went to the Immaculate Conception Seminary in Conception, Missouri, but the assassination of Reverend Dr. Martin Luther King, Jr., forced him to reevaluate his life. Moving to Holy Cross College in Massachusetts, Thomas embarked on a long road that led him first to embrace black separatism and the Black Panther movement and, eventually, after graduating from Yale University Law School, to become a conservative Republican. He got a job working in the office of fellow Yale alumnus and Missouri Attorney General John C. Danforth. Three years later, Thomas was hired by the Monsanto Company as an attorney working on pesticide issues.

After two years at Monsanto, Thomas went to Washington to work as an aide to Danforth, who had been elected to the U.S. Senate. In 1980, following a Thomas speech at a black conservative conference in San Francisco, *Washington Post* writer

Juan Williams wrote a long article on Thomas. The article caught the eye of someone in the recently elected Reagan administration, and Thomas was appointed to a job in the Department of Education as the assistant secretary for civil rights. Thomas was in the post for only eight months, but his work impressed those he worked with. In 1982, Reagan nominated Thomas to be the chairman of the Equal Employment Opportunity Commission (EEOC). In his eight years in the position, Thomas, as the second highest ranked black in the Reagan administration, came under fire from civil rights leaders because he did not push affirmative action programs as strongly as they would have liked. Other actions, such as the abandonment of any set timeframe for ending discrimination in the workplace, infuriated liberals as well. Nevertheless, in 1990, President George Bush nominated Thomas for a seat on the D.C. Court of Appeals, where he ruled in only 27 cases in his brief tenure before being placed near the top of President Bush's list to succeed retiring Supreme Court Justice William Brennan. Upon the retirement of Justice Thurgood Marshall in 1991, Bush nominated Thomas for the vacant seat. In the confirmation hearings there was heavy opposition to Thomas from civil rights organizations, as well as a now-infamous scandal involving allegations of sexual harassment from a former co-worker, Anita Hill; Thomas was confirmed to the high court. In his first two years on the bench, he allied himself to the Rehnquist–Scalia wing of the Court on many issues.

See also Equal Employment Opportunity Commission.

Till, Emmett (1941–1955)

The murder of Emmett Till in Mississippi triggered a national debate on lynchings in the United States. Till was born and raised on Chicago's South Side, attending McCosh Elementary School. In August 1955, he went to Mississippi to visit his cousin's relatives, near the town of Moncy. Till drove his cousin's grandfather's 1941 Ford to Money, where he stopped at Bryant's Grocery and Meat Market. Getting into a conversation with some boys outside, Till was dared to go and talk with the white woman inside the market. Apparently, Till walked in, bought some candy, and said, as he left, "Bye, baby." Little did Till know that the woman was the wife of owner Roy Bryant, and Roy Bryant wanted "niggers in their place," as he later told *Life* magazine. Three days later, Roy Bryant and his brother-in-law, J. W. Milam, took Till on a ride, tortured him, and when he refused to beg for mercy, shot him in the head. A 75-pound cotton gin fan was tied around his neck, and his skull was crushed for good measure. Dumped into the Tallahatchie River, Till's mutilated body was found three days later.

Emmett Till's violent death shocked the nation. Put on trial for murder, Bryant and Milam were acquitted by an all-white jury, which deliberated for about an hour. The verdict, coming just two weeks after Till was buried, fueled the nascent civil rights revolution that shook the South and the nation.

Toure, Kwame (1941–)

Kwame Toure was born Stokely Carmichael in Port-of-Spain, Trinidad, on 29 June 1941. While in college in the early 1960s, he joined the Congress of Racial Equality (CORE), but during a voter registration drive in Lowndes County, Mississippi, he joined the more radical Student Nonviolent Coordinating Committee (SNCC). He served in the SNCC for three years, became president of the group in 1966, and later joined the Black Panther Party. He rose in the organization to become its prime minister, but after the Panthers' decline, he moved to the African country of

Guinea in 1973, having changed his name. He later was arrested there for allegedly advocating the overthrow of the Guinean government, but was released after a few days.

Tourgee, Albion Winegar (1838–1905)

Albion Tourgee was the white New York attorney who defended Homer Adolph Plessy in the latter's unsuccessful attempt to get the Supreme Court to outlaw separate but equal accommodations in railroad travel. Tourgee was born on 2 May 1838, in Williamsfield, Ohio, the first and only surviving child of a French Huguenot father and a German mother. Although his family moved to Kingsville, Ohio, in 1847, Tourgee himself went to live with an uncle in Lee, Massachusetts. He later returned to Kingsville and attended the academy there, eventually enrolling at the University of Rochester in 1859. In 1861 he dropped out to teach in Wilson, New York, but, three months later, with the beginning of the Civil War, he enlisted in the 27th New York Regiment. At the First Bull Run and at Perryville he was twice wounded in the spine, injuries from which he never fully recovered. Captured by the Confederates in 1863, Tourgee was later exchanged and saw more action at Missionary Ridge, Chickamauga, and Lookout Mountain. In December 1863, he resigned from the army to take up the study of law, and, in May 1864, he was admitted to the Ohio bar.

During the next several years, Tourgee was an attorney, newspaperman, and teacher. Eventually, he moved on to North Carolina, where he entered politics. In 1868, he was elected to a superior judgeship and served until 1874. After a failed run for Congress, he went to New York and made that state his home.

Tourgee's entry into the area of civil rights was brief. In 1879, he was the author of *A Fool's Errand*, a castigation of segregation, a book many Southerners felt slandered their region. In 1896, incensed over the treatment black railroad passenger Homer Plessy had received because of his race, the nearly 60-year-old Tourgee defended litigant Plessy as high as the U.S Supreme Court, which held in the case of *Plessy v. Ferguson* that separate but equal facilities were constitutional. It was President William McKinley who saved Tourgee from debtor's prison, when he named the attorney in 1897 as U.S. consul to Bordeaux, France, where Tourgee remained until his death on 21 May 1905.

See also Plessy v. Ferguson.

Trumbull, Lyman (1813–1896)

Lyman Trumbull was the Illinois senator who, as one of the radical Republicans in the Senate, helped draft the Thirteenth Amendment to the Constitution. Trumbull was born in Colchester, Connecticut, on 12 October 1813. He attended the Bacon Academy in Colchester, then taught for three years in Greenville, Georgia. After reading the law, he was admitted to the Georgia bar in 1836.

Trumbull entered politics almost as soon as he set up his law office in Belleville, Illinois. Elected to the state House of Representatives as a Democrat, he resigned soon after to accept a position as the Illinois secretary of state, but in 1843 was removed from his post by the governor. He then practiced law until his election as a justice of the state supreme court, in which position he served until 1854. In that year, he was elected as a Democrat to the U.S. House of Representatives, where he opposed the entry of Nebraska into the Union as a slave state. In 1855, he was elected to the U.S. Senate with the aid of Abraham Lincoln, campaigning that year as an antislavery Whig. Over the next 18 years in the Senate, Trumbull was a Democrat, a Republican, and a Liberal Republican. During the "Bloody Kansas" controversy, he opposed allowing that state to submit a proslavery constitution. With

Lincoln's election to the presidency, Trumbull became one of his most important supporters in the Senate.

In 1864, as chairman of the Senate Judiciary Committee, Trumbull introduced legislation that was later to become the Thirteenth Amendment to the Constitution. With Lincoln's assassination, he was opposed by President Andrew Johnson in his attempts to strengthen the Freedman's Bureau and to draft a civil rights act in 1866. However, when Johnson was impeached by the radical Republicans in Congress, Trumbull was one of seven Republican senators whose "no" vote helped spare the president and avert a constitutional crisis.

Trumbull became disillusioned with the scandal-ridden administration of President Ulysses S. Grant and turned to the short-lived Liberal Republican Party, supporting Horace Greeley in the 1872 election. After the movement collapsed, he finished his senatorial career in 1873 and left office. He later practiced law in Chicago and was the unsuccessful Democratic candidate for governor of Illinois in 1880. In 1894, he helped draft ideas for the platform of the then-popular Populist party. Trumbull died two years later, on 25 June 1896.

See also Thirteenth Amendment.

Turner, Benjamin Sterling (1825–1894)

Benjamin Turner was the first black to represent Alabama in the U.S. House of Representatives, serving a single term from 1871 to 1873. Turner was born into slavery in the town of Weldon, in Halifax County, North Carolina, on 17 March 1825, and taken to Alabama when he was five. There is little information about his early life. Turner appears to have run a livery stable in Selma and to have grown prosperous from the operation. In 1867, he entered politics and was elected tax collector for Dallas County, Alabama. In 1869, Turner was elected to the Selma City Council. In 1870, just three years after beginning his political career, he was elected to the U.S. House of Representatives. It was a remarkable feat, the more so because Turner could barely read and write.

Turner served only in the Forty-second Congress. In the first session of the Congress, Turner introduced three bills, two of which sought to restore suffrage to former Confederates. Congress did not vote on any of the bills, however. In the second session, he called for the refund of a cotton tax imposed on cotton field workers, many of whom, Turner claimed, were black. He further called for the federal purchase of land in the South, which could be given to newly freed slaves. Again, neither of these proposals received any action. In the election of 1872, Philip Joseph, a black independent, split the black vote with Turner, ensuring the election of Frederick G. Bromberg, the candidate of the Democrats and liberal Republicans.

Turner left the House in 1873. He resumed his career as a merchant and, for a time, became a farmer. His last political act was as a delegate to the 1880 Republican National Convention. Benjamin Turner died in Selma on 21 March 1894, just four days after his sixty-ninth birthday.

Twenty-fourth Amendment

The Twenty-fourth Amendment outlawed the poll tax as an unconstitutional barrier to voting. The amendment reads simply: "The right of citizens of the United States to vote in any primary or other election for President or Vice President, for electors for President or Vice President, or for Senator or Representative in Congress, shall not be denied or abridged by the United States, or any State by reason of failure to pay any poll tax or other tax."

See also Poll Taxes.

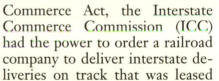

United States Civil Rights Commission

The U.S. Civil Rights Commission is the federal bipartisan panel that collects and disseminates information on civil rights. Established by the Civil Rights Act of 1957, the six-member group studies various ways civil rights can be enforced. Since its inception, there have been six chairmen of the commission. Dr. John A. Hannah, president of Michigan State University, who started a program of racial integration at his college, was appointed by President Dwight D. Eisenhower in 1957 and served until 1969. He was replaced by the Reverend Theodore Hesburgh, another member of the commission and president of Notre Dame University, who served until 1972. Stephen Horn was the third chairman; he served from 1972 to 1974. In 1974, President Gerald Ford appointed Arthur Fletcher as chairman. Fletcher stepped down in 1982. He was replaced by Clarence Pendleton, a member of the Urban League of California and the commission's first black chairman. Pendleton died in 1988 and was replaced by Fletcher, who is still chairman as of this writing.

The Civil Rights Commission has no enforcement authority. Through its six-member commission in Washington, D.C., several bureaus, and 50 state boards, it studies the problems associated with civil rights and reports its findings to the president and the Congress.

United States et al. v. Baltimore & Ohio Railroad Company et al. (U.S., 1948)

This Supreme Court case, while not dealing specifically with civil rights, established a precedent that became important in deciding civil rights cases. The high court held that under the Interstate Commerce Act, the Interstate Commerce Commission (ICC) had the power to order a railroad company to deliver interstate deliveries on track that was leased by a competitor. This case was the foundation for later civil rights cases, including *Boynton v. Virginia* and *Henderson v. United States*, in which it was argued that if the ICC had the power to regulate interstate commerce in the area of leased land, it could interfere when such land was used to discriminate, such as the creation of whites-only passenger waiting rooms in bus and train terminals.

See also Boynton v. Virginia; Henderson v. United States.

United States v. Cruikshank et al. (U.S., 1876)

United States v. Cruikshank et al. was the landmark Supreme Court case in which the Court decided that federal protections on the right to vote limited any prosecutions for infringing that right to matters of race only. The case originally was called *United States v. Columbus C. Nash et al.*, of which William Cruikshank was a party, and involved 98 men who stopped Levi Nelson and Alexander Tillman, two blacks, from voting in Louisiana in 1873. Tillman was murdered, so the defendants were indicted under section 6 of the Enforcement Act of 1870 for denying the men the right to vote, and under section 7 for murdering Tillman.

Of the 98 men named, 89 disappeared and were never brought to trial. One was acquitted of all charges, and, in a second trial (the first ended in a hung jury for eight of the defendants), Cruikshank and two others were found guilty of some of the charges. Cruikshank appealed his case to the U.S. Supreme Court, which ruled that the indictment under which the men had been tried and convicted was defective. Chief Justice Morrison R. Waite wrote the Court's decision. He ruled that race played no factor in the defendants' actions, and he discussed that the rights the men had been found guilty of denying to Nelson and Tillman—the right to peaceably assemble, the right to petition for the redress of grievances, and the right to bear arms—were "not covered by the Federal Constitution," and thus their violation could not be a federal matter.

United States v. Fordice, Governor of Mississippi, et al. (U.S., 1992)

In 1992 the Supreme Court ordered that states with dual, or segregated, higher educational systems must dismantle the facilities immediately. This case involved five black petitioners, one of whom was Jake Ayers, who, in 1975, sued the state of Mississippi because the dual system of almost all-white colleges and historically black colleges made education in the state separate and unequal. In 1990, with the election of Republican Kirk Fordice as Mississippi governor, the U.S. government intervened on behalf of the black petitioners and brought suit against Fordice and school officials in an attempt to end all school segregation. The Supreme Court held unanimously that Mississippi's segregated school system violated the *Brown* decision of 1954. Wrote Justice Byron White, who delivered the Court's opinion, "To the extent that the state has not met its affirmative obligation to dismantle its prior dual system, it shall be adjudged in violation of the Constitution and Title VI [of the 1964 Civil Rights Act] and remedial proceedings shall be conducted."

United States v. Guest (U.S., 1966)

In the case of *United States v. Guest*, the Supreme Court decided the question of whether persons whose civil rights were violated under the provisions of section 6 of the Enforcement Act of 1870 (now section 241 of Title 18 of the U.S. Code), and section 17 of Enforcement Act of 1870 (now section 242 of Title 18 of the U.S. Code) could sue in federal, and not state, courts.

There is a long line of cases involved with this question of law, including *United States v. Price, United States v. Williams,* and *Williams v. United States. Guest* concerned six men who stopped Lemuel Penn, a black teacher, while he was driving through Georgia and shot him. The state of Georgia tried two of the men for conspiracy to deprive Penn of his civil rights under section 6 of the Enforcement Act of 1870, but they were acquitted. In 1964, a federal grand jury indicted the two men under section 241 of the U.S. Code, but a district court threw out the indictments. The United States appealed the dismissal to the Supreme Court. In a judgment that was rendered by six justices, who joined in separate opinions, the Court ruled that interstate travel is a right secured in the Fourteenth Amendment, and the Court reinstated the indictments. Justice Potter Stewart, writing for the majority, said: "Although there have been recurring differences in emphasis within the Court as to the source of the constitutional right of interstate travel, there is no need here to canvass those differences further. All [of the justices] have agreed that right exists. Its explicit recognition as one of the federal rights protected by what is now section 241 goes back as least as far as 1904 .We affirm it now."

See also United States v. Price et al.

United States v. Harris (U.S., 1883)

United States v. Harris was the early Supreme Court decision that struck down section 2 of the Civil Rights Act of 20 April 1871 as unconstitutional. In August 1876, R. G. Harris and 19 others were charged with depriving four black men of the equal protection of the laws, attacking and beating them while they were under arrest and in the custody of a deputy sheriff in Crockett County, Tennessee. Harris and his cohorts were charged under the 1871 Civil Rights Act, which reads in part: "If two or more persons in any State or Territory conspire or go in disguise upon the highway or on the premises of another for the purpose of depriving, either directly or indirectly, any person or class of persons of the equal protection of the laws each of said persons shall be punished by a fine of not less than $500 nor more than $5000, or by imprisonment, with or without hard labor, not less than six months nor more than six years, or by both such fine and imprisonment." As the case came before the trial court, the defendants' lawyers, as well as two judges, felt that this part of the act might be unconstitutional and sent the case to the Supreme Court for review of this question. Justice William Burnham Woods wrote that Congress had no power "to enact a law which would punish a private citizen for an invasion of the rights of his fellow citizen, conferred by the State of which they were both residents," thereby striking down the law.

United States v. Mosley (U.S., 1915)

United States v. Mosley was the Supreme Court case that decided whether section 5508 of the Revised Statutes (1873), the statutory embodiment of section 6 of the Civil Rights Act of 1870, applied to state officials who deprived persons of the right to vote. Tom Mosley and Dan Hogan, members of the Blaine County, Oklahoma, Elections Board, failed to count several hundred votes from the 1912 congressional election and statewide referendum. All of these votes were Republican—some black, but most white. United States Attorney General Homer Boardman took the two men to court. They claimed that the miscount

had been ordered by the Democratic governor and the state Democratic Party organization, that the blacks who did vote had not needed to pass a literacy test, and that most of the votes that had been thrown out had been from whites, thereby defusing any prosecution because of race discrimination. Both men were convicted under section 5508, which prohibits a conspiracy to deny others the right to vote, as well as section 19 of the Criminal Code. A district court, however, overturned the men's convictions. The United States appealed the case to the Supreme Court, where the Court ruled 8–1 (Justice Joseph Rucker Lamar dissenting) that, under section 5508, Mosely and Hogan were guilty. Wrote Justice Oliver Wendell Holmes for the majority: "Just as the 14th Amendment was adopted with a view to the protection of the colored race but has been found to be equally important in its application to the rights of all, section 6 had a general scope and used general words that have become the most important now that the Ku Klux Klan have passed away."

United States v. Paradise et al. (U.S., 1987)

United States v. Paradise et al. was the Supreme Court case in which the Court limited the use of race-based promotions to overcome past discriminations. In 1972, a number of black plaintiffs sued the Alabama Department of Public Safety (ADPS), alleging that there was wide discrimination in hiring. A trial court agreed and ordered several remedies. In 1974, the trial court found that the ADPS had artificially restricted the size of the police force to limit the number of blacks hired. In 1977, the plaintiffs again sued for relief, claiming that remedies for an end to hiring discrimination were lacking. Two years later, the court consented to a plan in which the department would create a fair hiring procedure within one year. In 1981, testing of applicants without regard to race was instituted, but only several black applicants passed.

In 1984, 12 years after originally hearing the case, the court ruled that the new standards were failing to work and ordered a one-to-one hiring procedure, in which one black would be hired and promoted for every white hired and promoted. After eight blacks and eight whites were hired under this plan, the court suspended the new order, requiring only that 13 new officers be hired in this manner. The U.S. government asked for the court order to be continued, but the Eleventh Circuit Court of Appeals affirmed the lower court's ruling. The U.S. Supreme Court, in a 5–4 decision, upheld the trial court's order. The four dissenters—Justices Byron White, Sandra Day O'Connor, Antonin Scalia, and Chief Justice William Rehnquist—all opined that under the "strict scrutiny" analysis of such cases, the trial court had gone too far in its 1984 order.

See also Affirmative Action.

United States v. Price et al.
(U.S., 1966)

United States v. Price et al. was the Supreme Court case involving the murders of civil rights workers Andrew Goodman, James Chaney, and Michael Schwerner. On trial for the crime was Cecil Ray Price, deputy sheriff of Neshoba County, Mississippi. Price was indicted for allegedly arresting the three men in Neshoba County, setting them free, then following them in an official sheriff's car and picking them up again. The men were then taken to a secret place, where others joined Price and murdered the three civil rights workers. At issue in this Supreme Court case was whether Price had conspired to deprive the three men of their Fourteenth Amendment rights, as well as other technical matters. Also involved in the case were Neshoba Sheriff Lawrence Rainey and Philadelphia,

Mississippi, policeman Richard Willis, as well as 15 other "private" individuals. Indictments handed down against the 18 defendants included violations of the Fourteenth Amendment and conspiracy. A district court dismissed the charges against the 15 "private" individuals because it found that they were "not acting under the color of the law." In this matter, the U.S. government sued for relief to the U.S. Supreme Court to get the charges reinstated. As for Price, Rainey, and Willis, the district court dismissed their indictments because the Fourteenth Amendment did not, by their standards, list violations of civil rights. Again, on this point, the government asked the Supreme Court to restore the indictment. Solicitor General Thurgood Marshall argued the case for the government. In the former case, the Court held that the indictment must be reinstated. Justice Abe Fortas wrote the opinion that "to act 'under color' of law does not require that the accused be an officer of the state. It is enough that he is the willing participant in joint activity with the state or its agents." As for the latter case, Fortas wrote, "There is no doubt that the indictment [against Price, Rainey, and Willis] sets forth a conspiracy within the ambit of the Fourteenth Amendment. Like [the other indictment which the Court restored] it alleges that the defendants acted 'under color of law' and that the conspiracy included action by the State through its law enforcement officers to punish the alleged victims without the due process of law in violation of the Fourteenth Amendment's direct admonition to the States."

United States v. Reese et al.
(U.S., 1876)

United States v. Reese et al. was the Supreme Court case in which the Court ruled that sections 3 and 4 of the Enforcement Act of 1870 were unconstitutional. The government sued Hiram Reese,

Matthew Fourshee, and William Farnaugh, election inspectors in Lexington, Kentucky, for failing to allow William Garner, a black man, to vote in municipal elections in 1873 because he had allegedly failed to pay his poll tax. Reese, Fourshee, and Farnaugh were charged under sections 3 and 4 of the Enforcement Act of 1870, which stipulated that if such "capitation" or poll taxes were to be utilized, they could not be based on race; if so, they violated the Enforcement Act, and punishment was prescribed. All three men were convicted of violating the Enforcement Act. Their attorney, former Attorney General Henry Stanbery, appealed to the Supreme Court for relief. He was opposed by U.S. Attorney Gabriel C. Wharton. Stanbery argued that Reese and the others did not deny Garner the right to vote because of his race but because he failed to pay his poll tax. The Court ruled not on the merits of Reese's case but on the constitutionality of the two sections, and struck them both down. Chief Justice Morrison Waite wrote the opinion of the Court. He ruled that the Fifteenth Amendment gave the Congress the right to enact appropriate legislation to enforce the amendment, but that the Court felt the two sections "overreached" federal power into areas not covered by the Fifteenth Amendment. "We are not able to reject a part which is unconstitutional, and retain the remainder, because it is not possible to separate that which is unconstitutional from that which is not," Waite wrote.

United States v. Reynolds (U.S., 1914)

United States v. Reynolds was the second key Supreme Court test of the abolition of the peonage, or wage-slavery, system. The case involved Ed Rivers, a black man in Alabama, who was convicted in a state court of a minor crime. Unable to pay court costs and a hefty fine, the court in effect "sold" his labor to J. A. Reynolds until the costs could be worked off. This was known as the criminal-surety system. Reynolds and another man were indicted and convicted of involuntary servitude. With the help of various Alabama officials and U.S. Attorney General James Clarke McReynolds, the case came before the U.S. Supreme Court. Justice William Rufus Day read the unanimous opinion (8–0, as McReynolds removed himself from the case) of the Court, which upheld Reynolds's conviction and struck down the criminal-surety system as a violation of the Thirteenth Amendment. Although Justice Oliver Wendell Holmes agreed with the decision, he wrote a lengthy opinion that argued that the criminal-surety system was a legal use of a state's right to make contracts.

United States v. Rhodes (1867)

United States v. Rhodes was the second key test of the constitutionality of the Civil Rights Act of 1866. It involved a man called Rhodes who, along with two friends, had robbed a black woman, Nancy Talbot. As Talbot could not get justice in the state courts of Kentucky, where just a short time earlier she was considered property, the United States took Rhodes to a federal court as prescribed by section 3 of the Civil Rights Act of 1866. The court's inquiry was whether federal courts had jurisdiction over such a crime, and whether the section of the act was constitutional. Benjamin Bristow, an attorney, discovered that in a prior case, *United States v. Ortega* (1826), such federal prosecution of a state case was overturned by the Supreme Court. Justice Noah Swayne, on circuit duty in Kentucky, ruled alone that the Ortega case was not relevant to Rhodes. He further opined that the provision in the Civil Rights Act of 1866 with respect to state matters in federal courts was constitutional; unsure of how his colleagues on the Court might feel, however, he asked for Supreme Court review if such was necessary. The Court never took up the case, leaving the 1866 act and the Rhodes case unchallenged.

United States v. Scotland Neck City Board of Education (U.S., 1972)

The Scotland Neck case addressed the question of whether a school district could separate itself from another school district to avoid desegregation. The case involved a state statute that allowed the Scotland Neck, North Carolina, Board of Education to separate itself from the larger Halifax County system to which it belonged, at a time when Halifax was under a court order to desegregate. Up until 1965, although Halifax schools were 77 percent black, the law still required that they be segregated by race. A freedom of choice plan and busing had had a minimal impact upon segregation. By 1968, nearly 99 percent of the white students attended all-white schools, and 97 percent of the blacks attended all-black schools.

In 1968, the federal government intervened to force Halifax County to desegregate more rapidly. Then, in January 1969, the state legislature passed a bill allowing Scotland Neck to form its own school system—in effect creating an all-white enclave free from government intrusion. A district court found that by allowing the Scotland Neck Board of Education to form its own school district, the state paved the way for other school districts to become independent to avoid desegregation orders. The court of appeals reversed the lower court's ruling. The U.S. Supreme Court took up the case and, on 22 June 1972, decided unanimously that the Scotland Neck Board of Education plan was unconstitutional. Wrote Justice Potter Stewart: "We have today held that any attempt by state or local officials to carve out a new school district from an existing district that is in the process of dismantling a dual school system must be judged according to whether it hinders or furthers the process of school desegregation. ... [The state

law] was enacted with the effect of creating a refuge for white students of the Halifax County School system, and [thus] interferes with the desegregation of the Halifax School system."

United States v. The Litigants and Claimants of the Schooner Amistad (U.S., 1842)

In the *Amistad* case the Supreme Court held that slaves held aboard a foreign ship and brought to the United States in violation of the ban on the importation of slaves were not property but free men. The schooner *Amistad*, a Spanish vessel, was sailing from Havana to Puerto Principe, another Cuban port, when the slaves aboard the vessel, who had been taken in Africa, revolted and killed the captain. They then attempted to force two Spaniards—the ship's owner, Jose Ruiz, and Pedro Montez—to take them back to Africa. Ruiz and Montez instead sailed toward America, and landed off the shore of Long Island. The craft and its cargo of slaves was captured by the brig *Washington* and held by the U.S. government in Connecticut. Ruiz filed a motion to retrieve his "property." Other slaveowners backed Ruiz, claiming that the right to own slaves was fundamental, and removal of such ownership was unconstitutional. A group of abolitionists in New York sued to obtain the slaves' freedom. The U.S. government, pressured by the Spanish government to return its citizens' property, asked a district court to deal with the matter. The court found that the slaves were not free, but property. The district attorney for the Connecticut district where the slaves were being held sued a circuit court, but that court upheld the judgment. The United States, now the plaintiff, sued to the U.S. Supreme Court. With the recent death of Justice Philip Barbour and the illness of Justice John McKinley, the high court heard the case with only seven justices. They ruled 6-1 (Justice Henry Baldwin dissenting) that the slaves were free to live in the United States as free men because their importation was illegal. Justice Joseph Story wrote the Court's opinion. Eventually, the former slaves were returned to Africa by abolitionist missionaries.

United Steelworkers of America v. Weber (U.S., 1979)

In *United Steelworkers*, the Supreme Court ruled that agreements between workers and companies that set up racial quotas and/or timetables are constitutional, thereby instituting what has come to be known as "affirmative action." The case involved a 1974 agreement between the United Steelworkers of America (USWA) and the Kaiser Aluminum and Chemical Corporation mandating that 50 percent of the positions in the company's craft training programs must go to black employees. The controversy arose at Kaiser's Gramercy, Louisiana, plant. Chosen first for the training program were seven blacks and six whites. Several white employees, who wished to get into the training program but were turned away, had more seniority than the black employees chosen for the program. Among them was Brian F. Weber. Weber sued in district court to obtain relief from the union's agreement with Kaiser. The court ruled that the agreement violated section 701(a), 42 U.S.C., which stipulated that it was unlawful for an employer "to fail or refuse to hire any individual, or otherwise to discriminate against any individual, with respect to his compensation, terms, conditions, or privileges of employment, because of such individual's race, color, religion, sex, or national origin." The Fifth Circuit Court of Appeals affirmed the ruling, so the USWA took the case to the U.S. Supreme Court. Justice William Brennan wrote the 5–2 decision (justices Lewis Powell and John Paul Stevens did not participate, and Chief Justice Warren Burger and Justice William Rehnquist dissented), which ruled that because the

contract agreement was not state action and was entered into by the members of the union voluntarily, there was no violation of any law, including the equal protection clause of the Fourteenth Amendment.

Universal Negro Improvement Association (UNIA)

The brainchild of Jamaican-born Marcus Garvey, the Universal Negro Improvement Association (UNIA) was a movement that promoted black social and moral independence within white society. The organization, which started in 1911, strove, especially through its official journal, *Negro World*, to instruct and inform American blacks on their rights and how to be "race-conscious."

See also Garvey, Marcus Mosiah.

University of California Regents v. Bakke (U.S., 1978)

The Bakke case was the landmark reverse discrimination case, in which the Supreme Court struck down in part the use of quotas for admission to colleges. The case involved 37-year-old Alan Bakke. In 1976, he attempted to enroll at the University of California Medical School at Davis. The school, which set aside 16 of every 100 places in its classes for minorities, denied him admission as all the places not reserved for minorities were filled. Bakke sued, claiming that he was denied the equal protection of the laws, and that among the minority applicants accepted into the school, several were less qualified than he was for enrollment. The California Supreme Court ruled in favor of Bakke, and he was allowed entry to the school. The school did, however, appeal the case to the U.S. Supreme Court, although it was not heard until two years later, when Bakke was nearing the completion of his degree. The case's outcome, then, was more symbolic for Bakke than substantive. The Supreme Court ruled 5–4 (with Justices William

Brennan, Byron White, Thurgood Marshall, and Harry Blackmun concurring in part and dissenting in part) that the denial of admission to Bakke on account of his race was a violation of the equal protection clause of the Fourteenth Amendment. It also ruled, however, that a school may use race as a basis for an admissions policy. Writing for the majority, Justice Lewis Powell, Jr., wrote: "The fatal flaw in Petitioner's [the University of California] preferential program is its disregard of individual rights as guaranteed by the Fourteenth Amendment.

Such rights are not absolute. But when a State's distribution of benefits or imposition of burdens hinges on the color of a person's skin or ancestry, that individual is entitled to a demonstration that the challenged classification is necessary to promote a substantial state interest. Petitioner has failed to carry this burden."

See also DeFunis v. Odegaard.

Urban League
See National Urban League.

Vance, Zebulon (1830–1894)

Zebulon Vance was the Redemption governor of North Carolina who belonged to the Ku Klux Klan but also was involved with civil rights. Vance was born in Buncombe County, North Carolina, on 13 May 1830. He studied law at the University of North Carolina from 1851 to 1852 and served as solicitor of Asheville, North Carolina in 1852. He served a single term in the North Carolina House of Commons as a Whig, was the editor of the Asheville *Spectator*, and ran an unsuccessful campaign for the state legislature in 1856, running as a member of the "Know-Nothing" party. Vance lost a bid for the U.S. House of Representatives in 1857, but was elected in a special election and served a single term, 1858–1861. When the Civil War started Vance considered himself a Unionist, but soon returned home and organized a company of Confederate troops. He fought in the New Bern and Seven Days' battles. Although history books refer to him as "General Vance," he actually finished his military service as a colonel. In 1862, he was overwhelmingly elected governor of North Carolina. When he sparred with the Confederate government over conscription and the writ of habeas corpus, he was accused of harboring pro-Unionist sympathies. Although he was reelected in 1864, Vance realized the Confederacy was finished and tried to sue for a separate peace for his state. Instead, he was arrested and served two months in prison. Out of public life, he began a law practice in Raleigh. He was elected to the U.S. Senate in 1870, but his service for the Confederacy prohibited him from taking his seat. He later ran for Congress but was defeated. In 1876, he was named the Democratic candidate for governor of North Carolina, and was reelected. In this second term, which came immediately after the end of Reconstruction, he created normal schools for both races. Many histories of the Ku Klux Klan, however, list him as being a member. In 1878 Vance was elected to the U.S. Senate, where he served until 1893. In the last year before his death, he took to the lecture circuit to deliver various speeches, including one on Jewish history. Vance died in the nation's capital on 14 April 1894.

Village of Arlington Heights v. Metropolitan Housing Development Corporation (U.S., 1977)

Village of Arlington Heights was the Supreme Court case in which the Court decided whether a city, town, or village may refuse to zone an area for the building of racially integrated low-cost housing. In the end, the high court sidestepped the issue, leaving it unresolved. The Metropolitan Housing Development Corporation (MHDC) purchased a 15-acre property in the village of Arlington Heights, Illinois, and then asked the city officials to rezone it from an area for single-family residences to one of public housing. After a series of heated town meetings, the village refused the rezoning. MHDC sued to have the village rezone the area. The district court hearing the case found that the rezoning refusal was based not on racial grounds but on the reasoning to preserve home values in that particular area. The MHDC appealed the ruling in the Seventh Circuit Court of Appeals, which overturned the lower court's ruling. The village of Arlington Heights then turned to the U.S. Supreme Court. The Court ruled on 11 January 1977 that because there had been no hearing to decide whether the refusal to rezone was a violation of the 1968 Fair Housing Act, the case would have to be sent back to the lower courts, leaving in doubt the central issue of the case.

Virginia v. Rives (U.S., 1880)

See Ex Parte Virginia.

Voting Rights Act of 1965

Signed into law by President Lyndon B. Johnson on 9 August 1965, the Voting Rights Act was the first national law to guarantee fully the voting rights of all people. Codified into law is the following provision: "All citizens of the United States who are otherwise qualified by law to vote at any election by the people in any State, Territory, district, county, city, parish, township, school district, municipality, or other territorial subdivision, shall be entitled and allowed to vote at all such elections, without distinctions of race, color, or previous condition of servitude; any constitution, law, custom, usage, or regulation of any State or Territory, or by or under its authority, to the contrary not withstanding." Other sections of the act ban literacy tests other than those given to all voters or to people of special needs, such as the blind; prohibit the use of intimidation in voting; and uphold the rights of the U.S. government to sue on behalf of injured parties.

Walker, David (1785–1830)

David Walker was a slave known for his antislavey pamphlet, *David Walker's Appeal*, which was widely distributed in the South. Walker was born a slave, to a slave father and a free mother, in Wilmington, North Carolina, on 28 September 1785. Around 1827, he escaped to Boston, where he opened a used clothing shop on Brattle Street. John Brown Russworm and the Reverend Samuel Cornish had just begun printing *Freedom's Journal*, the first black newspaper, and Walker became the paper's Boston agent. He also made several written contributions to the publication. In 1829, he began publication of his famous work, *David Walker's Appeal: In Four Articles together with a Preamble to the Colored Citizens of the World, but in particular and very expressly to those of the United States of America*, a 76-page pamphlet that made a powerful appeal for the end of slavery through any means necessary, including the use of violence. Many abolitionists decried this call for violence, and Walker's publication was shunned. A large number of Southerners were angered at his work, and some threatened him. In March 1830, Walker published a third edition of the *Appeal*, this time even stronger than the first two. Three months later, he was found dead in the doorway of his shop. It was rumored that slaveowners had poisoned him, but this was never proven. He left behind a wife, known to history only as "Miss Eliza." Edwin Garrison Walker, later born to Miss Eliza, is presumed to have been David Walker's son.

See also Walker, Edwin Garrison.

Walker, Edwin Garrison (1831?–1901)

Edwin G. Walker was one of the first blacks in American history to be elected to a legislative seat. Walker was born in 1831, according to some sources, and supposedly was the son of famed abolitionist David Walker, who had died in 1830. Edwin Walker's precise birthdate and paternity have never been verified.

Edwin Walker was born out of wedlock, and sometime afterward his mother married a man named Dusen and moved from Boston to nearby Charlestown, Massachusetts. Edwin Walker attended the local schools there and became apprenticed in the leather goods trade. By 1857, he owned his own leather goods shop in Charlestown. He seemed set for success. Following in the footsteps of his famous father, however, he was a vocal proponent of the abolition of slavery. He traveled to Boston on several occasions to hear and deliver abolitionist speeches. He was also interested in the law and, sometime in the late 1850s, he purchased a law book and began to study law. In 1861, he was admitted to the Massachusetts bar, apparently the first black man to be so honored in that state.

At the end of the Civil War, Walker became interested in politics. As the friend of Robert Brown Elliott, a future congressman from South Carolina, Walker studied the workings of the Massachusetts state legislature and decided to run for election, winning the seat representing the Third District of Middlesex County in the lower house of the Massachusetts legislature.

Walker spent much of his term working for women's suffrage and against a proposed merger of Charlestown and Boston. Intending to campaign for reelection in 1868, he found himself facing strong opposition from the Republican Party because of his opposition to the Fourteenth Amendment; he ultimately chose not to run. He joined the state Democratic Party and continued practicing law. In 1883, he was named as a municipal judge in Charlestown, but Republican pressure and Walker's support for Democrat Ben Butler for governor led to Walker's defeat. Instead, another black, George L. Ruffin, was named to the judgeship.

In his final years, Walker was involved in the Equal Rights League and had been proposed as president of the Colored People's National Party; however, his death at his home in Boston on 13 January 1901 meant that he was never able to fill that position.

Wallace, George Corley (1919–)

Former Alabama Governor George Wallace is perhaps most famous for his unsuccessful bids for the U.S. presidency and his stand, literally, in a doorway at the University of Alabama, against desegregation. Wallace was born in Clio, Alabama, on 25 August 1919. He attended local schools, then received his law degree from the University of Alabama in 1942. During World War II, Wallace served in the U.S. Air Force, rising to the rank of flight sergeant. Upon his return, Wallace served for a year as assistant attorney general of Alabama (1946–1947), and six years as a member of the Alabama House of Representatives (1947–1953). From 1953 until 1962, he was a judge in the Third Alabama Judicial District.

Wallace first entered statewide politics in 1958, when he unsuccessfully sought the Democratic nomination for governor. He tried again in 1962 and was elected. During his term, Wallace led the movement to stop lawful desegregation of Southern schools. In 1963, when Vivian Malone and James Hood, two black students, tried to enroll at the University of Alabama, Wallace made headlines by standing in the doorway of the school and blocking their entrance. Deputy Attorney General Nicholas Katzenbach tried to get Wallace to move away, but the Alabama governor refused.

During the confrontation, it was University of Alabama President Frank A. Rose who mediated. Rose, who was neither an integrationist nor a segregationist (he described himself as a "realist"), told the Justice Department that when the black students were finally admitted, he would see to it that the law was carried out, and that peace would be the norm on the University of Alabama campus. Wallace, however, became the darling of Southern conservatives for his stand against desegregation. In 1968, he ran for president on the independent ticket and received several million votes. In 1972, when he was poised to run again, a would-be assassin, Arthur Bremer, shot Wallace, paralyzing him from the waist down. Wallace completed his gubernatorial term. He ran again in 1982 and was elected, serving until 1987. Today, he is considered a reformed segregationist, and drew many black votes in his last two campaigns for governor.

See also Alabama; Johnson, Frank Minis, Jr.

Walls, Josiah Thomas (1842–1905)

Until 1992, Josiah Walls was Florida's only elected black representative in the U.S. House of Representatives, and he remains the only member of that body twice unseated by his opponents, who alleged that Walls had stolen his elections. Walls was born on 30 December 1842, although the place of his birth, thought to be somewhere near Winchester, Virginia, and whether he was a slave or free, remain in doubt. When he was an infant, Walls's parents moved to the small town of Darkesville, Virginia (the town is now in West Virginia). Walls had little if any education; one source says he briefly attended the county normal school in Harrisburg, Pennsylvania, which was paid for "by a private source." Although there is some controversy as to the facts, history says that Walls was "impressed" into the Confederate army in 1861. He fought for the South for two years, until he was captured by a Union regiment at the battle of Yorktown in May 1862 and began fighting for the Union forces. In July 1863, in Philadelphia, he enlisted as a private in the Third Regiment of United States Colored Troops. In October of that year, he was promoted to the rank of corporal. In February 1864, the unit, under the command of Colonel Benjamin Tilghman, was posted to Florida. Although Walls did not take part in the Battle of Olustee, he did participate in the occupation of Jacksonville until the war ended. In late 1865, he was released from the army, and decided to stay in Florida.

After he settled down in the inland area of Alachua County, Walls worked for a time as a teacher in the town of Archer, and as a lumberer on the Suwannee River. In 1867, he was part of a biracial delegation sent by Alachua County to the Republican state platform committee and the state constitutional convention in 1868. Although many blacks refused to sign the moderate state constitution, Walls did, thereby assuring his political survival. In 1868, he was nominated and elected to a seat in the Florida state assembly. Later that same year, he was also nominated and elected to a seat in the Florida state senate. In 1871, as a delegate to the Southern States Convention of Colored Men, he requested that Ulysses S. Grant, the Republican presidential nominee in 1872, select black Virginia Congressman John Mercer Langston as his running mate.

In August 1870, at a Republican state convention, Walls was nominated by the Republicans for a seat in the U.S. House of Representatives. He won a narrow victory and went to Washington. His Democratic opponent, Silas L. Niblack, contested the election. In early 1873, the House Committee on Elections declared Niblack the winner. This was a moot point, however, for, in November 1872, Walls had once again defeated Niblack, and the defeated Democrat was only able to serve two months of his disputed term. In the House, through a total of three

terms (the Forty-second through the Forty-fourth Congresses), Walls introduced bills relating to pensions for Seminole War veterans, federally financed education for black students and for internal improvements in Florida, and gave moral support to the Cuban freedom fighters striving to end Spanish slave rule over the island of Cuba. In 1874, under mysterious circumstances, Walls's reelection to the House was thrown out by a House committee of six Democrats, with the one Republican voicing a loud dissent. Walls's congressional career was over.

Walls returned to Florida. He ran for reelection to Congress in 1876, but was defeated. Instead, he was elected to the state senate, but left before his first term was over and never returned. He went back to Alachua County and started a successful lettuce and citrus farm. In 1884, he ran as an independent candidate for the U.S. House, but again was defeated. In 1890, he ran his last campaign, an ill-fated attempt at the state senate. Walls spent his last years on his farm and, when a freeze destroyed his crops, served as manager of the farm at the Florida Normal College (now Florida A & M University). He was plagued by ill health and eventually died alone, on 15 May 1905, at the age of 62. He was buried in a black cemetery in Tallahassee, which no longer exists.

Wards Cove Packing Company Inc. et al. v. Frank Atonio et al. (U.S., 1989)

Wards Cove Packing Company was the controversial Supreme Court case that led to the enactment of the Civil Rights Act of 1991. The Wards Cove Packing Company was one of two companies operating seasonal salmon canneries in remote areas of Alaska. Work at the canneries fell into two distinct job types: cannery line jobs, which were mostly unskilled and held by Filipinos and by Alaska natives from local villages; and noncannery workers, usually engineers and bookkeepers, the majority of whom were white. The noncannery jobs generally paid more than the cannery jobs. Frank Atonio and other cannery liners sued the companies, alleging discrimination based on race, under Title VII of the 1964 Civil Rights Act (now 42 U.S.C. 2000e-2(a)). A district court sided with the companies; on appeal, however, the Ninth Circuit Court of Appeals overturned the lower court's judgment. The canneries appealed to the U.S. Supreme Court. Overturning the appeals court, the high court ruled 5–4 that the racial imbalance was not evidence in itself that the companies were discriminating in their employment practices, and that the burden of demonstrating discriminatory employment practices lay with the employees.

The Supreme Court ruling on *Wards Cove Packing Company* was later cited by Congress in the 1991 Civil Rights Act, which made it illegal for employees to carry the burden of proof of discrimination to win a civil rights lawsuit.

See also Civil Rights Act of 1991.

Waring, Julius Waties (1880–1968)

Julius Waties Waring was a federal judge who used all of his court's powers to end segregation and other discrimination in the South. Waring was born into an old, aristocratic Charleston, South Carolina, family on 27 July 1880. His father and two of his uncles served in the Confederate army. Later in life, Waring described the three men as "fine, decent slaveholders. But even where the relationship was pleasant, it wasn't right and therefore could not be tolerated." Waring received his first lesson in racial harmony as a child, describing, in an interview in the 2 November 1948 New York *Post*, his loving "Dah," his black "mammy." This relationship, he said, changed his attitude on the question of racism.

When he was only 11 years old, Waring entered the Student University School in Charleston. He went on to enroll at the College of Charleston, from which he earned his bachelor of arts degree in 1900. At the end of his senior year, he decided to enter the legal profession. His maternal great-grandfather, Thomas Waties, a delegate to the state constitutional convention that ratified the U.S. Constitution, had been an equity court officer; his grandfather had been an attorney. Waring studied in the offices of various lawyers and, in 1901, was admitted to the South Carolina bar. He maintained a private practice between 1901 and 1914; then in 1914, he became the assistant U.S. attorney general for Charleston, a post he held until 1920. From 1920 until 1942, Waring served both as a member of a prestigious Charleston law firm and as the city corporation counsel.

In 1942, at the age of 62, Waring was appointed to a seat on the Court of the Eastern District of South Carolina. It would have been an honorable way for Waring to end his career; Waring's career was just beginning, though. In 1938, he had been an advisor to the campaign of "Cotton" Ed Smith, the vitriolic segregationist senator from South Carolina. It was natural to assume, therefore, that he was a "safe" vote on the district court in matters of race. In 1947, however, a young black man petitioned the district court to attend law school. Waring ordered the state to let the man attend the University of South Carolina Law School. Instead, the state built an all-black school. In 1948, when a new test oath ("I believe in and will support the social and educational separation of the races") was implemented by the state Democratic Party, Waring warned party leaders that he would throw into jail any election officials who turned blacks away from the polls. As a result, there was no attempt to stop blacks from voting that year. During the next several years, Southern politicians unsuccessfully tried to remove Waring from the bench. In one of his last acts as judge, Waring combined a local school desegregation case with one from Topeka, Kansas; both were later considered together in *Brown v. Board of Education*. Waring left the bench in 1951, following an attempted bombing of his home in Charleston. He and his family moved to New York, where he became an advocate of civil rights and equality. Julius Waties Waring died in New York City on 19 January 1968, at the age of 87.

Washington, Booker Taliaferro (1856?–1915)

Booker T. Washington was the founder and first president of Tuskegee University, as well as the author of *Up From Slavery*. The date and place of his birth remain in doubt. What is known is that he was born into slavery somewhere in Virginia before the start of the Civil War. Freed at the end of the war, Booker and his mother went to Malden, West Virginia, where Booker's father had been kept as slave. In Malden, although the family lived in a crude shack, Booker began to study books and other literature to enhance his education. Working as a servant, he earned enough money to enroll in the Hampton Normal and Agricultural Institute in Virginia. Graduating in 1875, Washington returned home to Malden and was hired as a teacher.

In 1881, the Alabama legislature established a normal school at Tuskegee for the purpose of training black teachers. Washington was selected as principal. He took up the post in Alabama immediately, thereby changing the course of black education and American history.

Eager to make the school into a university, Washington sought the financial support among Southern whites. Although the school opened as a small, ramshackle place, Washington's fundraising soon allowed the school to recruit new students and teachers and to expand into Tuskegee University. With the opening of Tuskegee University on 4 July 1885, Washington utilized his special talents as a teacher and educator to

Booker Taliaferro Washington

pave the way for blacks to be educated to degree level.

Washington's influence steadily grew beyond the Tuskegee campus. In 1900, he was a founder of the National Negro Business League, formed to improve entrepreneurial opportunities for black Americans. Toward the end of his life, Washington was increasingly criticized by other black leaders, particularly W. E. B. DuBois, who called him "the Great Compromiser" because he refused to condemn Southern whites for their adherence to racial segregation. Washington saw things differently, however, feeling that a collaboration of power among whites and blacks in the South would allow the region to prosper. The philosophical basis for Washington's beliefs arose from the Protest Collaboration Movement, which was backed by noted black educator William Hooper Councill. The philosophy centered on the belief that black people should get along with and work with whites. Despite criticism, it was a belief that Washington continued to espouse his whole life. Washington died in Tuskegee, Alabama, on 14 December 1915, following a collapse in New York.

See also Councill, William Hooper; Protest Collaboration Movement.

Washington v. Davis (U.S., 1976)

Washington v. Davis was the Supreme Court decision that upheld as constitutional the use of job-related tests to hire employees, even if these tests proved to be discriminatory. The case involved several black applicants to the District of Columbia police force. All applicants were required to take and receive a score of 40 out of 80 on "Test 21," an examination that measured their reading, verbal, and comprehension abilities. More blacks than whites were failing the course, and Davis, among several failed applicants, sued the police force. A district court found the test to be constitutional, but an appeals court reversed the decision. The Supreme Court granted a review. The Court ruled 7–2 that, because the test was not discriminatory on its face, it was valid. Justice Byron R. White read the majority decision. "Reading ability is manifestly relevant to the police function; there is no evidence that the required passing grade was set at an arbitrarily high level; and there is sufficient disparity among high schools and high school graduates to justify the use of a separate uniform test."

See also Griggs v. Duke Power Company for a comparison of Supreme Court decisions on competency tests.

Watson, Thomas Edward (1856–1922)

Thomas E. Watson was the fiery Georgia populist orator whose actions during the 1915 Leo Frank case led to the reemergence of the Ku Klux Klan. Watson was born near Thomson, in Columbia County, Georgia, on 5 September 1856, the son, nephew, and grandson of Confederate war veterans. The war shaped and molded much of Watson's upbringing. Throughout his life, he faulted northern capitalists and their Southern allies—freed slaves—for ruining the South's agrarian way of life.

Watson was an angry young man during his youth. After spending some time at Mercer University in Macon, Georgia, and privately studying law, he was admitted to the state bar. In 1882, he was elected to a seat in the state assembly, and proceeded to challenge the party leadership as a freshman Democrat. In his speeches, he exhorted farmers of the South and the West to unite and build a politically strong agrarian organization. The result was the formation of the Farmer's Alliance, one of the most powerful political organizations in the western part of the United States. Watson advanced the idea that capitalism creates animosity between races, leading to racial turmoil.

In 1890, Watson was elected to a single term in the U.S. House of Representatives, where he became the father of the rural free delivery mail system. Watson ran unsuccessfully for reelection in 1892 and 1894 and was one of two vice presidential losers on the Democratic ticket in 1896. In 1904 and 1908, he ran as the populist candidate for president, but earned few votes. His political career uncertain, he then turned his attention to editing *Tom Watson's Magazine*, an influential populist journal dealing with political and economic reform.

In 1913, Leo Frank, a Jewish businessman from New York who ran a prosperous pencil factory in Atlanta, was charged with the rape and murder of 14-year-old Mary Phagan, a factory worker. Frank was convicted on circumstantial evidence and sentenced to death. The matter seemed to be closed, and Watson wrote an editorial calling for Frank's immediate execution. However, when the governor commuted Frank's sentence to life in 1915, Watson was outraged and gathered together a group of followers to form the Knights of Mary Phagan. They rode on horseback to the prison where Frank was incarcerated, kidnapped the prisoner, and lynched him. The Knights later became identified as the reformed Ku Klux Klan, a white supremicist organization that had died out in the 1880s. Thomas Watson was elected to the U.S. Senate as a Democrat in 1920, but he died on 26 September 1922, before completing his term. His impact, however, was felt for a long time. The reemergence of the Klan as a potent political force in many states paved the way for the spate of lynchings in the United States during the 1920s and 1930s.

See also Frank v. Mangum.

Watson et al. v. City of Memphis et al. (U.S., 1963)

The Supreme Court's decision in *Watson et al.* established that, under the Fourteenth Amendment, segregation of public accommodations is illegal and that the city of Memphis must proceed with desegregation of such facilities with "all deliberate speed." In 1960, several black citizens of Memphis, Tennessee, sued the city to quicken the pace of the desegregation of public parks and other publicly owned or operated public accommodations from which the plaintiffs alleged they were still excluded in whole or in part. The city countered that it was proceeding with a slow and gradual desegregation of these facilities for public safety and calm. Further, the city questioned whether the Fourteenth Amendment covered the matter of segregation in public accommodations. A district court hearing the case denied the petitioners immediate relief, but ordered the city to present a plan to the court in six months' time laying out in detail their plans for the rapid desegregation of the facilities. When the Court of Appeals for the Sixth Circuit upheld this judgment, the petitioners appealed the judgment to the U.S. Supreme Court. On 27 May 1963, the Court held that segregation of public accommodations was a violation of the equal protection clause of the Fourteenth Amendment, and as such had to be remedied immediately. Justice Arthur Goldberg wrote the Court's decision, in which he said: "Constitutional rights may not be denied simply because of hostility to their assertion or exercise .The city has failed to demonstrate any compelling or convincing reason requiring further delay in implementing the constitutional proscription of segregation of publicly owned or operated recreational facilities."

Wells-Barnett, Ida Bell (1862–1931)

Ida Bell Wells-Barnett was a social and civil rights activist who made it her life's labor to work for the passage of an anti-lynching law in the United States. Born during the Civil War in a small town in Mississippi, Wells began to teach in small schools when she was only 14. In 1884, she began to attend Fisk University in Nashville during the summers, when she didn't teach. While at Fisk, she became embroiled in a lawsuit over a whites-only segregated railroad car, and she lost her teaching job. Instead, she began to work for a black weekly, *Living Word*. In 1894, she became the co-owner and editor of another black weekly, *Free Speech and Headlight* in Memphis, Tennessee. While working at this paper, she wrote a strongly worded editorial opposing lynchings in the South, which led her to flee to New York, her life now in danger in Memphis. In New York, she was hired by T. Thomas Fortune of the New York *Age*. While a writer, Wells began a tour of the Northeast to lecture to audiences on lynching. In 1895, she married Frederick Barnett of Chicago. Barnett owned the Chicago *Conservator*, a black paper, and Wells-Barnett was its key writer. Wells-

Ida Bell Wells-Barnett

Barnett was a Republican and met and discussed black issues with President William McKinley. In her last years, she formed women's clubs and fought to have antilynching laws passed. Ida B. Wells-Barnett succumbed to the effects of uremia on 23 March 1931.

White, George Henry (1852–1918)

George H. White was the last former slave to serve in the U.S. House of Representatives when he sat during the Fifty-fifth and Fifty-sixth Congresses (1897–1901). White was born a slave on 18 November 1852, in Rosindale, Bladen County, North Carolina. After he was freed, sometime in 1962, White attended local schools in North Carolina for a short time while helping his family make wine casks. In 1873, he enrolled in Howard University as a medical student, but went on to receive only a normal certificate in electrical engineering. For the next two years, he studied law at various colleges and received a doctorate from Alabama A&M College. In 1879, he was admitted to the North Carolina bar and set up a law practice in the town of New Bern. While practicing his craft, he also served as the principal of the Normal School of North Carolina at New Bern. He became successful in real estate and, by 1880, owned more than $15,000 in property.

In 1880, White was elected to a seat in the North Carolina state House of Representatives, where he pushed for the creation of four normal schools for the instruction of black teachers. He later served as the principal of one of the four schools. In 1884, White was elected to the state senate, one of two blacks so elected, where he served on the all-important judiciary committee. In 1886, White moved to Edgecombe County and set up his law practice in the town of Tarboro. That year, he was elected as the solicitor and prosecuting attorney of the Second District of North Carolina. He was reelected in 1890.

In 1894, White sought the Republican nomination from the Second North Carolina District for a seat in the U.S. House of Representatives, but he was defeated in the primaries by Henry Plummer Cheatham, ironically White's brother-in-law. In 1896, White was a delegate to the Republican National Convention. That year, he ran again for Congress and defeated Cheatham in the Republican primary. He went on to win the general election by 3,000 votes over his Democratic opponent, incumbent Frederick A. Woodard, even though the black majority in the district was only 128. In his two terms in Congress, White attempted to get relief for depositors in the failed Freedman's Bank, worked to get financial help for former Congressman Robert Smalls of South Carolina, and proposed an antilynching bill. Although he won reelection in 1898, White foresaw that the passing of Jim Crow and other racist legislation in North Carolina would make winning a third term impossible. Two days after the election, a race riot broke out in Wilmington, Delaware. On 29 January 1901, in his final speech in the House, entitled "Defense of the Negro Race: Charges Answered," White lambasted his opponents, including racist politicians and newspapers, and "made a plea for the colored man." He decried the fact that his exit from Congress would leave that body without a single black member, but he predicted, rightly as it turned out, that blacks would some day return as representatives.

White spent his last years as a businessman and attorney. He opened law firms in Washington, D.C., and Philadelphia, and carried on successful real estate businesses in both cities. In 1907, he founded the People's Savings Bank, the first black-owned bank in Philadelphia. He later founded an all-black town in Whitesboro, New Jersey. In his last years, declining health forced him to give up his rigorous schedule. He died in Philadelphia on 28 December 1918, just 10 days after his sixty-sixth birthday.

See also Cheatham, Henry Plummer; Smalls, Robert.

White, Walter Francis (1893–1955)

Walter Francis White was the executive secretary of the National Association for the Advancement of Colored People (NAACP) from 1931 until his death in 1955. White was born on 1 July 1893 in Atlanta, Georgia. He had light skin, blond hair, blue eyes and mostly Caucasian features; as the *New York Times* speculated on his death, he could have slipped into the white world and would have never been challenged as to his color. White, however, was angered by the racial injustice around him and decided to go through life as a black man. His father, a postman, died when he suffered an injury and could not get help because of his color. At age 13, White witnessed the bloody Atlanta riots and was nearly killed when a white mob looking for blacks invaded his home. "That

night," White said in an interview years later, "I discovered what it meant to be a Negro."

White attended local schools, then enrolled at Atlanta University, from which he graduated with a bachelor's degree in 1916. When the Atlanta Board of Education threatened to end schooling for blacks after the sixth grade, White helped form a local branch of the NAACP to fight the threat. As branch secretary, he spoke out at a series of highly charged meetings of the board of education, arguing so persuasively that the board finally backed down. NAACP National Field Secretary Charles Weldon Johnson was so impressed by White's work that he offered the young Georgian the position of assistant secretary of the national NAACP.

White began work in 1918, charged with the task of helping NAACP branch offices get started. He was also involved with the antilynching campaign of the organization. During the Chicago riot of 1919, White was in Chicago helping blacks accused of crimes get fair representation. When he posed as a white reporter for the Chicago *Daily News* to get closer to the action, he was recognized and himself nearly lynched. The apocryphal story of his trip ends with him escaping Chicago on a train just moments ahead of a lynch party. In the 1920s, White dealt with other lynching cases, which he wrote about in books and articles. When James Weldon Johnson succeeded white social worker John R. Shillady as the NAACP's first black secretary in 1920, White became Johnson's immediate right-hand man. He served as Johnson's assistant until the latter became ill in 1929. White was named temporary head of the NAACP. In 1930, White led the NAACP in testifying against the appointment of Supreme Court nominee Judge John J. Parker, whose antiunion and anticivil rights record was exposed by the NAACP and the American Federation of Labor. White mobilized NAACP branches across the United States and lobbied key senators, all of which was key to Parker's eventual confirmation defeat. In 1931, the NAACP executive board elected White executive secretary of the organization.

White served as head of the NAACP until 1955. In those 24 years, he worked with Congress and several presidents on civil rights legislation. In 1944, he was largely responsible for Franklin Roosevelt's Fair Employment Practices Commission. In 1948, it was White who persuaded Harry S Truman to bolt from the Southern Democrats and support a civil rights plank in the Democratic platform that year. During the Harlem riots of 1943, he toured with New York Mayor Fiorello LaGuardia in an open limousine to call for calm. From 1943 to 1945, he served as a special war correspondent for the New York *Post*, and in 1945 acted as consultant to the American United Nations organization committee.

As more power was concentrated in his hands, some of the heads of the NAACP, who had always been suspicious of White, began to criticize him. When he divorced his black wife of 27 years to marry a white woman in 1949, he was criticized openly. When White returned as head of the NAACP in 1950 after a year's rest, he was challenged by several members who supported Roy Wilkins, who would eventually succeed White as head of the NAACP. White fought heart disease during his last years, succumbing to the illness on 21 March 1955, at the age of 61.

See also National Association for the Advancement of Colored People.

Wilder, Lawrence Douglas (1931–)

The first black man ever to be elected governor of a state in a popular vote, Lawrence Douglas Wilder was born in poverty in Richmond, Virginia, on 17 January 1931 (some sources list 31 January as his birthdate). Wilder was exposed to racial discrimination as a youngster

when his mother prevented him from taking one of the front seats, which were reserved for whites, on a city bus. Wilder attended local schools, then entered all-black Virginia Union College after his mother refused to sign him up for the U.S. Navy. When he graduated from Virginia Union in 1951, with a degree in chemistry, Wilder was drafted into the army. He served two years in Korea during the war, earning the Bronze Star for valor. In 1953, he was honorably discharged. When he returned to Richmond, he got a job in the state medical examiner's office as a chemist checking blood alcohol samples. In 1956, he took advantage of the G.I. bill and tried to enroll at the University of Virginia Law School. Because the state barred blacks from its law schools, Wilder instead studied law at Howard University, obtaining his law degree in 1959.

Wilder opened a law practice in the poorer section of Richmond, but soon found the pay woefully inadequate. He turned to more lucrative clients and specialized in criminal law and personal injury cases. In 1969, sporting wild Afro hair and an angry attitude, he was elected to a seat in the state senate—the first black to hold such a seat since Reconstruction. Wilder spent much of the next 16 years in the state senate arguing on racial matters. He tried to get the state song, *Carry Me Back to Old Virginia*, modified to exclude references to "darky" and his "massa"; proposed a statewide holiday honoring Reverend Dr. Martin Luther King, Jr.; and called for fair housing legislation. He was a staunch opponent of the death penalty, even casting the only vote against a senate bill calling for death for the killers of police officers.

In 1984, Wilder entered the race for the lieutenant governorship. It was a daring move in a state with a population that was only 20 percent black and that had once been the capital of the Confederacy. Wilder would need a substantial number of white voters to trust him as a politician, not just a black politician. With the

Lawrence Douglas Wilder being sworn in as governor of Virginia

backing of the county sheriff, Wilder faced down his opponent, Republican state senator John Chichester, when Wilder was accused of being against the death penalty. In November 1985, Wilder won a close victory, with 51 percent of the vote. It was a stunning upset.

Wilder was now the second highest official in the state, but he ached for higher office. In 1989, at the state Democratic convention, he was nominated for governor. He was opposed by Republican Marshall Coleman, a former state attorney general. The campaign was brutal. Wilder accused Coleman of waffling on the abortion issue, while Coleman de-

cried Wilder's change of heart from opposition to the death penalty to firm support of it. Although some polls on election eve gave Wilder a 4 percent to 16 percent lead, the results were much closer. Wilder was finally declared the winner by less than 7,000 votes, or one-third of 1 percent. It was, however, a historic moment. For the first time in American history, a black man, the grandson of slaves, had been popularly elected as the governor of a state.

When a recession hit, the new governor was forced to cut spending, including aid to schools, as well as to lay off state workers. He even showed a break with the past when, in 1992, he refused to give last-minute clemency to a death row inmate who declared his innocence. Wilder now had the highest office in the land in his sights. In 1991, he announced that he was running for the Democratic Party's nomination for president in 1992. His inability to raise sufficient campaign funds and a poor showing in the polls finally drove him out of the race—the first candidate to withdraw from the 1992 presidential primaries. Wilder is still anxious to hold a national office and is considered a possible choice for president or vice president in the future.

Wilkins, Roy (1901–1981)

Roy Wilkins was the executive director of the National Association for the Advancement of Colored People (NAACP) from 1955 until 1977. He was born in St. Louis, Missouri, on 30 August 1901, the son of a Methodist minister. His mother died when he was four, and he spent his early years under the care of his aunt and uncle in St. Paul, Minnesota. There, he was taught that blacks would get ahead if they adopted the attitudes of middle-class whites, i.e., by obtaining a good education and exhibiting moral behavior. In 1923, Wilkins graduated from the University of Minnesota with a major in sociology and a minor in journalism. During his college career, he worked on the St. Paul *Appeal*, a black newspaper, and served the local NAACP branch. He then went to Kansas City, where he worked on the local black paper, *The Call*, using the journal's pages to rail against a racist senator. The senator's electoral defeat at the polls is attributed widely to Wilkins's strong appeals to black voters. The exposure led NAACP Executive Secretary Walter White to invite him to New York in 1931, to serve as his chief assistant.

Wilkins's work in exposing inadequate working conditions for blacks in Mississippi led to congressional action for im-

Roy Wilkins

provement. In 1934, Wilkins succeeded W. E. B. DuBois as editor of *The Crisis*, the official organ of the NAACP. In 1949, Wilkins served for a year as executive secretary of the NAACP, then five years as minister of internal affairs. Wilkins gradually was made minister of internal affairs of the NAACP; however, in 1955, upon Walter White's death, Wilkins was actually elected executive secretary. He held the post for the next 22 years.

In those two decades of service, Wilkins led the fight for a federal anti-lynching bill, worked for the desegregation of schools and public facilities, and lobbied for the enactment of a voting rights act to guarantee the franchise for blacks. In 1977, as his health began to fail, Wilkins resigned as head of the NAACP and was succeeded by Benjamin Hooks, a member of the Federal Communications Commission (FCC). In his last years, Wilkins suffered from various illnesses. He died of kidney failure and uremia on 8 September 1981, just a week after his eightieth birthday.

Williams, Daniel Hale (1856? or 1858?–1931)

A noted black surgeon, Daniel Hale Williams was the founder of Provident Hospital, the first training school for black nurses in the United States, and was a founding member of the National Medical Association, a black counterpart to the American Medical Association. Williams was born in Hollidaysburg, Pennsylvania, on 18 January 1856 or 1858. After his father's death, Williams and his family settled first in Rockford, Illinois, and then Janesville, Wisconsin. Williams and his sister attended the prestigious Haire's Classical Academy in Janesville: he studied to be a barber; she investigated the hair care industry. After graduation, Williams hoped for a law career, but turned to medicine when he came under the eye of Dr. Henry Palmer, who had served as Wisconsin's surgeon general. Williams began to study medicine in Palmer's office in 1878, later entering the Chicago Medical College and graduating with a doctorate in 1883.

After an internship at Mercy Hospital in Chicago, Williams opened a medical office in an integrated area of that city. He also worked as attending physician at the city's Protestant Orphan Asylum, among other civic positions. In 1889, he was named to the Illinois Board of Health. Williams, however, had his heart set on opening a training hospital where black doctors could be schooled in medicine and black nurses could receive the necessary education and skills. In 1891, his idea culminated in the opening of Provident Hospital in Chicago, the first institution of its kind. He enlisted the aid of several Chicago philanthropists, including meat packer Philip Armour, to give generously to Provident. As head of the hospital, Williams made history in

1893, by becoming the first doctor to close a heart wound with stitches. In 1895, he was one of the founding members of the National Medical Association, a medical society for black doctors. Among his articles are "Several Cases of Inflammation Starting in the Caecum and Vermiform Appendix" and "A Report of Two Cases of Caesarean Section under Positive Indications with Terminations in Recovery."

Williams's last years were marked by personal tragedy and poor health. He died at his summer home in Idlewild, Michigan, on 4 August 1931, at the age of 73, and was buried in Chicago's Graceland Cemetery.

Williams, George Washington (1849–1891)

George Washington Williams was a black minister and historian who wrote several works on black life in America. Williams was born on 16 October 1849, in Bedford Springs, Pennsylvania, the son of black parents of mixed Welsh and German backgrounds. When George was three, the family moved to New Castle, Pennsylvania, where the future historian attended school. Later, he attended a private academy and was taught by a private tutor in Massachusetts.

When he was 14, Williams ran away and, lying about his age, joined the U.S. Army. He served during the Civil War under the name of one of his half-uncles and was promoted from private to sergeant major. Later, during the Mexican War, he joined the Mexican army. Then, after the fall of the Emperor Maximilian, Williams returned to the United States. He was not yet 20.

In 1874, Williams was ordained a minister, after attending the Newton (Massachusetts) Theological Seminary. From 1874 until 1876, he was involved as a journalist, working with the likes of John Mercer Langston and Frederick Douglass. In 1876, he went west to the Union

Baptist Church in Cincinnati, Ohio, where he held a pastorate for two years. Before he left Ohio, he served a term in the state legislature. An address in 1876, during Fourth of July celebrations, led him to begin a study of black history, which culminated in the publication of his two-volume *History of the Negro Race in America from 1619 to 1880*. Later, while living in Boston, he wrote *History of Negro Troops in the War of the Rebellion* (1888).

In 1890, Williams was appointed minister to Haiti by President Benjamin Harrison. It was while he was traveling in Africa that Williams caught African fever. Taken to London for care, he, nevertheless, died of his illness on 2 August 1891.

Williams v. Mississippi (U.S., 1898)

In *Williams v. Mississippi* the Supreme Court found that literacy tests used in jury selection did not on their face violate the equal protection clause of the Fourteenth Amendment, as long as the tests were applied equally. Plaintiff Henry Williams was indicted in Washington County, Mississippi, for a murder he had committed in 1896. He asked at trial that the indictment be dismissed on the grounds that the grand jury that returned the indictment was all white. The court found no evidence to dismiss, and, in trial, Williams was convicted. He sued to a district court and appeals court, which denied his appeal. Williams then turned to the U.S. Supreme Court. On 25 April 1898, the Court unanimously upheld Williams's conviction. Accepting the argument that the grand jury was drawn from voter registration rolls, the Court looked at how the rolls were made. It found that the literacy test used by the state to qualify a juror, elector, or voter constituted no violation of the equal protection clause because it was applied to both whites and blacks. The Court held that "it has not been shown that their [the literacy tests] actual ad-

ministration was evil; but only that evil was possible under them."

Williams v. State (1955)

Williams v. State dealt with the death sentence imposed on a black man, Aubrey Williams, in Georgia. In March 1953, Williams was sentenced to death in the electric chair for murder. The Supreme Court, in *Avery v. Georgia*, had overturned another black man's murder conviction in the same county because of the biased treatment of blacks in the jury selection process. Avery's conviction was overturned because the Court said he had been denied the equal protection of the laws. Williams claimed that he, too, had been denied equal protection. A state law enacted after the *Avery* decision, but before Williams's trial, held that for a defendant to claim bias in a trial, the claim must be made at the time of conviction. Williams's attorney waited eight months after his conviction to claim such bias. Williams sued the state for relief from the state jury bias statute and his conviction and death sentence. Justice John Marshall Harlan of the U.S. Supreme Court appointed his clerk to look at the issues in the Williams case and to come to a conclusion. The clerk concluded that Williams was indeed guilty, had received a fair trial, and was not being denied the equal protection of the laws. The Supreme Court decided, on the advice of Justice Harlan, not to review Williams's case. On 30 March 1956, Aubrey Williams died in Georgia's electric chair.

Woodson, Carter Godwin (1875–1950)

Carter Godwin Woodson was a noted black author and historian who, in 1915, established the Association for the Study of Negro Life and History and served as the first editor of *The Journal of Negro History*. Woodson was born the son of former slaves in New Canton, Virginia, just 10 years after the end of the Civil War. Due to his family's financial situation, he had to work at an early age and did not receive any education until he was 20 years old. By the time he was 28, he had received his high school diploma and a degree from Berea College in Kentucky. He then served four years in the Philippines as a school supervisor. Woodson returned to the United States and was awarded a master's degree from the University of Chicago in 1908. That year, he was hired as a professor in Washington, D.C., while he completed studies for his doctoral degree from Harvard University in 1912. Three years later, Woodson founded the Association for the Study of Negro Life and History. In 1916, he began publication of the Association's organ, *The Journal of Negro History*. From 1918 to 1922, Woodson headed three different educational institutions, including Howard University in Washington, D.C. In 1922, he founded the Associated Publishers, Inc., a press that published works specifically aimed at black audiences. Woodson served the rest of his life as editor of the *Journal of Negro History* and leader of the Association for the Study of Negro Life and History. He died on 3 April 1950, at the age of 75.

Wygant et al. v. Jackson Board of Education (U.S., 1986)

Wygant was the Supreme Court case in which the Court ruled that the laying off of white teachers with more seniority to preserve the jobs of minority teachers was unconstitutional. As part of its bargaining agreement with the teacher's union, the Jackson, Michigan, Board of Education agreed that if it became necessary to cut teachers, it would first fire white teachers with more seniority rather than newly hired teachers, most of whom were minorities. When these layoffs were instituted, among the affected teachers was Wendy Wygant. She, along with several other white teachers, sued the board of education on the grounds that the bargaining agreement clause was a violation of their Fourteenth Amendment rights. The District Court for the Eastern District of Michigan dismissed the complaint, ruling that such "remedies" were necessary to overcome years of discrimination. The Sixth Circuit Court of Appeals affirmed the judgment. The plaintiffs then appealed to the U.S. Supreme Court. Although the Court could come up with no universally accepted opinion, five justices, among them Justices Lewis Powell, Sandra Day O'Connor, Byron White, William Rehnquist, and Chief Justice Warren Burger, struck down the layoffs as a violation of the plaintiffs' rights under the equal protection clause of the Fourteenth Amendment. Among several points noted in the Court's opinion, it held that "a school board's interest in providing minority faculty role models for its minority students in an attempt to alleviate the effects of societal discrimination is insufficient to justify racially discriminatory practices in the hiring and layoff of teachers."

Young, Andrew Jackson, Jr. (1932–)

Andrew Young is the noted black politician who has served in the U.S. House of Representatives, as mayor of Atlanta, Georgia, and as U.S. ambassador to the United Nations. Young was born in New Orleans, Louisiana, on 12 March 1932, the first of two sons of a prosperous dentist. Growing up in a middle-class suburb of New Orleans, Young was shielded from much of the antagonistic racial atmosphere of the Deep South, but he did attend a segregated school and a private school. He enrolled at Dillard University in New Orleans in 1947, but after a year transferred to Howard University, earning a bachelor of science degree in 1951. His first thoughts were of following in the footsteps of his father and becoming a den-

tist, but he came under the influence of a clergyman and decided to enter the ministry. He entered the Hartford Theological Seminary and graduated with a bachelor of divinity degree in 1955. Ordained in the United Church of Christ, he toured the South until he was hired in 1957 by the National Council of Churches to work with white youths in New York City.

Young's first brush with the civil rights movement came in 1956, when he met and worked with Reverend Dr. Martin Luther King, Jr., then leader of the Southern Christian Leadership Conference (SCLC). In 1961, Young joined the SCLC and was responsible for organizing several peace marches in the South, including a walk in which police in Birmingham, under the direction of Eugene "Bull" Connor, hosed down and set attack dogs on demonstrators. In 1968, following King's assassination, SCLC President Reverend Dr. Ralph David Abernathy named Young as his second in command. Young served in this post until his unsuccessful run for a congressional seat in 1970. In 1972, he ran again and was elected, thus becoming the first black to represent Georgia in the House of Representatives since Franklin Long in 1871. In Congress, Young spoke out against strip-mining in his state and asked for the end of sugar quotas imposed on South Africa in an effort to encourage reform of the apartheid system in that country.

Young was reelected in 1974 and 1976. He played an important role in the election of Jimmy Carter to the presidency in 1976, when he served as a conduit between Carter and the black community. When Carter was elected, he rewarded Young for his help by asking the civil rights advocate to accept the post of U.S. ambassador to the United Nations.

Andrew Jackson Young, Jr.

When Young presented his credential to the United Nations on 31 January 1977, he became the first black to hold the post.

In 1979, Young ran into serious trouble when he met with officials from the Palestine Liberation Organization (PLO), a violation of United States law at that time. Under pressure from American Jewish groups, President Carter asked for and received Young's resignation. Embittered, Young ran for mayor of Atlanta in 1981, winning election that year and reelection in 1985. In 1990, he left the mayoralty, but remains a leading civil rights figure.

Young, Plummer Bernard, Sr. (1884–1962)

Plummer B. Young, Sr. was the fiery black editor of the Norfolk (Virginia) *Journal and Guide* whose politics were shaped by Booker T. Washington. Young was born in Littleton, North Carolina, on 27 July 1884, the son of Winfield Young, a former slave. In the 1890s, Winfield Young became entranced by the message of empowerment through education and self-help that Booker T. Washington was offering. He started a small weekly temperance paper, *The True Reformer*, on which his sons, among them Plummer Bernard, worked. In 1907, Plummer Young moved to Norfolk, Virginia, where he took a job as plant foreman of the *Lodge Journal and Guide*, the official organ of the local Knights of Gideon. Three years later, the lodge lost its mortgage, and Young purchased the rights to the paper. Dropping the lodge from the masthead, he began publication of the Norfolk *Journal and Guide*, the largest black-owned weekly in the South, with a circulation that, at one point, reached 55,000.

Thus began Young's 36 years as editor of the *Journal and Guide*. The impact of Booker T. Washington upon Young's paper was reflected in the publication's motto: "Build up, don't tear down." As a

protégé and follower of the great educator, Young was involved in turning Washington's words into actions in Norfolk. In 1913, he toured parts of Virginia with Washington. After Washington's death in 1915, Young was at the head of a movement to raise funds for a memorial for his mentor.

In 1943, Young accepted a position on the Fair Employment Practices Committee in response to an invitation from President Franklin D. Roosevelt. Young served for two years. In 1946, he handed over almost all control of the *Journal and Guide* to his two sons, although he retained the title of editor. Plummer Bernard Young, Sr. died of a respiratory illness on 9 October 1962.

Young, Whitney Moore, Jr. (1921–1971)

Whitney Young, Jr., was the fourth executive secretary of the National Urban League (NUL). Young was born in Lincoln Ridge, Kentucky, on 31 July 1921. His father, Whitney Young, Sr., was the president of the Lincoln Institute, an all-black boarding high school. His mother, Laura Ray Young, was a schoolteacher. As a result, Whitney, Jr., and his two sisters grew up in an atmosphere of learning. Whitney, Jr., attended Lincoln, then enrolled at the Kentucky State Industrial College, a historically black school located in Frankfort. In 1941, he earned a bachelor of science degree in natural science.

Young had planned to become a physician, even taking a premedical course at Kentucky State. Yet, after graduation, he took a job as assistant principal and athletic coach at Julius Rosenwald High School in Madison, Kentucky. In 1942, he was drafted into the U.S. Army and spent two years at the Massachusetts Institute of Technology, training to be an engineer. In 1944, he was sent to Europe, where he served as a private in the all-black 369th Regiment of the Anti-Aircraft Artillery Group. The outfit was

Whitney Moore Young, Jr.

the NUL branch in St. Paul, Minnesota, as its industrial relations secretary. In 1950, he was appointed head of the NUL branch in Omaha, Nebraska. He served in this post until 1954. While head of the Omaha branch, Young worked as an instructor at the School of Social Work at the University of Nebraska. In 1954, he left the NUL to become the dean of the School of Social Work at Atlanta University, an all-black school. In early 1961, he took a leave from this post to attend Harvard University as a visiting scholar on a grant from the Rockefeller Foundation.

On 29 January 1961, the NUL announced that Young had been chosen to succeed Lester Blackwell Granger as the organization's executive secretary. Young assumed his duties that August and served 10 years in the post. During that time, he gained prominence as one of the key black leaders during the March on Washington in 1963, advised the White House on various civil rights issues, and wrote a syndicated column that appeared in newspapers nationwide from 1963 until 1971.

In March 1971, Young traveled to Lagos, Nigeria, to attend a conference on African–American Dialogue, which discussed relations between the peoples of the two continents. On 11 March, Young, taking time out from the meeting, took a swim in the Atlantic Ocean. Apparently, he had a heart attack and drowned. Friends with him were unable to rescue him in time. Whitney Young, Jr., was dead at the age of 49.

See also National Urban League.

commanded by a strict white Southerner, and Young got his first insight into racial bigotry. Young stepped forward and helped out in situations that dealt with race, becoming the unit's "diplomat of race relations." This new embrace of social issues changed Young's perspective. When he returned to the United States, he entered the University of Minnesota and was awarded a master's degree in social work in 1947.

Whitney Young's climb to national prominence began in 1948. He joined

Chronology

1619 The first black indentured servants arrive in the New World.

1650 Chattel slavery is recognized by law.

1712 A slave revolt in New York is suppressed; six of the rebels commit suicide and twenty-one are hanged.

1741 A second New York slave uprising is put down; 13 are executed.

1770 Crispus Attucks, a free black man, is among five people killed by British troops in the Boston Massacre.

1774 Rhode Island becomes the first colony to ban slavery.

1775 The first Abolition Society is organized in Philadelphia, Pennsylvania.

1777 The state of Vermont bans slavery.

1794 The first independent church for free blacks is founded in Philadelphia by Richard Allen, a freed slave. Allen becomes the first bishop of the African Methodist Church in 1816.

1808 The importation of slaves is banned by Congress.

1810 The third census reveals that one of every seven people in the United States is a slave.

1812 Louisiana is admitted into the Union as the eighteenth state. The right to own slaves is explicitly written into the state constitution.

1817 The American Colonization Society is founded by whites to recolonize free blacks in Africa. The society begins this process by purchasing land near present-day Monrovia, Liberia.

1820 Congress passes the Missouri Compromise, which allows Missouri to enter the Union as a slave state but bars slavery elsewhere west of the Mississippi and north of the line of 36° 30'.

1822 A planned revolt by slaves in Charleston, South Carolina, led by Denmark Vesey, is suppressed by white slaveowners; Vesey and over 30 others are hanged.

1827 *Freedom's Journal*, published by John B. Russworm and Samuel E. Cornish, becomes the first newspaper printed by blacks in the United States.

1831 William Lloyd Garrison begins publication of his fiery abolitionist journal, *The Liberator*.

A slave rebellion in the Virginia tidewater led by Nat Turner leads to the deaths of over 50 whites and many blacks; Turner is eventually captured and executed.

1833 Abolitionists William Lloyd Garrison and Arthur and Lewis Tappan found the American Anti-Slavery Society.

1835 Oberlin College in Ohio becomes the first major educational institution to admit black students.

1837 Abolitionist newspaper publisher Elijah Parish Lovejoy is shot and killed by a proslavery mob in Alton, Illinois, on 7 November, after Lovejoy prints an antislavery editorial in his newspaper, the *Alton Observer*.

1840 Congress votes to refuse to accept any resolution or petition regarding the ending of slavery. The rule is dubbed the "gag rule" by abolitionists.

1842 In *Prigg, Plaintiff in Error, v. Commonwealth of Pennsylvania, Defendant in Error* the Supreme Court rules that states may not enact laws bypassing the Fugitive Slave Act of 1793.

1849 Californians vote to prohibit slavery in the state.

1850 Congress passes the Compromise of 1850, which recognizes California as a free state. The slave trade is ended in the District of Columbia, but the hated Fugitive Slave Law, which compels Northerners to return escaped slaves, is strengthened.

1852 Harriet Beecher Stowe's abolitionist novel *Uncle Tom's Cabin* is published in Boston. Within one year, 300,000 copies are sold.

1854 The Republican Party is founded by members of the Free Soil and Liberty parties in Ripon, Wisconsin.

The Kansas–Nebraska Act, which allows for a popular vote on slavery in Kansas and Nebraska, becomes law.

1855 Proslavery forces succeed in passing a Kansas state constitution that allows slavery.

1856 On 21 May, Northern settlers in Lawrence, Kansas, are attacked by proslavery mobs.

On 22 May, Senator Charles Sumner of Massachusetts, having spoken out three days earlier in a speech on "the crime against Kansas," which denounced slavery and included some personal invective against Senator Andrew Butler of South Carolina, is attacked and severely beaten in the Senate chamber by Butler's nephew, Congressman Preston Brooks of South Carolina. Sumner is nearly killed but will recover from his injuries to author the Civil Rights Act of 1875.

On 30 August, militant abolitionist John Brown and other anti-slavery activists attack and kill several slaveowners in the "Osawatomie Massacre" in Kansas.

The Republican Party's first candidate for president, John Charles Frémont, is defeated in the November election by Democrat James Buchanan.

1857 The Supreme Court holds in *Dred Scott v. Sandford* that blacks are not citizens, and, as Chief Justice Roger Taney says in the majority opinion, they "do not have rights any white man is bound to respect."

1859 On 16 October, abolitionist John Brown launches a raid against the federal arsenal at Harpers Ferry, Virginia; he is captured the next day and executed on 2 December.

1860 Following the election of Republican Abraham Lincoln to the presidency, South Carolina becomes the first state to secede from the Union, on 20 December.

1861–
1865 Civil War rages over the secession of the slave states and the issue of slavery itself.

1863 On 1 January, President Abraham Lincoln issues his Emancipation Proclamation, which frees all slaves in the Confederate states.

1865 The Bureau of Refugees, Freedmen, and Abandoned Lands, known more commonly as the Freedmen's Bureau, is established by an act of Congress.

The Thirteenth Amendment to the Constitution, which outlaws slavery, takes effect.

The Ku Klux Klan is founded in Pulaski, Tennessee.

1866-
1877 The process of Reconstruction takes place in the Southern states, effectively making them conquered territories of the United States. It ends with the election of Republican Rutherford B. Hayes in 1877.

1866 Congress enacts the Civil Rights Act of 1866, which explicitly grants the full rights of citizenship to all persons born in the United States, and protects the rights of freedmen in the courts.

1867 Congress passes the Peonage Abolition Act to end attempts to reinstitute slavery-like work for freedmen in the South.

1868 The Supreme Court finds in *Georgia v. Stanton* that a Southern state may not challenge the constitutionality of Reconstruction.

The Fourteenth Amendment to the Constitution, granting full American citizenship to the freedmen, becomes law.

1870 The Fifteenth Amendment to the Constitution, protecting the right to vote, becomes law.

The first Enforcement Act is enacted by Congress to support the Fifteenth Amendment.

1871 The second Enforcement Act is passed by Congress to protect the right to vote for freed slaves by bringing all state and local elections under federal observation.

The third Enforcement Act, also known as the Ku Klux Klan Act, is passed by Congress to deal with the growing menace of the Klan.

1872 The Supreme Court strikes down the 1866 Civil Rights Act in the case of *Blyew v. United States*.

1875 Congress passes the Civil Rights Act of 1875, which outlaws discrimination in public transportation and accommodations.

1876 On 27 March, the Supreme Court rules in *United States v. Cruikshank* that the U.S. Constitution does not cover some violations of voting rights based on race. That same day, in *United States v. Reese*, the Court finds that state officials cannot be punished for refusing to allow a citizen to vote on the grounds that the person failed to pay a poll tax.

1880 The Supreme Court rules in *Ex Parte Virginia* that the mere absence of blacks from a grand or petit jury does not in itself constitute evidence that a jury is tainted. On the same day, it decides in *Strauder v. West Virginia* that blacks may not be excluded by law from juries.

In *Ex Parte Siebold*, the Supreme Court holds that the federal government has a right to oversee local and state elections so that blacks could vote free from intimidation.

1881 Tennessee becomes the first state to pass a "Jim Crow" law when it mandates the segregation of whites and blacks in first-class railway cars.

1883 The Supreme Court rules in *United States v. Harris* that federal law prohibiting "persons in disguise" from violating the civil rights of others is unconstitutional.

In *Pace v. Alabama*, the Supreme Court allows states to ban interracial marriages.

In the "Civil Rights Cases," the Supreme Court largely overturns the 1875 Civil Rights Act.

1884 In *Ex Parte Yarbrough*, the Supreme Court finds that a conspiracy to deprive blacks of the right to vote is a violation of the Fifteenth Amendment to the Constitution.

1885 Booker T. Washington founds the Tuskegee Institute for black students in Alabama.

1887 The Interstate Commerce Commission finds in the case of *Councill v. Western & Atlantic Railroad Company* that while railroads may not segregate black customers into railroad cars that are unequal to white ones, segregation is allowable if the accommodations are equal.

1888 In *Heard v. Georgia Railroad Company*, the Interstate Commerce Commission strikes down "separate and unequal" accommodations in interstate travel.

1891 Georgia passes a law segregating streetcars.

1896 In *Gibson v. Mississippi*, the Supreme Court finds that the mere absence of blacks on a jury does not in itself entitle a black defendant to a new trial.

The Supreme Court rules in *Plessy v. Ferguson* that "separate but equal" facilities for blacks and whites are constitutional.

1898 In *Williams v. Mississippi*, the Supreme Court finds that literacy tests used to compile voter registration rolls are not on their face unconstitutional.

1900 Congressman George H. White of North Carolina introduces the first federal antilynching bill in the House of Representatives, but it dies in committee.

In *Carter v. Texas*, the Supreme Court finds that the deliberate exclusion of blacks from grand juries is unconstitutional.

1903 W. E. B. DuBois's landmark book, *The Souls of Black Folks*, is published.

1904 The American Teachers Association is founded as the first black teachers' union.

1905 Prominent black and white civil rights activists under the leadership of W. E. B. DuBois meet in Niagara, New York, and form the Niagara Movement.

1906 A riot in Brownsville, Texas, is blamed on black troops of the First Battalion, Twenty-fifth Infantry; 167 men are dishonorably discharged. Their records are not cleared until 1972, when all but one have died.

1908 Members of the Niagara Movement and others committed to solving the nation's racial problems meet in New York at the National Negro Conference. The groundwork is established for the later founding of the National Association for the Advancement of Colored People.

In *Berea College v. Commonwealth of Kentucky*, the Supreme Court finds that state legislatures may impose segregation on schools.

1909 The National Association for the Advancement of Colored People is established. Publication begins of the NAACP's journal, *The Crisis*.

1910 The Committee on Urban Conditions Among Negroes (CUCAN), the forerunner of the National Urban League, is established.

1911 The Supreme Court holds in *Bailey v. Alabama* that peonage laws are unconstitutional, thus effectively overruling its 1905 decision in *Clyatt v. United States.*

1913 In *Butts v. Merchants & Miners Transportation Company*, the Supreme Court strikes down the public accommodations clause of the Civil Rights Act of 1875 as unconstitutional.

1914 In *Jones v. Jones,*, the Supreme Court holds that former slaves not named in a will cannot inherit property.

The Supreme Court holds in *United States v. Reynolds* that peonage laws are unconstitutional.

In *McCabe v. Atchison, Topeka & Santa Fe Railway*, the Supreme Court rules that persons must actually suffer under a segregation law before they can challenge it in the courts.

1915 D. W. Griffith's silent film epic, *Birth of a Nation*, based on Thomas Dixon's *The Clansmen*, receives mixed reviews because of its heroic depiction of the Ku Klux Klan, but spawns the second rising of the Klan.

In *Guinn and Beal v. United States*, as well as in *Myers et al. v. Anderson*, the Supreme Court strikes down the notorious "grandfather clauses," restricting voting rights, as unconstitutional.

In *United States v. Moseley*, the Supreme Court holds that section 6 of the Civil Rights Act of 1870 prohibits violations of the right to vote by state officials.

1917 The Supreme Court strikes down segregated housing zones in *Buchanan v. Warley.*

1919 The Chicago Riot starts when a black youth is stoned to death on a whites-only beach. More than 30 people are killed and 500 injured.

In *Corrigan v. Buckley*, the Supreme Court finds that racially discriminatory covenants cannot be used to stop a landowner or homeowner from selling real property to a black person.

1927 In *Nixon v. Herndon*, the Supreme Court strikes down a Texas law that limits black participation in the primary system. The ruling would be upheld later in *Nixon v. Condon.*

1929 The Reverend Dr. Martin Luther King, Jr., is born in Atlanta, Georgia, on 15 January.

1931 Nine black youths are arrested near Scottsboro, Alabama, on the charge of raping two white women, touching off the "Scottsboro Boys" affair.

The Supreme Court holds in *Aldridge v. United States* that the attorneys for black defendants have a right to question prospective jurors about their racial attitudes.

In *Nixon v. Condon*, the Supreme Court strikes down the Texas primary system, which excluded black voters by setting voting qualifications based on race.

1935 The Supreme Court finds in *Grovey v. Townsend* that primary elections that exclude black voters are not unconstitutional, as such elections do not contitute state action.

In *Hollins v. State of Oklahoma*, the Supreme Court rules that the deliberate exclusion of blacks from juries solely on account of race is a violation of the Fourteenth Amendment.

1936 In *Brown et al. v. Mississippi*, the Supreme Court finds that if the only evidence against a defendant is a coerced confession, any conviction arising from that confession must not stand.

1938   The Supreme Court strikes down the systematic exclusion of blacks from juries as unconstitutional in *Hale v. Commonwealth of Kentucky*.

In *Missouri ex rel Gaines v. Canada*, the Supreme Court holds that where "separate but equal" educational laws exist, the black institutions must be equal or the laws are unconstitutional.

1940   The Supreme Court holds in *Chambers et al. v. Florida* that convictions in state courts that are the result of coerced convictions must not stand.

1941   In *Mitchell v. United States et al.*, the Supreme Court upholds the right of blacks to sue for damages resulting from discrimination in interstate travel.

President Franklin D. Roosevelt signs Executive Order 8802, which establishes the Fair Employment Practices Committee (FEPC) and attempts to end discrimination in the defense industry.

1944   The Supreme Court reverses the *Grovey* decision of nine years earlier in *Smith v. Allwright*, holding that state primary elections are state action and as such are regulated by the Fourteenth and Fifteenth Amendments.

In *Pollock v. Williams, Sheriff*, the Supreme Court upholds its 1911 antipeonage decision in *Bailey v. Alabama*.

1946   President Harry S Truman signs Executive Order 9808, which establishes the President's Committee on Civil Rights.

1947   In *Patton v. Mississippi*, the Supreme Court rules against the systematic

exclusion of blacks from grand and petit juries.

1948   In *Sipuel v. Board of Regents of the University of Oklahoma*, the Supreme Court rules that states must provide equal access to education for "qualified" black students.

In *Bob-Lo Excursion Company v. Michigan*, the Supreme Court holds that Article 1, section 8 of the U.S. Constitution bars racial discrimination on ferries that travel from the United States to other countries.

The Supreme Court finds in *Hurd v. Hodge* and *Shelley v. Kraemer* that courts cannot uphold racially restrictive covenants in housing.

President Truman signs Executive Orders 9980 and 9981, which establish the Fair Employment Board on the Civil Service Commission and the President's Committee on Equality of Treatment and Opportunity in the Armed Forces.

1950   In *Cassell v. Texas*, the Supreme Court holds that the unlawful exclusion of blacks from a grand jury voids the indictments against blacks handed down by the grand jury.

The President's Committee on Equality of Treatment and Opportunity in the Armed Forces releases its final report, *Freedom to Serve*.

The Supreme Court decides in *Henderson v. United States et al.* that separate dining tables for blacks and whites on railroad cars doing interstate travel is unconstitutional.

In *Sweatt v. Painter*, the Supreme Court holds that separate and unequal educational facilities violate the Equal Protection Clause of the Fourteenth Amendment.

1951   Florida civil rights activists Harry and Harriette Moore are mortally injured by a bomb explosion in their home; the Ku Klux Klan is suspected in the attack.

1953 The Supreme Court strikes down the use of "private clubs" to deny blacks the right to vote in *Terry v. Adams*.

The black residents of Baton Rouge, Louisiana, stage a bus boycott to protest discrimination; although only partially successful, the boycott lays the foundation for the Montgomery Bus Boycott two years later.

1954 The Supreme Court strikes down separate but equal facilities in education nationwide. The cases dealt with are *Bolling v. Sharpe*, *Briggs et al. v. Elliott et al.*, *Davis v. County School Board of Prince Edward County, Virginia*, and particularly *Brown v. Board of Education of Topeka, Kansas*.

1955 Emmett Till, a black youth 14 years of age, is kidnapped, tortured, and killed for whistling at a white woman. His accused killers are found not guilty by an all-white jury.

The Interstate Commerce Commission decides in *NAACP et al. v. St. Louis–San Francisco Railway Company et al.* that separate waiting rooms in train stations for black and white train riders violate the Interstate Commerce Act of 1887.

Seamstress Rosa Parks is arrested on a Montgomery, Alabama, city bus for refusing to move to the back of the bus. Her arrest touches off the Montgomery Bus Boycott.

1956 Nineteen senators and seventy-seven representatives sign the "Southern Manifesto," explaining how they will use every congressional method to fight implementation of the Supreme Court's *Brown* decision.

The Supreme Court strikes down the segregation of the Montgomery, Alabama, bus system.

1957 Martin Luther King, Jr. Joseph Lowery, Ralph David Abernathy, Fred Shuttlesworth, and other civil rights leaders organize the Southern Christian Leadership Conference on Transportation and Nonviolent Integration.

President Dwight D. Eisenhower signs the Civil Rights Act of 1957, which establishes the U.S. Civil Rights Commission and establishes new protections for the right to vote.

Eisenhower dispatches federal troops to Little Rock, Arkansas, to safeguard the entry of nine black students into all-white schools.

1958 In *NAACP v. Alabama ex rel. Patterson, Attorney General*, the Supreme Court overrules its 1928 decision in *Bryant v. Zimmerman* and strikes down a state law requiring an organization to open its membership lists.

In *Cooper v. Aaron*, the Supreme Court finds that schools cannot use the excuse of potential mob violence to avoid desegregating schools.

1960 Students from North Carolina A & T College in Greensboro protest segregation in public dining areas with the first "sit-in" protest.

In *Gomillion v. Lightfoot*, the Supreme Court strikes down all voting boundaries based on race.

1961 The Supreme Court holds in *Burton v. Wilmington Parking Authority* that businesses that rent land from state agencies must adhere to state antidiscrimination statutes.

The Interstate Commerce Commission finds that segregation in interstate bus terminals is illegal.

The Albany Movement is founded in Albany, Georgia, by civil rights activists in response to the Interstate Commerce Commission's 1 November ruling banning segregation in interstate transport bus terminals.

1962 The Supreme Court holds in *Baker v. Carr* that states must reapportion their congressional districts to reflect a "one man, one vote" formula.

President John F. Kennedy signs Executive Order 11063, which attacks racial discrimination in housing.

1963 In *Goss et al. v. Board of Education of Knoxville, Tennessee et al.*, a system of "voluntary student transfers," which would allow white students to leave desegregated schools, are struck down as unconstitutional by the Supreme Court.

Medgar Wiley Evers, field director for the NAACP in Mississippi, is killed by an unknown assassin in Jackson, Mississippi.

A quarter-million people march on the nation's capital in the March on Washington for Jobs and Justice. Martin Luther King delivers his famous "I Have a Dream" speech.

1964 The Twenty-fourth Amendment to the Constitution, which bars the use of the poll tax, is ratified.

In *Griffin et al. v. County School Board of Prince Edward County et al.*, the Supreme Court finds that a school board may not close a school to circumvent a desegregation order.

President Lyndon B. Johnson signs the Civil Rights Act of 1964, which bars discrimination in public accommodations and strengthens the right to vote.

Civil rights leader Dr. Martin Luther King, Jr., is awarded the Nobel Peace Prize.

In *Heart of Atlanta Motel v. United States*, the Supreme Court upholds the right of the government under the public accommodations clause of

the 1964 Civil Rights Act to force hotels to admit black customers.

1965 Malcolm X is shot to death in a hall in Harlem, New York.

Protestors rally for voting rights in the Selma to Montgomery March.

In *Harman v. Forssenius*, the Supreme Court strikes down the poll tax as unconstitutional.

The Equal Employment Opportunity Commission, established by the Civil Rights Act of 1964, begins its work.

President Johnson signs the Voting Rights Act of 1965 into law.

In *United States v. Price et al.*, the Supreme Court rules that the Fourteenth Amendment prohibits conspiracies to violate civil rights.

1966 The Georgia legislature refuses to seat activist Julian Bond because of his opposition to the Vietnam War; the action will be overturned by the Supreme Court later in the year.

Dr. Robert Weaver is confirmed as Secretary of Housing and Urban Development, the first black man to sit in the cabinet.

In *Harper et al. v. Virginia State Board of Elections*, the Supreme Court rules that following passage of the 24th Amendment, which bars poll taxes, and its 1964 decision in *Harman v. Forssenius*, any state action to reimpose a poll tax is unconstitutional.

The Supreme Court finds in *United States v. Guest* that the right to interstate travel is fundamental, and any imposition on that right is a violation of the Constitution.

The Supreme Court finds in *South Carolina v. Katzenbach* that the 1965 Voting Rights Act does not place an undue burden on the states.

In *Katzenbach v. Morgan*, the Supreme Court finds that literacy tests utilized for voting are unconstitutional.

Extremists Bobby Seale and Huey Newton establish the Black Panther Party.

1967 Congressman Adam Clayton Powell is denied his congressional seat because of allegations over the misuse of travel money. He will later be removed from Congress, but will win the special election to fill the vacant seat.

In *Reitman et al. v. Mulkey et al.*, private discriminations in the area of housing are deemed by the Supreme Court to be unconstitutional.

In *Loving v. Virginia*, the Supreme Court strikes down state bans on interracial marriage.

Race riots sweep through Newark, Detroit, and other cities; President Johnson appoints the National Commission on Civil Disorders.

Thurgood Marshall is sworn in as the first black man to sit on the Supreme Court.

Carl B. Stokes of Cleveland, Ohio, and Richard G. Hatcher of Gary, Indiana, become the first black mayors of major American cities.

The U.S. Census reports that 81 percent of black students in the South still attend segregated schools.

1968 The National Commission on Civil Disorders, also known as the Kerner Commission, releases its final report in which it states, "Our nation is moving toward two separate societies, one black, one white—separate and unequal."

Dr. Martin Luther King, Jr., is assassinated in Memphis, Tennessee, while attending a strike by sanitation workers. Rioting follows in many U.S. cities.

President Johnson signs the Fair Housing Act of 1968, which outlaws discrimination in all forms of housing.

In *Green v. New Kent County School Board, Virginia*, "freedom of choice" school attendance programs are struck down by the Supreme Court as unconstitutional.

The Supreme Court strikes down racially restrictive covenants in *Jones v. Alfred H. Mayer Co.*

Black Panther Party leader Huey Newton is convicted of manslaughter for killing a policeman in a shoot-out. A "Free Huey" campaign begins.

1969 Fred Hampton, head of the Chicago arm of the Black Panthers, is shot to death by police in his home.

1971 The Supreme Court finds in *Griggs v. Duke Power Company* that tests of workers that discriminate on a racial basis are unconstitutional.

The Supreme Court holds in the three cases of *Moore v. Charlotte-Mecklenburg Board of Education, North Carolina State Board of Education et al. v. Swann*, and *Swann v. Charlotte-Mecklenburg Board of Education* that school busing to achieve desegregation is constitutional.

In *Griffin et al. v. Breckinridge et al.*, the Supreme Court finds that violations of civil rights laws may be committed by individuals not necessarily working under the color of state action.

In *Palmer et al. v. Thompson, Mayor of the City of Jackson, et al.*, the Court finds that when a public facility is closed to everyone to prevent it from being desegregated, there is no denial of equal protection.

1972 Alabama governor George Wallace, while campaigning for the presidency, is shot and wounded by an assassin in Laurel, Maryland.

The Supreme Court rules in *Moose Lodge #107 v. Irvis* that private clubs with no connection to the state cannot be held liable for discrimination.

In *United States v. Scotland Neck City Board of Education et al.*, the Supreme Court finds that school districts cannot separate themselves to form new districts for the purpose of circumventing desegregation orders.

1973 In *Keyes v. School Board No. 1 of Denver, Colorado*, the Supreme Court finds that school boards complying with desegregation orders are under no obligation to do away with segregation based on housing patterns or other outside factors.

1974 The Supreme Court fails to rule on racially based affirmative action programs in schools in *DeFunis v. Odegaard*.

In *Milliken v. Bradley I*, the Supreme Court finds that unless a school board institutes segregation by law, it cannot be forced by a court to desegregate.

1975 In *City of Richmond v. United States*, the Supreme Court holds that cities may annex land that dilutes the political strength of minorities only if those minorities have full political representation afterward.

1976 In *Hills v. Gautreaux*, the Supreme Court rules that government sponsored housing programs that separate the races are unconstitutional.

1977 *Roots*, a television miniseries that graphically depicts slavery in the United States, appears in eight episodes.

In *Dayton Board of Education v. Brinkman*, the Supreme Court strikes down the use of "optional attendance zones," which had allowed white students to decide whether or not to attend desegregated schools.

The Supreme Court narrowly strikes down the use of quotas in educational institutions as reverse discrimination in *University of California Regents v. Bakke*.

1979 The Supreme Court holds that racial quotas and timetables are constitutional in *United Steelworkers of America v. Weber*.

1980 The Supreme Court upholds the constitutionality of municipal at-large elections in *Mobile v. Bolden*.

In *Fullilove v. Klutznick*, the Supreme Court holds that Congress may pass laws that allow racial quotas to remedy past discrimination.

1983 In *Bob Jones University v. United States*, the Supreme Court finds that the government can deny tax-exempt status to a private, sectarian university that discriminates racially.

1984 In *Palmore v. Sidoti*, the Supreme Court holds that there can be no challenges to the custodial rights of a parent based on the parent's residence in a multiracial household.

1986 The Supreme Court rules in *Batson v. Kentucky* that a prosecutor may not strike potential black jurors from a prospective jury on account of their race.

In *Wygant et al. v. Jackson Board of Education*, the Supreme Court finds that white teachers with more seniority may not be fired to prevent the termination of black teachers.

1987 In *United States v. Paradise et al.*, the Supreme Court limits the use of race-based promotions to overcome past discriminations.

1989 In *Wards Cove Packing Company v. Atonio*, the Supreme Court holds that employees claiming discrimination on the job must show that such discrimination was the intent of the employer.

1991 President George Bush signs the Civil Rights Act of 1991, which seeks to undo the effects of the Supreme Court's *Ward's Cove* decision.

1992 In *Freeman et al. v. Pitts et al.*, the Supreme Court finds that school districts plagued by segregation due to residential patterns are not at fault if the *de facto* segregation continues.

In *United States v. Fordice, Governor of Mississippi, et al.*, the Supreme Court holds that dual state school systems—including white state universities and historically black colleges—are unconstitutional.

1993 The Supreme Court finds that racially based congressional apportionment boundaries are unconstitutional in *Shaw et al. v. Reno, Attorney General, et al.*

Bibliography

Ambrose, Stephen A. *Eisenhower: Soldier and President.* New York: Simon and Schuster, 1990.

Bass, Jack. *Unlikely Heroes: The Dramatic Story of the Southern Judges of the Fifth Circuit Who Translated the Supreme Court's Brown Decision into a Revolution for Equality.* New York: Simon and Schuster, 1981.

Belz, Herman. *Reconstructing the Union: Theory and Policy during the Civil War.* Reprint ed. Westport, CT: Greenwood Press, 1979.

Billington, Monroe. "Freedom to Serve: The President's Committee on Equality of Treatment and Opportunity in the Armed Forces, 1949–1950." *Journal of Negro History* 51(4): 262–274.

Bishop, David W. "Plessy v. Ferguson: A Reinterpretation." *Journal of Negro History* 62(2): 125–133.

Bittker, Anne S. "Charles Richard Drew, M.D." *Negro History Bulletin* 36(7): 144–150.

"The Bomb Heard Around the World: The Murders of Harry and Harriett Moore." *Ebony* 7(5): 15–22.

Borome, Joseph A. "Robert Purvis and His Early Challenge to American Racism." *Negro History Bulletin* 30(5): 8–10.

Bramlett-Solomon, Sharon. "Civil Rights Vanguard in the Deep South: Newspaper Portrayal of Fannie Lou Hamer, 1964–1977." *Journalism Quarterly* 68(3): 515–521.

Branch, Taylor. *Parting the Waters: America in the King Years, 1954–63.* New York: Simon and Schuster, 1988.

Brewer, J. Mason. *Negro Legislators of Texas and Their Descendants.* Dallas: Mathis Publishing Company, 1935.

Brewer, William M. "The Poll Tax and the Poll Taxers." *Journal of Negro History* 29(3): 260–299.

Cagin, Seth and Philip Dray. *We Are Not Afraid: The Story of Goodman, Schwerner, and Chaney and the Civil Rights Campaign for Mississippi.* New York: The Macmillan Publishing Company, 1988.

Catton, Bruce. "Dred Scott v. Sandford: Black Pawn on a Field of Peril." *American Heritage* 15(1): 66–71, 90–91.

Chase, Hal. "William C. Chase and the Washington *Bee.*" *Negro History Bulletin* 36(8): 172–174.

Chase, Harold W. and Craig R. Ducat. *Constitutional Interpretation: Cases-Essays-Materials.* St. Paul, MN: West Publishing Company, 1979.

Cheek, William F. "A Negro Runs for Congress: John Mercer Langston and the Virginia Campaign of 1888." *Journal of Negro History* 52(1): 14–34.

Christian, Marcus B. "The Theory of the Poisoning of Oscar J. Dunn." *Phylon* 6(3): 254–266.

Bibliography

Civil Rights Enforcement by the Department of Education. Hearing before the Subcommittee of the Committee on Government Operations, 100th Congress, 1st Session, 1987.

Contee, Clarence G. "Edwin G. Walker, Black Leader; Generally Acknowledged Son of David Walker." *Negro History Bulletin* 39(3): 556–559.

Couch, Harvey C. *A History of the Fifth Circuit, 1891–1981.* Bicentennial Committee of the Judicial Conference of the United States, 1981.

Currie, David P. *The Constitution in the Supreme Court: The First Hundred Years, 1789–1888.* Chicago: University of Chicago Press, 1985.

Cushman, Robert F. with Susan P. Koniak. *Cases in Constitutional Law.* Englewood Cliffs, NJ: Prentice Hall, 1989.

Dewart, Jane, ed. *The State of Black America 1989.* National Urban League, 1989.

Dewart, Jane, ed. *The State of Black America 1990.* National Urban League, 1990.

DiNunzio, Mario R. "Lyman Trumbull and Civil Rights." *Negro History Bulletin* 35(8): 186–187.

Dukess, Karen and Richard Hart. "The Invisible Man: Harry T. Moore." *Miami Herald Tropic Magazine* 16 February 1992: 12–21.

"Edward A. Bouchet, Ph.D." *Negro History Bulletin* 31(8): 11.

Feeley, Malcolm M. and Samuel Krislov. *Constitutional Law.* Boston: Little, Brown, 1985.

Fleming, John E. "Slavery, Civil War and Reconstruction: A Study of Black Women in Microcosm." *Negro History Bulletin* 38(6): 430–433.

Fleming, Walter Lynwood. *Civil War and Reconstruction in Alabama.* Reprint ed. Gloucester, MA: Peter Smith, 1949.

Floyd, Nicholas Jackson. *Thorns in the Flesh: A Voice of Vindication from the South in Answer to "A Fool's Errand" and Other Slanders.* Philadelphia: Hubbard Brothers, 1884.

Foner, Eric. *Reconstruction: America's Unfinished Revolution, 1863–1877.* New York: Harper & Row, 1988.

Foner, Philip S. "[John Mercer Langston]: The First Publicly-Elected Black Official in the United States Reports His Election." *Negro History Bulletin* 37(3): 237.

Franklin, John Hope. *Reconstruction: After the Civil War.* Chicago: University of Chicago Press, 1961.

Franklin, John Hope and Meier, August, ed. *Black Leaders of the Twentieth Century.* Urbana: University of Illinois Press, 1982.

Gaboury, William J. "George Washington Murray and the Fight for Political Democracy in South Carolina." *Journal of Negro History* 62(3): 258–269.

Garrow, David J. *Bearing the Cross: Martin Luther King, Jr., and the Southern Christian Leadership Conference.* New York: William Morrow, 1986.

"George Washington Henderson." *Negro History Bulletin* 32(2): 20.

Gilpin, Patrick J. "Charles S. Johnson and the Southern Educational Reporting Service." *Journal of Negro History* 63(3): 197–208.

Gilpin, Patrick J. "Charles S. Johnson: Scholar and Educator." *Negro History Bulletin* 39(3): 544–548.

Hertzberg, Steven. *Strangers within the Gate City: The Jews of Atlanta, 1845–1915.* Philadelphia: Jewish Publication Society of America, 1978.

"Hiram R. Revels, Blanche K. Bruce, and Edward W. Brooke: Three Negro Senators of the United States." *Negro History Bulletin* 30(1): 4–5, 12.

Howe, Irving and Coser, Lewis. *The American Communist Party: A Critical History (1919–1957).* Boston: Beacon, 1957.

Jackson, Luther P. "The Educational Efforts of the Freedmen's Bureau and Freedmen's Aid Societies in South Carolina, 1862–1872." *Journal of Negro History* 7(1): 1–40.

James, Joseph B. *The Framing of the Fourteenth Amendment.* Urbana: University of Illinois Press, 1965.

Katz, William. "George Henry White: A Militant Negro Congressman in the Age of Booker T. Washington." *Negro History Bulletin* 29(6): 125–126, 134, 138–139.

Kennedy, Robert F., Jr. *Judge Frank M. Johnson, Jr.* New York: G. P. Putnam's Sons, 1978.

Kennedy, Stetson. *Southern Exposure.* Boca Raton: Florida Atlantic University Press, 1991.

Kirkendall, Richard S. *The Harry S. Truman Encyclopedia.* Boston: G. K. Hall, 1989.

Klingman, Peter D. "Josiah T. Walls and the Black Tactics of Race in Post–Civil War Florida." *Negro History Bulletin* 37(3): 242–247.

Kluger, Richard. *Simple Justice: The History of Brown v. Board of Education and Black America's Struggle for Equality.* 2 vol. New York: Knopf, 1975.

Levstik, Frank R. "William H. Holland: Black Soldier, Politician and Educator." *Negro History Bulletin* 36(5): 110–111.

Levstik, Frank R. "David Jenkins: Eagle That is Forgotten." *Negro History Bulletin* 38(7): 464.

Lewis, Ronald L. "Cultural Pluralism and Black Reconstruction: The Public Career of Richard H. Cain." *The Crisis* 85(2): 57–60, 64–65.

Lissitz, Robert W. *Assessment of Student Performance and Attitude: St. Louis Metropolitan Area Court-Ordered Desegregation Effort.* Voluntary Interdistrict Coordinating Council, 1992.

Litwack, Leon and August Meier, ed. *Black Leaders of the Nineteenth Century.* Urbana: University of Illinois Press, 1988.

Lofgren, Charles A. *The Plessy Case: A Legal-Historical Interpretation.* New York: Oxford University Press, 1987.

Logan, Rayford W. and Michael R. Winston. *Dictionary of American Negro Biography.* New York: W. W. Norton, 1982.

Mann, Kenneth Eugene. "Richard Harvey Cain, Congressman, Minister and Champion for Civil Rights." *Negro History Bulletin* 35(3): 64–66.

Mann, Kenneth Eugene. "Oscar Stanton DePriest: Persuasive Agent for the Black Masses." *Negro History Bulletin* 35(6): 134–137.

Mann, Kenneth Eugene. "John Roy Lynch: U.S. Congressman from Mississippi." *Negro History Bulletin* 37(3): 238–241.

Marcus, Irwin M. "Benjamin Fletcher: Black Labor Leader." *Negro History Bulletin* 35(6): 138–140.

McFeeley, William S. *Frederick Douglass.* New York: W. W. Norton, 1991.

McPherson, James M. *The Abolitionist Legacy: From Reconstruction to the NAACP.* Princeton, N.J.: Princeton University Press, 1985.

Meier, August and Elliott Rudwick. *CORE: A Study in the Civil Rights Movement, 1942–1968.* New York: Oxford University Press, 1973.

Menard, Edith. "John Willis Menard: First Negro Elected to the U.S. Congress, First Negro to Speak in Congress." *Negro History Bulletin* 28(3): 53–54.

Menard, Edith. "John Willis Menard: 100th Anniversary of the Election of the First Negro to the United States House of Representatives." *Negro History Bulletin* 31(7): 10–11.

Mendelson, Jack. *The Martyrs: 16 Who Gave Their Lives for Racial Justice.* New York: Harper & Row, 1966.

Miller, M. Sammy. "Elliott of South Carolina: Lawyer and Legislator." *Negro History Bulletin* 36(5): 112–114.

Mills, Nicalaus. "Forgotten Greenville." *Dissent* 37(3): 333–337.

Murphy, L. E. "The Civil Rights Law of 1875." *Journal of Negro History* 12(2): 110–127.

Naison, Mark. *Communists in Harlem during the Depression.* Urbana: University of Illinois Press, 1983.

National Urban League. *75th Anniversary of the National Urban League: 1910–1985.* National Urban League, 1985.

National Urban League. *80th Anniversary of the National Urban League: 1910–1990.* National Urban League, 1990.

Nolan, Joseph R. and Jacqueline Nolan-Haley. *Black's Law Dictionary.* St. Paul, MN: West Publishing Company, 1990.

Nomination of Clarence Thomas To Be Associate Justice of the Supreme Court of the United States. Senate Judiciary Committee Report J-102-40, 102nd Congress, 1st Session, 1991.

Olsen, Otto H. *Carpetbagger's Crusade: The Case of Albion Winegar Tourgee.* Baltimore: Johns Hopkins University Press, 1965.

Ovington, Mary White. "The National Association for the Advancement of Colored People." *Journal of Negro History* 9(2): 107–116.

Page, Wilber A. "Notes on George W. Williams: Soldier, Minister, Orator, Lecturer, Historian." *Negro History Bulletin* 30(6): 12.

Perkins, A.E. "Oscar James Dunn." *Phylon*, 4(2): 105–121.

Purnick, Joyce and Michael Oreskes. "Jesse Jackson Aims for the Mainstream." *New York Times Magazine*, 29 November 1987: 28–31, 34–35, 58–60.

Ragsdale, Bruce A. and Joel D. Treese. *Black Americans in Congress, 1870–1989.* Washington: U.S. Government Printing Office, 1990.

Reid, George W. "Congressman George Henry White: His Major Power Base." *Negro History Bulletin* 39(3): 554–555.

Reid, George W. "The Post-Congressional Career of George H. White, 1901–1918." *Journal of Negro History* 61(4): 362–373.

Reid, George W. "Four in Black: North Carolina's Black Congressmen, 1874–1901." *Journal of Negro History* 64(3): 229–243.

Report of the Joint Select Committee on the Condition of Affairs in the Late Insurrectionary States. House Report No. 22, 42nd Congress, 2nd Session, 1872.

Robinson, Jo Ann Gibson. *The Montgomery Bus Boycott and the Women Who Started It.* Knoxville: University of Tennessee Press, 1987.

Sabljack, Mark and Martin H. Greenberg. *Most Wanted: A History of the FBI's Most Wanted List.* New York: Bonanza Books, 1990.

SCLC: The National Publication of the Southern Christian Leadership Conference 21(1).

Sewell, George A. "A Hundred Years of History: Alcorn A & M College Observes Centennial (1871–1971)." *Negro History Bulletin* 35(8): 78–79.

Sewell, George A. "Hiram Rhodes Revels: Another Evaluation." *Negro History Bulletin* 38(1): 336–339.

Sims, L. Moody. "A Voice of Dissent: John Jay Chapman and the 'Great Wickedness.'" *Negro History Bulletin* 32(3): 12–13.

Simmons, William J. *Men of Mark: Eminent, Progressive and Rising.* Reprint ed. Chicago: Johnson Publishing Company, 1970.

Singer, Donald L. "For Whites Only: The Seating of Hiram Revels in the United States Senate." *Negro History Bulletin* 35(3): 60–63.

Stampp, Kenneth M. *America in 1857: A Nation on the Brink.* New York: Oxford University Press, 1990.

Steamer, Robert J. *Chief Justice: Leadership and the Supreme Court.* Columbia: University of South Carolina Press, 1986.

Suggs, Henry Lewis. "P. B. Young of the Norfolk Journal and Guide: A Booker T. Washington Militant, 1904–1928." *Journal of Negro History* 64(4): 365–376.

Tidwell, Billy J., ed. *The State of Black America 1992*. National Urban League, 1992.

Trelease, Allen W. *White Terror: The Ku Klux Klan Conspiracy and Southern Reconstruction*. Reprint ed. Westport, CT: Greenwood, 1979.

Tribe, Laurence H. *American Constitutional Law*. Mineola, NY: Foundation Press, 1978.

Valien, Preston. "The Brotherhood of Sleeping Car Porters." *Phylon* 3rd quarter 1940: 224–238.

Walton, Norman W. "James T. Rapier: Congressman from Alabama." *Negro History Bulletin* 30(7): 6–10.

Washington, James Melvin, ed. *I Have a Dream: Writings and Speeches that Changed the World*. San Francisco: HarperCollins, 1992.

Weisbord, Robert G. "J. Albert Thorne, Back-to-Africanist." *Negro History Bulletin* 32(3): 14–16.

Weiss, Nancy J. *Whitney M. Young, Jr., and the Struggle for Civil Rights*. Princeton, NJ: The Princeton University Press, 1989.

Whalen, Barbara and Charles Whalen. *The Longest Debate: A Legislative History of the 1964 Civil Rights Act*. Cabin John, MD: Seven Locks Press, 1985.

Wiggins, Sarah Woolfolk, comp. *From Civil War to Civil Rights: Alabama, 1860–1960*. Tuscaloosa: University of Alabama Press, 1987.

Wilkerson, J. Harvie. *From Brown to Bakke: The Supreme Court and School Integration, 1954–1978*. New York: Oxford University Press, 1979.

Williams, Juan. *Eyes on the Prize: America's Civil Rights Years, 1954–1965*. New York: Viking Penguin, 1987.

Wood, L. Hollingsworth. "The Urban League Movement." *Journal of Negro History* 9(2): 117–126.

Woodson, Carter Godwin. "Fifty Years of Negro Citizenship as Qualified by the United States Supreme Court." The *Journal of Negro History* 6(1): 1–53.

Yarbrough, Tinsley E. *Judge Frank M. Johnson and Human Rights in Alabama*. University: University of Alabama Press, 1981.

Yarbrough, Tinsley E. *A Passion for Justice: J. Waties Waring and Civil Rights*. New York: Oxford University Press, 1987.

Yarbrough, Tinsley E. *John Marshall Harlan: Great Dissenter of the Warren Court*. New York: Oxford University Press, 1992.

Zangrando, Robert L. *The NAACP Crusade against Lynching, 1909–1950*. Philadelphia: Temple University Press, 1980.

Zipser, Arthur. *Workingclass Giant: The Life of William Z. Foster*. New York: International, 1981.

NEWSPAPERS

Ames *Daily Tribune-Times*
Atlanta *Journal*
Atlanta *Constitution*
Atlanta *Journal-Constitution*
Birmingham *Age-Herald*
Birmingham *News*
Chattanooga *News*
Chattanooga *Times*
Daily Worker
Harper's Weekly
Houston [Texas] *Informer*
Indianapolis *Recorder*
Jackson [Mississippi] *Clarion-Ledger*
Miami *Herald*
New York *Herald*
New York *Herald-Tribune*
New York *Daily Mirror*
New York *Daily News*
New York *Post*
The New York *Times*
New York *Tribune*
New York *World*
New York *World-Telegram*

Bibliography

New York *World-Telegram and Sun*
Pittsburgh *Courier*
St. Louis *Republic*
Washington *Post*
Washington *Post and Times Herald*
Washington *Tribune*

MANUSCRIPT COLLECTIONS

Walter Lynwood Fleming Papers. New York
    Public Library, New York

NAACP Papers (microfilm) Library of
    Congress, Washington, D.C.

Illustration Credits

Index

DATE			